Crafting a Republic for the World

Crafting a Republic for the World

Scientific, Geographic, and Historiographic Inventions of Colombia

LINA DEL CASTILLO

University of Nebraska Press
LINCOLN & LONDON

Library of Congress Cataloging-in-Publication Data
Names: Del Castillo, Lina, author.
Title: Crafting a republic for the world: scientific, geographic, and historiographic inventions of Colombia / Lina del Castillo.
Description: Lincoln: University of Nebraska Press, 2018. | Includes bibliographical references and index.
Identifiers: LCCN 2017026970 (print)
LCCN 2017031982 (ebook)
ISBN 9780803290747 (cloth: alkaline paper)
ISBN 9781496205483 (paperback: alkaline paper)
ISBN 9781496205834 (epub)
ISBN 9781496205841 (mobi)
ISBN 9781496205858 (pdf)
Subjects: LCSH: Colombia—Politics and government—1810-|
Colombia—Geography. | Geography—Political aspects—
Colombia—History. | Science—Political aspects—Colombia—
History. | Historiography—Political aspects—Colombia—History.
| Elite (Social sciences)—Colombia—History. | Republicanism—
Colombia—History. | Postcolonialism—Colombia—History. |
Nationalism—Colombia—History. | Colombia—Colonial influence.
Classification: LCC F2273 (ebook)
LCC F2273 .D45 2018 (print)
DDC 986.1/03—dc23
LC record available at https://lccn.loc.gov/2017026970

Set in Minion Pro by E. Cuddy.

For my childhood's guardian, Gary J. Greenberg
and for my life's love, Jorge Cañizares-Esguerra

Contents

Illustrations

Tables

Acknowledgments

It takes a community to support the long-term production of a book. I received important financial and institutional support from the University of Miami's History Department and Center for Latin American Studies, the National Science Foundation's Dissertation Improvement Award, Iowa State University's Big 12 Faculty Fellowship Program, the Fulbright Scholar Program of the United States Department of State's Bureau of Educational and Cultural Affairs, the Teresa Lozano Long Institute for Latin American Studies—Benson, the History Department at the University of Texas at Austin, the Kellogg Institute for International Studies at the University of Notre Dame, the School of Advanced Study's Institute of Latin American Studies at the University of London, and the President's Office of the University of Texas at Austin's subvention grant program. Erin Greb's cartography that illustrates this text helped me see trends that otherwise would have remained occluded.

Words cannot express my gratitude for the inspiring people who have contributed to my book's community by reading chapters, listening to presentations, discussing various parts of this manuscript with me, suggesting further readings and archival documents, and challenging me to think deeper, all the while encouraging me to follow through. The list of debts is long, and I apologize in advance for any oversights. Many thanks to Mary Roldán, Michael LaRosa, Germán Mejía, Steve Stein, Bruce Bagley, Martha Few, Raymond Craib, Mauricio Nieto Olarte, Muriel Laurent, Ana María Bidegaín, Victor Uribe, Claudia Leal, Shawn Van Ausdal, Noble David Cook, Robin Bachin, Eduardo Elena, Ashli White, Guido Ruggiero, Laura Giannetti, Marten Brienen,

Efraín Sánchez, Daniel Gutierrez Ardila, Sergio Mejía, Francisco Ortega, Lucía Duque, Fernán González, S.J., Guiomar Dueñas-Vargas, Alfonso Múnera, Kristen Block, Marcela Echeverri, Joanne Rappaport, Brett Troyan, Hayley Froysland, Meri Clark, Rebecca Tally, Joshua Rosenthal, Nicola Foote, Aims McGuinness, Jane Rausch, Catherine LeGrand, Peter Henderson, Miguel Cuadros-Sánchez, Eduardo Posada-Carbó, Paola Ruiz Gutierrez, Matthew Edney, Barbara Mundy, Pete Sigal, Sebastián Diaz, Héctor Mendoza Vargas, Juanita Rodriguez Congote, Santiago Muñoz, Eden Medina, Karen Racine, Ernesto Bassi, Santa Arias, Neil Safier, Iris Montero, Felipe Martínez Pinzón, Adrián López-Denis, Matthew Crawford, Carla Lois, Ryan Kashanipour, Jennifer Derr, Jim Akerman, Roger Kain, Karl Offen, Jordana Dym, Zeb Tortorici, Adam Warren, Julia Rodriguez, Karin Rosemblatt, Sebastián Gil-Riaño, Christopher Heaney, Vanesa Miseres, Juan Vitulli, Karen Graubart, J. Samuel Valenzuela, Carlos Jáuregui, Carlos Abreu Mendoza, Carolina Alzate, Tatiana Botero, Angel Tuninetti, Florencia Quesada, April Eisman, John Monroe, Chrisy Moutsatsos, Jacqueline Jones, Xaq Frohich, Megan Raby, Sam Vong, Brent Crosson, Abena Dove Osseo-Asare, Julie Hardwick, Jeremi Suri, Mark Thurner, Leoncio López-Ocón, and Juan Pimentel. Jorge Orlando Melo, Angela Pérez Mejia, Martha Jeanet Sierra, and Mauricio Tovar aided my searches through Colombian archives and special collections. The kindness of the Ancízar family for opening Manuel Ancízar's archive to me, and the Restrepo family for allowing access to José Manuel Restrepo's archive have been inordinately important. Ernesto Capello offered welcome feedback on an earlier version of the manuscript. Rebecca Earle, Jamie Sanders, and Marixa Lasso also offered invaluable insights on the full manuscript. Seth Garfield's laser-like targeted reading powers helped me see much more clearly the significance of my research. Nancy Appelbaum generously has seen this project develop, and has read, critiqued, suggested sources, and offered timely advice throughout my writing process. Thanks are also due to Ana María Camargo Gómez, head of publications at the Banco de la República de Colombia, and to Bridget Barry and the folks at the University of Nebraska Press for their hard work to ensure this project arrived at the finish line. Finally, my deepest appreciation for the many enthusiastic graduate and undergraduate students that over the years have helped me clarify my arguments and gain greater understanding.

Friends and family are the sustaining life force behind often-isolating academic endeavors. My mother, Martha Senn, has been a boundless source of love, inspiration, and support. Her partner, Juan Sebastián Betancur, has listened and provided guidance when I've most needed it. My father, José María Del Castillo, and his wife have been keen enthusiasts of my historical meanderings. So have my siblings, Javier, Catalina, and Federico, and stepkids, Sebastián and Andrea. My grandmother, Dilia Rodríguez de Senn, encouraged me with her good humor and good sense, and the playful spirit of my grandfather, Nicolás Senn, lives on in my son. Family trees sometimes grow roots and branches in the places you least expect. Gary and Miriam Greenberg opened their home to me in 1980 when I first arrived in the United States from Colombia. In the fall of 2001, when I began graduate studies, Gary was diagnosed with melanoma. Despite failing eyesight, Gary proofread each chapter of the dissertation upon which this book is based. He died only a few months after my defense. But without Jorge Cañizares-Esguerra, this book would not have been possible. His nimble mind, challenging questions, incisive critiques, and amazingly useful suggestions and edits on several drafts of the manuscript have transformed this book. His love has transformed me. This book honors Gary's memory as it embraces Jorge's love.

Crafting a Republic for the World

Introduction

Postcolonial Inventions of Spanish American Colonial Legacies

There are no colonial legacies in Spanish America. Yet, this book is about them. It tells the tale of nineteenth-century Spanish Americans whose remarkable creativity and deep engagement with on-the-ground realities allowed them to craft a republic that the world would seek to emulate. I investigate a world they created of postcolonial sociological, political, and economic speculation that engendered new social sciences and new technologies to overcome alleged colonial legacies. This creativity was inspired by the sociopolitical and spatial revolutions unleashed by Spanish American independence and early processes of republican state formation. Spanish Americans marshaled in new histories, new sciences, and new geographies that offered radical new ways of understanding the past. This body of knowledge would allow them to propel economic development. Through detailed knowledge of local realities, Spanish Americans would best manage how territorial sovereignty would intersect with individual sovereignty in their present and future republics. These stories have long been buried under enduring narratives of nineteenth-century chaos, Liberal versus Conservative caudillos, aloof, disconnected elites who preferred Eurocentric models to local needs and realities, and, of course, colonial legacies.[1] Scholarship continues to uncritically consume a historical construct of Latin America as a region stymied by intractable intellectual intolerance, racism, political absolutism, and capitalist dependency, all attributable to the period of Spanish monarchical rule.[2]

This book argues that if it were not for the deep cultural work carried out by nineteenth-century Spanish Americans such as those considered here, the very category of colonial legacies would not exist. But the kind of "legacies" Spanish Americans invented did not cede the creation of key political and scientific categories to "Europe." They saw themselves as emerging from imperial structures, not nation-states. As inheritors of polycentric empires, the margin-periphery dichotomy made no sense.[3] This was the framework within which early to mid-nineteenth-century Spanish Americans operated. They committed themselves to a republican-liberal project that actively invented an array of narratives about what the colonial legacy meant, what it entailed, and how it needed to be addressed. Distinct inventions of the colonial legacy drove folks to do battle in the voting booth, on the battlefield, in courtrooms and legislative chambers, on church altars, in classrooms, and in the court of public opinion. These struggles reflected Spanish American efforts to define the global meaning of republicanism and how it should be expressed territorially, constitutionally, and culturally. There was no actual "colonial legacy" that hamstrung nineteenth-century state formation outside of the language discourse and the sociological imagination that these historical actors unleashed. The "colonial period" is, in a sense, a liberal-era invention.

A second related aim of the book is to show how, by the mid-nineteenth century, Spanish American experiments with republicanism had no models to follow. From their perspective neither the ossified aristocratic regimes of Europe nor the racist antebellum United States had been able to produce political and racial equality through republicanism.[4] Spanish Americans had reason to believe that their republican experiments were on the vanguard of political modernity.[5] To best experiment with political modernity, Spanish Americans turned to science. This book demonstrates how the language of nineteenth-century science permeated the thinking, methods, and practices that experimentally sought to craft a modern republic for the world. The "crafting" explored here underscores the material culture and practical handiwork that was central to the production of early to mid-nineteenth-century scientific knowledge.[6] This crafting of scientific knowledge was critical at a time when there was a lack of disciplinary coherence to the diverse sciences that Spanish American intellectuals and government officials developed for the purposes of republican governance.

It is in this line that the book engages in a focused demonstration of how nineteenth-century elites were, in fact, profoundly engaged with the deep, revolutionary transformations occurring in the region. Until the 1850s in New Granada, engagement meant a drive to expand the franchise by expanding the number of corporate bodies of political representation—the municipalities. The abolition of slavery and universal manhood suffrage came soon thereafter. The arrival of popular sectors into the political process exploded in the 1854 Civil War, and the nature of regional elite engagement changed. Postcolonial elites thereafter spent significant energy and imagination figuring out ways to limit what they considered to be the ill effects of the colonial legacy in the mind of the electorally mobilized masses.

The book demonstrates how postcolonial elites engaged with local realities by first tracing out the spaces of sociability where party leaders found common ground. Leaders from across the political spectrum interacted with each other not only in the halls of Congress and provincial legislatures, but also in scientific societies. Only a handful of scholars have explored mid-nineteenth-century Latin American scientific societies, and when they do, they tend to offer only a passing and often-dismissive reference to these midcentury spaces of sociability.[7] Rather than offer a contextualized reading of the forms of knowledge that these spaces allowed, scholars have simply shrugged off mid-nineteenth-century innovations produced through these spaces as hopelessly derivative, Eurocentric, and detached from local realities. These dismissive readings trivialize both the spaces of sociability and the kind of knowledge production they facilitated, and ignore the political training ground that scientific societies offered during this critical period. Such dismissive approximations are in part due to historical actors who trivialized cross-party spaces of sociability when reflecting on the mid-nineteenth century from their late nineteenth-century position of entrenched political party strife.[8]

Taking Colombia as a case in point, my book centers on how scientific sociability produced a remarkable consensus among historical actors that included lawyers, merchants, government officials, military engineers, religious leaders, architects, naturalists, journalists, and educators. They agreed that the republic needed to find ways to foment circulation by dismantling blockages supposedly produced during the period of monarchical rule. This perspective challenges narratives of sharp, regional partisanship pitting Liberals versus Conservatives, or centralists versus federalists bent on expanding plantation economies for export. I underscore instead the powerful state building force that emerged out of a remarkable midcentury consensus around a circulatory project aimed at developing internal markets. Regional elites came together around the need to engage in a sustained scientific effort to know and map the national territory and the people and resources it contained. The forms of knowledge production and practices that these bipartisan postcolonial elites produced toward that end included the land survey techniques developed specifically for New Granada efforts to map, measure, and distribute indigenous lands held in common; midcentury political ethnographies documenting New Granada popular culture in the provinces; the emergence of New Granada's "science of constitutionalism" and political administration; and the geographic writings, texts, and maps produced of New Granada provinces. This book shows how spaces that facilitated elite consensus—regardless of political party or regional origins—were instrumental for promoting the expansion of suffrage. The also served another purpose: dismantling and repressing those social movements that sought to further the interests of more radical popular sectors. From this perspective, historiographical interpretations about long-standing ideological divides between Liberal and Conservative party leaders that were rooted in the period of independence, and that were disconnected from local realities, begin to lose their explanatory power.[9]

This is not to say that conflict did not occur among Spanish American elites. Of course it did. But those contests were less about entrenched ideological differences than manifestations of elite efforts to mobilize and bargain with popular sectors so they would go to the voting booth or onto the battlefield.[10] Consider, for instance, the historiographical truism that posits a Liberal-

Conservative split over questions of centralism versus federalism.[11] The territorial and constitutional changes of the mid-nineteenth century are much more interesting when seen from the vantage point of ideological consensus and engagement with realities on the ground. Rather than resulting from an ideologically driven and disconnected Liberal push toward federalism versus a blindly reactionary Conservative push toward centralism, we should understand these fundamental territorial and constitutional changes and concomitant political party strife in terms of how Liberals *and* Conservatives were focused on figuring out ways to expand the circulation of people, products, and ideas while also controlling political participation.

New Granada offers an illuminating case in point. Greater circulation required greater participation in the republic by peoples in far-flung, often difficult-to-reach regions. The nineteen New Granada provinces of 1832 that had a voice in the national Congress, and whose representatives elected the president, mushroomed into thirty-six provinces from 1845 to 1853. This transformation occurred at a moment when cities, not individuals, carried political rights. The result was a marked expansion of political participation by people in newly enfranchised townships. Newly minted municipalities within the new provinces brought to political office folks whose kinship networks had previously been excluded from the national scene. These new political players saw allies in the Liberal Party, founded in 1848, precisely because the bulk of the new territorial divisions occurred under the first president to run on a Liberal Party ticket.

Members of the Conservative Party, for their part, began to see how they and their kinship networks were losing political ground. The political rights afforded to the newly formed provinces and municipalities that favored the Liberal Party needed to be quashed. Rather than act as staunch retrograde reactionaries who refused the expansion of suffrage, Conservatives enthusiastically embraced the most radical liberal republican measure at the time: universal manhood suffrage. That is because Conservatives counted on their alliances with the Catholic Church and popular religiosity to return party members to political office.

They were right. Once universal manhood suffrage passed via New Granada's 1853 Constitution, in the wake of the abolition of slavery in 1851, the floodgates opened for competition between the recently formed political parties to mobilize newly enfranchised citizens to vote. Competition spilled over into the battlefield, unleashing the Civil War of 1854, one driven more by popular sectors than party elites.

Party leaders soon realized they needed to reach consensus to rein in violence and instability, and spaces of scientific sociability facilitated this consensus building. One result was that starting in 1855 the many municipalities of the thirty-six provinces were subsumed into nine overarching, sovereign, centralizing states. Political party influence in each of these states was negotiated among elites and territorialized. By 1863 these states developed their own constitutional limits on individual suffrage rights without fear of a challenge by the national government.

In short, party leaders were deeply engaged with the effects that their experiments with republicanism had on the ground. The stakes were too high to ignore local realities. Although competition clearly existed between political parties when it came time to mobilize popular sectors, the differences between party leaders were not primarily ideological. Violence, inequality, questions of sovereignty, circulation of trade, civil wars, slavery, emancipation, struggles over land held in common by indigenous communities, and the role of the Catholic Church in state formation all enter into my analysis precisely because of the ways the variety of actors considered here grappled with these realities and their implications.

This book is thoroughly and unapologetically eclectic regarding methodology, allowing each chapter to best identify the many colonial legacies postcolonial elites invented and the various technologies they used to overcome these alleged legacies. I draw on methods developed through studies on the history of the book, print culture, and the public sphere to reconstruct the ways postcolonial elites invented a colonial legacy of scientific ignorance out of a world that, under Spanish monarchical rule, had been teeming with naturalists. Through prosopography, I reconstruct the regional rosters of a major scientific society that served as the institutional embodiment of the elite, the *Instituto Caldas*, and in doing so demonstrate how the postcolonial circulatory project reflected bipartisan consensus. I engage the methods of social history to identify the techniques used to transform the colonial-era "indio" into the postcolonial "indíjena," in order to demonstrate how the litigiousness of the colonial state was adapted and adopted to legitimate the new republic. Techniques of social history also help demonstrate how secular normal schools came to replace church-centered education as some elites identified clerical corruption as the egregious colonial legacy that caused false consciousness in the voting booth. I engage methods from more traditional constitutional history to demonstrate how, in the flurry of midcentury constitutional writing, there emerged technologies intended to defang the unpredictable partisan electoral results brought by widespread political mobilization created by the abolition of slavery and universal manhood suffrage. I employ analytical methods developed by cultural historians to engage in a detailed reading of cartography that reveals the emergence of early republican ideas about Bogotá as a microcosm of national circulation and inward-looking integrated market economies designed to overcome a legacy of regional fragmentations. Finally, I engage the tools of literary analysis to discover the functions of *costumbrismo* as a technology of political ethnography designed to overcome the colonial legacies that manifested themselves in the pedestrian, the quaint, and the self.

This book engages with postcolonial and subaltern histories of science by showing how the "postcolonials" studied here operated outside of dichotomous understandings; they saw themselves as creators of modernity and republicanism. Postcolonial histories of science may elaborate nuanced theoretical positions seeking to blur dichotomies through the notion of hybridities, but in practice these works have produced dichotomous narratives of west/nonwest, subaltern/elite, center/periphery, local/global, and so forth.[12] More importantly, they have ceded categories such as "Western Civilization," "centers of calculation," "reason," and "enlightenment" as the limited creation of societies that happen to be located in the North Atlantic.[13] Critics like Fredrick Cooper have questioned the underlying assumptions of the contemporary "postcolonial" by demonstrating how attempts to "provincialize Europe" have, in effect, rendered invisible the processes of global cocreations in which colonies were as important as imperial metropoles in the invention of categories such as citizenship, reason, ecological domination, capitalism, industrialization, and unions.[14] It is in this line that this book gives voice to an array of actors that long-standing, dominant historiographies have rendered voiceless: provincial leaders, educators, intellectuals, journalists, government officials, religious figures, historians, military engineers, naturalists, land surveyors, and novelists.

This book examines how these Spanish American creators of new, autochthonous sciences, historical writings, and geographic practices did not envision their productions as peripheral forms of knowledge that occurred far from important centers of calculation. They instead affirmed that these forms of knowledge production were proper to a Spanish American republic on the cusp of becoming the model other places needed to emulate. In short, Spanish Americans adopted a broad, flexible array of technologies and scientific methods to produce modern democratic republics.

Although the historiography on colonial and postcolonial science from the "periphery" has so far largely missed this dimension to New Granada science, this body of scholarship nevertheless is now in a position to recognize it. Scholars have long argued that there is no such a thing as periphery.[15] We now know that all modern sciences were cocreated by centers and peripheries through forms of transnational accumulation of information produced through the work of invisible technicians and centers of calculation.[16] This historiographical trend acknowledges that "excellence" was not just the monopoly of metropolitan centers of calculation.[17] And yet, studies that examine examples of scientific excellence on "peripheries" like Latin America are few, and they are generally predicated on competitive geographic advantage; rarely could such practices be replicated elsewhere.[18] The sciences explored in this study do not fit this model. The men that developed the sciences of republican nation building in New Granada believed others could emulate their scientific practices and disciplines. And they did.[19]

Spanish American elites, through prisms of their invented colonial legacies, saw their path toward modernity as riddled with the obstacles of the past. The spatial order that would structure the newly emerging republican system and the historical narratives that legitimated both became prime sites of experimentation. New histories and original contributions to scientific practices, including geography, cartography, land surveying, ethnography, constitutional science, sociology, and the calculation of equity through land reform, would pinpoint remnants of the colonial legacy and root out colonialism's adverse effects. These phenomena occurred throughout Spanish America.

To highlight the spatially grounded dimensions of these revolutions, this book takes as a case in point the generations of Bogotá-centered elites, who were not necessarily from Bogotá, but who developed these sciences of the republican vanguard from that capital city. Regional and national elites believed that Bogotá was ideally positioned to foment the circulation of people, technology, goods, capital, and ideas. But from 1821 to 1863, Bogotá served as the capital city of at least four different republics, each with its own distinct constitutional and territorial configurations. The book demonstrates how these changes in territoriality were not gratuitous, or pointless. Instead, they responded to transformations in forms of popular political mobilization that were remarkably engaged with elite efforts to manage, enhance, or restrain that mobilization.

A few words on Colombia's constitutional, territorial, and economic changes may help situate the reader in the fast-paced transformations considered in this book. The reader must bear in mind, however, that any synthesis of scholarship on nineteenth-century Colombia that tries to re-create an overarching sense for "what actually happened" on the ground, including the next three paragraphs that follow, is unavoidably informed by the very categories invented by the nineteenth-century actors considered in this book. As nineteenth-century actors identified new colonial legacies and the means to overcome them, they produced wide-ranging mountains of knowledge: economic, statistical, cartographic, historiographical, and ethnographic. This is the archive historians have subsequently used to reconstruct the period. This archive unwittingly frames our vision of Colombia as a nation of regions struggling to overcome legacies of ignorance, absolutism, corruption, partisanship, and dependency. Mid-nineteenth-century postcolonial elites would have been delighted to find out that generations of historians after them have compliantly acquiesced to their demanding narratives.

Officials of the first Republic of Colombia (1821–1831) proposed a centralizing constitutional order to facilitate the mobilization of troops and resources needed to establish independence for a vast territory encompassing the former Captaincy General of Venezuela and the former Viceroyalty of New Granada (roughly today's Colombia, Panama, Venezuela, Ecuador, and parts of Guiana and Brazil). Bogotá became the default capital city during these moments of instability, when sovereignty by the pueblos was still up for grabs.[20] When the threat of Spanish restoration abated by 1826, cities chafing under Bogotá's rule, such as Valencia, Caracas, and Quito, pulled away from that first Gran Colombian Republic. The republics of Ecuador, Venezuela, and New Granada (roughly today's Colombia and Panama) emerged in its wake. Bogotá's role as capital city for New Granada during the 1830s–1850s oscillated between that of a centripetal force drawing the regions in toward Bogotá's sphere of political control to that of a circulatory mechanism that diffused economic and political power to other regional capitals.[21] By 1858, this regional, city-driven process created the short-lived Confederación Granadina, or Granadian Confederacy, which only lasted as long as the civil war that tore it apart. Nine new states emerged in its wake to form a federal pact launching the United States of Colombia in 1863 that lasted until 1886.[22]

These dynamic constitutional and territorial changes are suggestive of the dramatic social-political and economic transformations that occurred in Colombia during the first half of the nineteenth century. Available economic histories tend to examine the latter half of the nineteenth century into the twentieth, when Colombia was more firmly engaged as an exporter of coffee and other commodities.[23] These works together with the precious few studies that emphasize the first half of the nineteenth century critically depend on the sources produced by many of the provincial government functionaries, lawyers, merchants, religious leaders, diplomats, writers, military engineers, and government officials considered here.[24] The economic picture that emerges from these studies tends to show economic segmentation and stagnation for reasons similar to those given by nineteenth-century historical actors. In part that is because Colombia's geographic terrain was and is undeniably significant in shaping economic, social, cultural, and political patterns and movements.[25] The massive Andean mountain range, which splits into three *cordilleras* that are divided by the Cauca and the Magdalena river valleys, produces remarkable climatic variation and makes overland travel difficult.

The challenges of a difficult geographic terrain were exacerbated by considerable international debt incurred during the period of independence. Conditions of fragmentation, stagnation, and poverty became central issues of concern.[26] Efforts to privatize communal land holding had a transformative effect on indigenous communities and on properties held in mortmain by the Catholic Church.[27] The gradual transition toward the abolition of slavery also transformed the economy and thousands of lives.[28] Although a somewhat smaller segment of the national economy, the economic lives of artisans also played a significant role in urban politics in Bogotá and at the national level.[29] Throughout this period, the Panamanian isthmus tantalizingly promised easy connections between the Atlantic and Pacific and therefore played an important role in the territorial and constitutional logic of the republic at midcentury.[30] Although beyond the scope of this study, international interests in canal building together with internal strife culminated in Panama's independence from Colombia by 1903.[31]

Chapter Outline

Six thematically and temporally interlinked chapters explore the consensus, continuities, and contentions that drove the dramatic territorial, constitutional, and sociopolitical changes that shaped Colombia during the nineteenth century. Each chapter reconstructs how different groups of Spanish Americans turned to geography, historical writing, and innovative scientific discourses to invent discrete "colonial legacies" and, in doing so, legitimate claims to rule and enact policy. Educators, intellectuals, government officials, and religious leaders deployed what they understood to be modern scientific technologies to either root out these negative colonial legacies or to enhance those invented legacies of Spanish culture and Catholicism that lent morality and inclusiveness to a developing Spanish American republicanism.[32]

The first chapter argues officials of the first Colombian Republic deployed print culture as a technology to erase evidence of the Spanish monarchy's support for Enlightenment science in the Americas, thereby legitimating independence from supposed monarchical tyranny and obscurantism. Print culture was relatively new to Spanish America by the 1820s.[33] Before then, communities of governance were imagined through the circulation of manuscripts.[34] At a time when independence was still up for grabs, republican officials deployed print culture to found a republic that was supposedly a complete departure from Spanish colonial rule. Examining early republican erasures of historical memory deepens our understanding of the role the press played in the invention of nations.[35] Colombian officials edited, reframed, and reprinted the writings of *criollos*, or the descendants of Spaniards born in the New World who proclaimed themselves the nobility of the continent. Colombian officials were especially eager to reprint the work of criollos whose participation in the early period of independence culminated in their execution by Spanish armies, most notably, Francisco José de Caldas. Caldas, prior to execution, had joined the hundreds of naturalists, mineralogists, military engineers, and botanists who participated in the massive Bourbon project of reform and information gathering through botanical expeditions, coastal soundings, mappings, and centralization of archives.[36]

Yet, in the hands of republican officials, Caldas, the martyred criollo savant, stood alone. His execution proved the Spanish monarchy was obscurantist and feared enlightened knowledge. No longer would Caldas be just one among hundreds of agents whose scientific work was supported by the Crown. For early republican elites, Caldas became the martyred patriotic father of Colombian geography whose enlightened knowledge was extinguished by the Spanish Army. The chapter signals a second and related kind of historical manufacturing that emerged during this period through the juxtaposition of Caldas with editorial commentary through print culture. Historians have recently demonstrated how the 1808–1815 dissolution of Spain's Spanish Atlantic monarchy had at its core the territorial logic of sovereignty reverting back to the pueblos.[37] Early republican writers erased that complex history to instead convey a story of the "Patria Boba" or foolish fatherland of chaotic federalism versus civilized centralism. Although the first Colombian Republic was a different polity than that of the New Granada Republic, the opening chapter underscores the emphasis that 1820s patriot leaders placed on Caldas's prescriptions for how good governance would come through scientific expertise deployed to truly know the territory. Republican leaders in New Granada continued to cherish this ideal for generations.

The second chapter moves forward in time to demonstrate how, a generation after independence, New Granada elites invented an entirely new legacy for Spanish colonialism that, instead of breaking with the past, displayed continuities that needed to be rooted out. For them, the principle legacy of the Spanish colonial period was that it created blockages to circulation. Midcentury government officials, educators, intellectuals, religious leaders, architects, engineers, and military generals agreed: republicanism needed to dismantle the blockages to progress created by the Spanish monarchy by fomenting the circulation of people, products, ideas, and capital throughout the national territory. Circulation and integration would flow more easily across regions through the imposition of homogeneity in currency, units of weights and measures, language, morality, and values. Roads, canals, ports, and educational infrastructure would allow New Granada to become the international hub it was meant to be. Provincial officials circulated through Bogotá and inaugurated educational institutions and scientific societies that further established Bogotá as a critical circulatory center for future generations of provincial leaders. The chapter argues that this cultural project of circulation, one shared by elites from a variety of New Granada provinces and whose loyalties crisscrossed the political party spectrum, marked a distinct moment in New Granada's invention of nationalism.[38] As such, this chapter challenges readings of the 1840s-1850s that focus on chaos, instability, elite detachment, and the supposed ideological divides between Liberals versus Conservatives or federalists versus centralists.[39]

Significantly, this bipartisanship and consensus developed a project of circulation that pointed inward. Midcentury postcolonial elites showed no interest in connecting out to world markets by building up plantation economies for export. For them, this outward orientation was a colonial legacy to be overcome.[40] They were well aware of the contemporary North American experiment to build an export-oriented republic on the back of racialized, industrial slavery, namely the Cotton Kingdom.[41] Several postcolonial Spanish Americans openly and loudly rejected this model and advocated for slave emancipation and the abolition of slavery. New Granada elites saw themselves as better positioned than the United States to be at the vanguard of world republicanism.

The chapter also contributes to studies that seek to show how space, place, and setting have always been culturally produced, socially negotiated, and historically shifting.[42] It does so by illustrating how this midcentury shared cultural project led to the invention of a circulatory function for national space through the geographic and cartographic training that future generations of provincial elites received in the Colegio Militar. A deep reading of the cartography that these cadets produced reveals the kind of cultural, economic, technological, spiritual, and gendered meaning midcentury actors embedded in Bogotá as circulatory capital for New Granada regions. Some Colegio Militar students went above and beyond required assignments and produced whimsical mental maps of New Granada that further reveal the remarkable engagement these actors had with global trends affecting New Granada realities.

Chapter 3 opens by considering a critical task set before graduates of the Colegio Militar: the surveying and partitioning of lands held in common by indigenous communities. Efforts to privatize indigenous communal lands were met with significant obstacles throughout Spanish America.[43] Among the most oft-cited reasons for delays: a lack of trained expertise.[44] New Granada was no different. The chapter shows how, by midcentury, graduates of the Colegio Militar, the best of the best, were ready to take on this task. These well-trained experts nevertheless failed miserably. The chapter contextualizes these failures by exploring the nineteenth-century invention of the "indíjena" that replaced the colonial-era *casta* category reviled by republicans: the "indio." Republicans repeatedly denounced the ineffectual Spanish colonial state that solved nothing and was mired in corruption. They argued that the miserable "indio," under the Spanish Crown, suffered exploitative tribute and was submerged in ignorance through settlement into *resguardos*, or lands held in common by indigenous peoples. "Indíjenas" would be different. The republican state would send surveyors trained in relevant laws, trigonometry, arithmetic, a republican calculus of equity to ensure that the partitioning of communal lands among indigenous communities would be equitable according to environment, land uses, and social relations. And yet, the invented trope of the *indíjena* became useful not only for republicans seeking to privatize resguardos, but also for those who wished to protect indíjenas by delaying privatization. Elite indigenous families seeking to maintain control over resguardo lands, popular indigenous folks seeking a measure of sustenance for themselves and their families, as well as neighboring mestizos and elites, all deployed the trope of the "indíjena" to support their case. The chapter traces out how, from the 1820s into the 1870s, the republican state produced a plethora of often-contradictory legislation, presidential decrees, and juridical dictates that reflected these tensions over the *resguardos de indíjenas*.

The engineers and land surveyors who would partition resguardo lands had to be well versed in these laws. New generations of surveyors also learned an elaborate and original calculus of republican equity that would grant land parcels of equal value to all members of indigenous communities. These innovative technologies and scientific practices would transform New Granada, and the rest of Spanish America that implemented this calculus, into the democratic vanguard that it needed to become. As such, the chapter challenges historical interpretations of nineteenth-century Spanish Americans who sought to privatize communal land holding as racist elites seeking to impose useless foreign models on local realities.[45] The radical measures they developed for local realities were nevertheless met with overwhelming resistance, but resistance notably did not come in the form of massive civil wars. Rather, conflict resolution was sought out through the assorted emerging levers of the state at the local, provincial, and national levels. These mechanisms often favored the interests of elite whites, but elite indigenous families who had long asserted control over resguardo land use also found ways of defending their interests. So did the neighboring white and mestizo families claiming rights to resguardo lands, and the poorer, unmarried indigenous women seeking ways to ensure sustenance for their families through resguardo land claims. The decentralized, multipolar system of justice gave all litigants hope, and, through litigation, the republican state's legitimacy was gauged and engaged. This form of legitimization through arbitration bore an uncanny similarity to how the Spanish colonial state had functioned.[46] As for the attempted surveys by Colegio Militar graduates, the chapter highlights how the division of the Bogotá province into smaller provincial jurisdictions, together with conflict over who was included and excluded from the census, meant that, despite expertise, the resguardos that Colegio Militar graduates surveyed were still in litigation well into the 1870s and beyond.

Chapter 4 addresses an important paradox: at midcentury, just as elites across the political spectrum and from the majority of New Granada provinces found spaces of sociability that facilitated a shared ideological republican project that was deeply engaged with local realities, the two most resilient and antagonistic political parties, Liberals and Conservatives, burst onto the scene. At the heart of that paradox, I argue, is the way spaces in New Granada carried political rights up until 1853. From the period of the dissolution of the Spanish monarchy, republican constitutions conferred political representation to urban municipal spaces, that is, the pueblos.[47] With New Granada's Constitution of 1832, the most significant space carrying representative weight within the republic continued to be the municipality. As noted above, from 1845 through 1853 the Executive Power dramatically increased the number of provinces to thirty-six, and with that expansion the number of municipalities also grew. The cumulative political effect was that greater numbers of people from around New Granada that previously had been excluded from participation in national politics had gained a significant voice. This transformation came at the same time that a vast infrastructure of print newspapers emerged, facilitating public reading in public spaces. This was also the moment when the scientific society appropriately named the Instituto Caldas was founded in Bogotá in 1848 and inspired hundreds of provincial elites, from across the emerging political spectrum, to form and join local chapters. This network of provincial elites laid the foundations for the Chorographic Commission; one of the most impressive, large-scale scientific expeditions of the nineteenth century.[48] The commission was supported by the national government no matter which political party held control, in large part because of the shared pan-regional, cross-party consensus created at midcentury through the Instituto Caldas.

The fourth chapter also contributes to literature on the Chorographic Commission by focusing on two underexplored dimensions: how it facilitated the political rights granted to newly created municipalities and its contributions to political ethnography. From 1850 to 1853 the commission was deployed to the provinces that the Liberal-led regime had recently carved out, including provinces that had exploded in civil war in 1851 because of the new divisions. This multiplication of municipalities and provinces emerged out of the Instituto Caldas's project to foment cultural and economic circulation. The Chorographic Commission was simply the coordinating administrative structure encouraging the new town and regional elites to collect statistics and introduce entrepreneurial republican virtues through education, religion, and the public sphere. Regional elites were bipartisan and avidly encouraged the spread of popular political participation within ancien régime logic, at least a first. The categories of individual rights, sovereignty, and the franchise were not yet the preferred framework of republican mobilization. Political rights spread because municipalities and provinces multiplied. Space had political rights, not individuals. The chapter then turns to the materials produced by the Chorographic Commission that circulated in print during the early 1850s, focusing on the travel narrative penned by the secretary of the commission and founder of the Instituto Caldas, Manuel Ancízar. I argue that Ancízar's narrative needs to be read as an early form of political ethnography, and he was not alone in the adoption of this scientific technique at midcentury. This cultural current proper to the nineteenth century is more commonly known as "costumbrismo," and literary critics have largely dismissed it as a nonsensical, derivative genre.[49] I argue that as members from the emerging Liberal and Conservative parties wrestled with the implications of expanded political participation by popular sectors, intellectuals and writers from both parties developed costumbrismo as a science of political ethnography. This science was meant to be read publically and widely, and the expanded public sphere of print by midcentury facilitated this intended purpose. Costumbrismo became a technology of transcendent surveillance intended to pinpoint and transform the national self.

Depictions of everyday life and customs would reveal how "colonial mentalities" produced absurd behavior that needed to be extricated from the republic. Liberals such as Ancízar used costumbrismo to condemn wasteful, impious, and irrational religious processions as a holdover from the more immoral aspects of Spanish colonialism and called on religious leaders to discipline their flock to worship more productive saints such as San Isidro Labrador, the patron saint of farmworkers. Conservative writers like Eugenio Díaz Castro deployed costumbrismo through fictional novels like *Manuela* to respond to Liberal Ancízar's critique by championing popular religious processions as innovative political speech. What Díaz Castro found absurd was how Liberal elites (like Ancízar) who sought to mindlessly adopt foreign models and graft them onto local realities missed the creativity of popular sectors. The legacy of Spanish colonialism as developed by Ancízar for the Chorographic Commission, and Díaz Castro's elaboration of the neocoloniality of the eurocentric Liberal operated through the national self. Both were pointing to *costumbres*, or behaviors that replicated oppression within the self. In this sense costumbrismo offers the nineteenth-century discovery of psychological oppression rather than the oppression of economic dependency. These techniques of reading everyday behaviors asked strikingly similar questions to those posed by postcolonial critical theorists such as Frantz Fanon, Albert Memmi, and Aimé Césaire one hundred years later.[50] The categories that nineteenth-century writers used to think through coloniality, however, were very different and produced remarkably innovative and creative answers.[51] Rather than cede the "West" to genealogically inherited, unchanging racial traits that drove the imposition of colonialism onto others, these thinkers thought of themselves as imbricated in the creation of modernity.

Chapter 5 explores the territorial, political, and constitutional revolution that occurred at midcentury in New Granada. By this period, elites developed what they called a "science of constitutionalism." This innovative approach to constitution writing allowed them to think through and experiment with the balance of sovereignty in a republic. The new science of constitutionalism introduced universal manhood suffrage in 1853, in the wake of the abolition of slavery in 1851. This represented a major departure from political mobilization. Prior to this change, enfranchisement occurred through the multiplication of corporate municipal rights. Faith in the wisdom of universal manhood suffrage was short-lived, however. The chapter argues that the introduction of universal manhood suffrage was not a radical Liberal Party project, but rather one that enjoyed widespread support from the same bipartisan, moderate elites—including Conservatives—that bolstered the Instituto Caldas and the Corographic Commission. Whereas in the early 1850s the balance tipped increasingly toward depositing sovereignty in individuals, midcentury civil wars and party strife forced the scales firmly in favor of a state sovereignty that trumped both individual and national sovereignty. The men most active in these constitutional-territorial experiments were also the men most engaged with local realities through the Instituto Caldas and the Chorographic Commission. Their constitutional experiments first yielded the Constitution of 1853 that sanctioned the abolition of slavery, universal manhood suffrage, and the popular election of the president, Congress, the Supreme Court, and provincial governors. This change meant, in effect, that individual political rights usurped a half-century-long constitutional order that made municipal and provincial governments the principle carriers of political rights.

The result was that overwhelming numbers of Conservatives assumed provincial and congressional offices. Popular and traditional Liberal elites were radicalized against this change. Elite Liberals blamed the colonial legacy: popular sectors voted against their own interests due to corrupt indoctrination by the Catholic Church. Popular Liberals, especially urban artisans and lower-ranking military officials, saw the Conservative-dominated Congress begin to develop legislation that worked against their interests, and they took action. By April 1854, and with the help of a handful of the more traditional leaders of the Liberal Party, they orchestrated a coup against the Conservative-dominated Congress. This uprising forced the majority of elites, Liberal and Conservative, to lose control of the national government. This popular movement, however, was at a distinct disadvantage. It lacked the spaces of scientific sociability and deep territorial knowledge that elites from both political parties enjoyed. A coalition that included the leader of the Chorographic Commission, Agustín Codazzi, repressed the popular uprising militarily on the ground. When back in control, Liberal and Conservative party leaders deployed the technology of constitutionalism to create Estados Soberanos, or sovereign states, starting with Panama in 1855. The chapter demonstrates how those elites most engaged with local realities, especially members of the Instituto Caldas and the Chorographic Commission, led this process, culminating in a new constitution that brought forth the Grenadine Confederacy starting in 1858. Framing the 1854 Civil War in this way allows for a clearer understanding of the deep constitutional, political, and territorial impact of this conflict, one usually read as a confusing one-off urban coup launched by an alliance of military officers united with disgruntled artisans that was supposedly limited to Bogotá.[52]

Despite elite agreements, party strife continued and again exploded in civil war from 1859 to 1862, bringing the confederacy's end. Conservative and Liberal party elites agreed to divvy up their regional sites of political control, bringing forth the United States of Colombia (1863–1886), a federation that granted even greater sovereignty to the states than the confederacy. Universal manhood suffrage enshrined in the Constitution of 1853 no longer was either universal or enforceable. Each individual state issued a new constitution. Such partisan control was nevertheless negotiated with popular sectors, especially in those sovereign states where the Liberal Party depended on mobilized popular armies. This explains why the hard-won right to universal manhood suffrage was not given up so easily in states like Cauca.[53] This also explains why the story was different in states like Boyacá, where the Conservative Party competed with the Liberal Party for dominance. The chapter shows how, by the 1860s, the science of constitutionalism, after facing the challenge of popular mobilization, yielded a national state that lost the right to intervene in state-level electoral processes, even if an election with national implications was conducted under massive electoral fraud. Cross-party elite unity of purpose and fears of uncontrollable, unpredictable popular sectors proved more significant than ensuring universal manhood suffrage. The technology of shaming the coloniality of the mind through costumbrismo in the public sphere proved insufficient. Constitutional science became the answer. Somewhat ironically the Liberal versus Conservative political party strife that forced the creation of the sovereign states yielded another casualty: the 1840s ideal of circulation throughout the republic. The chapter ends by showing how, throughout this period of party strife and constitutional and territorial changes, the Chorographic Commission continued, and debates raged over how materials would be presented to a more general public.

The sixth and final substantive chapter offers a nuanced exploration of how the Olimpo Radical, or the Radical Liberal Olympus, challenged the economic, cultural, and ideological power of the Catholic Church through the twinned policies of disentailment and public education, and lost. This defeat, occurring in the broader context of the late nineteenth and early twentieth centuries, marked the end of the elite republican project examined in this book. The beginning of the end had already been in the works as the shared ideals of universal manhood suffrage, internal circulation of goods, ideas, and people, and the separation of church and state were rolled back in the wake of violent civil wars.

The creation of nine sovereign states that made up the United States of Colombia starting in 1863 allowed the Radical Liberal Olympus to dominate national politics from the 1860s through the 1880s.[54] The former president and general, Tomás Cipriano de Mosquera, inaugurated the Radical Liberal Olympus after toppling the first president ever to be elected through universal manhood suffrage in the Western Hemisphere, Conservative Party founder Mariano Ospina. The United Sates of Colombia inaugurated under Mosquera transformed the very foundations of political economy. Ever since Caldas, the project of the provincial elites, including Mosquera, had been that of promoting integrative circulatory systems of all kinds. The raison d'être of the Instituto Caldas and the Chorographic Commission had been to promote the gospel of integration by smashing "colonial" barriers getting in the way of standardization and circulation within the nation and by the local accumulation of a bank of statistics meant to be shared. The United States of Colombia threatened a fragmented landscape of independent, sovereign islands loosely connected by a weak national government. The new balkanized state did not resemble that of the past, and spaces of sociability that cut across party lines like that of the Instituto Caldas were dismissed as useless utopias. Despite this tendency toward balkanization, Liberals in control of the national state nevertheless tried to maintain some circulation through the nation, especially when it came time to establish a national system of public education. The only way to establish such a system, as they saw it, was targeting the wealth that the Catholic Church held in mortmain.

Mosquera and other fellow elite Liberal Party members were concerned that the Catholic Church's affinity with the Conservative Party was dangerous and represented a nefarious colonial legacy of corrupt parish priests wrongly indoctrinating their flock. That was what explained the Conservative Party triumphs at the voting booth. Liberals argued that Catholic clergy, sustained by the landed wealth accumulated during the period of monarchical rule, perpetuated ignorance among popular sectors at the pulpit, induced their innocent flock to vote for the Conservative Party, and had themselves taken up arms and destabilized constitutional rule. The best way to assure Catholic Church clergy respected the republic was by allowing the republican state to gain the rights of *patronato* over the church. As in other Spanish American republics, Conservatives challenged the call to patronato by championing the separation of church and state.[55] Although Liberals and Conservatives may have disagreed on patronato, the chapter nevertheless demonstrates how Conservatives agreed with Liberals on implementing a key policy: disentailment of the Catholic Church's vast wealth in properties held in mortmain.

The final chapter therefore offers an overview of church-state relations to underscore points of consensus and contention among members of the Liberal and Conservative parties, focusing on the 1860 through 1880s. Liberals and Conservatives had long identified the Catholic Church as responsible for coordinating and reproducing immiserating landholding patterns. Republican elites across the political spectrum had tried to expropriate landed church wealth to create a circulating rural land market since the period of independence, to no avail. The chapter shows how, even though Liberals waxed triumphant in the wake of the Civil War of 1859–1862, their victory nevertheless conceded political control to Conservatives over some states. Elite Liberals needed to negotiate with Conservatives to implement the policies that targeted the Catholic Church throughout Colombia. Although met with some obstacles, the Liberal regime succeeded in disentailing several church properties, even in Conservative Party–dominated states. Conservative officials in the states also agreed with the Olimpo Radical that one of the best uses that disentailed wealth could be put to was expanding the national system of public instruction. Problems arose when it came time to decide on the content of public education and who would teach that content to popular sectors.

Whereas in the 1840s and 1850s partisan battles over the soul of popular folks played out through public gatherings of partisans who listened to newspaper costumbrista vignettes, by the 1860s through the 1880s classrooms became the prioritized spaces where students memorized lessons on geography and history. The national spatial network of normal schools and the interior spaces of these centers that were intended to educate future citizens reveal some continuities with the 1840s project of circulation of people, ideas, and print culture from Bogotá and out to each region and back. Midcentury mappings and geographic writings of the Chorographic Commission circulated throughout the normal school system. Codazzi's manuscript maps were nevertheless divested of the rich, detailed information produced through the Chorographic Commission. The dissemination of sanitized printed maps and atlases, cleansed of local details and placed at the front of normal schoolrooms formerly occupied by crucifixes, would magically work on popular imaginaries. State and national community ties would come to be more significant than municipal loyalties or religious piety. Printed geographies, educational manuals, and maps for consumption in a widening network of public schools would help manufacture communities of consent among popular sectors across generations and would ensure long-term Liberal dominance over the Conservative Party.

The chapter shows how, although many Conservatives negotiated with Liberals on disentailment and the expansion of public education, they drew the line at ideological indoctrination. Attacks by Liberals on the church sparked intellectual battles. Some Conservative voices, such as historian of the Catholic Church José Manuel Groot, articulated a narrative that resoundingly countered Liberal Party accusations of the church as perpetuator of a colonial legacy of backwardness. He demonstrated that, far from being the epitome of colonialism, the church during the colonial period was actually the epitome of modernity given its ability to foment the production of knowledge, engage in economic development, and serve as the testing ground for constitutionalism and democracy through inclusiveness. These intellectual battles were taken to the actual battlefield. The expansive secularization of education was bad enough. Conservatives could not stomach the Radical Liberal decision to bring in German Protestant normal school teachers to teach Colombian teachers how to teach. This move sparked the most devastating civil war in Colombia during the period of the Olimpo Radical. Although Liberals won the 1876 Civil War, they were significantly weakened and would soon lose hold of national power. By the 1880s the vision Mosquera had of a Catholic Church completely subordinated to the state through patronato and the expansion of a public education that put civic religion at its center rather than Catholicism was resoundingly defeated. Instead, the new Colombian Republic signed the Concordato, granting the church ample power to maneuver without state intervention. Furthermore, Colombia ceded control over frontier missions to the church as well as public instruction. These changes, together with the export-oriented economies that came to dominate Colombia's political economy, the devastating War of a Thousand Days, and the secession of Panama marked the death of the republican project of the 1840s and 1850s.

The book concludes by returning focus on how midcentury Spanish Americans had nevertheless crafted their republican experiments as models for the world to emulate. I take as a case in point the comparative sociology offered by one of the many vanguard republican scientists considered in this book, José María Samper. During his travels to Europe at the end of the 1850s, Samper was struck by the emerging racial discourse that pitted a supposed "Latin" race against a supposed "Anglo-Saxon" race. Writing in 1858, the year Franz Boaz was born, Samper boldly argued against emerging ideologies positing that "racial" traits were biological and inherited. Samper instead argued that "race" was culture and that the origin of exclusions and inequalities did not lie with the color of one's skin but in history and institutions.[56] Samper denounced the genealogical racial traits suggested by a "Latin" America and offered instead "Hispano-Colombia." This was a modern, republican continental Colombia with ties to a modern Spain. What tied the region together were shared cultural traits rooted in a resilient, modern Catholic Church. Samper's striking interventions and prescriptions, much like those of his Spanish American early republican cohort, are largely unknown. The conclusion explores the longer-term political effects of this remarkable historical loss of memory on how we understand the region.

CHAPTER 1

Gran Colombian Print Culture and the Erasure of the Spanish Enlightenment

Colombians have long known that "El Sabio" Francisco José de Caldas (1771–1816) was the patriotic founding father of Colombian geography at a time when geographic knowledge, and the Colombian Republic, were both in a state of infancy. Universities, plazas, streets, monuments, scientific networks and institutes, and even a territorial department and several municipalities have all been named in honor of El Sabio Caldas. Popular Colombian narratives of Caldas portray him as the self-taught genius from Popayán who developed interests in natural history, geography, and astronomy. Because of El Sabio's dangerous passion for knowledge, Spanish general Morillo ordered Caldas's execution. When Caldas pleaded for his life, Morillo is rumored to have coldly sealed Caldas's fate with the words "Spain has no need for *sabios*."[1] Several historical events between 1808 and 1816 helped invent this narrative of Caldas. Indeed, Caldas was from Popayán. He had penned several treatises about geography, astronomy, and natural sciences. Caldas's role in Santafé de Bogotá's declaration of independence has tended to overshadow the fact that, in 1812, Caldas had called for independence from the Spanish Cortes, not Fernando VII. The Spanish king's deployment of Reconquista armies to South America radicalized Caldas against monarchy. By 1816 Caldas and several other prominent members of New Granada society were arrested, and the massive collections of botanical specimens, drawings, and maps held in the astronomical observatory were confiscated. Caldas was executed. The vast collection of materials was sent back to Spain.[2]

The lionizing of "founding" individuals for specific disciplines is by no means unusual. Scholars have long noted how "inventions of tradition" have been employed by scientific societies and other social and cultural groups around the world to create a sense of historical legacy and legitimacy for specific intellectual and political endeavors.[3] Recent scholarship on the history of geography and cartography has therefore rightly stepped away from conventional hagiographic accounts of a small number of important founding fathers—and even fewer mothers—whose work progressively improved cartographic accuracy in order to instead engage in a more complex and critical reading of the discipline's past.[4] In Colombia, partly due to his popular, nationalistic appeal, Francisco José de Caldas and his writings have become the object of rigorous intellectual inquiry along these lines.[5] And yet these and other studies in the history of exploration, cartography, and geography place an overwhelming focus on the power-laden discourse of maps themselves, or specific expeditions that produced cartographic knowledge, or individual mapmakers.[6]

This chapter offers a different methodological approach toward understanding the significance of Caldas, his work, and his writings. Rather than taking Caldas's original writings as the focus of analysis, this chapter parses out the specific circumstances behind early 1820s efforts to edit and reprint Caldas in ways that produced him as Colombia's founding father of geography. Caldas's execution by Morillo's armies allowed early republican print culture to manufacture, for the first time, the narrative of Caldas as the lone savant working without any institutional support from the Crown. The feat is remarkable. Early republican leaders sought to convince a society that had recently witnessed a massive buildup of cartographical, geographical, and natural history knowledge under the Bourbons that the Spanish monarchy created a regime of ignorance. Caldas, to be sure, was no lone pioneer. He was one of hundreds who, in the late Bourbon period, collected statistics, wrote natural histories, drew maps and chorographies, explored odd geological landscapes, and engaged in historical research. New Granada was a land teeming with people like Caldas. And yet Caldas has emerged as the lone, autodidact martyr who exemplified the barbarism and obscurantism of the Spanish monarchy. Examining the historical framing—and erasures—produced in print during the 1820s reveals an under-appreciated dimension to the critical role print culture played in early Spanish American republics. The lionization of Caldas as martyr of knowledge, forgotten and marginalized by Spain, emerged in the early republic's press to erase the wealth of knowledge produced and supported by the Crown. Caldas became the Galileo of the first Colombian Republic. Despite this repudiation of the Spanish Crown, Colombia's official newspaper's editors drew on the natural knowledge produced through the Crown's support to argue that Colombia's centralized political economy would best extricate wealth from natural resources and circulate diverse populations. The Colombian Republic thereby legitimated itself as the antidote to a colonial legacy of superstition and persecution while asserting its claims to centralized rule for wealth extraction and circulation.

The chapter demonstrates how early republican leaders edited and reprinted Caldas's words to set in stone priorities for the new republic. Those priorities still resonate with some Colombians, as can be seen in the photograph in figure 1. This massive slab of words greets visitors to Colombia's Instituto Geográfico Agustín Codazzi (IGAC). Originally penned by Caldas in 1808, these words have been quoted time and again to elicit a patriotic drive to acquire knowledge of "our" mountains, rivers, coastlines, and territories. At the time of his writing, Caldas lamented that geographic knowledge about his place of birth was in its infancy. He argued no expense should be spared to ensure the production of a stately, dignified, detailed map, a "magic painting" that would attract the brightest minds and foment industry, navigation, education, transportation, and production and extraction of natural resources. Caldas warned against the humiliation, lethargy, and poverty created by geographic ignorance. Caldas's words, along with several other excerpts from his *Semanario del Nuevo Reino de Granada*, the scientific journal Caldas edited from 1808 to 1810, have been decontextualized, edited, and reprinted time and again. In the 1820s, Caldas, the lone savant, became the patriotic genius who proposed the free circulation of commodities and technical knowledge that the early Colombian Republic needed. The life of Caldas as the

> QUE LLEVEMOS NUESTRAS MIRADAS AL NORTE, QUE LAS LLEVEMOS AL MEDIODIA QUE REGISTREMOS LO MAS POBLADO, O LOS DESIERTOS DE ESTA COLONIA, EN TODAS PARTES NO HALLAMOS SINO EL SELLO DE LA DESIDIA Y DE LA IGNORANCIA. NUESTROS RIOS Y NUESTRAS MONTAÑAS NOS SON DESCONOCIDOS, NO SABEMOS LA EXTENSION DEL PAIS EN QUE HEMOS NACIDO, Y NUESTRA GEOGRAFIA ESTA EN LA CUNA. ESTA VER= DAD CAPITAL QUE NOS HUMILLA DEBE SACARNOS DEL LETARGO EN QUE VIVIMOS: ELLA DEBE HACERNOS MAS ATENTOS SOBRE NUESTROS INTERESES, LLEVARNOS A TODOS LOS ANGULOS DE LA NUEVA GRANADA. PARA MEDIRLOS, CONSIDERARLOS Y DESCRIBIRLOS; ESTA ES LA QUE, GRABADA EN EL CORAZON DE TODOS LOS BUENOS CIUDADANOS, LOS REUNIRA PARA RECOGER LUCES, HACER FONDOS, LLAMAR INTELIGENTES, Y NO PERDONAR TRABAJOS NI GASTOS PARA EL ESCRUPULOSO RECONOCIMIENTO DE NUESTRAS PROVINCIAS ★ NO SE TRATA YA DE UNA CARTA COMUN: ESCALAS REDUCIDAS Y TODO LO QUE TENGA APARIENCIA DE PEQUE= ÑEZ U ECONOMIA DEBE DESAPARECER DEL ESPIRITU DE NUESTROS COMPATRIOTAS. ★ DOS PULGADAS, POR LO MENOS DEBEN REPRESENTAR UNA LEGUA DE TERRENO. AQUI SE HAN DE NOTAR LAS COLINAS, LAS MONTAÑAS, LOS PASTOS, LAS SELVAS, LOS RASTROJOS: LAGOS, PANTANOS, VALLES, RIOS; SUS VUELTAS Y VELOCIDADES, ESTRECHOS, CATARATAS, PESCA: TODAS LAS POBLACIONES, TODOS LOS ESTABLECI= MIENTOS DE AGRICULTURA, MINERALES, CANTERAS; EN FIN, CUANTO PRESENTA LA SUPERFICIE DE NUES= TRO SUELO. REUNIDOS ESTOS CUADRADOS PRODUCIRAN UNA CARTA SOBERBIA Y DIGNA DE LA NUEVA GRA= NADA. AQUI VENDRA EL POLITICO, EL MAGISTRADO, EL FILOSOFO. EL NEGOCIANTE, A BEBER LUCES PARA EL DESEMPEÑODE SUS OFICIOS, AQUI EL VIAJERO, EL BOTANICO, EL MINERALOGISTA, EL QUE SE OCUPA CON LOS SERES VIVIENTES, EL MILITAR Y EL AGRICULTOR VERAN CON RASGOS MAJESTUOSOS PINTADOS SUS INTE= RESES, TODAS LAS CLASES DEL ESTADO VENDRAN A TOMAR AQUI LA PARTE QUE LES TOCA. ESTE ES UN CUA= DRO MAGICO QUE TOMA TODAS LAS FORMAS, Y SE ACOMODA A TODOS LOS CARACTERES. CADA PROVINCIA CO= PIARA SU DEPARTAMENTO Y LE GUARDARA RELIGIOSAMENTE. EN ESTOS TROZOS SE FORMARA LA JUVEN= TUD Y A LA VUELTA DE POCOS AÑOS TENDREMOS HOMBRES CAPACES DE CONCEBIR Y DE EJECUTAR GRANDES COSAS. POR TODAS PARTES NO SE OIRAN SINO PROYECTOS, CAMINOS, NAVEGACIONES, CANALES, NUEVOS RAMOS DE INDUSTRIA, PLANTAS EXOTICAS CONNATURALIZADAS; LA LLAMA PATRIOTICA SE ENCENDERA EN TODOS LOS CORAZONES, Y EL ULTIMO RESULTADO SERA LA PROSPERIDAD DE ESTA COLONIA.   F. J. CALDAS
> ★ MDCCCVIII

1. Photograph of the monument to Caldas at the entrance to Instituto Geográfico Agustin Codazzi. http://hugosalamancaparra.net/ComtlTerritorial.html.

martyred geographer conveyed the burden of colonial legacies and made the priorities of political economy transparent.

The first section reconstructs how Caldas formed part of a deep and wide network of naturalists, intellectuals, and merchant elites. Caldas drew on and contributed to a world of natural history and chorographic knowledge that was supported by the Spanish Crown. Archbishoprics, religious orders, the royal navy, newly founded universities, and the establishment of the first astronomical observatory in the hemisphere all formed part of an extensive, and expensive, push by the Spanish monarchy to expand natural knowledge production. Caldas was part of that cohort. The chapter draws on the work of others to show how, between 1808 and 1810, when the Spanish monarchy was in crisis, Caldas served as editor of the scientific journal *Semanario*, which fostered an existing elite community of reading. Much like his mentors before him, Caldas trained younger generations not just in natural knowledge production but also in the art of performing scientific neutrality.

The second section examines how some of the men closely associated with, and mentored by, Caldas deployed the performance of scientific neutrality for political ends. Many of these men came to form the core of what historians have described as the Partido de Libertadores, or Liberator Party, which supported Bolívar in the 1820s.[7] These men deliberately distorted Caldas's original writings to legitimize an independent, centralizing Colombian Republic. Antioquia's native son, José Manuel Restrepo (1781–1863) and his personal history of having been mentored by Caldas through the *Semanario* offers a compelling case in point. Restrepo, as minister of the interior and international relations for Colombia, oversaw the publication of Colombia's official newspaper, the *Gaceta de Colombia*, in the 1820s. The section demonstrates how Restrepo edited and reprinted selections from Caldas's *Semanario* in the *Gaceta* and suggests the two most significant, interrelated effects that the Liberator Party wished would result. First, by reframing Caldas as martyr of a barbaric Crown that sought to maintain political domination over its colonies by decimating Spanish America's few and isolated native-born geniuses, Restrepo erased the deep and long history of the Spanish Crown's support of natural knowledge production. Second, Restrepo deployed Caldas's geographic descriptions of New Granada to support the Colombian Republic's efforts to ensure that political authority would be centered in Bogotá, the national capital. Part and parcel of the Liberator Party's centralization project for the massive Republic of Colombia involved reigning in not just the smaller urban centers that claimed municipal status in the wake of Napoleon's invasion of Spain in 1808, but more significantly the claims to authority and capital status made by cities like Valencia, Caracas, and Quito, all of which threatened the newfound dominance Bogotá enjoyed. Through Caldas, the Liberator Party argued that only a centralizing national order could effectively bring together the variegated regions and peoples of Colombia. The reason was clear: Spanish reinvasion loomed. The *Gaceta de Colombia* deployed edited reprints of Caldas's works to help disseminate arguments in favor of a political order the *Gaceta* described as enlightened, neutral, and necessary to assure independence from a barbaric Crown. José Manuel Restrepo played a leading role in efforts to memorialize Caldas for these purposes, and he was not alone.

The third section considers a broader set of related practices that reflect how Restrepo, along with other members of the Liberator Party, operationalized recommendations made by Caldas and his cohort prior to independence regarding the expansion of geographic knowledge and public education. Adherents to the centralizing, pro-Bolívar view of the Colombian Republic understood that the work of geography could convincingly name, lay claim on, and order nature and society in ways that served specific political needs. Caldas's proposals for an all-encompassing map that revealed the country's natural wealth inspired the Liberator Party. They hired French-trained naturalists to teach enlightened Colombian citizens as they scientifically mapped the country's mineral and natural wealth. Colombian government officials complemented the work of foreign naturalists with detailed geographic reports from provincial governors. Decrees demanding maps with astronomical measurements and information on the local population yielded hundreds of reports and maps sent from the provinces to the Executive Power in Bogotá.[8] Compliance by provincial officials suggests a dynamic of centralizing state building. And yet local conflicts regarding control over land, people, and resources could not be included on the kind of map that the Liberator Party needed. Their project required a map that assured the stable unity of the republic for foreign audiences and culminated in the 1827 Parisian printing of the first atlas dedicated solely to portraying an independent Spanish American republic.[9]

The Liberator Party not only worried about foreign recognition and investment; it also demanded a patriotically educated citizenry to sustain their centralizing republican project. Primary school geography textbooks honored Caldas as the "father" of Colombian geography. Pedro Acevedo y Tejada, a veteran of independence wars and a colleague of Restrepo's in Colombia's National Academy, developed a well-regarded geography primer that the Liberator Party disseminated throughout Colombia's fledgling national public school system, a system modeled on the one described in Caldas's *Semanario*.[10] Despite these seeming continuities with pre-independence Caldas, the third section underscores how the wars of independence required that the Liberator Party significantly edit Caldas's proposals regarding New Granada populations. They tried legitimating their project before popular audiences by underscoring how theirs was a republican nation of equal citizens rather than a kingdom with a distinct *casta* hierarchy as Caldas had explained. From their point of view, the Spanish monarchy illegitimately ruled by dividing the population into castas. Caldas's descriptions needed to be updated to reflect how changes in institutions through revolution and bloodshed produced new races of men: either the moral citizens who supported independence, or those who could not escape the ignorance imposed upon them by the Spanish Crown and preferred monarchy.

This chapter plumbs the depth of the Liberator Party's engagement with the lessons they learned from Caldas yet emphasizes the new political circumstances of the1820s as compared to those Caldas encountered a decade earlier. These new circumstances were fundamentally territorial in nature. These men reworked the significance of Caldas's life, his death, and the content of his writings so as to legitimate the territorial-political order they proposed and sought to impose. The martyred Caldas emerged as the lone, patriotic founding father of geographic sciences. This was held true even as the Liberator Party's multipronged efforts to enlist geographic knowledge toward legitimating the centralization of political power in Bogotá became moot. With the threat of Spanish reinvasion gone, cities like Valencia, Caracas, and Quito derailed the centralizing political project the Liberator Party had in mind. The memory of Caldas nevertheless continued to loom large among educated elite New Granada government officials and among the new generation of citizens educated through the public school system.

As such, the chapter as a whole fine-tunes Benedict Anderson–inspired explanations for the rise of nationalism in the region.[11] Beyond peripatetic patriot criollos, this chapter underscores the strategic ways early nineteenth-century New Granada print culture founded new national imaginaries. Those in charge of shaping public opinion sought to erase the massive scale of Bourbon natural history research by inventing Caldas as a martyred father of geography. They nevertheless drew on knowledge produced under the Spanish Crown to legitimate a centralized Colombian political economy that could most effectively extricate natural wealth. They went further by criticizing any attempts by large cities to gain autonomy from Bogotá as evidence of failed "federalism" that hearkened back to the early period of independence when Spain had easily reconquered New Granada and killed its sabios. These erasures and inventions through print culture would indelibly chisel a particular kind of independence, republicanism, enlightened thought, and centralism onto national memories, especially for elites in Bogotá.

Caldas Mentors Criollos in Tumultuous Times

In the wake of his travels through South America, the Caribbean, New Spain, and the United States from 1799 to 1804, Alexander von Humboldt impressively noted how no other Crown in the world supported natural science expeditions like the Spanish Crown.[12] Humboldt had a point. Throughout the period of Spanish monarchical rule, the Crown supported deep, long-term endeavors to know and map the extension of the empire.[13] Archbishoprics, religious orders, the royal navy, and, by the eighteenth century, extensive botanical and scientific expeditions served as the major institutions that facilitated the production of natural knowledge.[14] During 1760–1808, New Granada's Botanical Expedition alone employed hundreds of artisans, artists, naturalists, and other men of letters and produced close to thirteen thousand botanical images.[15] Francisco José de Caldas was just one of thousands of people who had engaged in producing natural knowledge for the Spanish Crown over the course of generations.

Francisco José de Caldas edited the *Semanario del Nuevo Reino de Granada* during a critical turning point for the Spanish monarchy. The periodical's first installment ran in January 1808, just months before the Spanish kings' abdications at Bayonne. This timing, together with Caldas's need for support from royal authorities, explains the deference and loyalty that his *Semanario* displayed toward the monarchy well into 1810. Caldas was not staking out epistemological independence from Spain for elite criollos in his journal. On the contrary, his was a decidedly patriotic publication that championed enlightened knowledge and positioned criollos as cocreators of that knowledge. Caldas's patriotism was not just about duty to the land of a person's birth (specifically, the Kingdom of New Granada), but also to the Spanish monarchy. Caldas and his cohort extolled the valuable role of circulation from New Granada to European cities in gaining and disseminating skills and learning.

Powerful teleological narratives that project the independent Colombian Republic back into the past often obscure this overarching context of loyal, monarchical patriotism for the *Semanario*. The first instance of such reframing is explored further below. During 1808–1810, however, Caldas, through his *Semanario*, celebrated the scientific achievements of his fellow "good citizens" of the Spanish monarchy, especially those who remained loyal despite the political turmoil threatening to tear the monarchy apart. In doing so, Caldas mentored his readers on how to deploy their enlightenment knowledge to ensure patriotism, loyalty, and monarchy.[16]

Consider how Caldas effusively celebrated José María Cabal's return after seven years studying chemistry in Cadiz, Madrid, and Paris. Cabal's was an act of a "Good citizen," one who "abandoned Europe and all of its pageantry in order to bring to the heart of his fatherland needed enlightenment."[17] Historians have recently, and accurately, read Caldas's report on Cabal's return as articulating an elite creole belief in their sacred civilizing mission to educate.[18] Caldas's championing of Cabal's return also evinces deep loyalism to the Spanish monarchy, that is, if we read between the lines. Cabal's return to New Granada in 1809 was remarkably patriotic beyond the reasons Caldas explicitly cited. Several French-trained Spanish chemists like Cabal, who learned from the same French authorities, chose to remain in Europe in support of the Bonaparte regime in Spain. These men, later known derisively as the "afrancesados," won high positions in Madrid under Bonaparte.[19] Cabal could have joined his fortunes with those of the afrancesados. He did not. Caldas did not mention Bonaparte or the afrancesados in his *Semanario*. Patriotism (as well as vigilant censorship) meant Caldas made only oblique references to the prestige and honors

Cabal renounced by leaving Europe and a Madrid dominated by the Bonaparte regime.

The *Semanario*'s deafening silence on the dire circumstances that the Spanish monarchy faced in Europe during 1808–1810 did not mean its editor and contributors were detached from the political turmoil that exploded throughout the Spanish Atlantic monarchy. By 1809, the year of Cabal's arrival, Caldas and his cohort had received conflicting news of Napoleon's invasion. Elites in Santafé knew about the abdications of Charles IV and Fernando VII, they knew about the regime set up in Madrid under Napoleon's brother, Joseph Bonaparte, and they knew about the resistance movements sprouting up against Napoleon throughout the Spanish Empire.[20] They also knew and worried about the Spanish Cortes. Caldas, in protest against the *mal gobierno* of the Cortes, played a key role in the installment of Santafé's junta on July 20, 1810, yet he remained loyal to Fernando VII. That same year Caldas declared his disaffection with the Spanish junta in the *Semanario*, if only in the tiny lettering of its footnotes.[21] Caldas stopped work on the *Semanario* in 1810. He joined Joaquín Camacho at the *Diario Político de Santafé de Bogotá*, a paper dedicated to winning public opinion in favor of the Santafé 1810 Junta, its declarations of loyalty to Fernando VII, and its calls for autonomy from the Cortes in Spain. In short, Caldas witnessed—and participated in—significant political changes during his editorial position at the *Semanario*. As it turned out, the political changes occurring under Caldas's feet were fundamentally territorial in nature.

Recent studies have rightly emphasized how the political crisis engendered by the Napoleonic invasion of Iberia ignited an explosion of sovereignties throughout the Spanish Empire.[22] When faced with crisis, Hispanic legal scholars argued that in the absence of the legitimate king, sovereignty reverted to the "pueblos." The result was a vertiginously growing number of cities that claimed the right to municipal government. Towns that previously lacked a political voice within the empire took advantage of the crisis. Instead of pleading with the urban centers that traditionally had dominated them, these smaller cities represented their interests directly to the provisional government in Spain. The cities that most came to resent the Spanish Cortes therefore tended to be the historically dominant ones. Caracas, Quito, and Santafé (de Bogotá) were most radicalized against the Spanish Cortes. They formed their own juntas. Caldas led the charge in Santafé, declaring independence from the mal gobierno of the Cortes in Spain as a manifestation of loyalty to Fernando VII. And yet the territories under the jurisdiction of Santafé broke up into dozens of city-states. Some remained royalist and others declared independence, but, more significantly, each declared the right to form its own juntas with municipal power, often in a bold declaration of autonomy from Santafé. This mushrooming of municipal governance was especially intense in New Granada Viceroyalty, and it should be understood in the context of the dynamic—and contentious— formation of new cities from the time New Granada was erected as a viceroyalty in the early eighteenth century up through the Spanish monarchical crisis.[23] The sheer number of townships seeking autonomy from Santafé's junta forced that city's *cabildo* to worry that its dominance over neighboring regions and towns was under threat. Juntas like those of Santafé wrote constitutions and held elections as part of a strategy to reassert control over the towns that had found autonomy through the Napoleonic crisis.[24]

Caldas's public writings in the *Semanario* during 1808–1810, along with his private correspondence, offer a powerful avenue for understanding how he and his cohort tried to assert legitimate political control in a time of crisis: through the neutral, detached language of science. Mauricio Nieto Olarte has astutely observed how, through the publication of the *Semanario*, Spanish American *ilustrados*, or enlightened ones, were able to assert their interests as if they represented the universal needs of the entirety of the Kingdom of New Granada. This was precisely because of the scientific neutrality that the *Semanario* could claim. By constructing the *Semanario's* methods and ends as neutral, absolute, and universal, and as the product of trained, qualified minds, Caldas placed control over New Granada's nature in the hands of the "good Citizens" who contributed to the publication.[25] The dozens of good citizens Caldas mentored in this practice of performing neutrality through the *Semanario* included the young José Manuel Restrepo.

The kind of mentorship that the young, Antioqueño criollo, José Manuel Restrepo, received from Caldas during 1808–1810 helps us better understand several of the key territorial nation-state building actions that the Liberator Party carried out a decade later. Three dimensions to Caldas and his approach to mentoring Restrepo stand out. First, Restrepo paid close attention to Caldas's emphasis on the value of neutrality in the production of knowledge. Second, Caldas's direct mentorship of Restrepo's cartographic and geographic representations critically influenced Restrepo's later work overseeing the Colombian Republic's first national mapping endeavor. Finally, Caldas's interest in geography went beyond training experts; he made a strong case for patriotic public instruction in his *Semanario*. Restrepo, together with key members of the Liberator Party, put these recommendations into practice starting in the 1820s.

The key element behind Caldas's performance of neutrality in the *Semanario* was his open admission that he could not effectively produce valuable knowledge in isolation. On the contrary, Caldas openly stated that he would not have been able to write his first essay, "The State of Geography," much less produce the *Semanario* itself, without the strengths and talents of others. The value of the *Semanario* lay in the fact that it brought together "various subjects who are lovers of the fatherland," who "know and understand the obligations of a good Citizen, all those who, ultimately, desire, as they should, the honor, the prosperity, and the advantages of the country they inhabit."[26] Exemplary men who understood the duties and responsibility of citizenship within the Kingdom of New Granada would transmit their knowledge through the *Semanario*'s pages. Several social settings outside of the *Semanario* facilitated Caldas's efforts, most notably *tertulias*.[27] These exclusive face-to-face meetings, together with subsequent epistolary correspondence, helped cement relations of trust and authority between Caldas and the men whose contributions he highlighted. Focused, enlightened discussion among a community of actively engaged citizens generated the kind of useful, "neutral" knowledge that the kingdom needed. This was as true for the Kingdom of New Granada as it was for the Spanish monarchy as a whole.

Let us return, then, to Caldas's mentorship of José Manuel Restrepo in particular. Restrepo wished to be part of the *Semanario*'s exciting intellectual community and sought out Caldas for mentorship. Restrepo drew several maps and plans of his natal province and consulted their accuracy with Caldas.[28] Caldas congratulated Restrepo on his astronomical and geodetic measurements. He took the liberty of showing the young Antioqueño's findings to José Celestino Mutis, leader of the Botanical Expedition in New Granada. This move would have sealed the kind of patronage network that Restrepo avidly sought. Mutis's death later that year, and Caldas's continued directorship of the Astronomical Observatory nevertheless changed the expected patronage dynamic. If Restrepo wanted to pursue his geographic interests, he would need to depend more than ever on Caldas's goodwill and intellectual generosity. And, as Restrepo increasingly corresponded with Caldas, he deepened his own understandings of geography and how to convey these understandings to a knowledgeable community.

Caldas took his mentorship role with Restrepo seriously and rigorously critiqued the young Antioqueño's cartographic work. Although he considered Restrepo's original map of Antioquia exemplary, it could nevertheless be improved. Caldas recommended that Restrepo draw a new map with the same astronomical and geodetic material, but suggested that Restrepo represent geographic morphology differently.

> The mighty rivers like the Cauca should be drawn with four parallel lines; the lesser rivers that feed them with three; those that branch off further with two, and, finally the streams with one. The boundaries of provinces like this:-.-.-.-.-.-. The roads like this: . . . . The places fixed through astronomical observations should be indicated with a little star.[29]

Besides correcting Restrepo's use of map symbols, Caldas also suggested what kind of information needed to be included on the map.

> You neglect too much the physical contents of the country; it is necessary to signal the location for minerals like salt, iron, marble

and stone quarries, and differentiate the countries covered by jungle from those that have cultivated grasses. Those difficult portions of the Cauca that you communicated to me in your beautiful letter should be identified precisely on your map with the greatest care.[30]

Caldas offered one simple but important solution to the several inaccuracies he identified on Restrepo's map: increase the scale, and all will be remedied. Restrepo complied.[31] These suggestions reveal how Caldas tried to define a set of cartographic conventions for the cohort of enlightened criollos he mentored and networked in New Granada at a time when cartographic conventions around the world were still fluid.[32] Doing so enhanced the kind of prestige and authority Caldas wielded among his peers subtly, by appealing to the benefits that would come from effective abstract representations of territory. Despite the errors that Caldas found in the young Restrepo's cartographic abilities, he nevertheless considered that Restrepo's contributions were immensely valuable. This fact is evidenced by the extensive quotations of Restrepo that Caldas included in his *Semanario*—especially in the footnotes.

Despite the oft-quoted phrase by Caldas noting how geographic knowledge in New Granada was in its infancy, the bulk of the *Semanario*'s main text attested to the long historical legacy of existing geographic knowledge about New Granada. The footnotes revealed the most recent news about New Granada's geography that Caldas had received from qualified, expert citizens of the kingdom through epistolary exchanges and privileged access to geographic reports. Caldas's footnotes encouraged his readers, who also belonged to the same privileged elite clique, to read the most pertinent of these recent reports. Joseph Ignacio de Pombo's 1807 essay regarding the potential for a canal that would link the Atlantic and Pacific Oceans in Panama became required reading. So did the recent survey of the Juntas de Dagua by the royal Alfares of Cali, Don Manuel Caicedo y Tenorio. Caldas also briefly noted how he benefited from the navigational knowledge for the River Patia that was provided to him in December of 1807 by noted Payanés elite Don Gregorio Angulo. Neither could readers ignore information about the Magdalena River produced by the distinguished

Baron Alexander Von Humboldt. And yet each one of these contributions received no more than a brief acknowledgment line in Caldas's footnotes.

José Manuel Restrepo's letter to Caldas recounting local knowledge around Antioquia and Cauca was another matter. Caldas's fourth volume dedicated almost three pages of footnote space to the findings of "the hard working, enlightened youth, D. Joseph Manuel de Restrepo."[33] This extensive acknowledgment was followed a year later by Restrepo's featured contribution to the *Semanario*. Titled "Essay on Geography, Production, Industry, and Population of the Province of Antioquia," this work served to catapult Restrepo into the highest, respected echelons of New Granada inteligencia.[34]

Caldas's critical comments on Restrepo's maps of Antioquia, together with his championing of Restrepo's geographic contributions, need to be read in light of Caldas's exacting criteria for the most pressing need he considered that the Spanish Kingdom of New Granada had: a large-scale map. Over the course of the first six installments of his "State of Geography," Caldas underscored the heroic efforts of enlightened Spanish minds.[35] His weekly publication detailed existing knowledge about New Granada that had been acquired over the course of centuries. Caldas also championed the findings of contemporary provincial Spanish American elites in this journal. Why, then, after recounting the deep legacy of geographic knowledge in New Granada, and after synthesizing contributions to that knowledge by contemporary good citizens like Restrepo, would Caldas assert that "The State of Geography" in New Granada was humiliatingly one that was still in its infancy? The short answer is simple: Caldas was pleading with a Spanish monarchy that was already inclined to support these geographic endeavors to go further.

Caldas argued that a detailed and thorough mapping expedition would remedy the untenable situation of geographic infancy. The Spanish monarchy should spare no expense to carry it through, given the benefits it would bring to the colony. Caldas demanded a scale for the project that would reveal all the natural wonders the New Granada colony had to offer: two inches per league of territory.[36] Efforts to produce such a map, as well as the map itself, would bring the most enlightened minds to work in New Granada, from the politician to the magistrate to philosophers and businessmen, so they could "drink the lights they need for their endeavors." The uses such a map could be put to were legion. New Granada would see the arrival of travelers, botanists, mineralogists, zoologists, military men, and agriculturalists as a result of the accurate display of their interests majestically painted on the map. Caldas evocatively described the proposed image's versatility and power: "This would be a magic painting that could take on all possible forms, and would accommodate all different characters. Each province would copy their department from it, and would guard [that copy] religiously."[37] These provincial maps would, in turn, educate the good citizens of the future. The result would be that throughout the colony of New Granada construction projects for new roadways and canals would abound. So would experimentation for the development of new branches of industry and agriculture. "The patriotic flame will ignite in all hearts and the ultimate result will be the prosperity of this colony."[38]

The kind of geographic knowledge that Caldas accumulated from previous geographical endeavors and from provincial elites like Restrepo was the basis upon which Caldas proposed this transformative plan to Spanish monarchical authorities. Existing geographic knowledge in New Granada needed to be expanded and translated into the powerful, talismanic vision that only a large-scale map of the kingdom could provide.

Accurate cartographic knowledge among elite mapmakers and a large-scale magical map were not enough, however. The geographic project required a much larger, literate citizenry that could also read maps. What better way to "engrave" upon the hearts of citizens the need to know the geography of New Granada than to do so through public education of the kingdom's youth? Caldas joined his elite circle of enlightened criollos in championing just such a proposal for expanding public instruction. The anonymous "Amigo de los niños" penned these proposals for the *Semanario*. Over the course of seven installments, the treatise defended a system of free public education called the Patriotic School, detailing pedagogical approaches and educational content. The Patriotic School would be overseen by the viceregal government in New Granada and would emphasize equality, Christianity, and patriotism. The classroom, as proposed by the *Semanario*, would become the preeminent space where future "good citizens" of the kingdom could receive the kind of patriotic education that could best uphold the colonial social order. And that social order, according to Caldas, could be easily and coherently described.

In the first installment of the *Semanario*, Caldas explained that all inhabitants of colonial New Granada were divided into two distinct categories: savages and civilized men. "While the first were those nomadic tribes that had no other art besides hunting and fishing, no other laws besides their customs, who maintained their independence through barbarism, and who possessed no other virtue other than lacking some of the vices of civilized peoples." These were the peoples who inhabited the Darien, Choco, Orinoco, Guajira, and other frontier regions he had described in "The State of Geography." The second category of peoples, according to Caldas, were those who were "united in society under the gentle and humane laws of the Spanish Monarch." Caldas described how even among these civilized men, three races could be distinguished based upon their different origins: "the indigenous Indian of this country, the European who conquered him, and the African introduced after the discovery of the New World." Caldas then went on to describe the casta system that resulted from the interactions of these races of "civilized" men. For Caldas, the casta system merely reflected a social reality, one that conveniently served the privileged interests of himself and other elite descendants of Europeans in the New World. "I understand Europeans to be not just those who were born in that part of the world, but also their children who, conserving the purity of their origin, never mixed with the rest of the castas." These upstanding moral folk were known as the "Criollos, and they constituted the nobility of the new continent when their parents had enjoyed such status in their country of birth." The rest of the less noble yet nevertheless "civilized" peoples mixed with each other to produce the castas that formed the lower rungs of colonial society.[39] Caldas supported and derived privilege from the casta system and the social order it facilitated. This was the social order that the *Semanario* argued needed to be upheld through public, patriotic education within the Spanish monarchy.

Caldas's work for the *Semanario* was not just about the content and proposals that it provided its readers. As Nieto Olarte has shown, the collective nature of the enterprise had the effect of constructing a trustworthy, politically powerful group of elite Spanish American criollos. This social group defined itself as the "good citizens" of the kingdom, with the responsibility to dictate the policies that would allow their patria to flourish.[40] This point is critical, and well taken. But there is also a geographical dimension to the construction of this social group's power. The production of the *Semanario* was itself an exercise in circulation, but one that necessarily had to flow through Bogotá as the heart of that circulation. That was because the *Semanario* was edited from Santafé.

Caldas's efforts to synthesize all existing geographic knowledge on New Granada meant he needed to be located in the physical capital of the viceroyalty, where he could access the printing press. The dynamics of mail collection and distribution also allowed him to more easily collect information from various informants in different provinces from Bogotá. Santafé also was the main site of the social gatherings in private homes where scientific and geographic ideas were discussed. Elites from the provinces, like Restrepo, upon receiving recognition for the information on the territories they described in the *Semanario*, often would be drawn to the cultural and scientific center of Santafé. The essays and treatises Caldas edited and printed in his *Semanario* worked to generate the conventions that described, delimited, and claimed New Granada's territory in ways that implicitly and explicitly put Santafé at the center of the activities of enlightened New Granada Spanish American criollos.

The hierarchical social and political order that neutrality and scientific knowledge assembled during the late colonial period had placed Spanish American creole elites at its top, and Santafé de Bogotá at its center. Many of these same elite Spanish American criollos assumed positions of political leadership during Colombia's early republican period. As the following section shows, Restrepo offers us the most shining example of this dynamic. The experiences José Manuel Restrepo had with Caldas, both as his mentee and as one of his contributors to the *Semanario,* significantly shaped how a new generation of Spanish Americans reformulated this earlier era of scientific knowledge production. They did so to legitimize a new, centralizing independent political order that sought to make Santafé de Bogotá the "natural" cultural, political, and intellectual center of the new, fledgling, yet massive Colombian Republic.

Caldas as Martyr for the Colombian Republic

Caldas's death at the hands of the Spanish Reconquista armies in 1816 allowed surviving pro-independence patriots to go beyond criticizing the mal gobierno of the Cortes and radically denounce Fernando VII himself. That king, after all, had sent these sanguinary armies. The execution of enlightened New Granada men of science underscored the savagery of the Spanish Crown, shaping public opinion about the morality of Colombian independence, one that asserted republicanism as opposed to, and wholly different from, monarchy.

Take, for instance, how Venezuelan republican patriot Manuel Palacio Fajardo described Spanish general Morillo's rule in Santafé. London audiences in 1817 read with horror about the six hundred victims executed and exiled, most of whom had occupied the highest echelons of New Granada society and government. Victims included José María Cabal, the same patriotic New Granada native son Caldas had celebrated for refusing the honors the Bonaparte regime would have bestowed upon him in occupied Madrid. Among the "many other learned and valuable personages" that were executed was, of course, Francisco José de Caldas.[41] News of Morillo's sanguinary tactics and actions was disseminated quickly on both sides of the Atlantic.[42] Outrage at Spanish violence, especially against the learned men of New Granada (and their wives), easily fit already existing tropes of the Spanish black legend in Great Britain and the United States. Asserting this moral high ground to audiences outside the Spanish monarchy paid off; monetary and logistical support for independence poured in after news of Morillo's actions spread. Palacio Fajardo's account also became useful for another purpose and audience: rousing anti-Spanish sentiment among Spanish Americans at home. Venezuela's radical pro-independence newspaper, the *Correo del Orinoco*, quickly reprinted Palacio Fajardo's account in 1818.[43]

By March 31, 1822, Caldas's death at the hands of Morillo's armies was hardly news to Spanish American audiences, yet the newly formed Colombian Republic's national newspaper, the *Gaceta de Colombia*, stoked readers' outrage at Caldas's martyrdom, one that had occurred six years earlier. Why bring Caldas back to Colombian readers' attention? Part of the reason was because a disciple of Caldas had recently assumed the editorial helm of the *Gaceta*. That man was José Manuel Restrepo, Colombia's first minister of the interior.

This section traces out the ways in which Restrepo and the Liberator Party drew on and redeployed Caldas's lessons and his writings for two interrelated facets of Colombia's early republican processes of territorial nation-state formation. First, they sought to assure Bogotá's status as the national capital city at a time when its capital status was uncertain. Second, they wished to legitimize a centralizing national government that brought together the former Captaincy General of Venezuela with the former Viceroyalty of New Granada (roughly today's Colombia, Panama, and Ecuador). Restrepo emerges as a major figure in this two-pronged effort, but given the array of forces working against these projects, Restrepo did not act alone. A few words on the deep territorial transformations and political divisions that emerged over the course of the 1810s will help explain why Restrepo and the Liberator Party needed to work so hard to convince general public opinion within the Colombian Republic to support a centralized state with Bogotá as its capital.

By 1810 the perceived illegitimacy of the Spanish Cortes, together with the mushrooming of municipalities in Spanish America, forced the capitals of colonial-era *partidos, corregimientos, capitanias,* and viceroyalties to try to re-create the administrative spatial hegemonies lost to the political turmoil unleashed by Napoleon. They negotiated constitutional arrangements with emerging communities of *vecinos* in countless towns with newly minted *municipalidad*, towns that these larger cities considered their hinterlands. Several newly founded cities were determined not to lose their recently acquired rights of political representation during the early period of independence. The pressures of war, insufficient resources, and decimated populations nevertheless forced many to the negotiating table. The Foundational Law of December 1819 asserted the Colombian Republic's right to represent the interests of all the municipalities encompassed by the former New Granada Viceroyalty and the Captaincy General of Venezuela, as well as the Audiencia de Quito—despite continued control over Quito by the Spanish Crown. This bold proposition for a Colombian Republic worked for smaller municipalities as well as larger cities as long as the threat of Spanish reinvasion loomed.

The Foundational Law was signed in the city of Santo Tomás de Angostura on the banks of the Orinoco River in Venezuela, in the wake of Bolívar's decisive August 1819 military triumph in the Battle of Boyaca. That victory secured patriot control over Santafé de Bogotá and the densely populated Cundiboyacense high plains in New Granada. Royalist troops fled the region. Royalists nevertheless maintained control over key cities, most notably the ports of Cartagena and Santa Marta on the Caribbean, Coro and Maracaibo on Maracaiblo Lake, Guayaquil and Quito in the south, the Panamanian Isthmus, and several key locations in the interior of New Granada on the banks of the Cauca and Magdalena river valleys and beyond Colombia along the Pacific, forming the Pacific block. The generals and supporters of Bolívar who signed onto the Foundational Law agreed: unity was the only way for Venezuela and New Granada to consolidate their sovereignty and have it be respected. The Foundational Law united the two republics' outstanding international debt and offered a provisional territorial division for the newly formed and expansive Colombian Republic. Three departments, each with its own capital city and headed by its own vice president, comprised Colombia: Venezuela, with its capital in Caracas; Quito, with its capital in the eponymous city, and Cundinamarca, with its capital in Bogotá. The 1819 law envisioned a new capital city for all of Colombia, one that would carry the Liberator Bolívar's name. The first general Congress, according to that law, would determine the location and layout of the city "under the principle that [this new capital] would be proportionately suited to the needs of all the three Departments and to the greatness to which this opulent country has been destined by Nature."[44]

The first general Congress met in the city of Cucuta on the border between Venezuela and New Granada starting July 12, 1821, and approved Colombia's first constitution six weeks later. The new constitution offered only provisional definitions for the territory of Colombia and its internal divisions. Similarly, the capital status of Bogotá was still far from a foregone conclusion. In fact, the Cucuta Constitution was itself provisional. Its legitimacy depended primarily on Colombia's ability to expel royalist forces. The constitution's article 191 stipulated that within a period of ten years, if royalist forces were defeated, then the constitutional order of Colombia could be revisited and changed.[45] Lawmakers in 1821 anticipated several "inconveniences" to the union of Venezuela and New Granada. They had witnessed the violent recent history of autonomy and independence that cities throughout Spanish America sought out in the wake of the Napoleonic invasion of Iberia. More often than not, towns declared their independence from—or loyalty to—the Spanish Crown primarily as a way of finding autonomy from dominant urban neighbors. The centralizing constitutional-territorial organization of the Colombian Republic may have worked to mobilize resources quickly to the places that needed defense against the royalists, but that order made lawmakers nervous. Those from Venezuela were especially worried about the dominance Bogotá could display over other cities if royalists were defeated. Creating a provisional constitutional-territorial union allayed some of these fears.

Consider the problem of the national capital city, together with the new territorial divisions the General Congress developed for Colombia. On October 11, 1821, the General Colombian Congress, after considerable debate, passed a decree establishing the provisional residence of the capital in the city of Bogotá. This was because founding a new "Ciudad Bolívar" that could effectively serve the needs of all Colombian departments was still too difficult given continued circumstances of war. In the meantime, the best alternative became Bogotá.[46] Beyond offering a working solution regarding the location where the national government would reside, the Cucuta General Congress also resolved that, to best meet the demands of war, a strong central government was required. In territorial terms this meant dividing the three large Departments of Quito, Venezuela, and Cundinamarca into six smaller units that would allow for an "easier" political administration.[47] The location of the provisional capital, together with the new territorial division, centralized national political power and influence in Bogotá.

The Liberator Party that emerged in New Granada became a champion of this arrangement. They denounced calls for the kind of federalism that came from cities that competed for prominence in Colombia, most notably Quito, Valencia, and Caracas. Yet, the federalism these cities sought was precisely the kind of autonomy and self-determination that they had fought for throughout the wars of independence. After struggling against royalist forces, these cities did not want to be subordinated to the dominance of Bogotá. From Bogotá, the Liberator Party tried countering this continued pressure toward this kind of federalism by appealing to public opinion. The *Gaceta de Colombia*, as the national newspaper that enjoyed significant circulation at the cost of the government, was the organ the Liberator Party could most easily employ for the purposes of legitimizing a centralizing Colombian Republic whose capital resided in Bogotá.[48] José Manuel Restrepo, as the newly appointed minister of the interior, led this effort by strategically recalling the memory of Caldas and redeploying Caldas's enlightened, neutral geographic representations. And yet tracking down Restrepo as the person responsible for deciding to reprint Caldas requires a bit of digging.

As David Bushnell has shown, several different pro-independence leaders served as the *Gaceta de Colombia*'s editors.[49] While the Constituent Congress was still in session in Villa del Rosario Cúcuta, the radical republican Miguel Santamaría determined the

Gaceta's content from that city. By the end of 1821 Vice President Francisco de Paula Santander became acting president of Colombia and moved the paper's operations to Bogotá, the provisional capital city for the nation. Vicente Azuero, who had significant experience with newspaper production, became the interim editor early in 1822 but soon turned in his resignation to José Manuel Restrepo.[50] Restrepo scrambled to find a replacement. He suggested Casimiro Calvo, an official from his ministry, to Santander. The vice president agreed. To ensure that the paper reflected the government's official voice, Calvo's appointment required that Restrepo, as minister of the interior, "should know every detail that the printer publishes, should open all communications from the tribunals and courts to the writer of the *Gaceta*, and should create a stipend from the profits generated by the *Gaceta* for official work on the paper."[51] Restrepo therefore had significant influence over the information disseminated by the *Gaceta* after Casimiro Calvo's appointment in March 1822. This explains why the *Gaceta* did not initiate its reprinting of selections from Caldas's *Semanario* until the end of that month, when Restrepo was in control of the publication.

The first issue of the *Gaceta* printed under Restrepo's watch brought to the attention of Colombian audiences the martyrdom of the patriotic sabio Caldas. The *Gaceta* used anger and irony to describe Caldas's execution, hoping to stoke the same emotions in its readers: "our celebrated compatriot, C. José de Caldas, this wise, moderate and pacific man, who in the midst of torture received from the barbarism of General Morillo the cruelest of prizes for his lights and virtues."[52] The scientific virtues of Caldas underscored the violent horrors of Morillo. Caldas had consistently evinced a moderate temper to his mentees, the *Gaceta* editors wrote. He had been a peaceful man. What prize did the Spanish Crown give Caldas for his virtues and for his enlightenment? Spain "honored" Caldas with torture and death. The pithy, ironic statement denouncing Spanish cruelty and barbarism came six years after the torrent of condemnations that flooded international and national papers immediately in the wake of Morillo's reign of terror. The time lag suggests that pain at the loss of Caldas was not the main reason motivating Restrepo's editorial decision to reprint Caldas's works.

Restrepo had devised a new state-building purpose for Caldas's martyrdom by 1822. As the *Gaceta* explained, Colombia was opening its relations with all the peoples of the earth and needed to be known not just for its military triumphs and for its politics, but also for its "position, wealth, and natural advantages."[53] Restrepo shifted gears from outrage at Caldas's martyrdom to the benefits Caldas's unique descriptions would bring to the new republic. Restrepo chose key selections from Caldas's works to reprint in the *Gaceta* that emphasized Caldas's stand-alone genius. These selections also helped manufacture the innovative level of enlightenment, neutrality, and wisdom of the men supporting Simón Bolívar and a centralizing republican form for Colombia. The *Gaceta's* editorial voice in the shadow of Caldas projected itself as inheritor of enlightened knowledge, defender of the republic against the tyranny of the Spanish monarchy, and bastion of civility against the chaos of "federalism."

To best understand the content of Caldas's writings that Restrepo edited and redeployed for Colombian audiences, we must take into account the long-standing Spanish American tradition of natural history writings about the Andes produced during the period of Spanish monarchical rule.[54] This was a tradition founded in European encounters with Amerindian empires that controlled resources by occupying several ecological niches, or "vertical archipelagoes" along Andean mountainsides. Since the sixteenth century, naturalists such as José de Acosta (1540–1600) and Antonio de León Pinelo (1590–1660) wrote awestruck accounts describing how every conceivable terrestrial climate could be encountered as one traveled from Pacific and Caribbean coasts to Andean mountain peaks.[55] For these writers, the Andes were, quite literally, paradise.[56] This was the tradition in which Caldas wrote. His major contribution: arguing to his readers that providence had placed New Granada within an exceptional set of natural circumstances. The variety of Andean climates and fertile soils could produce any valuable commodity that existed on the planet. Located between the Atlantic and Pacific oceans, New Granada not only would supply all that it needed for internal consumption, but it also could provide the entire world with the goods it produced. All that was needed was precise knowledge of the provinces that would aid in their commercial integration and circulation. This was the tradition the Liberator Party learned from and perpetuated. But this was also a tradition they needed to tweak in order to adapt it for their own state-building purposes in the 1820s through the *Gaceta*.

Restrepo ensured a neutral voice for the "Geography of the former N.G." by editing out problematic sections of Caldas's original treatise. Rather than print the document in its entirety in a single issue, the *Gaceta* reprinted selections from the original in five installments.[57] The *Gaceta* reprint largely remained faithful to Caldas's original text, that is, up until Caldas acknowledged the young José Manuel Restrepo's geographic achievements in his footnotes. Restrepo demurred from reprinting accolades that would suggest his own vanity within the pages of Colombia's official newspaper. More important for Restrepo, and for the Liberator Party, was asserting the neutrality, legitimacy, and good governance of the Colombian regime. The Liberators, and the *Gaceta*, were best served by appearing to be neutral, enlightened, and universally useful to the needs of Colombian citizens rather than showcasing individual achievements.

A second change that suggests the Liberator Party's move toward neutrality through the reprinting of Caldas emerges in the title to the piece. The original full title read: "The State of Geography in the Viceroyalty of Santafé de Bogotá, with attention to economics and commerce."[58] The new title the *Gaceta* gave Caldas's essay in 1822 pointed to how Caldas needed to be repurposed. The new title read: "Geography of the former N.G [New Granada] that today forms a considerable part of the republic of Colombia."[59] The reasons for a new title to Caldas's essay may be obvious at first glance: New Granada was no longer a viceroyalty in 1822. Restrepo was right to signal that Caldas's writings were of the "Antigua" or pre-independence New Granada. Subtly, however, Restrepo eliminated the name for the viceroyalty that Caldas had originally given it: "Santafé de Bogotá." This may have been because "New Granada" was already a familiar name of the former viceroyalty. And yet, a more strategic reason was likely in play: Restrepo's new title for Caldas's work demurred from emphasizing outright the predominant position the city of Bogotá enjoyed over the entire former viceroyalty.

Restrepo recognized that readers in Caracas and Quito would be first to react strongly against such nomenclature. By changing the viceroyalty's name to N.G., readers would instead see Caldas's report as a matter-of fact, neutral geographic description of all of New Granada that did not feature Bogotá as the overwhelmingly dominant urban center. Legitimacy, as Restrepo had learned from Caldas, lay in the ability to appear enlightened, civilized, and, most importantly, neutral. Restrepo knew he needed to be careful how he used scientific discourse to naturalize Bogotá's ideal position as capital city for all of Colombia. Erasing Bogotá from the title offered one way to do so. Yet Bogotá nevertheless became, in Restrepo's reprinting of Caldas, an important and natural political center.

Restrepo began with the definition that Caldas gave of the New Granada Viceroyalty. "To avoid confusion, and simplify our ideas, I call New Granada all those countries subject to the Viceroyalty of Santafé, and under that denomination I include the New Kingdom, Tierra Firme (Panama), and the Province of Quito."[60] Caldas's words offered the *Gaceta*, and the Liberator Party, a neutral way to make expansive territorial claims for the Colombian republic. But this opening also offered a subtle way to underscore the taken-for-granted historical significance of the capital city of Santafé de Bogotá. The political dominance of Santafé as the capital city of the viceroyalty became a simple geographic fact; a point of departure for understanding what Caldas meant by "New Granada." Santafé de Bogotá was simply the capital city that could bring together and redistribute the vast wealth of all the countries over which it ruled. That was the naturalizing logic that drove the selections from "The State of Geography" that Restrepo reprinted in the *Gaceta*.

Restrepo reprinted for Colombian readers the geographic coordinates that scientifically naturalized the expanse of the city of Santafé's domain, including its coastlines, mountains, rivers, natural

phenomena, and, significantly, boundaries. The only other cities that appeared in this verbal map were used primarily to mark
off the boundaries under Santafé's jurisdiction. The cove of Tumbéz signaled the border with Costa Rica. Jaen de Bracamoros,
Loreto, and Yza traced the kingdom's claims along the Amazon
River. From the Amazon, Santafé's jurisdictions passed through
"unknown countries" until meeting the River Táchira (still the current boundary between Colombia and Venezuela), the source of
which lay within the mountain ranges of Cúcuta. The Llanos of San
Juan and Casanare marked off Santafé's jurisdiction in the eastern
plains that ran up into Guyana. Chocó, Barbacoas, Esmeraldas,
and Guayaquil were simply noted as the cities Santafé claimed to
the west until reaching the Pacific Ocean. Santafé's claims north
went up through the "mountains of the Motilones and Guajiros,
and following these ending at the Cabo de la Vela (Candle Cape)."[61]
In one broad sweep, the *Gaceta* reprinted Caldas's matter-of-fact
description of the "natural" territory of New Granada, one that
was, ultimately, subject to the city of Santafé de Bogotá.

This scientific naturalization of Santafé's jurisdiction in 1808
was extremely useful for the Liberator Party in 1822, a time when
Colombia still was in the process of shifting the location of its capital city. Reminding readers, if only subtly, of Santafé's historical
and natural status as a capital city went beyond merely allowing
Colombian citizens to know New Granada's portion of Colombia. It also worked to assure Bogotá's continued status during a
time when Bogotá had been chosen only as a provisional measure. The shifting location of Colombia's capital was not the only
factor that induced the Liberator Party to reprint Caldas's depiction of the "natural" contours of New Granada. The threat of federalism also played a significant role.

The federalism that threatened Colombia's unity in 1822 was not
the same fragmenting sovereignty characteristic of the period of the
interregnum (1808–1816) that Bolívar denounced in his Jamaica letter of 1815. After Morrillo's reign of terror and the significant losses
New Granada and Venezuela suffered at the hands of restoration
armies, smaller municipalities no longer saw advantages to asserting autonomy from larger urban centers as they did during the first

phase of independence. By 1822 the calls for federalism did not come from smaller municipalities seeking autonomy from larger, historically dominant centers. Instead, cries for federalism came from larger urban centers, those like Quito, Valencia, or Caracas that resented Bogotá's claims to dominance after the formation of the Colombian Republic. Several different newspapers called for constitutional reform, especially with respect to Colombia's territorial divisions. Despite this distinct change in the meaning of federalism, the *Gaceta* could not resist drawing alarming comparisons between the "federalism" of the period of the interregnum that resulted in the restoration, to the kind of "federalism" that larger urban centers proposed for the 1820s. Instead of casting the latter as an effort to win autonomy from Bogotá (which was the case), the Liberator Party simply rejected the small-mindedness of federalism in terms of the dire consequences it could bring for Colombia's independence.

Take, for instance, the *Gaceta's* editorial decrying calls for federalism, which ran shortly after it reprinted selections from Caldas's "State of Geography." It offered several powerful reasons "proving wrong the opinion that the current composition of the Republic should be discarded and instead organized in three large federated departments." The centralizing Constitution of 1821 had significant advantages to a confederation, the editorial argued. Without it, a Spanish reinvasion would be certain. The *Gaceta* proved its case to readers by appealing to the painful experience of the first period of the revolution. If Caldas's understanding of New Granada's providential spatial integration of several different ecological niches was not compelling enough of a reason to maintain all of Colombia together in a centralized government under the jurisdiction of Bogotá, then the difficult recent history of the interregnum would accomplish this task.

Instead of recounting stories of tensions and acrimony between specific cities and the larger, traditionally dominant capitals for this period, however, the *Gaceta* preferred to signal overarching patterns. The patterns it saw placed blame for the failure of the first revolutionary period squarely on the small-mindedness of nameless provincial authorities concerned only with the problems of their locality. Popular memory has come to call this period the "Patria Boba," and elites championing the early Colombian Republic contributed mightily to the "foolish fatherland" description of the interregnum. Federalism, they argued, was self-defeating in practice: "Congress (or the federal government) ordered one measure, the legislature (or the provincial government) contradicted it. The former contemplated one plan and outlined measures for its execution, and the latter offered up a thousand objections and suspended execution."[62] This kind of Patria Boba narrative obscured the struggles for autonomy and independence that smaller urban centers sought from historically more dominant cities during the interregnum. Invoking this argument against the federalism proposed by Valencia, Quito, and Caracas in the 1820s proved useful for the Liberator Party, at least until 1826. As long as the threat of Spanish royalism and Reconquista lingered in key cities of Venezuela, Quito, and Panama, the centralization of power in Bogotá made sense. Caldas's calls for the providential benefits that would come to a Kingdom located at the center of all the world's major trading routes, with its fertile mountainsides capable of producing every possible commodity on the face of the earth, became the carrot to the stick of the Liberator Party's Patria Boba.

There was a related benefit to the centralized state the Libertadores proposed: the civil war that federalism threatened would be averted. Drawing from Caldas's "The State of Geography" and other writings on the influence of climate on the human race, the *Gaceta* argued circulation through a centralized Colombia would bring political unity to a diverse population. "The current system [centralism] creates the conditions that allow for intimate ties to emerge between the inhabitants of the Orinoco with those of Guayaquil, the son of Caracas with that of Quito, the daring plainsman with the shy indigenous man, the inhabitant of searing sands of the coasts with that of the frozen mountaintops of Tunja."[63] The *Gaceta* argued to readers that the advantages to centralism for Colombia were clear, if folks took into consideration the heterogeneity of its population. Given these circumstances of diversity, it would be "almost impossible to maintain its equilibrium without the system that absolutely concentrates political and military power."[64]

Beyond averting civil war, and fomenting circulation of diverse populations, the kind of centralization the Liberator Party proposed would also bring the prosperity Caldas had envisioned. Each climate's peoples and productions needed to integrate with the others in order to produce the kind of autarkic polity that providence had designed for the future of the Kingdom of New Granada. And that was a critical point: for Caldas's writings during 1808–1810, New Granada was a Kingdom within the larger Spanish monarchy during a period of turmoil, when independence from the monarchy was not yet visible on the horizon. Caldas's writings were nevertheless easily repurposed by Caldas's mentees a generation later, when independence was not only thinkable, but also almost at hand. The Liberators adapted Caldas's writings on nature, territorial and human, in order to convince readers that centralism would defeat the Spanish while generating wealth and general well-being for all Colombians through the circulation it could facilitate. Caldas's disciples would, through the force of political, military, and territorial centralization, bring the providential future that the sabio had envisioned for New Granada to all of Colombia. Spanish forces would be defeated. Challenges to the Liberator's power from competing military generals in major cities would be squashed. The circulation of people and products would bring prosperity. Centralism could not go wrong with Bogotá, as the capital city, coordinating these moves.

Restrepo and the Liberator Party, in the pages of the *Gaceta*, reprinted Caldas selectively. These installments ran parallel to editorial columns underscoring the wisdom of a central government that brought diverse regions and peoples together, but only if the seat of government remained in Bogotá. The practice of editing Caldas's writings and publishing them parallel to "Patria Boba" interpretations of the recent past in the *Gaceta* helped the Liberator Party legitimate a centralizing republic whose capital needed to be in the "naturally" advantageous city of Bogotá. Where the capital city of a united Colombia would be had never been a foregone conclusion. Bolívar's Jamaica Letter of 1815, the first to explicitly announce the Liberator's plans to unify the former New Granada with Venezuela, had declared that the capital city would be either Maracaibo in Venezuela or another new city further to the north along the Goajira Peninsula.[65] From early on Bolívar preferred a capital city for a united Colombia that leaned closer to Venezuela, and that could be more easily defended against the Spanish. New Granada members of the Liberator Party, including Restrepo, nevertheless succeeded in shifting the legitimate center of political power to Bogotá by decree only a few years later. And yet public opinion more generally still needed convincing. Caldas's writings in the *Semanario* helped them accomplish this goal, at least for a few years.

Applying Caldas's Lessons on Political Economy

To effectively assert a neutral, scientific legitimacy for the centralizing Colombian government with its capital in Bogotá, Restrepo needed to go beyond selectively reprinting Caldas's text. Linking selections from Caldas with pro-centralist and anti-federalist editorials helped make his case, as the last section shows. Restrepo also adapted another key lesson from Caldas during his tenure as Colombia's minister of the interior: the need to make a powerful cartographic representation. As discussed below, other members of the Liberator Party adopted and deployed the cartographic and geographic knowledge produced by Caldas, which, in turn, had also drawn on a vast archive of maps and geographic descriptions, to reach children and instill in them patriotic values and love of country through geography primers on Colombia in the 1820s.

Restrepo employed the cartographic skills he learned from Caldas during his work overseeing the first official mapping endeavor for Colombia. On the one hand, the endeavor brought expert French-trained naturalists to Bogotá to map the country and educate its elite citizens in mineralogy, biology, chemistry, and other natural sciences.[66] On the other, the mapping project required provincial officials to send in geographic and statistical information to Bogotá, centralizing knowledge about disparate provinces in that city. These efforts culminated in an 1827 Parisian-printed atlas depicting Colombia's territory for international audiences, one that illustrated Restrepo's multivolume history of the Colombian Republic's revolution.[67]

The "patriotic" geographic education of young citizens ran parallel to that mapping project. Public elementary schools opened in Colombia during the 1820s. They were modeled on the "Patriotic Schools" contemplated in Caldas's *Semanario*. The content of public education, as evidenced by a widely used children's geography primer written by one of Caldas's disciples in the Liberator Party, Pedro Acevedo y Tejada, radically reformulated the casta-based social order that Caldas himself had championed. The geography of an independent Colombia, in this way, would be emblazoned in the hearts of future citizens. In short, this section demonstrates the practices through which Restrepo and the Liberator Party adapted the lessons they learned from Caldas to win patriotic support for an independent Colombian republic, nationally and internationally. Restrepo invited Colombian citizens who loved their country's prosperity to participate in a geographic and statistical information-gathering exercise. The *Gaceta* welcomed any information that would "contribute to making known some part of the territory of the Republic or its provinces."[68] As Rebecca Earle and others have correctly observed, the overwhelming majority of Colombia's population was largely illiterate around the time of independence.[69] Restrepo did not intend his petition in the *Gaceta* to go to just any person within Colombia's provinces, however. Restrepo knew how the *Gactea* circulated and who were its primary readers. Those who received the *Gaceta* were either government officials themselves, editors of other newspapers, or wealthy enough to have a privileged education and to afford a subscription. Influencing the opinion of these literate citizens proved crucial for the *Gaceta* and for the Liberator Party precisely because this readership was most involved in the business of politics. These citizens would make or break the Republic, at least from the point of view of the Liberator Party. Restrepo targeted his supposedly open appeal for geographic knowledge toward these valuable citizens. Voluntary information on Colombian geography from readers during the 1820s was less than reliable, however.

Restrepo launched a more systematic effort late in 1823 after the arrival in Bogotá of several French-trained naturalists who had been hired by Colombia's official diplomat in Paris, Francisco Antonio Zea.[70] Their charge: conduct systematic research on Colombia, teach its elites their talents, and map the extent of the new republic. Zea wrote to Colombia's minister of external relations about the value of hiring these men, not just for Colombian geography, but also for the purposes of international recognition of Colombian independence. "The enthusiasm that this expedition has excited among the wise men of Europe is incredible," he wrote. Zea noted how they believed the expedition proved Colombian independence augured well for the expansion of sciences and civilization more generally.

> The enlightened friends of our cause have overwhelmingly celebrated the fact that we provide this incontrovertible proof to Europe that, far from being barbarians incapable of ruling ourselves, as the Spanish and their supporters have obsessively tried to argue, we know the price and merits of enlightenment and we are quickly trying to contribute our part to the progress of human talent.[71]

This expedition of French-trained naturalists inspired the Liberator Party to put Caldas's 1808 proposals into effect.

The naturalists arrived in Bogotá and officially started work late in 1823. The Colombian government opened a natural history museum where the naturalists would train future experts in mining and natural sciences.[72] Given the cartographic dimensions of their charge, together with the minister of the interior's own geographic background and interests, the Colombian government passed decrees that would facilitate the work of these men in December 1823. First, Colombia needed a depository for "geographic and hydrographic charts, observations, and other important news for the formation of the general map of Colombia."[73] Second, the national government decreed that local officials turn in detailed maps and sophisticated geographic reports to Restrepo in Bogotá. Each governor needed to indicate navigable rivers, principle mountain ranges, ports, and major population centers. Separately, they needed to locate their province's latitude and longitude measurements, the approximate square area of their province in leagues, and its circumferential boundaries and to describe principle productions in ways that could identify the best strategies to enhance that province's prosperity. Local officials also were expected to include information on approximate population, differentiating between slaves and free people. It should not be surprising that the ideal, talismanic map described in Caldas's 1808 "Estado de la Geografía" served as the model for the kind of content that the provincial governors needed to include in their geographic report of their provinces.

Restrepo had learned from Caldas the value of having geographic information from several different regions centered in one place. This was, after all, a long-standing tradition within the Spanish monarchy. Restrepo sought to turn this information-gathering technique into a formal strategy for building state capacity. The Colombian Republic, through Restrepo, asserted the kind of cartographic conventions the state needed to make far-flung territories readable in formal decrees. Clear guidelines decreed in laws would allow local officials to follow a standardized method. The practice of gathering local geographical information, disciplining that information to suit the requirements of national decrees, and then submitting that information from the far-flung provinces to the central government in Bogotá appealed to the needs of a centralizing republican government regime. All the governors of every province would collect information from the cantonal political chiefs that they oversaw. They then would send any and all geographic information to their superiors. Reports from all cantons, provinces, and departments would, in turn, be centralized, processed, and archived by the office of the Ministry of Interior, headed, of course, by Restrepo.

The decrees worked. Over the course of two years, thousands of responses poured into Restrepo's office. The most active respondents were the *jefes politicos*, the highest executive power in municipal cantonal capitals.[74] More often than not, jefes politicos turned in a basic graph chart that explained what parish towns were within the jurisdiction of the canton they oversaw and that tallied the population of the canton, parish by parish. Occasionally, several jefes politicos did send in geographic map images, although they offered profuse apologies for the lack of geographic knowledge in their jurisdiction. The jefes politicos heading municipal government in the cantons seemed to have realized how the national government's decree offered a unique opportunity. Long-standing territorial conflicts would finally be resolved. Whoever had the ear of the central government likely would be most favored in those resolutions. While some jefes politicos decried the poor use of lands by indigenous peoples in resguardos, others claimed greater territory for the jurisdiction of their cantonal capital. But jefes politicos were not the only ones who sent in geographic reports.

Self-proclaimed cabildos made up of a town's local elite also sent in petitions illustrated by maps to Restrepo. Their petitions sought to convince the national government that their city required official municipal status, and these cabildos often cited the "patriotic" sacrifices their town made for the cause of independence.[75] The content of these numerous and intricate reports suggests that beyond supplying Restrepo and the Ministry of the Interior with graphic or descriptive verbal maps of local territories, these reports served a valuable political function. Most immediately, the reports allowed local government officials a sense that the central government in Bogotá would resolve territorial disputes and municipal jurisdictions in their favor. The central government in Bogotá, in turn, could not only gain knowledge about local conflicts over territory but also identify who were the most faithful and trustworthy local politicians. This information could be used as leverage: Bogotá could serve as the highest-level arbiter for local disputes, a role formerly served by the monarchy in Spain. This role secured Bogotá's legitimacy as Colombia's capital city at a time when its capital status was not secure. In short, the manuscript maps and reports sent by provincial officials to Colombia's Ministry of the Interior played a critical role in building state capacity for the centralizing republic, but more importantly, they assured a national capital status for Bogotá. What these maps did not do, however, was directly impact how the cabinet of cartographers in Bogotá drew out the national map of Colombia.

José Manuel Restrepo understood that the hundreds of sketches and reports sent in to the government in Bogotá would be impossible to include in the kind of cartographic project he needed for international audiences. Restrepo needed a scientifically informed map of Colombia that would help the new government win recognition of its independence from all foreign powers. Making visible the kind of local rivalries over jurisdictions that Restrepo had been forced to adjudicate from day to day would dangerously call into question the permanency of Colombia's territorial claims. That was why both the manuscript version of Restrepo's map, finished in Bogotá in 1825, and the printed version that emerged in Paris in 1827 underscore provinces rather than cantons as the smallest unit of territorial division in Colombia. Cantons are suggested on these maps, but clear differentiations between cantonal capitals and other important parishes are not consistently drawn out. In this way Restrepo and his cabinet of cartographers sidestepped the many unresolved disputes over cantonal jurisdiction, including efforts by some cities to gain cantonal status.

Rather than resolve local territorial disputes through a map of the Colombian Republic, Restrepo's project was primarily intended to underscore the reality of Colombia's revolution and serve as a visual aid for his historical account of it. The introduction to the atlas explained how the updated territorial divisions that the atlas displayed were complemented by how it marked off the places where the principle battles of the independence wars were fought. These details made the atlas "preferable to any other map has been published until the present day."[76] The printed version of this map became a multipage atlas of Colombia that indicated the locations of key battles of the independence war. As such, the atlas illustrated the historical account written by Restrepo and was geared toward an international audience that needed to better understand the revolution that had shaken South America.[77] Given Restrepo's training, it should not be surprising that geography deeply shaped Restrepo's historical narrative.

Restrepo insisted on his neutrality to establish credibility. Restrepo underscored how he personally witnessed several of the events he narrates, and yet he wrote, "Impartiality and truth: these are the two principals that I propose to give to everything

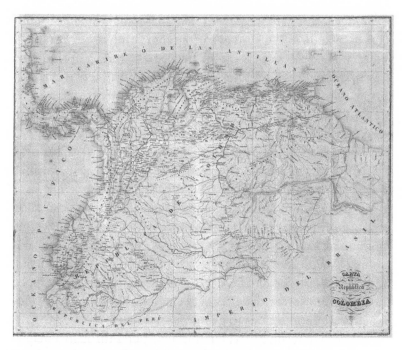

2. José Manuel Restrepo, "Carta de la República de Colombia, 1827." 49 x 60 cm. Scale: 1:5,500,000. Cadiz meridian. Paris: Libreria Americana. David Rumsey Map Collection, http://www.davidrumsey.com/maps3502.html. Courtesy of David Rumsey.

I write."[78] Restrepo relied on neutral language to offer a scientific territorial itinerary that marked off the boundaries of Colombia. Much like Caldas's original "Estado de Geografía," Restrepo offers readers a generous small-scale verbal map of Colombia's boundaries. Within these bounds, Restrepo underscores the different climates, topography, and natural products produced within the territory he described, as well as the character of its population "during the time that Spain governed these regions, and in the last years before the revolution began."[79] Caldas was an obvious source of information for Restrepo's illustrated treatise, but he was not the only one.

Restrepo understood that to best perform neutrality, one needed to credit the people and geographic findings that contributed to the geographic knowledge on display. Caldas was by no means the first or only informant on Restrepo's cartography, Restrepo also

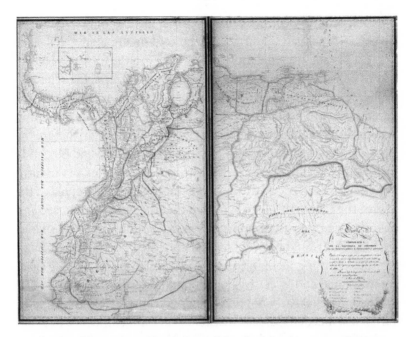

3. Colombia, "Carta Corográfica de la República de Colombia con sus divisions políticas de departamentos y provincias," Bogotá, 1825. Scale: 20 leagues to the degree. Two folios. Western half: 96 x 62 cm. Eastern half: 100 x 63 cm. Archivo Histórico Restrepo (AHR), Fondo XII.2, vol. 17, f. 11A–11B. Biblioteca Nacional de Colombia.

acknowledged that he was not alone in his design of the Colombian map. José María Lanz, the engineer hired in Paris by his old friend and colleague Francisco Antonio Zea, had drawn the original projection of the map on two large sheets. This was the first person Restrepo credited in the introduction to the atlas. But Lanz's absence from Colombia required that several other intelligent people continue the map.[80]

The three-page introduction to the atlas reveals the large cartographic repository at Restrepo's disposal. The great works of Humboldt, Caldas, and Talledo informed the content of the atlas. Restrepo's own expert knowledge and that of the recently arrived French-trained naturalists, Mariano de Rivero y Ustariz and J. B. Boussingault, corrected information from faulty Spanish maps and those of the Baron von Humboldt.[81] Restrepo, Rivero, and Boussingault, after all, had traveled through spaces that the baron missed during his South American sojourn. Restrepo confidently assured his readers that his atlas was the most exact source on the former Viceroyalty of New Granada because, according to Restrepo, the scientific pedigree of these maps was impeccable. Restrepo was nevertheless careful to point out the places that still required more exploration to establish precise knowledge. Such reasoned humility before the public sealed Restrepo's claim to expertise. Restrepo had diligently followed in Caldas's footsteps, drawing out an atlas his mentor would have been proud to see. More importantly, Restrepo and the rest of the Liberator Party expected that the world would see and acknowledge the cartographic knowledge produced by Colombia's leaders. This would be proof of their enlightenment and legitimacy to rule. Winning recognition for Colombian independence from international audiences was not enough, however.

The Liberator Party not only drew on Caldas's geographic methods; it also heeded Caldas's insistence on the significance of geography for national public education. The Liberator Party needed to inculcate future generations in the benefits of a centralized government and the wisdom of Colombia's leaders. Geography offered the most efficient and powerful way of naturalizing such an agenda for the classroom.

By 1824 Colombian leaders beamed that they had inaugurated the elite mining school, with classes taught by bright young naturalists originally trained in Paris. And yet, as Restrepo's introduction to his *Historia de la Revolución* explained, Colombia was still far from its goals of reaching the noble destinies that nature had in store. Restrepo argued this was because Colombia lacked trained experts, able jurists, magistrates, enlightened judges, professional politicians, economists, and mathematicians. The reason for this lack of trained professionals was simple, and Colombians should not be afraid to admit it:

On the one hand, our former colonial status as dependents on a metropolis that occupies the last rung among illustrated nations, and on the other, for the barbarous dedication with which Ruiz de Castilla, Boves y Morales, Morrillo, Enrile y Samano assassinated the most intelligent men that we had in Quito, Venezuela, and New Granada, decimating their number.[82]

Restrepo called for another generation to replace the martyred heroes, and Colombia's legislature needed to ensure measures that could secure the training of future experts more generally.

Despite Restrepo's anguished denunciation of the martyrdom of its ilustrado class, there was in fact no scarcity of prominent men dedicated to amassing geographical and natural knowledge for the emerging patria. A host of distinguished members of the Liberator Party were themselves geographers. Beyond Restrepo himself, we have the case of Pedro Acevedo y Tejada. Acevedo becomes important for this analysis because his geography primer was disseminated widely through the newly minted public education system. It too drew upon Caldas's writings to teach children about Colombia, including its racial composition. Despite this intellectual lineage, however, Acevedo's primer offered in print significantly different ideas about race than those offered by Caldas. In Acevedo's hands, geography would introduce the nation to new understandings of republican citizenship by doing away with the colonial-era casta system once and for all. The context of the independence wars forced Acevedo to transform the content of his children's geography primer with respect to Caldas's original racial formulations. This was precisely because Acevedo's strategy to rework the colonial-era casta system joined that of the rest of the Liberator Party in their efforts to inspire patriotism for a centralized Colombian state.

Acevedo was both a military man and a man of letters. He actively participated in the battles of independence, he was one of the signers on the declaration of independence, and he had a close relationship with General Francisco de Paula Santander.[83] Once royalist armies stopped posing a significant threat to Bogotá, Acevedo wrote his elementary school geography primer. He won support from Vice President Santander for the use of his book within the new public education system.

Acevedo's text was the first children's textbook to describe geography in terms of a territory ruled by the independent Colombian government. The book went through several editions including the 1825 versions published in Colombia and in London and the 1827 edition published in New York.[84] The cartographic information Acevedo used for his geography primer was essentially the same as Restrepo had used for his atlas. The geographies developed by Caldas, Alexander Von Humboldt, Jorge Juan Ulloa, and the Colombian colonel of engineers, José Lanz, all informed his work.[85] It stands to reason that Acevedo likely had been either in contact with or formed part of the cabinet of geographers that contributed to Restrepo's map of Colombia. At the very least, Acevedo's scientific credentials were cemented by the fact that he, along with Restrepo and several other of the republic's "enlightened minds" had been appointed by Santander to Colombia's National Academy.[86]

Acevedo's geography primer described the territories included in the Republic of Colombia. He praised the wisdom of Gran Colombia's political leaders holding off on determining exact boundaries. The Constituent Congress in Villa del Rosario de Cúcuta

> reasonably left for other circumstances the work of fixing the precise limits of Colombia. That was because Colombia possessed an immense frontier through unknown regions where other nations also arrive to lose their limits to their neighbors. Not a single one of the interested parties could make a clear demarcation without exposing themselves to crashing against justice or the pretentions of others, or to sacrificing their own interests.[87]

His intention was to convince new generations of citizens to trust their leaders and accept the territorial claims they made for Colombia, however fuzzy those claims were.

Acevedo's geography primer then turned to Colombia's human geography. In doing so, he completely reformulated Caldas's earlier writings on the casta system. Through human geography lessons, Acevedo tried to impress upon his readers the difference between an oppressive colonial regime and a democratic republican nation. The Spanish Crown's attempts to maintain caste divisions in its colonies signaled the oppressive nature of the Spanish government, argued Acevedo. In a Machiavellian move, Acevedo argued that casta divisions insidiously allowed the Spanish monarchy to maintain power, for this "sinister policy sought every means to sustain divisions, multiplying classes, and designating each one with particular and at times ridiculous denominations, creating between each group rivalries that would assure domination."[88]

This critique significantly departed from Francisco José de Caldas's explanation of the social differences that made up New Granada's population in 1808. As Acevedo explained to young pupils, the wars of independence transformed the nature of race in Colombia as originally described by Caldas. Criollos were no longer criollos, but rather they were "the white descendants of Europeans, who did not mix, that *before* were known as Criollos." The native population of Colombia also shifted in terms of their racial identity. "Indios" would no longer be called that name. By law, they would instead called "indíjenas."[89] The people transplanted from Africa and their pure descendants were, simply, "negros."[90] He pedagogically explained to his readers how "secondary castas" resulted from the mixture of the three "primary castas."[91] Instead of categorizing these mixed populations as "civilized" peoples, as Caldas had done, Acevedo considered that "at last all of them, mixing between themselves, are giving origin to individuals that are closer and closer to the European, and in their third or fourth generation do not present in their color or physiognomy, or at least only rarely, the Indian or African in their mix."[92] Acevedo confidently asserted that after Independence, in Colombia, there were no castas, no colors, nor any blood less noble than any other. This was because the blood of every man had been ennobled "after it was shed and mixed in defense of the fatherland, flooding those fields of battle. Each will equally receive the recompense of virtue, enlightenment, and valor."[93] The blood of Colombians had been ennobled through revolution. Race mixture and transformation could happen not just through sex and procreation, but through death and bloodshed in war. Young readers of all backgrounds could find their own nobility; that is, if they supported independence.

Physical, moral, and intellectual differences among humans during the post-independence period in Colombia, from the point of view of Acevedo, depended not on race but on the amount of support a group gave to independence. Indians who did not support the war were therefore profoundly different from other citizens, but through no fault of their own. "The opprobrium that breaks all of the soul's springs managed to sink them in the most profound abject poverty and in the most brutal of stupidity. . . . They have several times stained their hands with the blood of their compatriots."[94] Acevedo sought national and international acceptance and legitimacy for Colombian independence, much like Restrepo and other members of the Liberator Party. For New Granada geographers, citizenship depended solely on an individual's loyalty to the cause of independence. These pro-independence geography lessons reformulated the social order described by Caldas to legitimate the new republic that was Colombia.

This chapter began by interrogating the origins of Francisco José de Caldas's status as the founding father of Colombian geography. Ironically, Caldas would have probably characterized himself as an astronomer and botany expert before he would have called himself a geographer, despite the fact that his first essay in the *Semanario* centered on the value of geography for the New Granada Kingdom. A more significant historical irony is that Caldas did not seek independence from the Spanish monarchy in 1808. Neither did he have a republican "Colombia" in mind. His *Semanario* project was one of loyalty and affirmation of the Spanish Monarchy, and the place New Granada needed to have within the monarchical order. That was because prior to the Napoleonic invasion of Iberia, the idea of declaring independence from the Spanish monarchy lay far from the horizons of even the most enlightened of criollos.[95] Many criollo "sabios del reino" nevertheless did take up arms against Fernando VII's forces starting in 1815, including Caldas. Although Caldas along with other "sabios" were executed, not all members of this cohort were killed. Those who survived most easily transitioned into positions of political and cultural power after loyalist armies had been ousted from New Granada by 1819. The divisive, destructive, and deadly battles fought to win independence for Spanish America from Spain in large part help explain this dramatic change.

What has been less clear in historiographical terms, however, is precisely how criollos turned pre-independence scientific discourse, which was inspired by enlightenment thought, worked out by peoples in several different settings of the Spanish Empire, and supported either intellectually or economically by the Crown, into proof of the Spanish monarchy's efforts to instill ignorance among its subjects.[96] This chapter shows some of the key ways criollo ilustrados accomplished this task for their generation once independence was a fait accompli in the first Colombian Republic. By the 1820s Caldas's network of mentees turned Caldas into a lone savant who dedicated his time to natural wonders despite the Spanish Crown's refusals to support his explorations. Caldas's writings in the *Semanario* became prescient geographic representations that legitimated Colombian independence from a barbarous Spanish Crown and that championed Bogotá as the rightful, centralizing capital city that could bring the different regions together into a powerful republican force on the world stage. The men mentored by Caldas during the late colonial period carefully decontextualized Caldas's writings to assure a neutral, scientific legitimacy for a centralizing national government, one whose national capital rested in Bogotá.

Caldas himself was a provincial elite from Popayán. Several of the elites Caldas mentored, including Restrepo, were also from the provinces, not Bogotá. And yet Bogotá, as viceregal capital and possessor of one of the very few printing presses in the region, became the center of calculation for Caldas during the chaotic period of 1808–1810, when news of the Napoleonic invasion, abdications, and formation of the Spanish Cortes arrived. This social circle lived through and participated in the chaotic interregnum period from 1808 to 1816, when sovereignty, in absence of the legitimate Spanish monarchs, reverted to the pueblos. The "pueblos" became the townships that either enjoyed or sought out municipal sovereignty. The return of Spanish troops in 1816 destroyed dreams of municipal sovereignty and autonomy. Those who escaped Morillo's armies in New Granada joined the centralizing political project for a massive Colombian Republic headed by the "Libertador," President Simón Bolívar. This Liberator Party faced a complex task. They needed to legitimate the union of the Captaincy General of Venezuela, the Viceroyalty of New Granada, and the still-to-be-liberated Audiencia of Quito. They needed to do so before national, international, and future audiences. During the 1820s these men found in Caldas the kind of intellectual, geographic, and historical material they needed to assure that legitimacy.

Restrepo's editorial of Colombia's first official national newspaper, the *Gaceta de Colombia,* most clearly illustrated the ways in which Caldas's writings were edited and redeployed for the needs of a centralizing Colombian state, one that needed to legitimate Bogotá's role as capital city. The capital for Colombia had never been a foregone conclusion, especially given Venezuela's powerful role in its military defense. Already the national capital had shifted from the banks of the Orinoco in Angostura to Villa de Rosario de Cúcuta, a border city accessible to both Caracas and Bogotá. Precisely because Caldas offered a description of New Granada's providential spatial integration and ecological complementarity, Colombian government leaders who edited the *Gaceta* presented Caldas's findings to underscore the position of Santafé as the natural capital. *Gaceta* editors were also careful about what articles would go alongside the reprintings of Caldas's "State of Geography." Caldas's writings were tucked in alongside new laws, decrees, and, more importantly, editorials that underscored the neutrality and enlightenment of Colombia's leaders as compared to the Spanish, and the value of a centralized form of government centered in Bogotá, as opposed to the chaos of "federalism." Historical lessons of the Patria Boba' taught *Gaceta* readers what would happen if they did not heed Caldas's calls for unity around a Bogotá-centered national government.

Several members of the Liberator Party also learned an important lesson during the late colonial period with respect to geography and natural sciences. Those who could best represent a territory scientifically before an informed audience could most legitimately claim dominion. That was why the Colombian government hired French-trained naturalists. When members of the scientific commission arrived in Bogotá, Restrepo saw the opportunity to launch Colombia's first official mapping commission. Subsequent legislation and decrees supported the work of this commission by requiring local government officials to send in geographic reports to Restrepo. The content they needed to include, although it was not always meticulously followed, nevertheless was modeled on Caldas's cartographic proposals that would support a prosperous political economy. The way in which these reports reached Restrepo was also useful to the centralizing needs of the Colombian state—especially the national government apparatus located in Bogotá. The jefes politicos and self-fashioned cabildos of the cantons, who were most aware of territorial disputes among different parishes, reported their findings up a hierarchical chain that included provincial governors and departmental intendants. They, in turn, reported to Restrepo. Their petitions for recognition as cities with cabildos no longer went to Cádiz or Madrid; Bogotá would adjudicate the status of these urban populations. The wealth of geographic information local leaders provided may have served the interests of day-to-day state capacity building, but it did not necessarily result in inclusion within Restrepo's final map of the Colombian Republic. Intended for recognition of Colombian independence from international audiences, that map needed to elide the messy local territorial conflicts that riddled the Colombian state.

The decontextualization of Caldas by members of the Liberator Party explicitly sought to cast Spain as responsible for any ignorance still existing within Colombia. This was as true for Restrepo as it was for other members of the Liberator Party engaged in geographic practices. They repeatedly pointed to Spain's barbarous execution of Caldas and other men of letters as proof of the monarchy's desire to keep Spanish Americans in the dark. That barbarism was not just germane to the wars of independence; this was an essential component of Spain's colonial rule over Spanish America. New generations needed to know and understand this legacy, one that, as invented by these early republican leaders, legitimated their fledgling state form. Several members therefore adopted Caldas's proposals for free public education as the most powerful way to inculcate patriotism among future generations.

As Vice President Santander expanded the public education system, men like Acevedo developed schoolbooks that would teach children about the wisdom of independence leaders and the tyranny of Spain. Acevedo reformulated Caldas's writings on the castas to call to mind the popularity of Colombian independence for all peoples, or at least those peoples not mired in Spanish-induced ignorance.

This deep cultural transformation through print culture worked, but only as long as Spain continued to pose a looming threat to Spanish American independence. By 1826 battles on the ground had met diplomatic dealings abroad, settling the Spanish American question. Although Spain itself would not recognize New Granada independence until much later in the nineteenth century, it nevertheless largely agreed to stop trying to reconquer the mainland. Once the Spanish threat abated, internal contradictions within the Colombian Republic began to pull it apart. The goal of asserting Bogotá's "natural" status as a capital for Colombia, a republic that also included historically dominant cities like Caracas and Quito, seemed indisputable in 1825. The thousands of geographic reports and petitions for territorial claims sent in by various regions throughout Colombia suggested as much. And yet, the following year, crisis loomed. José Antonio Paez, an independence war hero whose base of support came from Apure and Valencia, understood the forces pulling Venezuela away from the Colombian Republic and took advantage of them for his own political gain.[97] By 1830, with the death of Bolívar, both Venezuela and Ecuador seceded from Colombia, bringing an end to that republic. Fearing efforts to force the unification of Colombia, Venezuela's political leaders quickly drew up internationally acclaimed geographic descriptions to forestall any such territorial incursions.[98]

New Granada was slower than Venezuela in its efforts to draw up a new geography after Colombia's dissolution. Not until the 1840s did geography enthusiast and military engineer General Joaquin Acosta (1799–1852) go beyond José Manuel Restrepo's cartography and territorial history of independence for Gran Colombia. After a deep exploration of European archives and after several conversations with European scientific elites, including a couple of the Colombian-hired French-trained naturalists who, by then, had returned to France, Acosta produced a dense collection of printed materials about New Granada. Acosta was especially interested in New Granada's colonial history. His historical geography, titled *Compendio Historico de Descubrimiento y Colonizacion de la Nueva Granada en el Siglo Décimo Sexto,* was intended to educate the future citizens of New Granada in the "ancient" history of their country.[99] Characterizing New Granada as a unified territorial entity helped make the fragmentation of the Republic of Colombia into New Granada, Venezuela, and Ecuador historically logical and acceptable. Acosta also produced a printed map of New Granada, one largely based on the findings from the commission of French-trained naturalists hired by Francisco Antonio Zea in the 1820s. Although well received internationally, some prominent New Granada citizens were deeply offended by Acosta's 1847 map.

Tomás Cipriano de Mosquera, patriotic geographer, military engineer, and former provincial governor turned president, criticized Acosta for his map's scale and for the overall presentation of cartographic information. Mosquera reserved his more scathing criticisms for the audacity of Acosta's dedication of the map. Acosta had honored a man who had personally supported Acosta's own scientific observations, Alexander von Humboldt. Humboldt, according to Acosta, was the man "to whom we owe the first positive notions of geographic and geological of this vast territory."[100] Mosquera would have none of it. Caldas, not Humboldt, needed to be credited as founder of geographic knowledge about New Granada. This criticism, published in the *Gaceta,* demanded that Acosta "correct this error of his dedication because it is offensive to an enlightened compatriot of ours whose merits Acosta knows well."[101] Mosquera would not allow Acosta to dethrone Caldas as the founding father of Colombian geography by championing the foreigner, Humboldt.

CHAPTER 2

A Political Economy of Circulation

S tarting in the 1840s, a generation of leaders operating in the wake of the dissolution of the Gran Colombian Republic decided to transform the nomenclature of Bogotá city streets.[1] The two axes of naming logic for Bogotá's urban space reflected how midcentury elites believed unity would come for New Granada: through the twin processes of circulation through Bogotá from the regions and back, and a shared cult to independence. Most of the new ninety-plus street names made Bogotá's San Francisco River and its central plaza the jumping off points from which roads, named for regional urban centers, departed. Bogotá denizens would move through urban space in ways that, at least through nomenclature, connected them to the major cities of New Granada's regions. Many of the new street names also sought to elicit the unifying national patriotism of independence. Ayacucho, Angostura, and Cariaco, all places by then in the Venezuelan Republic that had seceded from Colombia, nevertheless mattered to Bogotá for the independence history Bolívar made on their battlefields. Bolívar himself became central to Bogotá's urban space. The colonial-era Plaza Mayor, the city's administrative, juridical, and legislative center, was renamed Plaza de la Constitución, and a monument to Bolívar was unveiled in 1846. Soon the Plaza simply came to be called "Plaza de Bolívar." This new Bogotá became memorialized in a map created in 1849 by young cadets training in the newly founded Bogotá-based Colegio Militar. Although many of these cadets were the sons of prominent Bogotá families, there were several who participated in this mapping project who were from different New Granada provinces. All of them were part and parcel of the circulatory project envisioned for New Granada at midcentury.

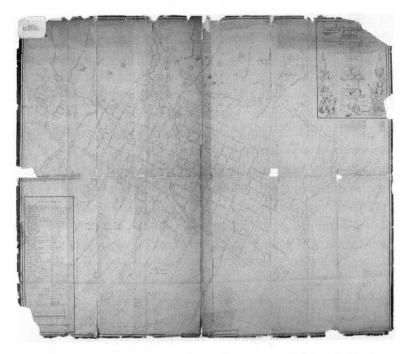

4. Colegio Militar, "Bogotá y sus alrededores," 1849. SMP 2, Ref. 1-21. Archivo General de la Nación, Bogotá.

The Mapa Topográfico de Bogotá of 1849 serves as a window onto a long forgotten and misunderstood world that conjured up a New Granada that needed to be freed from the burdens of the colonial past. Government functionaries for the New Granada that emerged out of the dissolution of Colombia in 1830 argued that their new republic was a nation of regions. This was true not just because nature made it so, but also because the colonial past was what had worked to keep New Granada fragmented and divided against itself. For these men, the colonial period of Spanish monarchical rule had left a legacy of blockages to circulation: a multiplicity of measuring units, legal codes, currencies, grammars, taxes, histories, sovereignties, and local traditions. The monarchy also left New Granada poor in terms of printing presses, roads, canals, ports, and bridges. The New Granada republic needed to be organized around a political economy of standardization and circulation. Granadinos from all provinces and occupations articulated a shared vision that sought to remove blockages to the circulation of things, peoples, and ideas. The political economy of circulation sought to create badly needed transportation infrastructure and technologies, such as steamboats, to move commodities and peoples around. This project of circulation demanded new institutions of learning and training to homogenize and standardize practices and units of measurement and currency. To break with a past that they saw as having produced fragmentation and isolation, the nation required circuits of pilgrimage by cadres of trained professionals: architects, engineers, land surveyors, cartographers, grammarians, mathematicians, journalists, and lawyers. Although it may at first seem paradoxical, this project needed a center, and that center became Bogotá. That is because Bogotá gave peripheries a voice and a role in the construction of a unified nation out of a polycentric, fragmented, colonial-era space.

Understanding this project allows us to supersede a well-entrenched historiography that sees early New Granada republican state formation as torn between centralist versus federalist ideals. The political economy of circulation was first articulated under President Tomás Cipriano de Mosquera's first presidential administration via a scientific society founded in 1847 that was appropriately called the Instituto Caldas. Mosquera's successor, General José Hilario López, was the first member of the Liberal Party to be elected to the presidency, and his administration supported the mission of the Instituto Caldas through its support of the Chorographic Commission, an extensive and thorough mapping endeavor to know New Granada regions that was first imagined by members of the Instituto Caldas. Neither administration saw New Granada through a Manichean prism of a national center versus federal states. Bogotá was never to be a centralizing Leviathan that would silence and discipline regional autonomies and economies. Instead, both posited a model where Bogotá would facilitate integration, pilgrimage, and circulation.

The Mapa Topografico de Bogotá captures rather well the late 1840s circulatory project that the Instituto Caldas proposed and that members of this institute intended for the Chorographic Commission. Its creators exemplified the circulatory ideal. The cadets involved in the project were provincial youths summoned and assembled in Bogotá for training. These military engineers would get technical training in cartography, land surveying, and engineering. They would create roads and infrastructure. Upon graduating, they would return to their home region. They would lead by example by creating a shared meritocratic culture of virtue. The content and image of the map seals this circulatory vision for New Granada, even though it only depicted Bogotá. By displaying the new nomenclature of the city and the newly founded universities and educational institutions, the map memorializes Bogotá's urban space as the symbolic microcosm of the New Granada Republic. On the map, there were no rivers and mountains blocking circulation between *calle* Antioquia and *calle* Popayán. There were no differences in systems of measurement and currency that got in the way of movement and circulation between the many different streets pointing the way to New Granada regions. This chapter shows how Bogotá itself came to stand as an ideal of unimpeded circulation and integration. For these men, Bogotá city space came to signify the republican triumph over the colonial legacy—as they imagined it.

The people involved in this renaming and re-forming of Bogotá were part of a larger community of people dedicated to advancing the circulation of people, capital, ideas, technology, and goods from the provinces through the capital city of Bogotá, and back. Few of these people were Bogotanos themselves, however. Most came from provinces distant from Bogotá. Take, for instance, President Tomás Cipriano de Mosquera, under whose administration this renaming of Bogotá city streets began. Mosquera came from Popayán, a city located in New Granada's southern region near the Cauca River Valley. In his 1852 geographic treatise on New Granada, Mosquera described the Cauca as the most fertile, healthy, intertropical "country" of New Granada, rich in mineral deposits, including gold, silver, and copper, with cattle-filled plains and five major urban centers (Buga, Cali, Cartago, Pasto, and Popayán).[2] It should not be surprising that Popayán's native son and champion of the Cauca would speak so favorably of his home region. And yet Mosquera's description of just the Astronomical Observatory in Bogotá roughly equaled the number of pages he dedicated to the entirety of Popayán.[3] Mosquera offered much more focused attention to the cultural, scientific, architectural, and industrial wealth of the capital city of New Granada than to any other place in the republic. Geographic treatises read before international audiences in 1852 were the logical ideological continuation of what Mosquera's first presidential administration, which ran from 1845 to 1849, had worked so hard to do for Bogotá.

Mosquera, his ministers, his advisers, his allies in Congress, and even his successor to the presidency, General José Hilario López, shared a view of economic, political, and historical geography of New Granada. President López, for instance, had continued the process of renaming Bogotá city streets according to the logic inaugurated under President Mosquera's administration. Both administrations and the many different journalists, intellectuals, religious leaders, military engineers, architects, chemists, merchants, and educators affiliated with them recognized the republic's deeply fragmented nature as stemming from the colonial period. They nevertheless saw in that very same fragmentation great untapped potential through complementarity. Like the Liberator Party generation before them, these men took up the mantle of Caldas by arguing that geography was key for understanding how to bring that potential to fruition. Unlike the Liberator Party, this generation argued that the republic did not offer a complete break with monarchy, that the legacy of Spanish colonialism ran too deep. Blockages to circulation were what the republic inherited, and these blockages needed to be toppled. Along with expanded infrastructure and a growing public sphere, this generation believed they needed to shape cultural and discursive geographic imaginaries so citizens understood why a fragmented New Granada needed to be connected. These men marshaled in geographic practices and representations to inspire all New Granada regions to have a stake in the new republic. Through geographically informed policies and practices, these elites tried to create a shared sense of space for New Granada's citizenry. One vital center where a sense of shared national space needed to occur was in the capital city of Bogotá.

Yet neither Bogotá nor New Granada were to be isolated from the world. The kind of political economy proposed by members of the Instituto Caldas, the Chorographic Commission that it launched, and the Colegio Militar took into account the geopolitical forces shaping New Granada. They understood the polity in a much wider spatial framework. Consider the slaveholding Cauca region, from which President Mosquera hailed. He was adamant about connecting the Cauca valley to the port of Bucaramanga. Cauca needed a port to connect the valley to Antioquia, Panama, Cartagena, and the rest of the regions that together made New Granada. Mosquera saw the Cauca and the Magdalena rivers as arteries of circulation that would be teeming with steamboats. But this circulation was not envisioned as a plan to subordinate regional economies to the pursuit of commercial global markets, however. Their republican project was tied to markets, but the markets to be prioritized were internal markets rather than global. Both the Mosquera and the López administrations were very much aware that the Anglo-Saxon republic to the north, the United States, was building a mammoth economy on the back of slaveholding plantations for export of commodities. Mosquera even admired the United States. After his first presidency Mosquera moved to Philadelphia to establish a commercial office. But Mosquera knew well that the key to his political heft in New Granada was the abolition of slavery, not its expansion. The Hilario López administration that succeeded Mosquera brought abolition to fruition. New Granada was no Cotton Kingdom, nor would it be. Bucaramanga was not New Orleans. Cauca and Magdalena were not to be the Mississippi either. New Granada government leaders at midcentury instead sought a political economy of circulation and the building of internal markets. Identifying internal markets, what products were traded from canton to canton and by what routes, came to be one of the central contributions of the Chorographic Commission in the 1850s.

Dominant historiography on Latin America has come to see liberals as a comprador bourgeoisie interested from the very inception of the nation in establishing global commercial connections and plantation economies. This was simply not the case in New

Granada at midcentury. The political economy of circulation of the 1840s and early 1850s would overcome what these leaders saw as a colonial legacy: dependency on exports. The Spanish monarchy had created blockages to internal trade so that it could siphon off New Granada wealth. The result was a fragmented polity of autonomous regions with their own currencies, units of measurements, dialects, accents, customs, and tolls precisely because the colonial period had privileged exports of gold, emeralds, and tobacco instead of fomenting the circulation of an integrated internal market. This framework explains Mosquera's decision to invest in the establishment of a brand new port on the lower Magdalena River near Barranquilla. Unlike Cartagena and Santa Marta, both of which are ports that openly face the Caribbean Sea and the greater Atlantic World beyond it, Barranquilla faces the interior, up the Magdalena. Mosquera thereby transformed the orientation of the economy inward, not outward as had always been the case.

New Granada nevertheless maintained connections to the Atlantic, the United States, and Europe to draw in expertise and capital. New Granada was a polity saddled with overwhelming foreign debt in the wake of independence and dissolution of Gran Colombia. To solve the problem of debt, the various governments of New Granada offered land as payment. Land would entice colonization and migration. The Instituto Caldas, the Chorographic Commission, and the Colegio Militar would bring in the experts who would train future technical experts who would then, in turn, survey state-owned lands that up until then were only vaguely known in their extent. These lands would be exchanged to pay off debts and welcome immigration. Trained surveyors would also measure and parcel out indigenous lands held in common. Both strategies, surveying state-owned lands to entice immigration and the breakup of communal land holdings, served the same purpose: to promote internal markets.

The first section of this chapter shows how people from a variety of New Granada provinces sought to forge a New Granada nation by centering Bogotá as the main conduit for the circulation of people, material goods, and ideas. This project took cues from U.S. industry, progress, and federalism, yet its expression had to contend with distinct New Granada realities. Morality would be the core value that would best bring the kind of modernization New Granada required. With the unique needs of New Granada in mind, elites founded the Instituto Caldas in Bogotá in December 1847. This scientific society, however, was not limited to Bogotá. The regional scope of the chapters that opened in the wake of the institute's founding points to the circulatory breadth of the shared elite project to tear down blockages to development supposedly created by monarchy, but in ways that were tuned into local realities. Founding members of the Instituto Caldas socialized with each other, invited foreign experts, and served as critical functionaries in the national government that passed legislation in support of the creation of new universities and educational institutions. These facilities were conceived as places where the best students from all the provinces could obtain the kind of education that would ensure New Granada's development.

This emerging culture of circulation, education, and morality was intrinsic to the founding of the Colegio Militar. The second section illustrates how the Colegio Militar became the site where the men most actively engaged in this circulatory national project imagined the place of Bogotá in New Granada through cartographic representations. The inspector-director of the Colegio, Agustín Codazzi, who also led the subsequent Chorographic Commission, deployed the most significant on-the-ground mapping project for the school. The cadet's survey work, together with Codazzi's expertise and the artistic license of drawing teacher Carmelo Fernandez, culminated in the "Mapa Topografico de Bogotá, 1849."[4] These mapmakers emphasized Bogotá's historically sanctioned role as a capital city, eliding the provisional capital status Bogotá endured during the First Colombian Republic of the 1820s. The map identifies the new pedagogies, entrepreneurial ethos, and technical practices that Mosquera's generation held dear. Furthermore, the ethnic and gendered ideas that infused the map of Bogotá reveal how the geographer corps was expected to understand, categorize, represent the regions of New Granada in the future and, through those representations, control them.

The last section explores the global, regional, and local dimensions of how this New Granada circulatory project was imagined. It does so by introducing a second map drawn in the Colegio that was unlike—yet deeply intertwined with—the 1849 topographic map of Bogotá. For their final capstone project, all cadets, following the apprenticeship-style pedagogy of the Colegio, needed to demonstrate their ability to draw a map at different resolutions and their dexterity at using cartographic conventions. The majority of students drew a series of nameless, imaginary landscapes. A sixteen-year-old cadet from Zipaquirá, Manuel Peña, went further, placing his own geopolitical imaginary onto the abstracted geographic landscape he drew. The imagined landscape reveals how Peña, like his classmates, encountered for the first time people and perspectives from several different regions of New Granada and the world. As his world expanded, it became filled with railroads, interoceanic canals, steamboat travel across oceans, and discoveries of gold in California. But it was also a distinctly Andean, landlocked place that witnessed warfare, dystopian and unconquerable natural features, and threatening global forces. Peña's mental map allows us to see the larger world in which the Bogotá-centered circulatory project made sense: a world of connections, migrations, markets, and the threats that warfare, foreign invasions, and natural obstacles posed. Peña's imaginary mental map offers a reading of local, regional, and global forces that are pulled into the center of his geopolitical vision. Bogotá, although not explicitly located on his mental map, is Peña's place of enunciation. In short, Peña's map reveals the global imaginaries that the Colegio Militar helped instill in their young cadets. The Colegio teachers trained these young men to be the engineers that would forge an integrated New Granada Republic out of the fragmented provinces left in the wake of the colonial period at a time when foreign invasion loomed.

Apprenticeship and Circulation

The opening of the Colegio Militar formed part of a larger national project that dreamed of a New Granada that was far more traversable, legible, interconnected, and open to internal trade and global connections.[5] After his travels through the United States in the

1830s, Mosquera found in that country's federal government useful strategies for how to achieve unity in diversity. With an eye toward turning Bogotá into the equivalent of Washington DC, President Mosquera brought a Danish Caribbean architect, Thomas Reed, to build Bogotá's capitol building; a massive neoclassical building not unlike those Mosquera had seen during his travels in the United States.[6] Mosquera also was thrilled by the technological innovation that facilitated circulation within the United States. Mosquera returned from his travels with a desire for canals that connected the rivers Atrato and San Juan in the Pacific. He wanted ports in Darien to move products from Antioquia highlands to national and international markets. His administration invested heavily in new technologies to transform the Magdalena into a new Mississippi, with steamboats plying the waters all the way to the newly founded port of Bucaramanga on the Caribbean. A federalism that suited the needs of New Granada's provinces and that was modeled on the United States required a grand, culturally dominant capital city that would pull all of New Granada together, and technology and innovation would make all this happen.

Washington DC helped Mosquera envision his national project, but it was not the only model Mosquera admired; Francisco José de Caldas clearly had also been on his mind. By the 1840s, with the threat of a Spanish reinvasion gone, and the goals of fomenting economic and political modernization for New Granada reinvigorated, Francisco José de Caldas's writings became useful once again. Caldas's 1808–1810 vision of the Kingdom of New Granada as perfectly poised geographically to produce all the world's agricultural commodities rang true. Mosquera and his generation were also inspired by Caldas's calls to ensure circulation throughout New Granada through construction of roads, canals, and other transportation improvements. Advancing geographic knowledge held the key to unlocking these improvements, and Mosquera's generation worked mightily to forge that key for New Granada in Bogotá.

The Mosquera administration knew that ambitious plans for infrastructural development were only possible through accurate geographical knowledge that could make the ground legible and transformable. A trained cadre of technical elites, well versed in related sciences and enjoying ample hands-on experience, and who themselves were from different provinces, would see the transformation through. That was the founding ideal behind the Colegio Militar, and it was also the founding ideal for several other institutions created during this period. Although it was true that the military institute at West Point clearly inspired the Colegio Militar, this was not the only model to which Mosquera turned. That is because at midcentury New Granada elites agreed that all of these educational experiments seeking industry and progress needed to be guided by a strong moral compass. This compass was provided by the single most important institute that brought together all those who founded and promoted these educational institutions, including the Colegio Militar. The institute was aptly named the Instituto Caldas.

Formally decreed into existence by Mosquera in December 1847, the Instituto Caldas was originally conceived of by one of Mosquera's closest advisers, his sub-secretary of state, Manuel Ancízar. The Caldas Institute, as Ancízar explained, was modeled on similar industrial societies in New York. With time and perseverance the institute, much like its sister New York societies, would reach admirable ends in agriculture, manufacturing, and arts.[7] The kind of progress and industry New Granada needed was different from the United States, however. The founding members of the Caldas Institute in Bogotá wished to connect industry and education to morality for all of New Granada provinces.[8] Every chapter in each province would promote a lay culture interested in the acquisition of new technologies, discovery, entrepreneurship, economic liberalism, and, above all, a strong moral education. Through these clubs, the learned, technical elites of the provinces would develop local industry and find solutions to the problems of geographic isolation. They would build new roads, canals, and even railroads. But unless producers were morally indoctrinated, they could succumb to the eroding forces of individualism that capitalism championed, bringing utter chaos to communities and the country as a whole.[9]

President Mosquera became the official director of the Instituto Caldas and offered a sumptuous banquet for the installation of the central chapter in Bogotá, where he honored the institute's namesake. Mosquera's speech reveals the new incarnation of Caldas that he deemed critical for a New Granada nation at midcentury:

> To promote and found any institute that has as its elevated purpose to maintain and disseminate notions of morality, public instruction, and advancing grenadine industry is to work towards the duties that institutions impose on a magistrate and that he must fulfill. But if that institute is joined to a great name, one that reminds the patria of the naturalist, the philosopher filled with virtues, the statesman, who was the victim immolated by foreign barbarity, then that institute acquires the consideration and prestige that patriotic enthusiasm grants to all who envelope themselves in its grandiose vision.[10]

Mosquera highlighted the attributes of Caldas and his various patriotic contributions in ways that went beyond those the Liberator Party employed for their geographic state-building purposes of the 1820s. Caldas's memory was itself evocative of the kind of morality, public instruction, and industry that New Granada leaders needed to promote. By 1848 the victimization of Caldas, in Mosquera's speech, was carried out by a nameless "foreign" power. The specific barbarity of Spain no longer mattered as much. Caldas's heroic founding patriotism was what mattered, and it was this tradition that would ignite patriotic passion in the hearts of New Granada citizens, regardless of political party affiliation. Mosquera knew whereof he spoke.

Strikingly, the founding members of Bogotá's Instituto Caldas came from across the political spectrum, not just because of the nonpartisan appeal of industry and development but also because of the moral improvements it promised for New Granada's population. Provincial chapters of the institute followed soon after Bogotá, and membership in the provinces also cut across party lines. Throughout 1848 and for some of 1849, while under the Mosquera presidency, province after province set up a chapter, naming dozens of prominent local learned elites to institute ranks.[11] Santander Province's Instituto Caldas most notably expanded education for women to train them in hat weaving, helping to transition the region away from a declining cottage weaving industry in cotton.[12] The founding Bogotá chapter further promoted the formation of provincial chapters by organizing annual industrial fairs in Bogotá that offered prizes for the best products exhibited by the attending provincial chapters of the institute.[13] Most members of the Instituto Caldas across New Granada belonged to a similar social and economic class and enjoyed exceptional educational backgrounds, yet they differed in their political leanings. What allowed them to rise above party differences was the fact that they all shared a similar goal for the institute: reaching the more humble, laboring free people of color and artisan classes, ostensibly to foment the skills needed for economic growth and the morality needed to create a nation.[14]

These patriotic goals were not without critics. Proponents of the Instituto Caldas launched a targeted defense of the enterprise, suggesting where the sites of weakness for the endeavor lay:

> Let it not be said that the Instituto Caldas is the fruit of an illusion and an unrealizable dream. For too long laziness has shielded itself behind such classifications. If anything, they represent an inertia of spirit: the day has come for recognizing such evasion as not only ridiculous but also anti-patriotic, given that the abandoning of our people to chance will bring grave consequences for the future of the patria as a free and civilized nation. The Executive Power is encouraged by the help of good citizens, those who love their country without limits in terms of time or in terms of individuals. They will bring excellent results to the Instituto Caldas.[15]

These official words shrouded the Instituto Caldas in a national, patriotic cloak. Only lazy individuals would dare criticize the endeavor.

With the end of the Mosquera presidency and the arrival of the José Hilario Lopez administration in 1849, the creation of new Instituto Caldas chapters nevertheless fell into a lull. José Manuel Restrepo, one of the Instituto Caldas's founding members in Bogotá, later recalled how despite the shiny picture Ancízar and Mosquera painted of the potential of this institute, "after a few and useless sessions, the Instituto Caldas disappeared, leaving no other memory than the decree of its foundation."[16] Although the Instituto Caldas itself may not have left a lasting legacy in Restrepo's oft-cited opinion, the individuals involved in the endeavor nevertheless were remarkably active in promoting a moral education that would readily produce industry for all of New Granada's provinces for a generation. Apprenticeship-style learning rather than abstract transmission of ideas became a central component of their pedagogical approach.

The Instituto Caldas offered a critical staging ground for hands-on apprenticeship training in the development of industry, both from Bogotá and in the provinces. Members of the Instituto Caldas in Bogotá were active in the formation of new educational institutes, schools, and centers during the Mosquera administration. With the help of Instituto Caldas members, Mosquera revived the Astronomical Observatory in Bogotá and founded an affiliated institute at the observatory intended to promote studies in mathematics, astronomy, physics, and natural sciences.[17] Mosquera also gave new life to the Natural History Museum and National Library, both located in Bogotá. Instituto Caldas members not only frequented both centers, but they also offered up their valuable collections of books and natural specimens to these repositories. Bogotá overwhelmingly became the city of residence for the technical experts the Mosquera administration hired from all over the world to head the plethora of schools and scientific studies programs.[18] The institutions at which these foreign experts worked included the University of the First District, the Colegio Militar, and the Astronomical Observatory. Men affiliated with Bogotá's Instituto Caldas helped facilitate communication across these educational facilities. French mathematician Aime Bergeron, for instance, not only had befriended Mosquera and Ancízar; he also became a member of the astronomical institute and gave astronomy classes in the observatory to Colegio Militar students as well as to those of the University of the First District.[19]

Members of the Instituto Caldas in regions far from Bogotá also helped network foreign experts with local elites and local needs. For instance, chemists Giuseppe Eboli and Bernard Lewy fomented production in the coining mints of Popayán and Bogotá, respectively, and also aided salt mine engineers in Zipaquirá fine-tune their practice. The physical presence of experts in the provinces, either imported from abroad or as local experts united in a provincial chapter of a society such as the Instituto Caldas, was not the only way that regions could benefit from Mosquera's measures. Precisely because Bogotá offered a dense conglomeration of experts, institutes, and educational facilities, regional elites sent their best and brightest to be trained, and the Instituto Caldas helped orient the training of these young provincial sons seeking expertise. Take, for instance, the influence that Thomas Reed, Danish architect and founding member of the Instituto Caldas, had in the training of young men from an impressive number of New Granada provinces. Provincial governors, only months after inaugurating an Instituto Caldas chapter in their capital cities, quickly named talented young men from their province to be trained in Bogotá under Reed.[20] Regional reach, however, was not the only goal; Reed emphasized the value of hands-on apprentice style education. He taught architecture and engineering to incoming students from the provinces at Bogotá's University of the First District and also taught practical masonry classes on the construction site of the emerging Capitol building.[21]

This model of regional diversity and apprenticeship-style education fomented by members of the Instituto Caldas through a variety of educational spaces also surfaced in the Colegio Militar. In fact, the Colegio embraced the regions from the moment of its very conception. Each of the twenty-two provinces that then comprised New Granada were guaranteed at least one of the forty fully funded admissions spots. Contrary to studies that overestimate the significance of Bogotá for this institution, the vast majority of provinces sent students to be trained in the Colegio, with only Choco and Panama abstaining.[22] The hands-on training cadets received came largely from the newly hired foreign expert brought from Venezuela to teach these students and to draw up a general map of New Granada: Italian military engineer Agustin Codazzi.

Codazzi was one of the most recognized and active of the dozen foreign experts Mosquera hired to come to New Granada.[23] Codazzi had grown familiar with Spanish America from the time of independence, having served as second in command on the *America Libre* captained by French privateer and patriot general Louis Michel Aury. Although Codazzi drew coastal maps of the Caribbean during his time with Aury, he did not build an international reputation as an expert geographer until the publication of his work surveying and mapping Venezuela during the 1830s. Manuel Ancízar, for his part, was intimately familiar with Codazzi's work. The two men had become friendly during Ancízar's years in Venezuela.[24] Ancízar and Mosquera's common interests in promoting scientific advancement and a rational understanding of the New Granada state resulted in their decision to offer Codazzi two posts in 1848.[25] Codazzi ambitiously accepted the directorship of the Colegio Militar and the leadership of the Chorographic Commission. Upon arrival, he met with his old friend from Venezuela, Tomás Reed. Students who took classes with Reed often would take classes with students of the Colegio Militar who were under Codazzi's direction.[26] Codazzi immediately instituted a regime of cartographic apprenticeship. One result was the map of Bogotá from 1849. It is to this map, finalized during the first months of the José Hilario Lopez presidential administration, that we now turn.

Drawing Bogotá as the Heart of the Nation

The Instituto Caldas played a crucial role in helping intellectual and cultural elites found various educational training sites, including the Colegio Militar. The press, especially the press controlled by the Instituto Caldas founder, Manuel Ancízar, enthusiastically greeted news that Colegio Militar cadets would survey Bogotá's lands for a future map. "If the students of the Colegio are determined to render this service for the country, thereby proving their knowledge and good intentions, we, for our part, offer to publish an etched and annotated 'Plano de Bogotá I sus alredededores, levantado por los alumnus del Colejio Militar.'"[27] Several Colegio Militar cadets agreed to join in on this national, patriotic endeavor. The result was the 1849 *Plano Topográfico de Bogotá i parte de sus alrededores.* Although now a rare map, two of the three existing lithographers in Bogotá published versions of this original map in 1852.

This section takes a close look at the 1849 *Plano Topografico of Bogotá* but goes beyond the contents of the map to highlight the people involved in its making. Doing so reveals how this map-making process reflected a concerted, cross-partisan elite effort to rework the urban space of Bogotá, and representations of it, so as to signal the place Bogotá needed to occupy in New Granada, historically, politically, economically, and culturally. The subtle transformation of Bogotá in this mapping endeavor was, at its core, an effort to begin to transform the entire New Granada nation more broadly. Therefore, analyzing this mapping process, from the people involved to the practices employed to the image drawn, sheds abundant light on three major, interconnected aspects of midcentury efforts to build a New Granada nation, efforts that had been developed by scientific and political elites who were in Bogotá yet were not necessarily originally from Bogotá. First, the diverse origins of the mapmaking cadre that mapped Bogotá's urban space and environs underscore how Bogotá increasingly was becoming, in effect, a unifying center for scientific elites from far-flung regions, and from around the world. Second, how the map was drawn reveals the idealized practical apprenticeship style of education inaugurated by Instituto Caldas members under the Mosquera administration. Third, the new technical, entrepreneurial, and nation-building priorities championed at midcentury by both the Mosquera and Lopez administrations are distinctly displayed on this map through the topographic information on the map's face that is made legible through the cartouche and map key.

Let us begin then, with the non-Bogotáno origins of the people who contributed to the making of the 1849 map of Bogotá. Agustin Codazzi reflects the mid-nineteenth-century iteration of this trend most clearly, especially since he was the director of the school and leader of this mapping endeavor. This Italian military engineer had recently arrived from a multiyear cartographic survey of Venezuela. His work for President José Antonio Paez in Venezuela began in 1830, in large part to mark off Venezuela's national identity from that of the former first Colombian Republic and, more importantly, from any effort by Bogotá to regain control over Venezuela. Codazzi's cartographic work for Venezuela culminated in a highly acclaimed atlas, one that was made patriotically meaningful through the allegorical drawings by Carmelo Fernandez Paez. As his maternal surname suggests, Fernandez Paez was not just a talented artist; this Venezuelan also happened to be the nephew of Venezuelan general and president José Antonio Paez. Codazzi had traveled extensively with Fernandez, including a Parisian sojourn to publish the Venezuelan atlas in 1840. The trust Codazzi had in Fernandez's talents meant the New Granada government was happy to hire this Venezuelan and bring him to Bogotá to teach drawing to Colegio Militar students.

These two Colegio Militar professors were not the only men foreign to Bogotá, of course. Miguel Bracho, the first drawing professor hired for the school, also hailed from Venezuela. Aime Bergueron, the astronomy professor brought by Mosquera from France, was added to the Colegio Militar ranks as mathematics professor. The original mathematics professor and champion of the school, Lino de Pombo, had been born in Cartagena and formally served in New Granada's legislature as a representative from Cartagena, yet his family wealth hailed from Popayán. In short, the principle faculty members teaching these students to draw a patriotically inspired map of Bogotá were not themselves from Bogotá. Codazzi and Fernandez, the two men most directly involved in the Bogotá mapping exercise, had built their professional reputations on their cartography of Venezuela and had close ties, either professional or by blood, to the Venezuelan general who had led the process of fragmentation of the first Colombian Republic. One would expect that these personal and professional backgrounds would cause these men to reject a project to convey the dominance of Bogotá. Instead, Codazzi and Fernandez were the men responsible for leading students, and map readers, toward this goal.

Although several students participating in this mapping endeavor lead by Codazzi and Fernandez were sons of elite Bogotá families, many were not. From the face of the map, we know the last names of the cadets who mapped the public lands of the city. The Bogotanos included Manuel Ponce de Leon, José Cornelio Borda, Joaquín Barriga (the son of the secretary of war), Ignacio Ortega (the former Colegio Militar director's son), Celestino Castro, and Félix Caro. There were some noted sons of provincial elites who happened to be in Bogotá as well. Rafael Pombo, for instance, was the son of Lino de Pombo, the Colegio Militar's mathematics professor who was originally from Cartagena. Significantly, humbler students from the provinces also made up the Bogotá mapmaking team. The first student recognized on the map for his contributions was Juan Esteban Zamarra, a young man from Antioquia. He had shown so much promise that, despite his humble origins, the bishop of Antioquia took Zamarra under his wing. The bishop mobilized alms collection in Antioquia to fund the boy's travel expenses to Bogotá.[28] In addition to Antioquia's sponsorship of Zamarra, several other provinces paid for the tuition and the room and board of deserving young men. This was the case for Antonio Merizalde, who came from Tunja, Juan Francisco Urrutia, from Popayán, and Manuel García Herreros, from Pamplona. José María Arrubla's origins as a "particular," or private student, meant that he did not enjoy a fellowship that paid for his studies at the Colegio, and so his origins are unclear.[29]

Apprentice-style training was at the core of the pedagogical approaches followed at the Colegio Militar. The mapping of Bogotá was an obvious way of displaying the value of the skills they acquired. The finished map to which the students contributed offered itself up as the first, choice harvest from the investments that national and regional governments had put into their education. Reading the content of the finished map backward helps us see what that apprenticeship-style education may have looked like on the ground.

As the map tells us, these twelve students surveyed *ejidos*, or public lands, found within the areas between La Peña, the Plaza de las Cruces, and "Tres Esquinas" until the River Fucha. The map identifies these public lands through geometric patches of what seem to be well-tended groves of agricultural production. They sprinkle up around the entire built-up area of Bogotá, but the students only surveyed a portion of these lands, including the fields nestled around the highest-elevation area of La Peña, near Monserrate on the top right-hand side of the map closest to the cartouche. They also surveyed the intersection of the three rivers located above the compass rose at the bottom of the map image. Finally, Colegio Militar students hiked around the lands surrounding the River Fucha, on the bottom right-hand corner of the map. Although they worked only a portion of the total lands surveyed by Codazzi for the city of Bogotá, the cadets' surveys of the ejidos offered up proof of the value that an engineering education provided the nation.

Codazzi, from the time he first arrived in Bogotá, argued to government officials that land surveys were the primary practical contribution that students trained in the Colegio Militar could offer New Granada.[30] With trained surveyors, territorial disputes over private property boundaries would be easily resolved. Furthermore, the national state could depend on these trained cadets to inventory nationally owned *baldio*, or uncultivated state-owned lands in a cadastre, allowing the state to dispose of those lands more easily. Codazzi taught these skills to Colegio Militar students through praxis. The map information that Codazzi and the other instructors helped students create was embedded in a complex and still evolving cartographic process whose conventions had yet to be defined. Codazzi and his students nevertheless understood that map information was created and re-created by a series of interpretive processes that included how the mapmaker represented territorial understanding on a map's surface, the clues provided on the map that help decipher its meaning, and the map readers' ability to understand the particularities of the specific map at hand.[31] Through the making and viewing of maps, cartographers and map readers in the mid-nineteenth century engaged in a process that structured visual field according to a set of agreed-upon rules. The map of Bogotá that the cadets helped produce evinces this hands-on, yet at the same time abstracted, process.

In mid-nineteenth-century New Granada, map readers and mapmakers tended to be a very small sector of the population. The cartographic language that Colegio Militar students and their instructors developed during the mid-nineteenth century linked into an emerging international code of cartographic conventions. In that sense these men were participating in and developing a common cartographic language that made the symbols and abstractions they used, if used correctly, believable and authoritative, irrespective of what the reality on the ground may have been. Although based in international trends, this language also necessarily formed an integral part of the cultural, social, political, and economic values of the emerging cartographer corps. The 1849 *Plano Topográfico* of Bogotá, which resulted from the surveys students and Codazzi conducted on the ground, the cartographic information Codazzi had on hand in Bogotá, and the artistic license Carmelo Fernandez took to represent the city, reveals key interactions between this internationally sanctioned yet still emerging cartographic language, and the kinds of mid-century New Granada nation-building propositions that these map makers were working to make a reality.

One can begin reading a map at any point, yet we can begin to decode this specific map according to the ways its makers tried to encode Bogotá's significant points of interest. Paying special attention to what map scholars have termed the "para map," or the texts and images that surround the topographic image, we can begin to better understand the meaning the mapmakers wished to inscribe upon the territory they depicted. The para map of the 1849 cartographic image occupies close to a fifth of the entire visual field and includes the allegorical cartouche on the top right, the commentary below the compass rose at the bottom center of the map, and the exhaustive list of places worthy of notice on the bottom left. The following close reading of the para map allows for a deeper understanding of the cultural and political milieu that shaped the territorial representations these men drew out and the kind of history they wished to embed within Bogotá's topography.[32] Overall, the resulting view for Bogotá evinces a concerted effort to recuperate New Granada's Spanish colonial heritage, to identify the kind of material progress and industry available since the time of independence, and to champion the kinds of projected reforms that not only were intended to transform the physical space of the city, but that would also patriotically unite the disparate provinces of New Granada through Bogotá.

The cartouche itself asserts its importance relative to the map through sheer size; it takes up almost an eighth of the entire map.

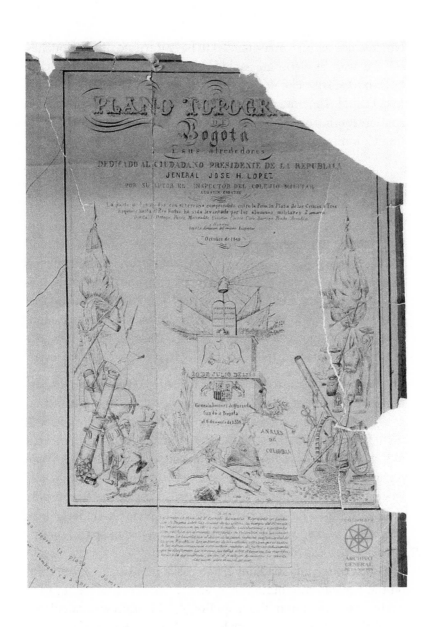

5. "Bogotá y sus alrededores," 1849 map detail. SMP 2, Ref. 1-21.
Archivo General de la Nación, Bogotá.

Nineteenth-century maps tended to have intricate title cartouches, but few were as elaborate as this.[33] Fernandez explained the symbols in his cartouche design through a long note underneath the map legend. The note underscores the historical, institutional, and spatial significance of Bogotá, including its role as capital for the first Colombian Republic:

> Note: the vignette is by Mr. Carmelo Fernandes. Represents the foundation of Bogotá over the ruins of the Indians, the times of the Viceroyalty, its emancipation in 1810, and its current institutions and political representation in the world. The annals of Colombia upon which the laurels and trumpet of fame rest indicate that it was the capital of that Great Republic. The emblems on the sides express that Bogotá is currently the center of ecclesiastical, military, judicial, and treasury administrations, and that within Bogotá flower the sciences, the fine arts, commerce, manufacturing, and agriculture. Finally, the frailejón plant [Espeletia grandiflora] demonstrates Bogotá's high elevation above sea level.[34]

This text and the cartouche image together reveal Carmelo Fernandez's argument for Bogotá's eminence as resting not just on geography, but also on history. The high elevation of Bogotá still mattered, as symbolized by the frailejón, a species of plant that only grows above two thousand meters in South America's Andean region. The high altitude suggested by this plant reflected the elevated location of Bogotá, a city that rose above the supposedly unhealthy, uncivilized lowland climates of New Granada. In fact, much like in colonial-era maps of Bogotá's urban space, mountains oriented the map. Bogotá was nestled between the twin peaks of Monserrate and Guadalupe, two easily identifiable mountains on the Andean mountain range, and the mountains, rather than north, are at the top of the map. Bogotá's location was calculated according to height above sea level and also in terms of its astronomical position relative to Paris. This allowed the mapmakers to characterize Bogotá as a temperate, cool city connected to Europe. Bogotá's civilized, elevated location serves as the principle backdrop to the rest of Bogotá's story, one elaborated upon by Carmelo Fernandez's cartouche. The cartouche itself is divided into three spaces, with the central composition showing the foundational pedestal supporting distinct stages of New Granada history and the two columns framing that pedestal represent the major institutions of culture, learning, science, religion, and order found in Bogotá.

The central column's base begins with the historical foundation of the city by Gonzalo Jimenez de Quesada, rises up through Bogotá's independence on July 20, 1810, and culminates with New Granada's pomegranate-decorated constitution topped by a Phrygian cap that shines with its inner light of republican liberty. This representative move signaled a shift in how New Granada elites were portraying that nation's relationship to Spain. Rather than continue the Partido de Libertadores's argument for the virtue of republicanism as opposed to the gruesome barbarity of Spanish colonialism that extinguished lights and learning, these midcentury elites found in New Granada continuities with its Spanish colonial past. That continuity embraced Quesada, New Granada's Spanish founder who had shattered the cultural artifacts, stone statues, tablets, and staffs representing indigenous culture. These broken pieces could vaguely refer to any indigenous culture, but the cracked tablet with a sun and a moon, images central to Musica cosmology, work to identify the Muiscas as grounded in the history of Bogotá. These broken symbols lend greater weight to a significant silence on this map. While the cartouche identifies the ejidos, or public lands, drawn by Colegio Militar students, nowhere does the map identify indigenous communal lands, or resguardos, within the vicinity of Bogotá. Through the cartouche's allegorical drawings and topographic image, the makers of this map relegated the indigenous population of Bogotá to the dustbin of history.

The ruins of indigenous culture also help point to Bogotá's longevity. The note below the cartouche pragmatically explains how Bogotá had long been the administrative center of justice, treasury, church, and army from the viceregal era. So solid is Bogotá's history as capital, that any challenge to Bogotá's status is completely locked out of the central image of the column. The declaration of independence in Bogotá on July 20, 1810, is etched onto the column side, elevating that city's significance to the republic,

while also erasing the memory of equally significant independence declarations that sprouted up among various cities in the
former viceroyalty. Focusing on Bogotá's date of independence
also allows the cartouche to forgo any discussion of the several
different cities surrounding Bogotá that declared their independence not from the Spanish monarchy, but from Bogotá itself. The
tumultuous interregnum (1808–1816), which brought competition
among urban centers, had called Bogotá's dominance into question. This cartouche's rendition of Bogotano history erases that
period of uncertainty. Skipping over the tumult of the interregnum, the cartouche instead offers a history book that identifies
Bogotá as the capital city for the first Colombian Republic. Doing
so usefully offers evidence of Bogotá's historically sanctioned place
as capital. The "Anales de Colombia," or history of the Colombian
Republic, is not constitutive of New Granada's founding column,
however. Instead, a victorious Colombian history, graced by lau-
rels and a horn, rests upon New Granada (and on Bogotá), but off
to the side, as a book that usefully broke the chains of the Spanish colonial period. After the first Colombian Republic dissolved,
Bogotá continued on in New Granada as the seat of culture, civilization, and political power for New Granada, and the two panels
that flank the central image further flesh out that story.

Framing this stable historical monument to Bogotá are two columns of symbols that speak to the new values of entrepreneurship and technical apprenticeship that midcentury government
elites wished to foment. To the left of Bogotá's central foundational history (right side of the image from the viewer's perspective) are the cardinal institutions for the nation that Bogotá housed
in 1849. The abundance of gold coins fresh from a gold-panning
plate spill out onto the ground beside what appear to be double-
entry ledger books. This image suggests Bogotá's efforts to make
rational sense of New Granada's treasury. A musical harp offers
a harmonizing force to the gears, pick axes, and shovels of industry. The symbol of pharmacopeia and the telescope suggest the
kind of scientific work that is carried out specifically in Bogotá
through medicine and the Astronomical Observatory. But this
map cartouche symbolizing Bogotá is not completely secular; it

cannot be, given Bogotá's singularly important role as an arch-diocese. The miter, crosier, incense burner, and stole symbolize the sacramental vestments that, together, only the archbishop can use, marking off Bogotá as the New Granada city with the highest level of church administration in the country. The scales above the church symbols famously represent the administration of justice. Rather than held by a blindfolded Lady Justice, however, these scales are tied to the background banner and the downward-pointing sword of punishment.

The absent body of Lady Justice visually parallels another absent body in the column of objects to the right of the central historical column (left side of the image from the viewer's perspective): the absent body of Bolívar. The Libertador's hat and sword mirror the angle at which the sword of justice and scales are presented. Although Bolívar's body is missing, a pair of slightly overlapping hands peeks out, seemingly from nowhere. Perhaps these hands gesture toward the handing over of military power (Bolívar's sword) to a civilian government? That a symbolic map in the cartouche lays on top of bayonets and horns of war suggests as much, as do the upright canons resting on the ground in disrepair. The brick foundry pouring out molten iron seems to be repurposing those old war cannons. A hammer and sickle underscore the kind of industry that Bogotá promotes. Pharmacopeia emerges on this panel too through the snake, mortar, and pestle. So do the arts: a mask for theater, an art pallet for painting, panpipes for Andean music.

Fernandez's cartouche image thus established Bogotá's republican history as founded in Spanish conquest, yet blossoming as a center of culture, industry, government administration, religious authority, and civilization for New Granada. The geographic information transmitted through other parts of the map reinforces the message, while also making a case for the need to engage in further reforms. Bogotá may have been the historical center of administration and industry, but much more work was needed in order to allow the city to perform even better as a capital for the New Granada republic. In many ways, that vision of industry and needed progress emanated from President Mosquera's first presidential administration. As noted above, Mosquera paid careful attention to the training of students in the Colegio Militar. This was evidenced not only by Mosquera's founding of the school itself and his hiring of technical experts for that school, but also by his gift of a dedicated map of the Magdalena to the students.[35] Codazzi and Military School students reflected the several urban changes that the Mosquera administration effected on Bogotá's urban space in their 1849 map.

Consider, for instance, how Mosquera spearheaded the reform of Bogotá's street nomenclature, transforming that city into a microcosm of the nation. Outsiders and long-term Bogotá natives, after 1846, would have to navigate the streets of Bogotá in ways that reminded them of that city's location with respect to all the other provinces of New Granada. The topography of Bogotá depicted on the 1849 map displays this new system. Streets with names such as Carrera de Pamplona and Carrera de Socorro, for instance, ran toward the north of the city in the direction of where those towns lay relative to the San Francisco River, the main river that ran through the center of Bogotá. On the other side of that river, those street names changed, reflecting a change in direction toward the south, and became Carrera de Popayán and Carrera de Tuquerres. Those were cities that lay, appropri- ately, to the south of Bogotá. The topographic image of the city, in conjunction with the cartouche, thereby synthesized the major efforts of the Mosquera administration to bolster the status of Bogotá as the unifying center of the disjointed political econo- mies that made up New Granada.

Mosquera's efforts to transform Bogotá were mostly followed by his successor, José Hilario Lopez, and the map also reflects this continuity. The map is dedicated to President Lopez and also champions the future projects to transform Bogotá that were pro- posed by Lopez appointees like Cundinamarca governor Vicente Lombana. Along the higher portion of the mountain range words snake around mountainous terrain, carving out the projected path for a future road by stating, "The current governor, Mr. Vicente Lombana, is having a public path built, one that will meet with another path, and both will emerge flat, wide, and elevated to over more than 100 varas over the Plaza, dominating the city and

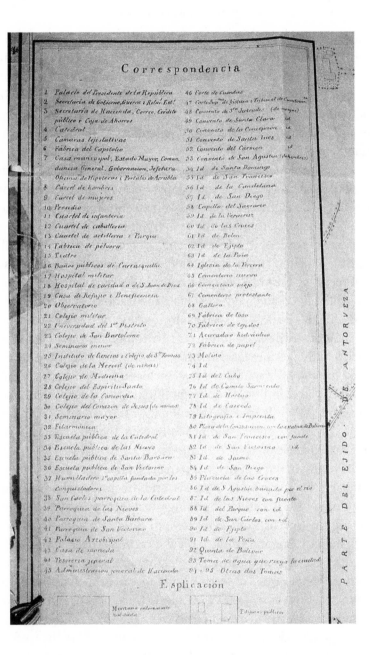

6. "Bogotá y sus alrededores," 1849 map detail. SMP 2, Ref. 1-21.
Archivo General de la Nación, Bogotá.

the plains." Just beneath and parallel to that path of words signaling a future roadway was another: "Path of the Agua Vieja that the current Governor, Dr. Lombana, will unite with that of Agua Nueva."[36] Codazzi and his students thereby displayed the utility of their cartographic representations for future development projects. They offered up this utility regardless of the political party that held national power.

The most notable way that Codazzi, Fernandez, and the Military School students adopted and adapted cartographic conventions from the late eighteenth and early nineteenth centuries is in their use of a map key to make the topographic image of Bogotá legible to map readers. The Esquiasi map of 1791, modified by Morillo during his occupation of the city in 1816, and Carlos Francisco Cabrer's 1797 map of Bogotá both would serve as models for Colegio Militar students.[37] Both Esquiasi and Cabrer's map keys identified religious buildings, such as the location of Bogotá's cathedral or religious orders, or important buildings for public services, such as jails and the slaughterhouse. Taking cues from Cabrer and Esquiasi, the Military School map included a map key that identified key places in Bogotá but went into far more detail than existing models. While in 1816 Morrillo, via Esquiasi, knew of at least eighty-five important buildings in Bogotá, the 1849 Colegio Militar map listed ninety-five locations.

Beyond schools, convents, parishes, jails, and plazas, infantry barracks, the cavalry barracks, and the artillery barracks, the 1849 map also identified buildings and institutions established during the first half of the nineteenth century. Doing so allowed this map of Bogotá to mark off the recent growth and change the city experienced during the early republican period. These included institutions of learning and research, such as the Astronomical Observatory (#20), the Colegio Militar (#21), and the newly founded Universidad del 1er Distrito (#22). Places of industry, such as the gunpowder factory (#14), the tile factory (#69), the weaving factory (#70), the paper factory (#72), and its hydraulic powered log yard (#71), also were listed and located. Mills peppered the city, yet of the six that existed, several were privately owned. Bogotá, as the cartouche suggested, was a center of culture and entertainment, as was plainly visible by the fact of its theater (#15), its philharmonic (#32), and cock-fighting pit (#68). The map key also located Bogotá's major institutional buildings that provided needed government services, including the palace of the president of the republic (#1), the secretariat of government, war, and external relations (#2), the secretariat of the treasury, postal mail, public credit, and savings (#3), the legislative chambers (#5), and the place where the future capitol building was being constructed (#6). The topographic image, the cartouche, and the map key all need to be read together in order to understand not just what Bogotá looked like in 1849, but also how mapmakers, and those who supported them, wanted Bogotá to look in the present and in the future. There still was some room for patriotic ambiguity, however. As mentioned above, the Plaza Mayor in Bogotá officially had its named changed to "Plaza de la Constitución," and by 1846 a statue of Bolívar watched over it. These midcentury mapmakers offered the official Plaza de la Constitución and identified the statue of Bolívar that it contained (#80). Concisely introducing references to the productive entrails of the city along with the old and the new buildings representing justice and politics, as well as an emerging, civil public sphere, this map made evident the new values of the Mosquera administration, the Instituto Caldas he had inaugurated, and the continuation of those values through the Lopez administration.

The image also inadvertently reveals a bit about the mapmakers' scientific geographic imaginations and self-fashioning. The perspective is that of a totalizing vision from above, a technique that involved sophisticated training in geometry and advanced mathematics, training only available to men. Though only men participated in these mapmaking projects, women and their separate spaces nevertheless had a place in these representations. Consider, for instance, how the map key also signaled which public spaces were either male or female. Students identified how the jail for men was separate from the jail for women, and indicated which convents housed nuns and which housed men. Of the fifteen schools listed in the map key only two were specifically signaled out as schools for women. These parenthetical explanations suggest that the other thirteen schools and universities were exclusively male. Female spaces were further differentiated according to the kind of women that inhabited them. Innocent *monjas*, or nuns, lived in convents, and respectable *niñas*, or girls, went to school. Less innocent *mujeres*, or women, were housed in jail. Men were always men, whether they were in jail, in a convent, or moving freely about the city. The fact that these mapmakers emphasized how public space in Bogotá was divided between male spaces and different classes of female spaces helps us understand how the larger nation-building project envisioned for New Granada was conceived as one that included women, but within confined, distinct spaces. Similarly, the imagined and scientific geographies these students developed for New Granada also included indigenous culture, but only mythically so. Rather than identify where indigenous peoples still held land, the map shows indigenous culture as simply having been shattered and controlled by Spanish American conceptions of time, history, and territorial organization.

The *Plano Topográfico* was both welcomed and challenged by different members of Bogotá society. Some sectors of Bogotá appreciated the hard work of the Military School students who accompanied Codazzi. As we read in the optimistic Neo-granandino passage that opened the section, those closest to the ideals of the enterprise, men like Manuel Ancízar, graciously offered to publish the work of these students as "the best retort to those that have criticized the School."[38] Once the map was finalized, it did make a splash in the Bogotano public sphere with two of the three printing presses in Bogotá publishing it simultaneously in 1852.[39] The civilian character of the work the Colegio Militar students carried out seemed to redeem the school in the eyes of influential people who denounced any effort to support the military. Those denouncing the military saw in the Civil War of 1854 justification for shutting down the school, a move that was further justified given increasing impoverishment at the national and regional state levels that made funding the school impossible. In 1852, before the school shut down, and in the same year that the map of Bogotá came out in print, several Military School cadets turned in their final mapping assignments, the capstone to their cartographic education. It is to these exercises, over a hundred of them, that we now turn.

Mapping Out Global, Regional, and Local Connections

Given the Military School's mission to train young men in the cartographic arts in Bogotá, and given the weight that their first "real-world" mapping endeavor placed on the space of Bogotá for the New Granada nation, one might be tempted to state unequivocally that the Colegio Militar was the critical site where an unquestioned Bogotá-centered construction of territory for New Granada was developed.[40] And yet a close analysis of the multiple abstract mapping exercises Colegio Militar cadets drew allows us a view of what went on in the classroom in ways that challenge this expectation. This section examines a unique example of these exercises, the mental map meticulously drawn out by sixteen-year-old Manuel H. Peña. As noted above, many students of the Colegio Militar, as well as its professoriate, hailed from a variety of places in New Granada and the world. Peña was himself from the neighboring province of Zipaquirá. Peña's map begins to suggest how different regional perspectives brought together in one place opened up students' geographic imaginaries. The section draws on Peña's mental map to demonstrate how students came to understand New Granada's place in global, regional, and local dynamics of circulation, population movements, and politics. Peña's mental map reveals how, rather than evincing a narrative of a centralizing Bogotá, cadets in the Military School brought in multiregional perspectives with sophisticated geopolitical readings of New Granada's place in the world. Peña's mental map also suggests the extent to which the students had acquired a solid grasp of the fissures and forces that worked against a New Granada circulatory national project, especially with respect to natural features, warfare, and potential invasion by outside powers.

The surviving 124 drawings by Colegio Militar students are gathered into eight files and preserved in the national archive of Colombia.[41] The overwhelming majority of these images are of nameless landscapes, mountains, and three-dimensional geometric figures. Instead of serving as navigation aids, these exercises were intended to prove a student's ability to portray cartographic language in a standardized fashion. Although a few, select students had gone out in the field with Codazzi to survey ejidos for the topographic Bogotá map of 1849, an undoubtedly useful hands-on experience, the actual drawing up of the ejidos was finalized by Codazzi. Therefore, before they could have a hand in drawing up the "real" places they surveyed, Military School students apprenticeship-style training meant that they needed to prove they mastered cartographic conventions. The mapping of "real" places, given their complexities, could potentially make a student's practical training in modes of representation even more difficult, at least during the early stages.

To graduate, students needed to demonstrate to their instructors that they mastered all modes of cartographic representation in a standardized, intelligible fashion. Much like artisans who display their mastery of carpentry with a final woodworked piece, Colegio students needed to demonstrate their cartographic dexterity. The series of mapping exercises in which students engaged allowed them to learn perspective, shading, and scale, how to use color, how to draw symbols to depict elevation, rivers, human settlements, and forests, how to create bounded regions, and how to demonstrate hierarchical relationships among different units. The majority of the early exercises did not emphasize accuracy with respect to a real place they surveyed and then mapped. Rather, the emphasis was on the development of a common cartographic language, a challenge given the lack of standardization in cartography around the world during this period.

"Planos humorísticos de Manuel Peña," drawn in 1852, although part of a cartographic education project in which all Military School students engaged, stands out from the group.[42] Born circa 1836, Peña was originally from the salt-producing town of Zipaquirá to the north of Bogotá, and his family belonged to this province's upper crust. Peña's demonstrated intelligence and aptitude won him a scholarship from Zipaquirá's provincial government to study in Bogotá's Colegio Militar. Peña's teachers hailed from near and far and included, of course, Italian-born military engineer Agustín Codazzi and Venezuelan artist Carmelo Fernandez, but also Ramón Guerra Azuola, an engineer originally from the small town of Tocaima, about a day's journey on mule back from

Bogotá. These instructors, together with the array of regions represented by fellow classmates, opened Peña's world to the significance of New Granada's place in the world. His imagined landscape
of 1852 reveals what that significance implied.

Peña includes four insets in his final mapping exercise. While
the two on the left depict unnamed imaginary landscapes much
like those of the other students, the two on the right do include
place-names. These names made Peña's map so unusual that an
unnamed archivist working for the Archivo General de la Nación
in Bogotá was struck by their originality, cataloged the exercise
separately, and named it "Planos humorísticos." It seems the archivist believed the map to be an act of whimsy because Peña's map
depicts a landscape with the names of places that existed in the
real world but re-arranged to form an imaginary place. The way
in which that Peña brings geopolitical information together on
his *plano* is more than whimsy. At the tender age of sixteen, Peña
evinced a deep level of historical, geographical, and geopolitical sophistication. Engaging in a close reading of Peña's imaginary landscape reveals how Colegio Militar students were very
much aware of the global and local forces that potentialized yet
also impinged upon the midcentury circulatory national project.

Although he did not join Codazzi on his survey and mapping
of Bogotá in 1849, Manuel Peña did manage to display his mastery of cartographic language much like other Colegio Militar students. Peña's 1852 plano is in many ways representative of other
charts drawn by his classmates. He used brown to differentiate
mountains from flatter areas, blue to identify the course of rivers
and mark off bodies of water from the contours of coastlines and
islands, and red squares to indicate human settlements. Orderly,
parallel rows of green bushes suggest lands that are under cultivation, and slightly larger bushes that play with green and blue
shadows, placed in a less orderly fashion, suggest uncultivated
forestland. Peña also evinces the different techniques students
learned to represent elevation, the most difficult and malleable of
cartographic conventions.

Peña's plano demonstrates his ability to convey elevation using
the two major cartographic conventions available at midcentury in

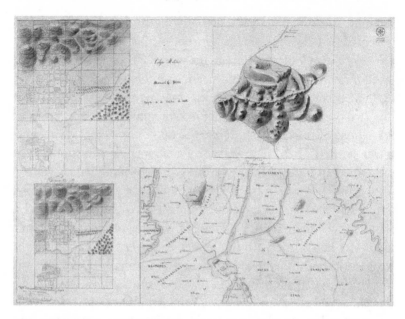

7. Plano Humorístico de Manuel Peña. SMP 6, Ref. 246. Archivo General de la Nación, Bogotá.

New Granada: "fish scales" and "hairy worms."[43] Fish scales were mostly used during the eighteenth century and consists of what look like undulating columns of curving stacked plates. The symbol does not reveal mountain peaks. Rather, mountain ranges tend to be cut flat at the point where the perspective for the map begins. Figures resembling hairy worms increasingly became the alternative to the stacked fish scales, especially for smaller-scale maps that depicted larger swaths of territory. The hairy worms eventually became Codazzi's preferred method for depicting elevation in his subsequent maps and tended to be the method many of his students adopted. Peña's map offers a kind of hybrid to represent his imaginary mountains he draws, although notably he prefers the fish scales option over that of hairy worms.

The cartographic conventions Peña used fell well within the acceptable requirements of the Colegio Militar. What differentiates Peña's plano from those of most other students, however, is his inclusion of place-names on the two insets on the right of his

plano. Peña's choices underscore how far removed from a concrete spatial reality these exercises were, at the same time that
they help us, as map readers, begin to see the kind of geopolitical world these young men were coming to see and understand in
1852. Before delving into how Peña's plano reflected the ideals and
problems of the midcentury project of circulation through New
Granada as Military School students understood them, consider
an important absence on Peña's plano. The capital city of Bogotá
is not explicitly identified anywhere on his map. Bogotá's absence
underscores how these professionals-in-training were learning
about the place of New Granada's capital city with respect to New
Granada's provinces and the world. Unlike the 1849 map drawn
by Colegio students, Manuel Peña's map decenters Bogotá. That
decentering does not undermine Bogotá's significance; rather, it
underscores how Colegio Militar students understood the critical circulatory function Bogotá was to have in ways that would
connect the world and the regions to internal, New Granada markets. Only from the city of Bogotá could Peña draw all these places
as being in a relationship with each other. Bogotá, as the place of
enunciation, is what makes Peña's reading of New Granada geopolitics possible. Rather than center on Bogotá, Peña's plano brings
far-flung provincial and world regions to the center of a map produced in Bogotá. Bogotá becomes less important as a dominant
centralizing force than as a place where global, regional, and local
dynamics converged and flowed.

Peña had a clear political scheme organizing the swath of territory depicted in the bottom right-hand panel. Peña did not depict
the contours of a stand-alone, bounded political unit. Instead, what
Peña shows us is a land-locked region, one that includes departmental boundaries, but not complete ones, and no clearly drawn
national boundaries mark off this place from another. Peña nevertheless does suggest hierarchical distinctions among territorial
units. The names Peña gives to the overarching and contiguous
departmental divisions, the stand-out capital cities, and the significant bodies of water and river ways help us see which "real"
places in the world, from Peña's perspective, mattered for New
Granada geopolitically. These places, though distant from each

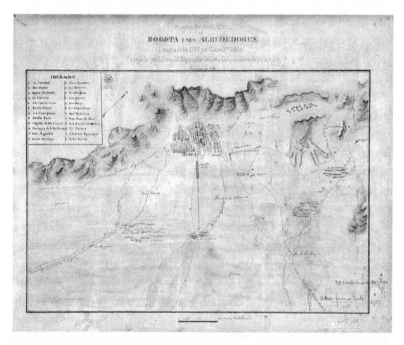

8. Fish scale mountain detail from "Plano topográfico, copiado por Indalecio Liévano," 1797. SMP 1, Ref. 143. Archivo General de la Nación, Bogotá.

other in the real world, are drawn together as a unified central landscape imagined from Bogotá.

The global place of New Granada in the world is made visible by Peña's inclusion of place-names that signal Western Europe, Africa, Russia, and the Americas. Londres (London), Paris, La Haya (The Hague), Francia (France), Castilla, and Mudarra share common space with California, Pichincha, Carabobo, Tucuman, Salta, Trinidad, and Lima as well as the historically significant Egyptian city of Alejandria (Alexandria). Rivers, roadways, and canals suggest easy connections among these and other places, and the names of rivers and lakes underscore global connections as well. Although the city of Bogotá is absent, its main artery, the Bogotá River, connects Paris, the Hauge, and the Rio Paraguai (Paraguay). A network of roadways link this portion of the territory to places like Lima and Mudarra, and from there via the Rio Rhin (Rhine) to California and the Magdalena River. The Lago de la Union, where the Island

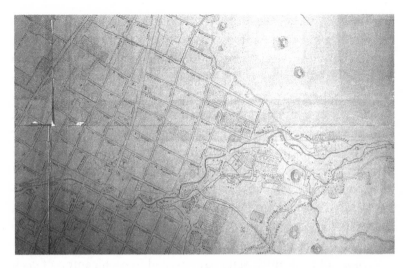

9. Hairy worms detail from "Bogotá y sus alrededores," 1849. SMP 2, Ref. I-21. Archivo General de la Nación, Bogotá.

of Trinidad floats, and where Russia's Rio Volga finds its headwaters, is networked in as well. Places where independence history was made, such as Carabobo and Pichincha, are woven in via this network of roads and rivers, and these places, in turn, connect to Londres (London) and eventually the Rio Tamesis (Thames).

History and geography lessons were, therefore, clearly on Peña's mind. By 1852 Peña and other students were exposed to the many instructors from around the world that had come to Bogotá to teach them. Cosmopolitan naturalists, engineers, mineralogists, and drawing instructors from around the world arrived in Bogotá, as did military men and not a few migrants seeking to settle agricultural lands. This trend had its origins in the independence period, was met with some difficulties during the dissolution of Gran Colombia from 1826 to 1830, and was revived during the 1840s–1850s.[44] Clearly, cadets like Peña learned from their teachers about independence, but the significance of independence was not an exclusive New Granada national story in the 1850s. Crossed swords strewn about the Peña's landscape, together with the names of independence battlegrounds outside of New Granada, signal a story that flows over national boundaries.

Similarly, rather than display the flow of goods and peoples outward from Bogotá and New Granada to far-flung cities in the world, the outside world is brought into the center. Cadets like Peña were, literally, positioning themselves with respect to the duties for which they were training. New Granada government officials believed they could pay off international debt, attract investment, and attract agricultural settlers through its vast stores of *tierras baldías*, or unoccupied lands claimed by the national state. These students were training how to draw landscapes precisely so that they could, as land surveyors, help the national state identify tierras baldías, settle boundary disputes along discrete land parcels, and take stock of indigenous communal land holding. The Colegio Militar's director, Agustín Codazzi, was most active in taking an inventory of how much state land existed in each canton of each province through the Chorographic Commission. As explored in chapter 3, he also surveyed indigenous resguardos, as did several top Military School graduates. That students understood that one of their future purposes would be linked to solving problems with respect to indigenous land holding emerges in Peña's map.

Consider how the place that Peña depicts is decidedly Andean, and not just because he draws a land-locked mountainous region. The Andean-ness of Peña's imaginary place is seen through the names of most of the smaller cities Peña included, which are Spanish-language versions of "real-world" indigenous Andean sites. Those also would have been the places with which Peña was likely most familiar given his early childhood in Zipaquirá, just to the north of Bogotá, nestled in the Andean high plains. Cities in this region had indigenous names, and Peña included several of them: Cunacua, Suta, Cogua, Cajicá, Boyacá, and Ubaté. They are not, however, concentrated in one department. These cities are sprinkled across all six departments. This hierarchy in representation, especially since it is of an imagined place, illustrates how Military School trainees included Andean territories in their mental maps of New Granada, but only in the position of subordination to Spanish American cultural notions of territory, as well as imagined domination and influence by Europeans (Londres) and North Americans (California). The ways in which these Andean, indigenous towns are nevertheless interconnected to the rest of the world also suggest how these students would help the national state create the fluid circulation of goods and people, for internal and global markets.

The Magdalena River has a prominent place in Peña's imagined landscape, and this fact should not be surprising. Students at the Colegio Militar learned how the buildup of infrastructure along that river would play a critical role in realizing a project that would allow the interior markets of New Granada to connect with each other and with the world. Consider, for instance the 1849 printed map of the Magdalena River that outgoing President Mosquera had bequeathed to the school.[45] The map, which Mosquera drew based on the astronomical measurements he took in 1842, 1847, and 1849, was intended to show the parts of the river that could be traversed via steamboat navigation. Mosquera's map also identified the astronomical and barometric readings of Sabanilla, the newly founded port city at the entrance of the Magdalena River. Mosquera ensured oversight and protection of trade via the Sabanilla port through the Salgar Castle, built in 1848 to combat contraband.[46] Sabanilla and its neighbor, Barranquilla, came to rival Cartagena and Santa Marta as critical port cities precisely because steamboat navigation allowed products to flow upriver into the interior of New Granada more easily. Peña, along with his classmates, would have studied Mosquera's map of the Magdalena River, and the Magdalena River is prominently displayed in his mental map. What may be a bit striking, however, is how Peña's imagined Magdalena River borders the California Department. On Peña's map, California is the only "Department" that is not based off of a real-world location in Spanish America. The 1849 discovery of gold in California had, after all, propelled the recent and ongoing construction of a trans-isthmian railroad by a U.S.-based engineering firm in Panamá. California thereby became a critical landscape drawn into the geopolitics of New Granada.

The vision Peña has for infrastructure development is not all rosy, however. Consider the Canal de la Mancha that connects the Thames River to the Volga River on Peña's map. Evocative of the ideas for canal building in Panama to connect two oceans, Peña's

Canal de la Mancha suggests how this may be, after all, a quixotic endeavor. Peña's plano further suggests some of the more difficult forces working against the idealized plan to foment circulation through Bogotá, to the regions, and the world. The mountainous terrain Peña drew in the top right inset, for instance, may at first seem like an ordinary, placid, large-scale rendition of the towns, roads, and rivers along a "fish-scaled" mountainside. Upon a closer reading this a rather dystopian landscape. Crossed swords pointing down and a single sword pointing up suggest that battles were fought, and few clear victories came of them. Evil forces riddle the natural features of this landscape. The "Dangerous River," for instance, connects the Magdalena River to the River Fucha, a river located in Bogotá's environs. Other streams feeding the Fucha River include "Horrible Ravine" and "Ravine of Beelzebub." The devil himself along with unspecified horrors seems to be poisoning the waters. This view was far and away distant from the optimism that Mosquera, his advisers, and his successors promised. The many sets of crossed swords underscore the violence etched onto the landscape of this dangerous place.

The crossed swords Peña inscribes onto the globally and locally connected landscape may point not just to independence battles, like that fought in Carabobo and Pichincha, but also to more recent warfare. Consider the departments of Socorro and Medellin. As discussed in more detail in chapter 4, both cities were embroiled in conflict regarding their status as provincial capitals, and Conservatives in both provinces had led a rebellion against the administration headed by Liberal president Lopez in Bogotá in 1851. The driving factor that exploded in civil war was how the national government divided the existing provinces into smaller units in ways that directly challenged the political dominance of the Conservative Party. Peña's decision to identify at least one town, with the place-name *gaznápiro*, or "fool" in Spanish, suggests Peña was at the very least poking fun at foolish attempts to map out New Granada's ever-shifting territoriality.

The question remains, was Peña's map surprisingly different from those of his cohorts? No lesson plans or private correspondence or journals exist that allow us to directly get at Peña's own agency or intentionality in his use of certain names for places. What is clear is that all images drawn by the students are similar in terms of color, map symbols, perspective, and scale. Most of the imaginary spaces drawn by other students included no place-names at all. Some students included the exact instructions they received from the instructors on their projects in order to show how they executed the requirements. Place-names were not required in these instructions.[47] The only other student whose work also included a similar imaginary map with place-names was Sixto Barriga.[48] Barriga did not use territorial divisions in his map, nor did his map include as many place-names as Peña had done. The few names Barriga did include were evocative of Venezuela and made no mention of Bogotá. And yet both men drew these maps precisely because they were in Bogotá. Though it is not surprising that elite mapmakers and surveyors carried their religion and Euro-peanized perspectives with them, the differences in how students conceived of spatial hierarchies for New Granada from Bogotá challenges the idea that elites in New Granada developed a uni-form and unquestioned geography with Bogotá at the center.[49] Instead, these regional elites were themselves participating in a project that brought Andean towns, New Granada regions, and the world together through Bogotá, but in ways that highlighted circulation rather than dominance by Bogotá over all others. And yet the young men trained within institutions located in Bogotá were also well aware of the forces that could pull apart this Bogotá-centered circulatory project.

Manuel Peña may have signaled the major global, geopolit-ical, and regional forces challenging a national project that put Bogotá at the center of a modernizing New Granada nation seek-ing to foment circulation. Bogotá nevertheless remained central to Peña's professional life. Peña did not hold elected political posts after graduating, but he did often serve as a representative of the national government on engineering projects, particularly for rail-road construction.[50] Peña was one of the few surveyors who adver-tised his services in the *Gaceta Oficial*, or New Granada's official newspaper printed in Bogotá, a strategy that brought him several surveying jobs over the course of the nineteenth century. Peña

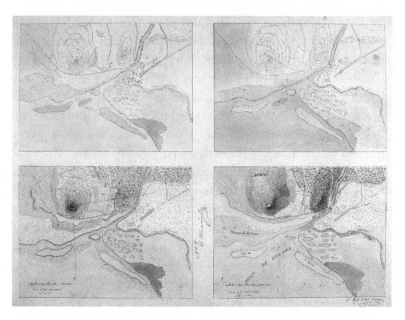

10. Topographic chart by Sixto Barriga, 1850, in Topographic charts and profiles drawn by students of Colegio Militar. SMP 2, Ref. 1246. Archivo General de la Nación, Bogotá.

surveyed public and private lands, including indigenous communal lands, national baldios, and national forest lands on or around the high plains surrounding Bogotá. During 1873–1874 Peña continued to advance his studies at the Ecole des ponts et chausses in Paris. His expertise qualified Peña to train civil engineers as a National University professor in Bogotá. By 1887 Peña published a well-regarded geometry and surveying textbook for Colombian engineers.[51] His manual built on the drawing techniques that he had first acquired as a young student at the Military School, and that he advanced through several years of practical, on-the-ground experience. Much of this experience, of course, depended on commissions he got from the national government, located in Bogotá, commissions he won, in part due to his training at the Military School also located in Bogotá.

New Granada mapmakers were not significantly different from other cartographers of the mid-nineteenth century. As J. B. Harley has suggested, cartographers tend to place themselves and their cultural values at the center of their representations through cartographic "rules" that highlight particular places in ways that set them off as special, better, dominant—in short—worthy of representation.[52] Mark Monmonier has also warned us that all maps are massive reductions of the reality they represent, and clarity demands that much of that reality be suppressed. In short, all maps are lies.[53] And from a more literary perspective on cartography, Jorge Luis Borges's famous imaginary all-encompassing map ultimately became unreadable, but its remnants did occasionally haunt unexpected corners of the empire.[54] Despite confounding and contradictory dimensions to map making, Colegio Militar students nevertheless worked hard to acquire these skills and hitched their future careers to this enterprise. The kind of cartographic "haunting" in which these young men would later engage would be indelibly marked by the kinds of strategies, experiences, techniques, and worldviews that were forged in the classroom, in the field under the supervision of their teachers, and challenged by their experiences in the real world. At its base, however, the common cartographic language students learned created an agreement among trained technicians with respect to the kind of abstract visual language that needed to be adopted in order to represent landscape, boundaries, productive lands, and territorial hierarchies. This supposedly neutral language was a central component of the kind of transformation that midcentury leadership wished to push through in New Granada.

The Colegio Militar was originally conceived in line with the kind of moral and practical transformative goals that patriotically tried to reach all New Granada provinces through institutions, academies, and the employment of international experts. It was also established at the same time that the overall size of the national army was shrinking. As Safford and Palacios point out, every government administration in New Granada since the dissolution of Gran Colombia in 1831 sought to keep the size of the standing army to a minimum.[55] By the 1840s Presidents Tomás Cipriano de Mosquera and José Hilario Lopez, themselves military generals, each reduced the 3,400-member national standing army by about

1,000, leading to protests by several military men.[56] Following this logic of reduction of the military, the Colegio Militar was not an institution set up for the rank-and-file members of the military. It was intended as an elite institution to train upper ranks of an ever-shrinking army.[57] President Mosquera, together with Lino de Pombo, further promoted the elite civilian nature of the school.[58]

As elite families learned of the high salaries paid out to foreign engineers on the infrastructural projects New Granada commissioned, they encouraged their sons to pursue training in the relatively new profession. To graduate, civil engineering students needed to pass classes in arithmetic, algebra, geometry (speculative, descriptive, analytical, and practical), trigonometry, mathematics, differential and integral calculus, astronomy, linear drawing, graphical resolution of geometric problems, cosmography, mechanics, architecture, and road building. Therefore, despite the school's military character, Colegio Militar students could opt to pursue a civil engineering degree with no military training. In return, the Executive Power would prefer these graduates for jobs related to their profession, including public instruction and official land surveys.[59] Of the eighteen students who were admitted in 1848, two graduated as both military and civil engineers and eleven graduated as civil engineers.[60] Despite these clearly civilian intentions, however, at the end of the day the school was a military academy.

The minds most actively imagining the role of the Colegio Militar in a productive, industrializing New Granada had trouble convincing all New Granada citizens of their vision, especially as far as the Colegio Militar was concerned. A significant paradox riddled the founding of New Granada's Military School: in most elite circles the strengthening of morality and civility meant that the military needed to be weakened. Civilian elite sectors of the Liberal political party in Bogotá feared a military school would strengthen and expand the military overall, threatening the stability of civilian governance.[61] For their part, the rank and file of the military, although initially pleased by the school as a way toward promotion, eventually came to resent the exacting academic requirements students needed to fulfill just to enter, not to mention the rigorous math and science curricula they needed to pass in order to graduate. The effect of these civilian-led policies was that it excluded the humbler military men that did not have access to the kind of early education that elite children enjoyed.[62] Furthermore, despite efforts to ensure regional representation among its students, even regional elites eyed the school with suspicion. They had reason to complain. Students from the provinces were in attendance, but most of those representing far-flung provinces were primarily the children of provincial elites who were drawn to Bogotá due to political careers.[63] Despite its efforts to train meritorious students from the regions, with the school's location in the center of Bogotá, many of the students educated in this nationally sponsored school came from that capital city's elite families.

By 1853 the Liberal Party's hostility toward the military joined the effects of fiscal decentralization, which cut the federal government's budget overall. Appropriations for the Colegio Militar were cut by 60 percent. The civil wars of 1851 and 1854 combined to further work against the funding and the justification of having a military school in the first place. In the wake of the Civil War of 1854, which had brought together urban artisans in Bogotá with members of the rank and file of the military, several civilian congressional representatives proposed plans to abolish the Colegio Militar. Some proposals offered to create regional civilian schools, with civil engineering, mathematics, and physical sciences in Bogotá, mining in Medellin, agriculture in Cali, commerce in Panama, navigation in Cartagena, and manufacturing in Socorro.[64] Despite these suggestions, it proved easier and more financially viable to simply close the school and shuttle students and instruments to the Central School of Mathematics in Bogotá.[65] The seven years during which this first incarnation of a Colegio Militar trained civil and military engineers nevertheless marked a significant moment for the history of geographic practices as they played out in New Granada. As the next chapter shows, several of the students trained in the Colegio Militar played a fundamental role in using geographic practices to try to solve one of the most difficult, paradoxical nation-state building efforts Latin American states faced over the course of the nineteenth century: measuring and dividing indigenous resguardo lands.

CHAPTER 3

Calculating Equality and the Postcolonial Reproduction of the Colonial State

I n his September 1852 address to Bogotá's Provincial Chamber, the newly appointed governor, Rafael Mendoza, celebrated the hiring of recent Colegio Militar graduates Joaquin Barriga, Manuel Ponce de Leon, and Joaquin Solano Ricaurte to measure and partition several *resguardos de indíjenas* along the fertile high plains surrounding the capital city. Resguardos were the land reserves officially destined to shelter and sustain "indíjenas," or the communities of folks previously known as "indios" during the colonial period. Nineteenth-century indíjenas, like colonial-era indios, held and cultivated resguardo lands in common rather disposing of them as individual private owners. As such, resguardos de indíjenas were the antithesis to a free land market. Mendoza, a young radical liberal politician, firmly believed that resguardos were a "holdover" from the colonial period that needed to be dissolved. Over the course of thirty years since the first legal effort to dissolve resguardos had taken effect, state officials had repeatedly identified a common problem: inadequately trained surveyors had botched resguardo surveys, causing interminable delays. Mendoza was pleased to report that the young engineers hired by Bogotá promised something different. "I have sound reason to believe that the contracted parties will carry out their duties with exactitude and success because they possess the scientific knowledge required for this matter."[1] By mid-nineteenth-century standards, Governor Mendoza's reasoning seemed sound.

Although Joaquin Solano Ricaurte's specific educational background is uncertain, the training and expertise of Manuel Ponce de Leon, Solano Ricaurte's associate, was clear.[2] Ponce had not only graduated from the Colegio Militar with honors, but he had also taught civil engineering classes. Joaquin Barriga, the son of the secretary of war, also graduated from the Military School with honors. Both men received national attention for their academic accomplishments.[3] While Barriga was hired to survey and partition the Anolaima and Zipacón resguardos nestled along the slopes of the central mountain range to the west of Bogotá's savannah, Solano and Ponce ambitiously agreed to work on eight resguardos running north to south along the high plains surrounding Bogotá: Ubaté, Cucunubá, Tocancipá, Cota, Suba, Engativá, Fontibón, and Usme.[4] Bogotá's governor boldly predicted positive results from the conscientious work of these trained engineers: "I have no doubt that after the course of one year, the period of their contract, not a single indigenous person will be left in the Province that will not be able to make use of their right to freely dispose of their properties, in line with the principles of a liberal system."[5] Not all provincial governors were as enthusiastic about the survey, partitioning, and privatization of indigenous resguardos as Mendoza, however.

As Governor Mendoza celebrated the renewed survey effort, Juan Miguel Acevedo, the governor of Zipaquirá, denounced it. Governor Acevedo pleaded with Zipaquirá's provincial chamber to do all within its power to stop the process. Acevedo defended the integrity of several resguardos, including that of Tocancipá, which was slated for survey and division by Ponce and Solano.[6] When Ponce and Solano signed their contract with Bogotá to survey Tocancipá in January of 1852, that resguardo lay under Bogotá's jurisdiction. But three months later the Zipaquirá Province assumed jurisdiction over Tocancipá. Governor Acevedo noted how the Tocancipá resguardo had already undergone a partial survey, and it had been a disaster for its indigenous populations. None other than José María Solano Ricaurte, the brother of Joaquin Solano Ricaurte, had conducted that survey in the 1830s. Several sections of the resguardo remained outside of Solano's purview, including the rocky terrain of Esmeraldas and Canavita, both on steep inclines, and the fertile pasturelands called Los Patos, Desbabadero, and La Comunidad," at the foot of Esmeraldas and Canavita.[7] La Comunidad was offered up in public auc-

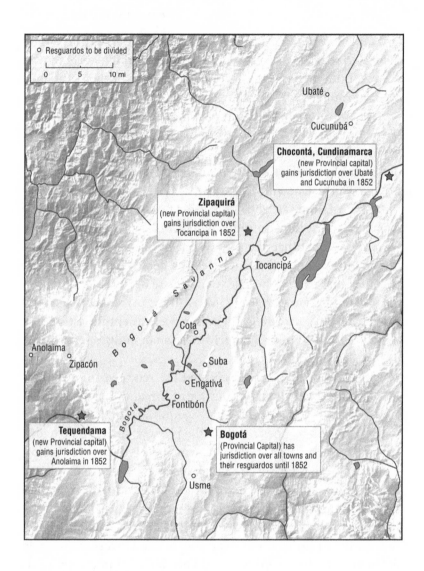

11. Map of indigenous resguardos located in the high plains near Bogota to be divided by Colegio Militar-trained surveyors. Territorial division changes based on SR, Fondo Gobernaciones, Catalogo Documental Tomo 1. Archivo General de la Nación, Bogotá. Map created by Erin Greb.

tion to pay for José María Solano's surveying work. He received $800 from its sale, an amount supposedly greater than what he was owed. When asked to return the excess money, Solano disappeared.[8] Governor Acevedo's address to the Zipaquirá Chamber signaled how another survey of Tocancipá would only have the effect of "encumbering those disgraced ones with yet another unbearable expenditure."[9] These directly opposing views and arguments of the Bogotá and Zipaquirá governors in 1852 reflect the schizophrenic reactions of state actors with respect to the polarizing, complex, and contradictory process of surveying, parceling, distributing, and selling off of indigenous communal lands during the nineteenth century in New Granada.

A robust body of literature has examined how abolishing indigenous tribute and privatizing indigenous communal lands influenced state formation and ethnic identity in various countries of Latin America.[10] While these works have increased our understanding about the effects of land reform on the cultural and political meaning of indigenous identity, the actual processes by which indigenous land holdings were measured, parceled off, and privatized are only now beginning to undergo examination.[11] During the nineteenth century, continuous interactions between indíjenas and non-indíjenas occurred at the local, provincial, and national level through petitions, complaints, and lawsuits. Several of these interactions came to have the force of national law or provincial ordinances. These trends shaped and reshaped the ways resguardo lands were surveyed and distributed, yet they did not culminate in the end of resguardos altogether. Scholarship on resguardos in the high plains surrounding Bogotá nevertheless insists that these communal lands disappeared during the nineteenth century.[12] More broadly, scholarship on resguardos has highlighted the malfeasance and ignorance of surveyors as major factors causing the impoverishment of indigenous people because they forced the sale of communal lands at a fraction of their actual value.

This chapter traces how the growing complexity involved in resguardo land partitioning in New Granada during the nineteenth century demanded an increasingly sophisticated cadre of surveyors who could survey, map, and distribute resguardos to deserving indíjenas. The category of "indíjena" emerged from this period as part of a discursive effort to distance the republican state from the era of Spanish colonialism. "Indios" no longer existed in the republic, as Pedro Acevedo y Tejada had explained in his patriotic 1825 elementary geography considered in the first chapter. The term "indio" became an insult. During the republican era "indíjena" came to idealize equity among all those who belonged to a resguardo, especially when it came time receive a parcel of resguardo land. Once all indigenous people obtained their rightful land parcel, then the "indíjena" identity could disappear. A republic of equal republican citizens would result.

Piecing together national legislation, provincial ordinances, governor reports, and surviving resguardo survey records reveals how government officials, former colonial-era indios, as well as other stakeholders with an interest in either maintaining or breaking up indigenous resguardos, actively cocreated an "indíjena" identity for the republic, one that riddled the resguardo privatization process with contradictions and delays. The trained expert was charged with equitably distributing resguardo land parcels to deserving indíjenas, but as legislation grew more complicated and contradictory at the national and provincial levels, proper surveys required increasingly sophisticated training. The chapter shows how, despite the availability of well-trained surveyors, the work of surveying and partitioning resguardos was consistently and continually subject to further delays and stoppages. In short, the legal cocreation of the republican indíjena joined the emergence of engineering expertise in ways that culminated in the utter failure of the New Granada state's effort to provide equitable distributions of resguardo resources so as to bring an end to resguardos as nontransferable corporate property. Indíjenas were not uniformly forged into undifferentiable republican citizens who could reap capitalistic benefits from the opening of a rural land market. This was not a failure of the republican state more generally. On the contrary, this chapter argues that increasing litigation by all stakeholders, including indíjenas, over resguardo-related questions, whether it was to impede or promote resguardo breakups, ought to be read as evidence of the growing legitimacy of the republican state.

The process of surveying, partitioning, and selling of indigenous communal land was unsurprisingly riddled with conflict, yet
this chapter underscores how attempts to resolve conflict were less
often channeled through violence than they were through the newly
established, and often changing, legal channels of the New Granada
state. The chapter follows a chronological structure, beginning with
the New Granada government's inheritance of the first Colombian
Republic's debate between Bolívar and Congress over resguardos.
While Bolívar sought to maintain and protect resguardos, thereby
receiving desperately needed indigenous tribute to help fund the
war effort, the Colombian Congress tried to dissolve resguardos
and tribute altogether. After Bolívar assumed dictatorial powers
in 1828, he decreed the reinstatement of resguardos and tribute for
Colombia. During 1831–1843, in the wake of the first Colombian
Republic's dissolution, New Granada renewed efforts to dissolve resguardos, yet conflict over dissolution resulted in perpetual delays.
At the core of these delays was a critical question: when, exactly,
would indigenous individuals and families be able to legally dispose of their allotted resguardo parcel as private property?

By midcentury, the national government of New Granada recognized that resguardo issues were so complex that only provincial governments could offer a solution. The province of Bogotá,
home to one of the densest areas of indigenous resguardos and to
the recently trained surveying experts from the Colegio Militar,
became the principle testing ground for resguardo dissolution in
the 1850s.[13] While the previous chapter considered how Colegio
Militar students acquired mapping skills and demonstrated their
abilities by mapping imaginary territories, this chapter returns
attention to the students' mastery of another skill: social arithmetic through tabulations, formulas, and charts that put several
variables visually in relation to each other. In the hands of trained
Military School students, complicated variables would be easily
charted and conflict resolved. That was because by midcentury
land surveyors were expected to know much more than basic trigonometry, geometry, and arithmetic to ascertain equitable land distributions. Elite republican ideology favored equity and demanded
the transformation of oligarchic indigenous communities led by

caciques and indigenous cabildo cliques into new rural polities of equal citizens. Equitable land division required complex calculations that included all sorts of historical and ecological variables that only expert social ethnographers with knowledge of disparate land values could determine. And yet, despite the Colegio Militar students' sophisticated training in social and territorial mapping, they too failed to effectively survey and partition resguardos along the Bogotá savannah. Several of those resguardos continue to exist today, if significantly reduced in acreage.

This chapter directly challenges the dangerously simplifying narrative trope of the undifferentiable, miserable, disappearing indíjena who was the victim of white and mestizo machinations on resguardos. It also complicates the figure of the scheming, immoral land surveyors, a trope that has permeated much of the scholarship on the subject. Instead, it offers a more nuanced view on this highly complex and politically charged process by focusing on how increasingly intricate and often contradictory laws and regulations at the national and provincial levels rendered the work of even these highly trained surveyors with impeccable honor surprisingly ineffectual.

Contradictory Colombian Laws and Decrees, 1821–1831

On May 20, 1820, the Liberator of Gran Colombia, President Simón Bolívar, issued a decree from Villa del Rosario de Cúcuta articulating the rights of the "naturales," or the indigenous populations in the Cundinamarca Department (former New Granada Viceroyalty). Bolívar refused to continue to adopt the Spanish colonial term "indio," a pejorative term. He argued that "naturales deserve the most paternalistic attentions on the part of the government because they were the most mistreated, oppressed and degraded [peoples] during the period of Spanish despotism."[14] With these words Bolívar initiated the creation of a new identity for indigenous populations under a republic. By 1820, after having defeated royalist armies on the battlefield, Bolívar needed to wrest away any remaining indigenous support for the Spanish Crown.[15] Bolívar's decree assured "naturales" would be like all other free men in Colombia since, as individuals, they could "come and go with their passports, engage in commerce with their fruits and possessions, taking them to the markets and fairs of their choosing, and practice their industry and talents freely, in the way that they choose without any impediment."[16] Unlike other free men, however, naturales had the right to have their colonial-era resguardos reconstituted, and Bolívar guaranteed equitable access to resguardos for each and every indigenous family on a resguardo. No one could freely dispose of communally held resguardo lands, however. Bolívar framed his decree as part of a republican effort to protect native populations, offering them clear reasons for joining the republican cause on terms that many would find appealing.

In Bolívar's decree local municipal authorities were most directly involved in day-to-day interactions between these naturales and the republican state. These "jueces politicos" would equitably distribute land parcels large enough to sustain entire families. If any lands remained after distribution, then the jueces politicos could auction those off to the highest bidder. The winner of the bid could legally rent these leftover resguardo lands, but not buy them. The juez politico needed to keep a detailed account of rents and tribute. Funds from rents would pay a schoolteacher to teach indigenous children about their "rights and obligations as citizens in Colombia."[17] Any additional income from rents could offset tribute payments owed by indigenous families to the republic. Bolívar's decree contemplated the protection of naturales from abuse by stipulating strict penalties if jueces politicos tried to force labor out of indigenous communities without proper payment. These penalties also applied to other actors who had business with the naturales, including Catholic Church clergy. Church functionaries could not withhold sacraments from indigenous people who did not pay the church tithe, nor could clergy force indigenous people to hold expensive religious celebrations. Bolívar required jueces políticos to instruct the naturales on the content of this decree, encourage the indigenous populations under their watch to defend their rights, and encourage indigenous people to denounce any infraction to the decree.[18] In other words, jueces politicos and parish priests, although charged with significant power over tribute-paying indigenous communities, were nevertheless made accountable to those same communities through the mechanisms Bolívar created for the newly founded republic.

Despite Bolívar's efforts to protect resguardos and the indigenous tribute that came with them, the Colombian Congress passed a law in October 1821 abolishing tribute and resguardos altogether, one that would take effect starting January 1822.[19] Instead of the continued cultivation of parcels of community land by tribute-paying indigenous families that Bolívar envisioned, Congress called for the end of tribute collection, with each family assuming full ownership and dominion over the lands assigned to them. This would occur "after circumstances permit, but before the end of five years."[20] In the meantime, until resguardos were divided and distributed as private property, the naturales could continue to use community lands according to existing regulations. Indigenous cabildos would also continue in the interim, but the law limited the function of cabildos specifically to ensuring better administration, concentration, and distribution of community property. These "pequeños cabildos" needed to be directly subordinate to parish judges.

Congress drew on the language of Bolívar's 1820 decree for legitimation, explaining how Colombia's indigenous people had been mistreated and oppressed by the Spanish government.[21] Ironically, Colombia's Congress was also drawing on the liberalism of the same Spanish government that it was fighting against. The Cortes de Cadiz had also abolished tribute in the Constitution of 1812. With the Cadiz liberal framework in mind, and with Bolívar's decree as a model, Congress thought it could score a moral victory against Spain by issuing a law that abolished the "tax known by the degrading name of tribute."[22] Francisco de Paula Santander, only days after assuming his post as vice president in charge of administering the nation while Bolívar was on the battlefield, approved the law.[23]

Congress understood Colombia's population of naturales to be in a state of *miseria*, or deep, miserable poverty as a result of Spanish colonialism. For that reason indigenous peoples would not have to pay parochial taxes, nor any other civil contribution related to resguardos for a period of five years. Neither would they have to pay any fees when engaging in civil or criminal suits. The law upheld the post of the *protectores de naturales*, or the legal representatives of indigenous peoples before the republic. To ensure that indigenous peoples would become in every way equal to other citizens, Congress also reiterated that labor could not be demanded from indigenous people without a salary.[24] And yet, unlike Bolívar's decree, this law stipulated that communities did need to pay parish priests for religious services. Furthermore, those indíjenas with private wealth were required to pay taxes just like other Colombian citizens.

One of the most complicated components to the 1821 law impacting resguardo privatizations for generations to come was its "liberation" of indigenous peoples from paying tribute. That was because only tribute-paying indigenous families could receive resguardo land parcels for the purposes of privatization. As far as implementation of this law during the 1820s was concerned, Congress put much weight on the national government to carry through the law. The law made the national government responsible for drawing up exact lists of eligible indíjenas. The national government also needed to provide information about the territorial extent of resguardos in ways that identified potential difficulties for dividing them. The national government had to develop the mechanisms that would verify resguardos had actually been divided. Finally, the national government would oversee the costs the process incurred and would offer sources of funding that could help cover these costs.[25] This extensive report was to be presented at the subsequent congressional session.

A report on resguardo divisions finally did come, but not until 1825, and it did not offer good news. By then jueces politicos were responsible for ensuring that resguardos were distributed equitably.[26] And yet the secretary of the interior reported interminable doubts over how resguardo lands needed to be divided and asked for another law that would allow the executive power to carry out this duty more effectively.[27] Rather than contemplate a detailed legal solution to the problems that resguardo divisions presented, it seemed Colombian congressional lawmakers defaulted to the status quo (a move permitted by the same law).[28] Few if any resguardos were distributed to indigenous peoples as private property during the five-year period contemplated by the 1821 law.

An 1827 report by Bolívar's secretary traveling through Boyaca underscored how, even though the departmental intendant did all in his power to obey national laws, his subalterns, especially the jueces politicos, eluded their responsibilities. Among the litany of civic sins committed by local authorities was the "apathy and indolence of the jueces politicos in carrying out their duties, [and] the lack of compliance with the law on the distribution of lands to the indíjenas."[29] Not only had lands not been distributed, but the suspension of tribute had had nefarious effects on departmental reserves. Take, for instance, the province of Pichincha, in the Department of Ecuador. After reporting on the fiscal damage that the law extinguishing tribute among indíjenas had caused, the Pichincha governor pleaded for reform.[30] Reform came forthwith, despite the 1821 law. Ecuador reported its income and expenses from June 1826 to June 1827. Of the $220,460 it received, the single largest source of income, $48,153, came from "indigenous contributions," the new republican name for tribute.[31]

Not only had tribute continued in the form of "indigenous contributions," and not only had resguardos remained undivided, but the Colombian government also established legal mechanisms that allowed the number of indigenous resguardos to expand. That was because the republican state needed to bring sovereign indigenous peoples in frontier areas into the fold of the Colombian Republic. The baldio lands Colombia claimed became essential in this regard. In 1824 the Colombian Congress passed a law addressing the needs of "gentile" indigenous tribes that "live nomadically within the limits of Colombian territory."[32] Several of these groups supposedly had made manifest their desire to enter into society under the Republican government. To do so, the executive branch could distribute up to 200 fanegadas (1384 acres/5.7 square kilometers) of baldio lands to each family of a tribe that wished to settle as a community in the republic. The republic could sweeten the deal with an extra grant of community land for grazing.[33]

The same year the law on "gentile" indigenous tribes was passed, Colonel Mauricio Encinoso petitioned the Colombian government so he could buy land on the Goajira Peninsula known to produce Brazilwood. He promised to use "soft means" to bring the "savage Indians" in the region to civilization.[34] After considerable debate Congress granted Encinoso his request, requiring he allow each indigenous family who settled in the community their own land parcel.[35] It is not clear if Encinoso was successful. His petition does suggest, however, that as efforts to dissolve resguardos in densely populated Cundinamarca failed, the national state was willing to create de facto resguardo-like communities in frontier regions. This fact points to the emerging republic's contradictory impulses when figuring out the place of indigenous peoples in the republic. It also reveals how closely the republican regime hewed to colonial practices that tried to incorporate sovereign indigenous nations into the polity.

By September 1828, after Bolívar assumed dictatorial powers, he returned to the question of indigenous tribute and resguardos. He observed how, far from having improved the condition of indíjenas, the law of 1821 seeking to abolish resguardos had worsened their lot.[36] He annulled the law. In its place Bolívar offered detailed regulations expanding his decree from 1820 guaranteeing the integrity of resguardos. Beyond the right to work their own resguardo plot as part of a community, indigenous people would also have the right to communal grazing lands. Any remaining lands could be rented as before, but resguardo community members would be the preferred renters. Finally, Bolívar demanded that the protectors of indíjenas encourage cultivation of common lands to benefit the community.[37] All these enhanced rights and protections were guaranteed in return for "the personal contribution of indíjenas," the nicer name for tribute.[38]

Bolívar has been famously remembered for stating upon his resignation on 27 April 1830 that he who serves the revolution is "plowing the sea."[39] And yet when it came to resguardos and personal contributions by indigenous populations, the Colombian government upheld Bolívar's 1828 decree. The collection of the "contribucion personal de indíjenas" continued as late as 1832 in New Granada, well after the dissolution of Gran Colombia.[40] Concerned with keeping a record of these transactions, the treasury department asked departmental officials in August 1831 if they received personal contributions from indíjenas, what measures they had adopted to do so, and if they had not collected the contribution, why not.[41] These records would be crucial as New Granada geared up for yet another round of efforts to abolish indigenous resguardos in what they considered to be equitable ways.

Calculus of Equity for New Granada Indíjenas

With the end of Bolívar's dictatorship and the dissolution of the first Colombian Republic came the constitutional convention to form New Granada. That convention immediately revisited the tribute and resguardo questions. Despite ratification of Bolívar's decree by the late Colombian government in 1828, and despite the continued collection of the indigenous personal contribution in Cundinamarca well into 1832, the convention came down hard against tribute and communal resguardo landholding. Or at least it seemed that way. Early in 1832, the convention claimed several Granadino citizens, "known by the name of indíjenas," complained about the imposition of a personal contribution by Bolívar's "dictatorial government."[42] The convention reiterated the constitutionality of the 1821 law that abolished tribute and dissolved resguardos, and deemed Bolívar's 1828 decree a flagrant constitutional violation. The 1832 law ended collection of tribute. The convention further argued that the only way to "emancipate" indigenous populations from the "degrading" state they occupied as a direct result of Spanish colonial rule was to distribute resguardo lands according to the precepts of the first Colombian Republic's 1821 law.

But wait. The New Granada government wanted to ensure a fair process of division, and that took time. Individual indíjenas and their families, barring some exceptions, would not be able to legally dispose of the lands they received in these divisions until ten years after the passage of the 1832 law. This delay effectively preserved communal ownership over resguardo lands over the course of that ten-year period. Indigenous cabildos, usually made up of the most politically powerful and wealthy male members of indigenous communities, maintained administrative power over how communal lands would be used during the interim. Furthermore, the 1832 law stipulated that indigenous cabildos needed to be consulted when it came time to select the impartial experts who would engage in the survey and partitioning of common lands.[43] The authority indigenous elites enjoyed over resguardos for generations was nevertheless challenged by the kind of legal equity among resguardo community members that was demanded by the republican distribution process. This challenge had first come from Bolívar's original 1820 decree. The laws the New Granada Republic passed in the wake of Gran Colombia's dissolution further challenged the control indigenous elite men and their families could maintain over resguardo lands. The laws of 1832 and 1834 illustrate this challenge clearly through the mechanisms they called for to divide and distribute resguardos.

Much like Bolívar's 1820 decree, the 1832 law stipulated that the resguardo lands eligible for distribution would be divided according to the number of indigenous families that formed the community. Each family headed by an eligible indíjena needed to receive a parcel that was roughly equal in value to all others, taking into account size, quality of land, and location. Precisely because the law delayed privatization of these resguardo lands for ten years, it contemplated how resguardo lands could benefit indigenous communities during the waiting period before privatization. First, at least eight to twenty fanegadas (28 to 570 square meters) would be separated off for an urbanization project to house all indíjenas from the community. The remainder would be divided in twelve portions of equal value. The production from at least one of these portions would pay for a parish school. Unlike Bolívar's decree, the law dictated that another of the twelve portions could be sold to pay for the costs of surveying and partitioning the resguardo, unless the community covered these costs themselves. If the latter was the case, then that portion would be incorporated back into the resguardo, expanding the total area to be parceled out. The 1832 law also recognized the improvements made by families who cultivated specific parcels of land, and so stipulated that families would receive priority for the lands they lived on and worked.

An Executive Decree supplemented the 1832 law and attempted to further level the negotiating ground between local government authorities and indigenous cabildos. Local officials needed to work closely with indigenous cabildos to identify an impartial expert to survey and appraise the value of resguardo lands.[44] Neither the

Congress of 1832 nor the Executive Power considered specific training was necessary for these experts, however. Neither did national
officials in 1832 contemplate who, exactly, counted as an indíjena
head of household eligible to receive a resguardo land parcel.

The wave of questions that followed the 1832 legislation was
overwhelming. Some questions, such as when, exactly, personal
contributions by indigenous people needed to end, were easily
dealt with. A sheet circulated to local officials simply stated that
indigenous people would pay a prorated contribution up until the
date when the law was made public in their canton. From then
on they would only pay the taxes other granadinos were required
to pay.[45] Ending the payment of "tribute" in the form of indigenous "contributions" was therefore easy. Other questions were
less easily resolved. Tribute, after all, determined who was eligible to receive a resguardo land parcel. And yet resguardos were
intricately woven into local economies well beyond the uses to
which indigenous families had put those lands. The 1832 legislation threatened to transform the warp and weft of those economies. Two years later, the New Granada Congress tackled the
questions that erupted head on with a new law.

The most difficult question the 1834 law tried to settle was
who was eligible to receive a parcel of resguardo land. Despite
New Granada's efforts to abolish it, tribute payments became the
principle way Congress could determine indigenous identity. The
problem was that only tribute-paying indigenous males or those
males who served on the indigenous cabildo and the families
of these individuals were eligible to receive resguardo lands.[46]
Tribute-paying men, irrespective of whom they married, could
claim lands for themselves and all of their legitimate children.
The sons of tribute-paying men who had not themselves paid
tribute due to "emancipation" did not have the right to claim resguardo lands for their children, but they could do so for themselves. Women did not pay tribute, but as daughters and wives
of tribute-paying men, they needed to count when parcels of
resguardo lands were distributed, especially if women were the
heads of a household.

The legislature therefore had to contemplate the rights of indigenous women's claims to resguardo lands. As it turned out, indigenous women could also claim resguardo lands for themselves and their children, even if they were not married to tribute-paying men. To claim lands, these women needed to meet complicated requirements. First, like "emancipated" non-tribute-paying indigenous men, women needed to demonstrate that their fathers were tribute-paying indíjenas. Also similar to emancipated males, women who were the children of single mothers needed to show that their maternal grandfathers were tribute payers. If these eligible indíjena women married "vecinos"—or non-tribute-paying men—then they had a right to resguardo lands for themselves, but not for the legitimate children born of that marriage. Only illegitimate children born by these eligible women, or those born of a marriage with tribute-paying indigenous men, had a right to resguardo lands. The gendered detail with which this legislation contemplated eligibility was based on Spanish colonial mechanisms for collecting tribute. And yet, the drive toward assuring equity among all deserving "indíjenas" was a kind of gendered revolution in land tenure. Families headed by single mothers with illegitimate children would have as equal a share in resguardo lands as the wealthiest married tribute-paying male or the most powerful indigenous male cabildo leader. After a period of ten years, that access to a resguardo land parcel would be transformed into private property rights.

The detailed stipulations of the 1834 legislation meant surveyors needed to be especially careful when it came time to properly allocate resguardo land parcels. Eligibility was not the only question surveyors needed to consider. The law required that a surveyor conduct a clear census of the total resguardo population to evaluate the actual size of the urbanization project intended to house resguardo community members and to determine how many shares of land needed to be contemplated in the division overall. The law also demanded that surveyors know which portions of the communal resguardo lands had been destined to pay for religious services by local priests or religious brotherhoods. Those lands were to rejoin the resguardo land total, but not if the donation had been certified by public notary prior to the law of

1832. The surveyor also needed to know what lands had a legal levy against them, for those could not be included in the division until the levy was paid off. When a surveyor came to a resguardo that had no lands, then the surveyor needed to identify nearby baldio lands and distribute those equitably among eligible families. In short, to legally divide resguardo lands to deserving indíjenas, a surveyor had to know all applicable national laws as well as all specific regulations issued at the provincial level that corresponded to the specific resguardo in question. All this knowledge needed to complement a deep understanding of applied trigonometry, geometry, and surveying techniques.

Up until 1834 no legislation contemplated the kind of expert knowledge resguardo land surveyors needed to possess. Conflicts at the local level regarding who, at the end of the day, was the most effective neutral party that could survey resguardo lands reached national legislative ears. The solution: scientifically trained surveyors were always to be preferred.[47] Such legislation was in the spirit of ensuring an equitable process. Trained surveyors, after all, would employ their sophisticated expertise in national and provincial legislation, as well as their land surveying skills, for the best possible results. The problem was that scientifically trained surveyors elevated the cost of conducting the survey, one born by the indigenous community in question. Although provincial legislatures set the salaries for evaluators and surveyors, those salaries could not exceed those stipulated in the 1824 law on duties.[48] According to that law, *practicos*, or untrained surveyors, could earn up to four reales for every hour of work. Trained surveyors, on the other hand, earned sixteen reales for every hour of work and eight reales for each fragment of hour thereafter.[49] Trained surveyors could legally stand to make a tidy sum off resguardo surveys and divisions, especially as compared to untrained evaluators.

Profit motive may explain why, the same year the detailed 1834 law on resguardo partitions was passed, Lorenzo María Lleras (1811–1868), a noted educator and intellectual, published a thirty-three-page booklet entitled *Catechism for Land Surveys, Appropriate for Use by Granadinos.*[50] In the preface Lleras wrote that "it is sad to observe the way in which the division and survey of resguardos has been carried out in some villages."[51] Lleras had worked as a provincial lawyer, had held several posts with the national government, and had worked with Bogotá's provincial government. These experiences meant Lleras well understood the unfortunate reality of indigenous resguardo divisions.[52] Several of Lleras's contemporaries agreed that properly trained surveyors would solve the problems associated with resguardo partitioning. The Colegio de San Bartolome, for instance, began holding public exams testing its students on a range of topics, including the surveying of indigenous resguardos.[53] Lleras issued his *Catechism* to help students understand how to effectively measure, divide, and allocate indigenous resguardos. His booklet briefly discussed the history of land surveys, the different standards of measurement used in Spanish America as opposed to Britain, the various kinds of tools surveyors needed to master, how to measure irregular tracts of land, and how to divide land into proper portions. This background prepared surveying students for the main lesson: how to partition "tierras comunes o de comunidad."[54] Lleras also sought to instill morality among those seeking to learn about the practice of surveying. The kind of honorable equity, morality, and precision surveyors needed to employ was rooted in Benthamism, especially in terms of the solutions that numerical abstractions could provide.[55]

Take, for instance, the numerical formula Lleras offered surveying students as a solution to the problem of determining how much land each indigenous family was allowed to receive. The formula that Lleras developed challenged the 1834 legislation for enacting gender equity in land distribution. Lleras's formula had as its base unit the single male with no family.[56] If a surveyor considered that different individual members of a family deserved less of a share of resguardo land than the base unit, then the surveyor could count those "less-deserving" individuals through fractions. The reason Lleras offered this option was because "if what was wanted was that the distribution was to be carried out equally among all individuals, then the law would have said so, without leaving any room for doubt."[57] Furthermore, available laws only noted how much land the head of a family could receive, whether the head of the family was a tribute-paying man, or an emancipated indigenous man, or the daughter of a tribute-paying indigena. These laws did not stipulate how much additional land needed to be allocated per each additional member of a family headed by any one of those individuals. Lleras considered that those parishes that allocated an equal share to each member of each indigenous family had produced unfair results, since "it does not seem fair that individuals that have such different rights and obligations in society should be equal to each other."[58] Lleras therefore offered what he considered to be a "prudent" alternative for calculating how much land each additional family member could receive so that "equity could be achieved without infringing the law."[59] Judging by how contentious was the process of resguardo divisions it is likely that scores of surveyors had already adopted Lleras's method for "equity" in land allocation.

Bogotá governors as well as indigenous cabildo members understood the significance of properly trained surveyors for dividing up resguardo lands. So much so that Governor José María Mantilla complained about the complications indigenous cabildos posed to hiring trained surveyors. In his 1835 report to the Bogotá Legislative Chamber, Governor Mantilla described the grave inconveniences that made it impossible to put New Granada laws of 1832 and 1834 into effect. Among other intractable problems such as inadequate salaries for the jefes politicos, or even for surveyors themselves, Mantilla explained how "the naming of surveyors, in part subject to the capricious will of the cabildos de indíjenas, is not carried out with corresponding rigor."[60] Mantilla described the cabildos de indíjenas as corporations made up of influential individuals that had long taken control over the majority of the territories in the resguardos. "It was natural that these corporations . . . resist a measure that was directly opposed to their personal interests," explained Mantilla. "For this reason," he continued, "not only do they not cooperate in any way, but also try to elude the division of the resguardo by suggesting individuals who are the least prepared to carry out the work of surveying in the way it should be done."[61]

Compounding this problem was the fact that individuals "who

ignore the most simple and trivial elements of geometry" abounded in their desire to find work dividing resguardos. Mantilla proposed the nullification of all contracts with existing surveyors. Four scientifically trained surveyors should replace them. With these men, and with clear instructions defined by the Bogotá Chamber, Mantilla believed Bogotá resguardos could be surveyed and parceled out within the year.[62] Upon succeeding Mantilla in 1836, Governor Ramón Villoría also insisted the delays in resguardo privatization were caused by the ineptitude and lethargy of the surveyors. The governorship needed total control over the naming of these surveyors without having to accept the proposals coming from the jefes politicos who, according to national law, needed to consult with the cabildo de indíjenas.[63] By October 1836 Bogotá's Provincial Legislature complied with the governor's recommendations, issuing an ordinance stipulating that "the Governor will name the surveyor to each parish without the need for proposals."[64] This essentially foreclosed indigenous cabildo consultation when it came time to select a surveyor, a measure that circumvented national law. Since national legislation stipulated that scientifically trained surveyors were always to be preferred, the Bogotá ordinance stood as long as governors trained surveyors.

So many complaints emerged across the nation from just the survey and partitioning process launched in 1832 that the 1834 Congress also contemplated outright suspension of resguardo divisions if provincial and national authorities thought it convenient. As Lino de Pombo, minister of the interior for 1834 (and future mathematics instructor for the Colegio Militar) noted, "experience has shown that each locality requires a modification of the law."[65] Those who were supposed to benefit from the law, explained Pombo, considered it diametrically opposed to their interests and looked upon the partitioning of the resguardo with repugnance. In the places where the repartimiento had been carried out, several indíjenas had been scandalously defrauded and suffered grave prejudices in spite of the precautions adopted over time.[66] Given the problems that appeared at the local level, the national government allowed provincial governments to opt out of the measure all together. Popayán, Tunja, Rio Hacha, Pasto, and Cartagena immediately petitioned to suspend the division of several resguardos in their provinces by 1838.[67] The national executive accepted their pleas. The executive power also sent commissions of experts to examine the procedures and rectify problems. This was the case for the towns of Ortega in Mariquita and Turmequé in Tunja.[68]

The result was that by 1839, seventeen years since the first national law on ending tribute and dissolving resguardos had been passed, the process of resguardo surveys and distribution was uneven at best. As Minister of the Interior Pedro Alcantera Herran noted, each province and even each canton within each province had different concerns and needs. He echoed provincial officials' complaints about the lack of trained surveyors and underscored how, even for trained experts, the job was complicated given the legal requirement that each indigenous family receive an equitable share of resguardo land. Several factors needed to be considered for ensuring equity, including discrepancies in land quality, the location of indigenous families' homes, and the actual size of a resguardo, which often was difficult to determine in the first place. Resistance from the indigenous communities also continued. Given all the complications, Herran proposed that the best measure would be to nullify existing laws and instead issue a new, broader law that allowed provincial authorities more leeway in determining how to carry out the process.[69] Furthermore, because so many provincial reports had identified cabildos de indíjenas as responsible for delaying the process of resguardo partitions, he suggested these pequeño cabildos be suppressed. The New Granada Senate in 1840 contemplated a bill to do so, but too many senators opposed this measure; the bill never became law.[70]

By 1843, the year that indíjenas would finally be able to assume private ownership of their land parcels across New Granada, Mariano Ospina became secretary of the interior. Ospina observed that the resguardo divisions had become so riddled with problems and injustices that he proposed indíjenas be prohibited from selling their resguardo parcels for an additional fifteen years. In the meantime the injustices could be most effectively resolved in favor of the needs of the "ignorant and miserable state to which indíjenas have been reduced."[71] The first new national law on indigenous resguardos since 1834 emerged in June 1843, and it was in direct conversation with Ospina. Titled "On the Protection of Indíjenas," the new law did not nullify previously existing laws on resguardo partitions (as per the recommendations of Minister Herran), but it did push back the date indigenous folks could assume private ownership over resguardo lands for another twenty years (until 1863). Congress then addressed the legal morass unleashed by the official ten-year delay stipulated in the 1832 legislation. Thousands of indigenous individuals had already begun to treat their allocated land parcel as their private property. Congress declared these sales illegal because, from the perspective of the national state, they harmed the interests of "miserable" indíjenas.

The 1843 law once again specified that indigenous people needed to be protected by an officially sanctioned spokesperson for each community. These spokespersons needed to be in close communication with local authorities and had the right to go before the provincial government in order to nullify or rescind contracts that sold indigenous resguardo lands. They also needed to provide reports to provincial governors on the effect of dividing the resguardos in each community. They were responsible for keeping track of the claims that emerged as a result of the divisions, their course and result, and based on this information, they could propose decrees helpful to indigenous communities. These reports and decrees would pass to provincial legislatures so that adequate ordinances could be issued. Furthermore, without consultation and approval from these pro-indíjena spokespersons, indíjenas could not rent their property. When rental agreements were approved for indigenous lands, none could be longer than three years, and indíjenas would not need to pay for any improvements renters carried out on resguardo lands. After some two decades of republican rhetoric on the virtues of a free market's ability to transform indíjenas into virtuous, independent citizens, New Granada returned to age-old colonial discourses, with a republican twist. The colonial practices of the Spanish had made indíjenas so miserable that they were like children in need of protection from the petty ambitions of cacique bosses and mestizo cliques of overlords whose rapine was depriving indíjenas of their only possible source of sustainable livelihood. The republican state swooped in to protect indigenous interests and, in doing so, sought to gain legitimacy with indigenous populations.

The 1843 law intended to "protect" indigenous populations had the effect of prolonging the integrity of indigenous resguardos in ways not unlike the original 1820 Bolivarian decree. For instance, the "extra" lands that in the 1830s could be legally sold to support the payment of a school for indigenous children could no longer be sold. Investment of lands in an endowment and rental agreements became the legal alternatives. If none of those options covered the cost of the school, then the lands would go back to the resguardo. Instead of land sales, all the vecinos, indigenous or not, would pay into a communal education fund. The 1843 law nevertheless did continue to require the equitable division of resguardo lands among eligible indíjenas for the eventual purpose of privatization. By then, however, a new problem emerged in terms of eligibility: some indigenous tribes, like the Goajiros, had never been under the control of the Spanish government and so had not paid tribute. The republican government, seeking to incorporate sovereign indigenous peoples into the nation, decided that tribute could not determine who was an eligible indíjena in those cases, but it did not offer any alternate ways of determining indigenous eligibility among recently incorporated resguardos like those of the Guajiros.

If one thing is clear by now, it should be that the trajectory of the national legislation on resguardo surveys and distribution from the 1820s until 1843 was, if nothing else, increasingly labyrinthine and always contradictory. The most fundamental contradiction emerged as lawmakers tried to transform communal land that had been so deeply embedded in non-indigenous local economies into private property and tried to do so in ways that benefited indigenous families equitably. This impulse toward equity, rooted in Bolívar's need to secure support for the independent republican cause, incited dramatic social and economic revolutions within resguardos. Most notably, the powerful indigenous cabildo leaders and the wealthiest indigenous families feared they would lose control over how resguardo lands could be used or rented while thousands of indigenous people who did not necessarily enjoy indigenous cabildo patronage had sold off the lands they had been allocated.

While it is likely that graft, greed, and corruption may have resulted in unfavorable circumstances for indigenous folks in many of these transactions, it is also worthwhile to note how many of these sales may have been carried out much to the chagrin of elite male indigenous cabildo leaders. Despite national efforts to suppress cabildos for their role in delaying resguardo partitions, indigenous cabildos nevertheless remained as the most critical corporations with which the republican government authorities could nego-tiate. It is likely that the economic influence and political power wielded by indigenous cabildo leaders at the local and national lev-els not only made equitable divisions of resguardos difficult by the 1830s; they also made legal privatization of resguardo land virtu-ally impossible. Despite significant blockages, individual indíjenas nevertheless did find ways of selling their resguardo shares. Ten-sions mounted. Cabildo leaders, spokespersons for resguardo com-munities, individual indíjenas, the array of state actors regulating resguardo partitions, and folks with no legal claim to indigenous identity yet whose economic interests where tied to resguardos increasingly faced off against one another. Governors bore the brunt of these claims, counterclaims, and complaints. Bogotá governor Alfonso Acevedo grumbled to the legislature how at least half his workday was dedicated to handling resguardo-related problems. His words echoed those of dozens of overwhelmed provincial gov-ernors: "The stupidity of the Indians, the avarice of some whites, and the ignorance of the majority of the surveyors have produced such commotion and confusion in the partitioning, that a mag-istrate dedicated solely to the quick execution of all the processes related to the survey and distribution of resguardos is needed."[72]

Trained Surveyors Available, Yet Ineffective

By 1848 the problems of surveying indigenous resguardos had so overwhelmed local government offices in Bogotá that Ordinance 47 of that year ordered that all resguardo surveys be suspended in the province.[73] The very next year, in 1849, newly elected gover-nor Vicente Lombana informed Bogotá's Provincial Chamber how "all that has been pondered in existing ordinances was enough to effectively carry out resguardo partitioning."[74] What could have changed so quickly? Governor Lombana explained that the most renowned, scientifically trained surveyors would soon be available as a result of the founding of the national Colegio Militar in Bogotá. These moral, upstanding, intelligent, and trustworthy young men would expedite the process and end the resguardo divisions once and for all. Governor Lombana's 1849 report to the Bogotá legislature was printed in the province's official newspaper, *El Constitucional de Cundinamarca*. By serendipitous coincidence, the edition preserved in the Biblioteca Luís Ángel Arango is autographed by Governor Lombana himself and is dedicated to "Commander Agustín Codazzi, Inspector of the Colegio Militar."[75] Governor Lombana understood that the Colegio Militar and its inspector would play a critical role in the survey and mapping of the province. As chapter 2 discusses, it was under Lombana's watch that Codazzi, along with several Colegio Militar cadets, mapped the urban space, rural ejidos, and proposed roadways in the national capital. The kind of sophisticated training the students received from men like Codazzi and former minister of the interior Lino de Pombo convinced the Bogotá legislature that surveys of resguardos finally would succeed.

Chapter 2 underscored the mapping and surveying skills Colegio Militar students received during their training. Another dimension of their studies is worth noting here: the emphasis that their civil engineering training placed on developing ways of working with complex, interrelated, yet often incommensurate variables. Whereas in the 1830s Lleras offered detailed, mathematically complex instruction to Granadino surveyors, his formulas considered only two major variables: how to measure and place a value on resguardo land and how to determine how much of that land each eligible indigenous family should receive.[76] By the late 1840s former minister of the interior Lino de Pombo, who was well versed in the plethora of complications and variables involved in resguardo partitions, had moved forward his proposal to make the Colegio Militar the country's most sophisticated center for training civil engineers. Pombo had a deep-seated patriotic conviction: advanced civil engineering would bring solutions to the problems of the early republic. He, together with instructors such as Amie Berguerón, developed a program of study for students that included standardization of measures through the metric decimal system.[77] Agustin Codazzi augmented the training of Colegio Militar students by teaching them how to develop increasingly complex tables that allowed several different variables to be shown visually in relation to each other. These tables offered a complement to the cartographic skills the Military School students acquired in the classroom and on the ground. Codazzi envisioned that graduates would tackle "the survey of all the territories of private parties, providing clear boundaries so as to avoid conflict"[78] President Mosquera, immediately drawing on the suggestions of Codazzi, was most enthusiastic about fomenting this dimension of student education. In his outgoing speech ending his first presidential administration from 1845 to 1849, Mosquera suggested that Colegio Militar education needed to expand to include important branches of education including social arithmetic, probability, calculus, statistics, and advanced geodesy.[79] Augmenting the curriculum in this way would perfect the training of Colegio Militar students.

By the late 1840s and early 1850s Lino de Pombo led the way toward this increasingly sophisticated training of civil engineers. As Frank Safford succinctly put it, although Pombo was never the schools' director, "he was the soul of the enterprise."[80] Pombo's push to emphasize academic rigor at the Military School meant that civil engineers learned more than just simple trigonometry, geometry, and mapping techniques; they also learned how to engage in multivariate social mapping through tabulations. Lino de Pombo had himself expertly developed such tables for the National Treasury in 1849 and published them in the official national paper.[81] These sorts of tabulations and complex mathematical calculations would allow Colegio Militar students to be the most exceedingly well-trained civil engineers to date. Only engineers trained at the Military School would be able to keep straight the plethora of variables involved in resguardo measurement and distribution. These included, but were not limited to, the value of land adjusted to local microclimates and types of crops that could be grown in each; the types of land tenancy within resguardo lands, including rental agreements with non-indigenous outsiders; lists of rightful tributaries; the history of previous land surveys and partitions; and liens and claims on resguardo lands by priests, cofradias, or renters. Of all possible candidates, Colegio Militar graduates possessed sophisticated training that would allow for the effective, fair, legal, and equitable division and distribution of resguardos once and for all.

More than one hundred young men had been trained in the Colegio Militar from 1847 to 1853. When rising tensions between the national army and some political leaders led to the closing of the school by New Granada's Senate in 1853, the Central School for Mathematical Sciences was opened in its stead. All the instruments, books, supplies, and archives of the Military School passed on to Central School as did the Colegio Militar cadets.[82] Therefore, although the Colegio Militar's closure complicated the continuity in education, this transition did not keep engineers and surveyors from being trained. In any case, by 1852, on the eve of the school's closure, several students had graduated, and did so with honors. The technological, political, and legal conditions at the provincial and national levels made it a natural inevitability that starting in 1852 these graduates would survey and partition several resguardos of the province of Bogotá. The location of the school in Bogotá made the logistics of hiring these individuals much easier in the *Altiplano Cundiboyacense* than in other areas.

This brings us back to the vignette that opened this chapter. The stage was set in the savanna of Bogotá for the positive role Colegio Militar–trained surveyors could play in the effective equitable distribution of resguardo lands, a process that included so many interlinked and complex variables. Manuel Ponce de León (1829–1899) led his classmates in taking on the resguardos in Bogotá's high plains. Ponce introduced himself to the Bogotá governor as a graduate and lecturer of the Military School, stating, "I cannot doubt the scrupulousness with which you will honor the contract I propose to you once I am named surveyor, a post that I have a right to as graduate of the Colegio Militar."[83] Ponce's proposal eventually became the template used for drawing up subsequent contracts for partitioning resguardos in Bogotá.[84] Ponce and his business partner, Joaquin Solano Ricaurte, won the contracts to measure and repartition the resguardos of Engativá, Suba, Fontibón, Cota, Usme, Tocancipá, Cucunubá, and Ubaté.[85] Joaquin Barriga, another noted graduate of the Colegio Militar, won the contracts to measure the resguardos of Anolaima and Cipacón nearby. Several of these resguardos had already been subject to surveys that generated interminable disputes, including the survey of Tocancipá by Solano Ricaurte's brother in the 1830s.

This new relationship between Colegio Militar graduates and the Bogotá Province inspired radical liberal Bogotá governor Rafael Mendoza to celebrate Bogotá's passage of ordinance 141 in October 1851. His celebration nevertheless evinced a level of paternalism and racism that current-day readers will find disturbing. According to Mendoza, liberal ideas would finally work "in favor of the indigenous class, and [the Province's] hard work will take this class out of that ominous abject state with which it has always been insulted and degraded to the extreme, at all times, given that this fraction of our political association has been judged incapable of managing its own affairs because of its lack of intelligence."[86] By the mid-nineteenth century liberal leaders had come to see the continued existence of resguardos as one of the reasons why indigenous populations had been mired in ignorance during the colonial period and why they continued to suffer during the republican era. Excising the colonial-era legacy of resguardos had become a liberal republican duty. Governor Mendoza joined elites championing effective probity and skills of Colegio Militar graduates as the class of surveyors who finally would seamlessly bring this colonial-era legacy to an end in Bogotá.[87]

And yet during the short time of Governor Mendoza's tenure, as the Solano, Ponce, and Barriga surveys were underway, problems emerged. Mendoza's description of those problems further underscores how, by the mid-nineteenth century, the identity of who was "indíjena" with the right to claim resguardo lands had become a complex, contradictory legalistic cocreation of the nineteenth century, one that stubbornly resisted even the most sophisticated of trained surveyors and confounded the most radical liberal of government officials. On the one hand, republican state makers such as Mendoza insisted that all indíjenas needed to be transformed into citizens equal to all other granadinos. Then again, from Mendoza's perspective, the legacy of resguardos had created deep inequities between indíjenas and granadinos. A grave problem emerged in the form of the owners of lands adjacent to that of the resguardos. These owners, according to Mendoza, "have appropriated resguardo lands with ease. As indigenous peoples are now on the same terms as the rest of the Citizens, with their same rights and obligations, they see themselves forced either to sell the small plot of land that they were adjudicated at a tenth of its value, or to fence the plot at a cost that is several times the value of their possessions."[88] These circumstances resulted in hundreds of complaints that indíjenas brought before Mendoza and his predecessors in Bogotá's governorship. The Bogotá governor argued that the province had resolved these claims in ways that were favorable to indigenous populations, but the national government overturned provincial decisions. To avoid future doubts and litigations on this issue, Mendoza recommended that the Provincial Chamber should issue an act that "defined once and for all resguardo borders in ways that put the best interests of that wretched class first."[89] The problems outlined by Mendoza were a harbinger of the obstacles to resguardo distribution that would continue well into the end of the nineteenth century, obstacles that ultimately bested Colegio Militar–trained surveyors.

Ponce de Leon and Solano Ricaurte had originally agreed in their 1852 contracts with Bogotá that they would conclude their operations within the year. But in February 1853 they requested a six-month extension, citing unseasonable rains as their excuse.[90] Nature was not the only force working against these surveyors. It seems that as soon the 1852 contracts with Ponce, Solano, and Barriga had been signed, several indíjenas did all they could to put a halt on these measurements and appraisals. These operations would mean more expenses and the loss of more resguardo lands, argued the indíjenas opposed to the measurements. The pressure was on, and newly redrawn provincial boundaries worked in favor of these indigenous litigants. By 1852, when Solano and Ponce began their work on the Tocancipá resguardo, Tocancipá no longer lay under Bogotá's jurisdiction. Instead, Tocancipá came under jurisdiction of the newly formed province of Zipaquirá. Zipaquirá's governor, Juan Miguel Acevedo, who had heard many complaints from indigenous peoples from the Tocancipá resguardo, did all in his power to put a stop to the new round of surveys.[91] These delays, petitions, and redrawing of provincial jurisdictions worked against the surveyors. By 1856 Ponce and Solano still had not met the terms of their contract, and Bogotá's governor's office rescinded it. Cota and Suba were the only resguardos that Ponce and Solano had managed to partition off to indigenous families during that five-year period. But even these partitions had to be revised because, according to complaints by several indíjenas, the surveyors had appropriated the best lands, leaving to the indíjenas "desolate terrain."[92]

As of April 23, 1853, Joaquín Barriga apparently had never showed up to survey and partition the resguardos of Anolamia and Cipacon. Changing jurisdictions may have also played a role in Barriga's apparent dereliction of duty. Barriga's contract from 1852 had been with the province of Bogotá. By 1853 Anolaima had passed to the jurisdiction of the newly created province of Tequendama. The Tequendama governor's office, frustrated with Barriga's no show, annulled his contract and opened up the bid in May 1853 to survey Anolaima.[93] The resguardos that Colegio Militar students were hired to survey and partition proved remarkably resistant to their work. Although several of those resguardos, such as those of Engativá, eventually were dissolved, many of the resguardos that Colegio graduates had been hired to break up continue to exist to this day.

The continued unsuccessful efforts at the complete dismantling of indigenous resguardos as envisioned by national and provincial government leaders during the early nineteenth century fall out of the preview of this study. While it is true that several resguardos were, in fact, dismantled by 1863, the dynamics that led to that dismantling were less about the effectiveness of trained, technological expertise, as republican leaders such as Mariano Ospina or educators like Lorenzo María Lleras would have their readers believe. Barriga and Pombo, after all, were the exemplary, honored graduates of the Colegio Militar. They were unable to carry out the work they thought they could so easily conclude within a year. What is worth noting, however, is not so much the failure of technical expertise, but rather how technical expertise joined legislative efforts and juridical decisions in a continued cocreation of an "indíjena" identity that allowed for the resilience of resguardos in New Granada. In doing so, these contradictory, litigious processes also lent legitimacy to the New Granada Republican state.

Resilient Resguardos Build the Postcolonial State

As a final case in point, consider the resilience of the Suba resguardo. As of 2014 the Suba indigenous cabildo still existed and included over 2,500 families.[94] This indigenous resguardo was nevertheless subject to countless surveys and partitions, including one by Solano and Ponce, whose unsuccessful survey demanded yet another revision, one conducted by José Leiva Millán, also a Colegio Militar graduate.[95] Leiva Millán's work also failed to dissolve the Suba resguardo. In the 1860s, anticipating the privatization wave of resguardo lands that would come with the end of a twenty-year grace period signaled in New Granada's 1843 legislation, lawmakers at the national and municipal levels again revised resguardo regulations. Another Suba resguardo partitioning took place in 1877. The procedures followed in the partitioning reflect changes to legislation in the 1860s.

After gathering together all the Suba *communeros*, or the people of Suba eligible to receive a resguardo land parcel, the surveyor of the resguardo read off names from his list. He needed to make sure that all communeros eligible to receive land parcels were on it. He invited those who thought they had been unjustly excluded to state their claims. Claims abounded. The ways the surveyor noted and resolved these claims is worth citing at length, for it evokes continuities with the ways surveyors were trained in the 1830s under Lleras's manual, while also suggesting the new ways folks understood indigenous identity after the tribute-paying generation had long died off:

> In effect, Juana Bulla claimed [resguardo lands] for herself and for her two children, Gregoria and Timoteo, and so did Antonia Nin-

que, who, because they were indigenous on both parental lines, were inscribed in the list under the first division. Eustaquio Cabiativa asked that his daughter, María, be inscribed in the first division, as a pure indígena, and she was immediately added because, in reality, she was. Santos Niviayo immediately followed by asking that her natural son, José Catarino, be included, and, this being true, he was included in the second division which lists the names of the natural children of single indígena mothers. Joaquin Mususú, indígena married to a white woman asked that his daughter, Rufina, be included as well, and she was under the third division that includes the names of the mestizos.[96]

By the late 1870s, eligibility requirements for resguardo land had changed. Eligibility was less rooted in proof of the tributary status of the father or maternal grandfather, and more in terms of "purity" of indigenous identity on both parental lines. By the 1870s, another notable change was that "mestizos," legitimate or illegitimate, finally could claim resguardo land rights as mestizos, even if their share was less than that of the "pure" indigenas, irrespective of the father's identity. What "purity" meant almost two generations after tribute had been abolished was up for interpretation. In short, the nature of the claims indígenas could make was still subject in part to surveyor calculations as to who could claim resguardo land and how much.

The mediation role of surveyors in the 1870s continued a trend from the division of resguardos starting in the 1830s, despite significant changes over the course of those forty-odd years. Surveyors continued to determine who was an eligible indígena, while also calculating what kind of land, and how much of it, different classes of eligible indígenas could obtain. Lleras and his students of the 1830s determined which individual indíjenas within a family were more deserving of resguardo resources given their sex, age, or status in the community, thereby impacting a family's overall claim on resguardo lands. Those decisions at the micro level had macro effects, precisely because of the leeway surveyors had when it came time to calculate a "fair" allocation, one that could count individuals in the family as fractions rather than as whole persons. By the 1870s, surveyors no longer determined how much resguardo land a family in the aggregate obtained by creating abstract families made up of fractions. Instead, surveyors needed to consider individual indígenas, one by one, yet individual lineages mattered for how those determinations and calculations would be worked out.

By the 1870s, individuals who could prove indigenous heritage on both parental lines, close to seven hundred individuals in Suba, received the largest share of land rights at 15.72 units of value. What these "units" of land rights translated to in terms of actual acreage was a direct legacy of the mathematical work that Lleras and granadino surveyors carried out. Like Lleras's 1830s granadino agrimensores, surveyors in the 1870s needed to ensure that all the units assigned to individuals equaled the total value of available resguardo lands. The value of distinct parcels of resguardo lands, in turn, depended on where in the resguardo the lands were located, their arability, improvements that existed on that parcel, and acreage. The "second division" received the same "units" as the "first division." The only difference between the two was that those listed as second-class resguardo members were conspicuously marked off as the illegitimate "hijos naturales de indígenas de Suba." Over eighty individuals assumed this status. The third division reflected an increasing legal preoccupation with "mestizaje," something absent from the provincial ordinances and national laws from the first half of the nineteenth century. Eighty-five individuals on the list were categorized as *mestizo* and were entitled to only half the units of value of resguardo lands that had been allotted to individuals who claimed legitimate blood lines on both sides, either as children of legitimate marriages or as illegitimate children.[97] The first division, then, obtained the best valued lands. Individuals in the second division received the same units of value, which meant perhaps more acreage that likely was located in less fertile or less advantageously located areas. "Illegitimate" indíjenas in the third division would similarly be allocated their smaller "units" of resguardo shares according to acreage and value. By 1888, despite the painstakingly detailed survey and parcelization of the 1870s, which included a public revision opportunity, several indigenous folks nevertheless challenged the Suba resguardo partitioning due to what they considered to be unfair practices. Their petitions were heard, and another revision of documents and land distributions went forward. Such success in petitioning by indigenous peoples, which delayed or rolled back resguardo privatization, points to how the early republican state functioned.

The greatest problem surveyors faced throughout the nineteenth century lay precisely in this conundrum: who got to determine what equity meant was always up for debate. This uncertainty was, in and of itself, an important aspect of republican national state formation. Surveyors were among the first state agents who arbitrated the value of resguardo land and then assigned land shares to the individuals deemed eligible indigenas. But as Raymond Craib has suggested, villagers were very much aware of the implications of surveys on the lands they inhabited and worked. Surveyors could potentially turn resguardos into discrete and legible plots of land that did not necessarily—if at all—coincide with the ways local people put land to use.[98] Select members of indigenous communities, especially those working in the *pequeños cabildos*, had access to the flow of information regarding upcoming resguardo surveys, and they most actively in participated in them. Indigenous cabildo heads were required by law to accompany the surveyor in order to explain to him the various aspects of community life that he might need to know, and they were to do so without any compensation.[99] The fact that indigenous cabildo members did participate in this task, despite their lack of compensation, points to the importance of the endeavor to key individuals of indigenous communities. Less influential folks within these indigenous communities nevertheless also would be informed of these operations, given the extensive censuses and implications of resguardo partitions for the entire community.

Indigenous awareness and participation in the resguardo division process meant that the governors of several provinces encountered complications, complaints, corruption, and conflict when the abolition of tribute and partitioning of resguardo laws went into effect within their jurisdictions. National laws, national courts, the national executive power, provincial ordinances, local jefes politicos, church leaders, provincial governors, provincial legislatures, judges, and local lawyers all offered distinct avenues that could allow an array of individuals, including indigenous people, to either contest or uphold the work of surveyors. The fact that these avenues existed points not to a failure of the early republican state to dissolve resguardos, but rather to the state's growing resilience. It was in the very failure of resguardo divisions, distributions, and privatizations that we can begin to see how the early republican New Granada state expanded its accessibility to a broad swath of actors, including a variety of folks from different economic strata who claimed an indigenous identity. The republican state came to be seen as offering legitimate forms of arbitration on this, one of the most contentious issues of the day.

Indíjenas were not the only ones who had recourse to the courts to block procedures. Renters, tenants, hacienda owners, priests, religious sodalities, surveyors, protectors of indíjenas, jefes politicos, governors, and provincial and national magistrates all launched complaints and legal challenges. Indíjenas as well as other resguardo stakeholders became deeply familiar with the intricacies of local, provincial, and national legislation on resguardos and employed multiple legislative contradictions to delay or move forward procedures, appealing to all three branches of the republican state. From local courts to provincial and national supreme courts, from appeals to the governor that reached the ears of provincial chambers, and from executive ministers of the interior to presidents, these indigenous and non-indigenous claims often translated into new national laws or provincial ordinances and decrees. Indíjenas had become Granadino republican citizens after all. They, much like their non-indigenous Granadino counterparts, understood the levers of power on which they could push to find resolution to their needs and concerns.

Non-indigenous government representatives did not see the plethora of complaints and countercomplaints as a state-building trend. Instead, they saw these complaints as indicative of a moral failing rooted in the opprobrium of New Granada's Spanish colonial past. The only way to address the problems of such a legacy was through appeals to the modernity and morality of science. Bogotá governors and its Provincial Chamber were not unique in their belief that only trained surveyors could solve communal landholding problems. Recent studies on Mexico have found that complaints about the lack of adequately trained surveyors were pervasive.[100] Both in New Granada and Mexico, the surveyors who had carried out partitioning were characterized as overwhelmed, unscrupulous, or incompetent. These striking parallels demonstrate that the Latin American republics that called for the breakup of corporate landholding in an effort to modernize the national state had an unshakable faith in modern scientific technologies. These were the talismanic-like methods that would expedite and legitimize this process.

All around the early Spanish American republics, scientific surveyors would transform the state's main source of revenue from colonial-era indigenous tribute and mercantile trade taxes on the property of those who would become, by virtue of their landholdings and tax contributions, the engaged citizenry of a modern representative state. Such work would itself take New Granada out of its colonial legacy and turn it into a true republic. Nineteenth-century state actors had difficulty fathoming the reasons for the failure of effectively and equitably dividing up resguardos for indigenous people. Blaming improperly trained surveyors offered one way of understanding the problem. The innocent ignorance of indigenous folks also helped explain subsequent complaints. These state actors tended to be blind to the deep legal knowledge of the republican system by indíjenas. It was literally unthinkable that certain indigenous people clearly understood the levers of power they could use to their advantage. Also unthinkable was the increasing ability of a New Granada state to address and incorporate the claims and complaints of its citizenry, indigenous and non-indigenous, through legislative acts and juridical decisions. Historiography has largely overlooked how the question of resguardo partitions was so riddled with conflict that postcolonial state-building emerged in part to help resolve that conflict. Instead scholars have tended to fall into the same blind spot that early republican state makers had. Resguardo surveys turned into botched endeavors carried out by craven surveyors causing indigenous communities to suffer. For elite nineteenth-century actors seeking to abolish resguardos, the failure of equitable resguardo distribution had one clear cause: the supposed colonial legacy of moral corruption and ignorance that had yet to be excised from Spanish America. Rather than place inordinate blame on surveyors, or on the corrupt predations of non-indigenous folks, or on the innocence of indigenous groups, this chapter has teased out the complex state-building dynamics that were set off during the process of land surveys. That state building ultimately mirrored the same tactics the Spanish monarchy used to expand its legitimacy in the New World during the colonial period.

This chapter's focus on the geographic practices involved in the privatization of indigenous resguardos pointed to how the elite invention of an idealized "indíjena" identity during the nineteenth century became a critical component of the dramatic social and political transformations occurring within a surprisingly resilient New Granada state. Sophisticated training in statistics, surveying, and mapping became the primary way to guide a kind of resguardo privatization that would produce the idealized, egalitarian indíjena communities that elites had in mind, and then break those communities apart so as to forge individual New Granada citizens with no claims to communal privileges, much less communal landownership. Ironically, these elite productions of idealized indíjena communities were themselves a critical reason why the supposed "objective" and "scientific" surveys of resguardos became so contentious and controvertible. Taking the case of resguardos in the fertile high plains surrounding Bogotá as a case in point, the chapter suggested how the notable "failure" of the New Granada state to systematically and effectively break up resguardos actually revealed the remarkable array of state mechanisms that a variety of folks had available to them. Nineteenth-century Granadinos pressed their particular claims on resguardo lands, irrespective of their self-identity as white, mestizo, or indíjena, man or woman, legitimate or illegitimate.

CHAPTER 4

Political Ethnography and the Colonial in the Postcolonial Mind

On the morning of January 21, 1850, the Chorographic Commission, led by Agustín Codazzi and Manuel Ancízar, left Bogotá and embarked on their first tour: to the northeastern provinces of New Granada then called Vélez, Socorro, Tunja, and Tundama.[1] They returned to this region for their second tour in January of the following year to study Soto, Ocaña, Santander, and Pamplona. These areas, taken together, roughly comprise today's Santander and Norte de Santander Departments. Ancízar strikingly recalled his passage out of the bustling city of Bogotá, the fragrantly fresh, breezy air of the neighboring countryside, and the dewy emerald green pastures expanding before his eyes, filled with the soft sounds of bleating sheep, grazing cattle, and the low voices of peasants at work. "Behind me I left to Bogotá everything that shapes the life of the heart and of the mind: before me lay the unmeasured regions and counties that I needed to visit during my long peregrination."[2]

Ancízar was technically correct in saying that he had set off to explore "unmeasured regions and counties." That is because several of the provinces that the Chorographic Commission set off to study did not exist prior to 1850. They had been created under the recently elected administration of Liberal president José Hilario López in part to help boost the Liberal Party's share of representation in Congress. And yet, despite the clear partisan interest that the López administration had in employing the Chorographic Commission to naturalize the newly created provinces, subsequent administrations, Conservative and Liberal, supported the Chorographic Commission's work well into the 1860s.

This chapter explains why by highlighting an often underappreciated moment in New Granada elite sociability at midcentury: the formation of the Instituto Caldas from 1847 to 1849. At the time of the institute's founding, political rights were primarily expressed through corporative bodies, namely municipalities and provinces. As new provinces were carved out of the national territory, new chapters of the Instituto Caldas also emerged. Several members of provincial chapters of the Instituto Caldas also played significant roles in provincial governments. The history of the institute offers a window onto the role that hundreds of provincial elites played in the constitution of the political and cultural economies of circulation first described in chapter 2. Circulation brought with it the creation of a growing number of provincial chapters of the institute, each with men who joined either the Liberal or the Conservative party. These teams of provincial elites devoted themselves to the accumulation of statistical and chorographic information and connected with other elites in newly formed municipalities within the growing number of provinces within New Granada.

This chapter teases out how the Instituto Caldas called for, and strengthened, a Bogotá-centered network of knowledge production and circulation upon which the Chorographic Commission built. Bogotá emerged as important for the commission and for the government leaders from different parties and regions that supported the enterprise, not so much because Bogotá was a centralizing capital. Instead, it was the circulatory model of knowledge production facilitated by the institute from Bogotá that allowed the commission to engage in knowledge assembly by connecting Bogotá elites to elites in provincial capitals. The circulatory rather than centralizing function of Bogotá facilitated the commission's work.

Along with the rapidly growing number of Instituto Caldas chapters, New Granada also witnessed the development of a vast expansion in the print culture of newspapers. Newspapers announced the membership and findings of the Instituto Caldas chapters. Although the Chorographic Commission's maps and lithographs were difficult to reproduce via existing midcentury technologies of print, newspapers nevertheless were able to publish some of the initial findings of the commission. These included the travel narrative written by Instituto Caldas founder and Chorographic Commission secretary Manuel Ancízar. Ancízar's writings resonated with—and spurred on—contemporaneous fictionalized ethnographic accounts of individuals and communities printed in newspapers and as stand-alone volumes. Scholars today call these ethnographic depictions "costumbrismo," suggesting the freezing of customs in time. The chapter argues that these stories, however, were not simply quaint, folklorist descriptions of behavior. Rather, they were descriptions of cultural traits that acted as barriers to republican development and the culture of circulation. Costumbrista vignettes acted as technologies of shaming and ironic self-recognition that worked through the public sphere to identify "colonial legacies" that needed excising. Listeners were prompted to find themselves in the vignettes and therefore change. Elites across the political spectrum deployed this technology. The different ways they did so helped mark off significant differences between Liberals and Conservatives at midcentury. In that sense we can think of costumbrismo as a form of political ethnography seeking to mobilize elite and popular sectors to one or another political party.

In previous chapters we have seen several discursive inventions of the colonial legacy during the early nineteenth century. The early republic legitimated itself by inventing a Spanish colonial period defined by obscurantism and tyranny. Midcentury republicans shifted gears to argue that Spanish colonialism produced bottlenecks to the free circulation of currencies, commodities, peoples, and knowledges. As we saw with the invention of the republican-era indíjena, nineteenth-century leaders argued that the Spanish colonial period had created oppressive corporate bodies that produced Indian rural oppression and backwardness, and republicanism demanded equity among all citizens. In this chapter we turn to a different way in which midcentury discourse of coloniality was deployed through costumbrismo: to solidify and mobilize political party identities. Costumbrismo writers did not simply seek to shame the "colonial" but the "neocolonial" as well. Liberal

Party–leaning costumbrista writers found in wasteful expressions of religiosity forms of false consciousness that either stimulated harmful economic behavior or that rendered populations vulnerable to manipulation. Conservatives, on the other hand, deployed vignettes to invent emerging narratives of Liberal elites as neocolonial dilettantes, enamored of foreign liberal fads and therefore blind to the republican virtues of popular Catholicism. Even though each found different expressions of the "colonial" mind, both deployed costumbrismo to pinpoint continued expressions of either coloniality or neocoloniality.

Highlighting the cross-party alliances that led to the Instituto Caldas and the deployment of the Chorographic Commission and then demonstrating how party competition informed the use of costumbrismo as a technology to eradicate "colonial legacies" of blockages to circulation and false consciousness help us begin to have a clearer understanding of midcentury Latin America in ways that go beyond New Granada. Dominant literature on nineteenth-century Latin America tends to overemphasize the ideological differences in programmatic positioning between Liberals and Conservatives.[3] "Liberals" have become a shorthand way to refer to those who championed the separation between church and state, religious pluralism, free markets, increasing political participation among popular sectors, and freedom of the press. "Conservatives," for their part, have come to stand for Hispanismo, the defense of Catholicism, the defense of national markets, a strong state that moralized by limiting freedom of speech, and a state that limited political participation.[4] The evidence presented in this chapter breaks with this tradition of facile ideological divisions between Liberals and Conservatives. Political parties and the strong identities that formed around them clearly existed. Entire regions went to war rallying around either end of the Liberal versus Conservative divide. This chapter demonstrates how those identities were not created over alternative programmatic visions of modernity.

This chapter underscores how Liberals and Conservatives together were cocreators of the new scientific techniques of governance that promised modernity and supported republicanism. Focusing on the founding mission of the Instituto Caldas helps reveal how party leaders shared a common republican project. Elites across the political spectrum and throughout New Granada provinces agreed on an overarching idea that had become a truism by midcentury: the new republic needed to excise the obstacles to modernity that had been set into place by Spanish colonialism. Sharp ideological differences were not the cause of conflict, at least among elites. When conflict between the two parties did erupt, it was not over ideology, but rather over whose political network, Liberal or Conservative, would control what towns, provinces, regions, and, ultimately, the nation.

The chapter begins by deepening our understanding of the Instituto Caldas as envisioned by Manuel Ancízar. From its very foundation the institute embodied New Granada's cross-party pan-regional republican project. Surprisingly, the founding members of the array of political parties that emerged at midcentury, the same leaders that had faced off against each other in civil wars, all had found common ground between 1847 and 1849 by joining the ranks of the Instituto Caldas. This unity of purpose helps explain why the Chorographic Commission that emerged from the institute continued to function with national and regional support, no matter what political party was in power during the ten-year period that the commission roamed New Granada and produced its findings.

The chapter then turns to Ancízar's *Peregrinación de Alpha.* The second section illustrates how the *Peregrinación* was a kind of chorography that sought to map a grandiose precolonial indigenous past of commercial prosperity that was annihilated by a short-term revolution of conquistador pillaging and violence. For his historical chorography of the paths that conquest took to exterminate entire commercial civilizations, Ancízar drew on the historical accounts, colonial chronicles, archeological studies, and linguistic findings of his contemporaries, most notably the geographer and historian Joaquin Acosta.[5] The third section continues the analysis of the *Peregrinación* but reads it as political ethnography. It highlights Ancízar's interpretations of two different religious processions through narrative description: the San Isidro Labrador procession in Charalá, which Ancízar identified as a useful celebration that reenforced a positive work ethic among villagers, and the Octava de Corpus procession in Soatá, which Ancízar considered the epitome of backwardness and immorality. Ancízar's writings had clear territorial implications, not only in terms of how national audiences would come to imagine the relative progress of specific towns and regions, but also in terms of how the national government could potentially invest in specific regions for the future. The chapter shows how Ancízar's contemporaries, many of whom either formed part of the Instituto Caldas or were close to those who were institute members, understood the potential implications of Ancízar's words.

The fourth section underscores how not everyone was pleased with Ancízar's specific findings or characterizations of people or regions. Elite writers, politicians, and thinkers who belonged to the Conservative Party creatively challenged Ancízar's unfavorable representations of popular sectors. Their rejection of Ancízar was not because Conservative writers were retrograde opponents to modernity. Instead, the section shows how Conservative elites adapted the very same scientific methods developed by Ancízar, the method of political ethnography, but did so to demonstrate how Liberals misunderstood the ingenuity and creativity of popular sectors. Reading costumbrismo literature as political ethnography reveals how this cultural movement was far more sophisticated than a simplistic literary effort to identify racial types and freeze them in time, as current scholarship on costumbrismo would have us think.

The final section shifts its focus from competing Liberal versus Conservative ethnographic narratives of provincial popular sectors to illustrate the dramatic territorial changes that had occurred under the Chorographic Commission's feet during 1849–1853. I show how the Chorographic Commission and members of the provincial chapters of the Instituto Caldas together played key roles in shaping (and contesting) the radical territorial divisions occurring at midcentury. From 1849 to 1853, Liberal-led territorial divisions in New Granada rewarded Liberal-leaning provinces while punishing those dominated by Conservative Party leaders. Provincial membership in the Instituto Caldas had become a critical site for elite mobilization either to embrace the new territorial divisions or to challenge them. The section highlights the case of Ocaña elites, who greeted the division of the northeast provinces with the immediate creation of an Instituto Caldas chapter in their capital city in 1849. Many of the Liberal Party members of Ocaña's institute went on to hold prominent posts in Ocaña's provincial government. The section then turns to Conservative Party members of the Instituto Caldas from Antioquia and Buenaventura, who had a very different reaction to the national government's division of Antioquia into smaller provinces. By 1851 these Conservative Instituto Caldas members assumed leadership roles in a civil war against the Liberal-led national government and cited the division of the province as their casus belli. In both these cases the rhetoric of the colonial legacy that had been invented through the political ethnography of costumbrismo became a useful tool for Liberals who controlled the process of divisions that undergirded their efforts to control New Granada's national government.

In short, this chapter demonstrates how the Chorographic Commission and the Instituto Caldas, which inspired the commission's creation, along with an expanding culture of print, played significant roles in representing the provinces to national readership in ways intended to spread a cultural project shared by elites of all political stripes. The original project sought to promote circulation, progress, and morality, yet, upon implementation, partisan conflict exploded. In part, conflict was due to the growing ability of the Liberal Party to draw on the geographic project of the Chorographic Commission to solidify the creation of new Liberal-leaning provinces. And yet Conservatives Party members also drew on the same scientific techniques developed by commission members to defend Conservative Party interests and appeal to popular sectors by inventing a neocolonial mindset for the Liberals. The chapter therefore sketches the evolution of new technologies to excise the colonial from the minds of the individual and the community. The colonial, by and large, came to be defined as behaviors that did not encourage circulation and participation, and these included not just immoral religious practices held over from the Spanish colonial period but also apish borrowings by Eurocentric elites. The colonial thus devolved into the neocolonial as Liberals and Conservatives began to combat each other through the public spaces of print and on the battlefield.

Cross-Party Support for the Instituto Caldas

This section maps out the ideological, political, and geographic network created by the Instituto Caldas. Historians of Colombia, if they address the institute at all, tend to characterize it as a utopian, short-lived, and largely useless endeavor.[6] The measurable success or failure of the specific activities that the Instituto Caldas conducted is less significant than the specific individuals that comprised it. Reconstructing the institute's membership at the national and provincial levels yields a veritable who's who list that reaches across New Granada's entire mid-nineteenth-century political spectrum. Precisely because elites from all political stripes signed on to the Instituto Caldas, we can begin to understand why the Chorographic Commission, which emerged from the institute, received support from the national government irrespective of what political party came to hold power. Understanding the Instituto Caldas's mission and the network it engendered also allows us to see how the workings of the commission mapped onto how Instituto Caldas members organized national space, with Bogotá at the center. Bogotá did not seek to dominate provincial elites. Instead, the Bogotá chapter worked with provincial chapters, recognizing, coordinating, and integrating the civilizing efforts of elites in provincial capitals. To begin to understand the Instituto Caldas, its links to the Chorographic Commission, and the cross-party and pan-provincial support that both projects enjoyed, we must turn to the members that comprised these enterprises. Let us begin with the first Instituto Caldas chapter, inaugurated in Bogotá in December 1847.

Table 1. Members of the Founding Bogotá Chapter of the
Instituto Caldas

Education Committee	Charitable Aid Committee	Development and Material Improvements Committee	Roadways, Immigration, and Statistics Committee
Dr. Alejandro Osorio	M. R. Arzobisbo M. J. de Mosquera	Dr. Rufino Cuervo	Dr. Florentino Gonzalez
Dr. José Manuel Restrepo	Dr. Joaquin J. Gori	Mariano Ospina	Lino de Pombo
Dr. Ulpiano Gonzalez	Jeneral Joaquin Barriga	Dr. Eladio Urisarri	Raimundo Santamaría
Dr. Lorenzo María Lleras	José Ignacio Paris	Juan Manuel Arrubla	Antonio Poncet
José M. Triana	Urbano Pradilla	Manuel Ancízar	José Eusebio Caro
Pedro Fernandez Madrid	Guillermo Iribarren	Tomás Reed	Dr. Vicente Lombana
Miguel Bracho	Dr. Justo Arosemena	Antonio M. Silva	Juan Antonio Marroquin

Source: "Clase de Educación," "Clase de Beneficencia," "Clase de Fomento y Mejoras Materiales," "Clase de Inmigración, Estadística i Vías de Comunicación," Manuel Ancízar, "Instituto Caldas" (Bogotá: Imprenta por V. Lozada, 1848), 6.

With historical hindsight the cross-party dimensions of the Instituto Caldas are striking. Consider how many of its members later came to devote their writings and activities toward fashioning the political agendas of distinct political party movements. Mariano Ospina and José Eusebio Caro, for instance, founded the periodical *La Civilización* and within its pages developed the Conservative Party platform in 1849.[7] Similarly, Florentino Gonzalez, at the time Mosquera's secretary of the treasury, became an intellectual leader of the "Golgotas," the Liberal Party's elite radical wing that adhered to internationally circulating ideals about liberalism, socialism, and the separation of church and state.[8] Vicente Lombana, the former governor of Bogotá who had encouraged the Colegio Militar's mapping of the capital city under Agustín Codazzi's direction, also served as rector of the National University, where he joined several young elite Golgota activists in establishing the Escuela Republicana. This elite radical Liberal group set itself off against the more popular Sociedades Democraticas of the Liberal Party.[9] Leaders of that more popular line of the Liberal Party are also represented among the original members of the Instituto Caldas. Lorenzo María Lleras, the writer of the 1830s catechism for New Granada surveyors, had assumed an early mantle of leadership for the "Draconianos," the Liberal Party faction that challenged the young, elite radical Golgotas to consider how popular sectors, especially artisans in New Granada, needed protection from cheaper foreign goods. The Draconianos increasingly appealed to middling urban artisans and lower-ranking military officers.[10] We will return to these growing political party fissures and tensions in the next chapter. For now it is worth noting that the founding fathers of New Granada's major political party movements all belonged to the Instituto Caldas, pointing to the ideological consensus elites shared given the mission of the institute as articulated by its founder, Ancízar.

For the foundation of the Instituto Caldas, Manuel Ancízar crafted a compelling narrative about the danger that a supposed "colonial legacy" posed to the workings of republicanism. When Manuel Ancízar penned the Instituto Caldas's founding mission, he had just recently arrived in New Granada from Caracas.[11] Although born near Bogotá, Ancízar's father, a Basque merchant who had served as a royalist Corregidor during 1816–1819, wisely left with his family for Cuba, fleeing patriot retribution. Once Ancízar completed his legal education in Havana, he continued his studies in the United States. From there Ancízar went to Caracas, where he wrote a treatise on moral psychology, founded magazines and newspapers, taught philosophy classes, and directed several schools.[12] Lino de Pombo, New Granada's envoy to Venezuela at the time, was impressed. He convinced Ancízar to come to New Granada and join Mosquera's first presidential administration. Ancízar brought along his printing press. His charge as interim secretary of foreign affairs and internal improvements became, on the one hand, helping the Mosquera administration create a propaganda campaign to attract foreign investment. On the other, Ancízar needed to develop a program that would yield effective internal improvements. He conceived of the Instituto Caldas to fulfill this goal.

A close look at the founding mission of the Instituto Caldas as penned by Ancízar reveals how members of the inaugural Bogotá chapter, despite political differences, shared common ideals regarding the role that science, technology, investment, aid, and education could play in allowing New Granada to surmount the obstacles of the colonial legacy.[13] Manuel Ancízar articulated clear reasons for creating the organization. Simply put, the pueblo Granadino needed "the preservation of *morality*, the diffusion of primary *instruction*, and the development of *industry*."[14] These values were intertwined with the work of decolonization, as Ancízar and his generation understood it. "The liberal laws, meditated upon by the Executive Power, and passed only yesterday, target the obstacles set up by a prior, ancient regime that blocked the industrial expansion of the country and, as such, blocked its intellectual development."[15] Independence had set free the liberalizing impulse, one that was gaining strength each day. But Ancízar warned that the desire to acquire could be as healthy as it could be pernicious. It just as easily could "create hardworking small property owners and strengthen good customs within them, as it could awaken a tenebrous lust for the foreign, causing the neediest to prostitute their souls."[16] Therefore, the general purpose of the Instituto Caldas was to guide a devout pueblo toward true morality through proper education that would undo the negative legacy of the colonial past by promoting progress, industry, and moral patterns of consumption.

Ancízar further explained how corrupt, colonial-era ideas had driven innocent populations, popular as well as elite, into the arms of ignorance and immorality. He noted how the pueblo Granadino was an innocent believer, yet, in some places ostentation, mechanistic rituals, and errant preaching had sapped belief and virtue from religiosity. The only way of undoing the damage propagated by corrupt religious leaders, a legacy of the colonial past, was through popular education that included moral instruction, paired with the careful government-guided strengthening of domestic industry. Compounding these local problems were the corrupt, Old

World ideas that continued to wash upon New Granada's shores, harming the Granadino youth. Ancízar explained how this youth, thirsty for knowledge, had "drunk from the gutters of a literature that lacked faith or virtue, and that was tossed onto an honest America from the other hemisphere by the insensitive hand of the European speculator."[17] Appropriate educational institutions, together with healthy books and newspapers useful for education and industry, were what New Granada needed to offer its citizens. These needed to be deep, autochthonous examinations and meditations on what the Granadian pueblo was, and what it needed, rather than a blind transference of European models. To begin to accomplish these tasks, Ancízar proposed that the wills united under the Instituto Caldas focus on four major interrelated fronts, or "committees": education; charitable aid; development and infrastructure; and roadways, immigration, and statistics. The regional chapters of the institute wholeheartedly embraced the gospel of circulatory political economy considered in chapter 2. As Table 1 shows, members signed up to work on these tasks accordingly. The names in the table also suggest the ways the Instituto Caldas helped foment the larger, longer-running project that later became the Chorographic Commission.

Manuel Ancízar himself was the most obvious contributor from the Instituto Caldas to the Chorographic Commission, but other members of the Bogotá chapter of the Instituto Caldas also collaborated, most notably José M. Triana and Miguel Bracho.[18] Codazzi, the leader of the commission, arrived from Venezuela only two months before Mosquera turned over his presidential administration to Liberal general José Hilario López in 1849. For that reason, Codazzi did not form the inaugural class of the institute in Bogotá, yet, through Ancízar, Codazzi was quickly made aware of its participants and activities.[19] Several other original Instituto Caldas members aided the commission by providing access to information on infrastructure and road-building projects, and by ensuring political and economic support at the national and local levels throughout the period of its fieldwork.

Take, for instance, how Vicente Lombana, governor of Bogotá in 1849, facilitated the Colegio Militar's mapping of Bogotá, the trial run for the national mapping commission Codazzi would come to lead.[20] Lorenzo María Lleras and Pedro Fernández Madrid together proposed a law to Congress in 1851 ordering all provincial governors and cantonal political chiefs to provide the Chorographic Commission with statistics and local reports and ensure that the commission's transportation and provision needs were offered at fair prices.[21] The law passed. Lino de Pombo supported the commission from his position at the Colegio Militar, and later from his eventual post as secretary of exterior relations under the interim presidency of Manuel María Mallarino (1855–1857). Mallarino, who developed a close friendship with Ancízar during their common work for the Mosquera administration in the foreign relations office, found little reason to object to the renewal of the commission's original contract in 1855, especially under the insistence of members of his cabinet. Those cabinet members included Lino de Pombo and Pastor Ospina Rodríguez, then secretary of state.[22] Mariano Ospina (brother of Pastor Ospina) won the 1856 presidential election conducted under universal manhood suffrage, and he too supported the commission's work, if perhaps not as enthusiastically as his predecessors. Influential intellectual elites with leadership positions in Bogotá's premier educational institutions as well as the major leaders of, and investors in, infrastructural development projects also joined the founding Instituto Caldas chapter in Bogotá and had a vested interest in the findings of the commission.[23] In short, individual members of Bogotá's Instituto Caldas, despite political party differences, supported the Chorographic Commission throughout the 1850s. This was because of the far-reaching consensus on the benefits that the commission would bring, given that it was rooted in the Instituto Caldas's founding mission.

The national official newspaper, the *Gaceta Oficial*, circulated Ancízar's reflections on the Instituto Caldas's mission, which included suggestions for how provincial sections of the institute could also help do away with the obstacles of the colonial legacy through science. Ancízar encouraged each provincial branch of the institute to organize itself according to local needs. Ancízar hoped that already established societies with related missions, such as the "Amigos del país," "Immigration," "Vaccines," or other related organizations in the provinces would incorporate themselves with the Instituto Caldas. This would allow for a network of previously disconnected corporations to join in a patriotic unity of efforts. Clear advantages came with such unity.[24] The institute could thereby produce an efficient network of folks eager for the circulation of accurate and detailed information from each province. Ancízar offered a unity of purpose and clear organization, one that would make the Instituto Caldas's central node in Bogotá the place of assembly and coordination. In this way, Ancízar's original vision for the institute underscored Bogotá's role in coordinating the knowledge that was to be gathered at the provincial levels, laying the foundation for the logistics of the Chorographic Commission. The model was identical to the circulatory cultural discourse first introduced by Mosquera's regime as discussed in chapter 2.

In 1848–1849 provincial governments responded positively and in droves to Ancízar's call. Of the twenty-two provinces that comprised the New Granada republic in 1848, fourteen established a chapter.[25] A political economy that saw development as shattering obstacles to the circulation of commodities, currencies, knowledges, and information spread like wildfire. The following year three more provinces were created, and one of them, Ocaña, also established its Instituto Caldas chapter. We return to the Ocaña later in the chapter, but for now it is worth noting that the overwhelmingly positive response by provinces to form Instituto Caldas chapters was due, in part, to the ability of Ancízar's vision to strike a chord with national and provincial elites through nationally circulating newspapers. Economic and political incentives promised by the Mosquera administration also helped.[26] The overarching network of urban provincial leaders who ascribed to the Instituto Caldas's mission was announced in the national press, including the provincial governors and their secretaries, who played an important role in selecting participants. The *Gaceta Official* proudly announced all of these Instituto Caldas participants within its pages. As the official voice of the national government from Bogotá, the paper dedicated several issues to information directly related to business of the institute, including geographic reports, discussions on roadways and steamship navigation, the expansion of public education, and charitable works. Already from 1848 to 1850 the network idealized by Ancízar began to work: provincial organizations gathered information at the local level and sent it to Bogotá, where intellectual and government elites went on to compile, edit, and print information from the provinces for national circulation. The Instituto Caldas was doing right by its namesake. The network that extended throughout New Granada functioned much like the network of "ilustrados" that Caldas had connected through the *Semanario del Nuevo Reino* that he edited and printed from Bogotá between 1808 and 1810.[27]

This bevy of circulating information on and by Instituto Caldas members through the national press peaked with the arrival of Agustin Codazzi and the Chorographic Commission in the provinces. One effect of the network was that several provincial elites associated with the Instituto Caldas created a positive feedback loop that aided the work of the Chorographic Commission and, in turn, promoted provincial development projects. Take, for example, the Socorro Province. On April 2, 1848, Governor Zoilo Silvestre announced the inauguration of an Instituto Caldas chapter in Socorro.[28] One year later Silvestre himself submitted a detailed geographic treatise on the Socorro Province to the national government, and the national government printed his findings in the official newspaper.[29] Socorro then became one of the first provinces to be visited by the Chorographic Commission, and Zoilo Silvestre's findings helped orient the commission's work. Dr. José María Villareal, also a member of Socorro's Instituto Caldas, was especially interested in the construction of a bridge in San Jil. As an informant for the commission's work in Socorro, it should come as no surprise that Villareal subsequently welcomed Agustín Codazzi's evaluations of that province. Villarreal included the Chorographic Commission's findings to support his report on the need for a bridge in San Jil to the central government.[30]

A network of like-minded elites of different political stripes and from a variety of provincial backgrounds was made visible in the national press, a fact that allowed commission members like Ancízar and Codazzi to chart out what elites in which cities would be most welcoming of their endeavor, even before they set out on their first expedition. Local elites, in turn, were ready for the commission to arrive. They believed, and rightly so, that the commission would aid provincial calls for investment in the development of infrastructure, trade, and education. The exchange between provincial Instituto Caldas elites and the central government in Bogotá also suggests that Ancízar's institute succeeded in offering a territorial organizational structure for the collection, analysis, and diffusion of scientific information on these provinces and their populations. Bogotá's centrality to the nation was less about a need to impose a centralizing government over the provinces. Instead, Bogotá would serve as a capital city that could bring unity and coordination to provincial development projects, much like the Bogotá chapter of the Instituto Caldas would bring unity and order to the work carried out by provincial chapters. The chapters that were set up in dozens of provinces in 1848–1849 accepted and promoted the original mission espoused by Ancízar for Bogotá's founding chapter. That shared pan-provincial, interparty mission would come to shape the means by which the Chorographic Commission established the logistical infrastructure it needed to conduct its work in the provinces and the kind of information it deemed worthy of gathering and presenting to national audiences.

Bringing the connections between the Instituto Caldas and the Chorographic Commission into high relief sheds light on the origins of the commission in ways that go beyond materials already examined, and eloquently so, by other scholars.[31] The Chorographic Commission itself, which ran well into the 1860s, was—and still is—impressive in its scope. It generated not only hundreds of geographic reports and dozens upon dozens of maps, but also botanical studies of over 60,000 samples of close to 8,000 different species collected by the naturalist José Jerónimo Triana, over 150 watercolor renditions by several different artists of the people and landscapes the commission encountered, and landmark travel narratives. The result has been that scholars of Colombian history, beginning in the late nineteenth century, highlighted the Chorographic Commission as the single most important effort by the national state to gather geographic and scientific information about the country, and championed Agustin Codazzi for his work as leader of the enterprise.[32] Efraín Sánchez's touchstone, in-depth study on the commission's origins, work, and legacy for the New Granada government and Olga Restrepo Forero's examination of the commission's contributions to the production of scientific knowledge represent the most thorough scholarship on this expedition.[33] Nancy Appelbaum's most recent study examines how the members of the commission tried to resolve a fundamental tension of nineteenth-century state formation: the desire for national homogeneity given the reality of diversity. As Appelbaum is right to argue, the commission's solution came through the creation of regions, each uniquely diverse, within the nation.[34]

The map in figure 12 provides a rough visual description of the commission's travels from 1850 to 1859, the year Codazzi died. The map clearly indicates one dimension of this itinerant scientific enterprise: the commission always started and ended its expeditions in Bogotá. Making Bogotá the center of operations for the commission made logistical sense. Not only was that city the nation's capital, but it also housed the Astronomical Observatory and the Colegio Militar. These institutions provided needed infrastructure and personnel that facilitated the compilation and analysis of the information collected in the provinces, transforming measurements, notes, and sketches into maps, charts, and geographical reports. Although commission members spent significant time in Bogotá, and this was the only city of New Granada that Codazzi mapped in detail, other provincial capitals became significant nodes in the commission's network. The capitals of each province served as discrete bases of operation for the commission when it was active in their regions.

Ancízar, as founder of the Instituto Caldas, and as secretary of the Chorographic Commission that emerged from it, proposed that a central contribution to this Bogotá-centered network of information on New Granada needed to be the production of sociological, psychological, and statistical studies of the Granadino pueblos. Ancízar and his contemporaries firmly believed statistics were the key to developing precise solutions to precise problems.[35] As previously described, statistics promised government

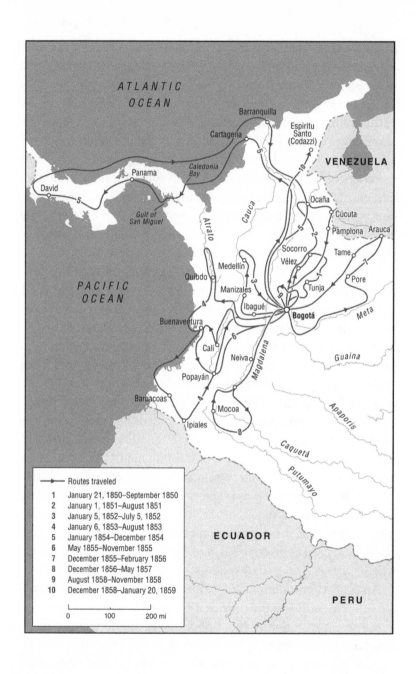

12. Comisión Corográfica: Routes traveled 1850–1859. Map created by Erin Greb. Based on Efraín Sánchez, *Gobierno y Geografía*.

elites and surveyors a language that would supposedly solve the problem of distributing indigenous resguardos equitably. Accurate statistics were needed for the nation far beyond resguardos, however. A government needed to promote the health of its nation, but without statistics it could not know the ills that afflicted it, nor the proper medicine required.[36] Ancízar also understood that studies in and on the provinces needed to comprehensively examine the extent to which each pueblo had worked to transcend the very many and deeply entrenched problems of the colonial legacy. Such information needed to be organized around discrete geographic sections of New Granada, that is, through a chorography detailing the social composition of New Granada towns and regions. Studies like these promised to offer the kind of critical information that would allow the national state, centered in Bogotá, to effectively legislate the measures that a fledgling republic needed. As the next section demonstrates, Ancízar provided a benchmark study that sought to fulfill these criteria in his *Peregrinación de Alpha*. His compelling travel narrative reconstructed through antiquarianism and ethnographic essays a chorography of the colonial legacy for New Granada. Ancízar's observations did not always sit well with readers, however. Those who challenged Ancízar did not challenge his methods. On the contrary, they embraced ethnographic writing as an expressive tool. They nevertheless employed this tool to show how much Ancízar himself had misread popular folkways, especially popular expressions of religiosity.

A Chorography of the Colonial Legacy

The scientific diagnosis of the colonial legacy was the driving purpose behind Ancízar's *Peregrinación de Alpha,* a travel narrative describing his two tours with the Chorographic Commission during 1850–1852 to the northeast provinces. The thrust of Ancízar's narrative systematically applied his analysis of the chorography of the colonial legacy to each and every region through which he passed, and did so by drawing on his knowledge of antiquarianism, his readings of history, and his interactions with everyday folk. Themes Ancízar had outlined in his writings prior to the commission emerge again in his *Peregrinación*, and forcefully so.

Most significantly, Ancízar evaluates the relative morality, education, and industry of local populations in the wake of republicanism's emergence from monarchical rule, offering ways to ensure progress for even the most 'backward' of regions.

Part of the appeal of Ancízar's narrative was its melancholic chorography of the archeological manifestations of an entrepreneurial Chibcha past and the various violent Spanish campaigns of conquest that wiped it out. It was the arrival of New Granada independence war veteran, military engineer, historian, and geographer Colonel Joaquin Acosta from Paris in 1849 that dramatically shaped these contours of Ancízar's chorography. Acosta's history offered a precolonial Chibcha splendor as the background for Spanish colonization and, in doing so, provided the historical threads that allowed Ancízar to weave his own narrative. Town by town, Ancízar drew on Acosta's history of colonization, coupled it with his own detailed analysis of landscape, and in this way set out to recover the exuberant evidence testifying to indigenous agrarian and commercial entrepreneurship and the material remains of conquest. Therefore, to best understand Ancízar's new science of the chorography of the colonial legacy, we need to understand what Acosta brought to Bogotá after years of study in Paris, and why.

Within the remarkable period of five years, 1845–1849, Acosta complied a massive amount of historical, scientific, geographic, and cartographic information on New Granada while in Europe. He built on a willing network of cosmopolitan printers and literati who helped him translate everything into Spanish and had these materials printed in Paris. Acosta then brought back several volumes to New Granada along with an impressive collection of scientific instruments and botanical samples upon his return in 1849.[37] Acosta's main contribution to the Chorographic Commission, and Ancízar's writing in particular, is best seen through two of the many published volumes and maps that Acosta brought back with him: the edited and annotated edition of F. J. Caldas's *Semanario de la Nueva Granada* of 1849 (*Semanario*) and the *Compendio histórico del descubrimiento y colonización de la Nueva Granada* of 1848 (*Compendio*).[38]

The structure and content of Ancízar's *Peregrinación de Alpha* reveal his close reading of these documents brought back by Acosta. Take, for instance, how the 1848 Parisian printed edition of Caldas's *Semanario* included a previously unedited travel narrative written by Caldas of his tour through territories surrounding Quito.[39] This text influenced the way Ancízar understood and operationalized chorography as a scientific method to study regions. Although Caldas's narrative emphasized a chorography of plants, he also included social commentary on different populations of the regions through which he passed. Inspired by Caldas, Ancízar structured his travel narrative as a chorography of the colonial legacy in New Granada society, one that mapped neatly onto the values and goals of the Instituto Caldas. The content of Ancízar's *Peregrinación* also suggests that he conducted a close reading of Acosta's *Compendio*, a text that at its core was a historical geography of Spanish sixteenth-century colonial depredations of a fabulous yet forgotten Chibcha civilization.

Acosta's *Compendio* painstakingly worked to highlight the significance of the Chibcha civilization and the devastating effects Spanish colonization had on the Chibcha "empire."[40] Acosta innovatively synthesized published accounts from the colonial period and weaved them together with previously unpublished and little-known manuscript chronicles of the *conquista* of New Granada, sources he found in Madrid's Historical Academy and the Archivo de Indias.[41] He drew on the archeological work of Manuel Vélez Barrientos, who "discovered" the ruins of a pre-Hispanic monument in Villa de Leyva that the people of the region called "El Infiernito."[42] This stone work, argued Acosta, was clearly a Chibcha temple that testified to that indigenous culture's high level of civilization.[43] Acosta also chronicled the cultural sophistication of the Chibchas by developing a grammatical guide analyzing their linguistic prowess.[44] In this sense Acosta's work anticipated that of Spanish naturalist Marcos Jiménez de la Espada during the second half of the nineteenth century.[45] And yet Acosta's historical treatise was not a Hispanophilic ode to the Spanish conquistadors. His was the first post-independence historical narrative on New Granada to deify the glorious past of the Chibchas, the indigenous group Acosta identified as dominating New Granada prior to Spanish colonization.[46] Acosta tried to fill a void in historical and geographical studies on what he characterized as the "third center of American civilization that was embodied by the dominium of the Chibchas o Muiscas."[47] French geographers took notice of his efforts.[48]

The problem was that Acosta not only had to grapple with the fact that the Chibcha were so little known among international elite circles; he also had to account for the seeming ease with which the Spanish colonized this remarkable culture. Acosta tackled both problems with a single argument: the Chibcha were decimated within the period of two generations. The Spanish deprived the Chibcha nation

> of its independence, its leadership, of its liberty, and even of its own language, due to the most cruel, blind, and perseverant impulses of persecution, which have managed to erase even [that nation's] name among from the catalogue of the peoples who existed, condemning its descendants to total ignorance of their origins, leaving that work to those who from now on occupy themselves with the antiquities of America.[49]

Acosta's narrative proved useful for Ancízar's aims. The speed with which Spanish colonization obliterated the Chibcha civilization meant that another revolution, one championed by both Acosta and Ancízar, could once again transform New Granada culture and society, and do so quickly. That revolution was embodied by Spanish American republicanism. And yet its success was threatened by the negative effects left in the wake of the colonial era.

Ancízar drew directly on Joaquin Acosta's historical writings to underscore how, prior to colonization, Chibchas were moral, productive, and educated. Colonization befuddled, demoralized, and nearly annihilated the Chibchas through violence. Any attempt at resistance to the Spanish proved futile. Ancízar cited Acosta to describe one such futile incident of resistance, when the Indians of Tausa, Suta, and Cucunubá fled the Spanish to the Peñon de Tausa with their wives and children, only to be decimated by Spanish forces from Santafé. "For many days, says Acosta, nothing else was seen in these places of desolation other than birds of prey, who gorged themselves on the cadavers of the destroyed Indians."[50] That anecdote allowed Ancízar to lay the narrative foundation for the violence colonialism wrought on indigenous populations, noting how these same scenes simply repeated themselves throughout the country of the "defenseless Chibchas."[51] For Ancízar, that violence explained why, by 1576, thirty-nine years after initial contact with the estimated two million Chibchas, only a handful of the original inhabitants remained. The speed with which colonization destroyed Chibcha civilization to the very core, as explained and documented by Acosta, became the mirror-opposite prefiguration of the positive changes initiated by independence in 1810 and the republicanism it brought to New Granada by 1849, thirty-nine years later.

Peregrinación de Alpha as Political Ethnography

Beyond evocatively and synthetically embedding Acosta's history of New Granada's pre-Columbian and colonial past in the landscape, Ancízar's Peregrinación also offered readers an extraordinary ethnography. He reconstructed how the colonial legacy manifested itself in the details of the mundane. Unlike political economies of the eighteenth century, which sought to study the general manifestations of colonial policies of trade, production, and taxation, Ancízar's ethnography displayed localized manifestations of a culture of languor, superstition, and dependency.[52] And yet much like monarchy and colonialism had annihilated the morality and productiveness of Chibchas within a period of thirty-nine years, republicanism had brought industriousness, education, and morality back to New Granada society within the same span of time. These changes, however, were unevenly distributed in New Granada.

Ancízar's meticulous report showed how the places that had embraced republicanism and rejected monarchy had benefited most. Good roads had facilitated this embrace. They helped local producers take their goods for trade to market and gave local residents access to republican education. The circulation of people, products, and ideas was especially important for the moral health of provincial populations. Circulation allowed local people to break through geographic isolation and the moral opprobrium of the colonial period in ways that brought folks closer to a productive republican ideal. Select individuals, especially parish priests, were most significant for ensuring proper moral development among rural populations. Local elites joined priests in their responsibility for fomenting moral, industrious education among popular sectors, including women. All these themes are evident throughout Ancízar's narrative, and they are meticulously drawn out through specific examples from the towns through which Ancízar passed. While some offered positive examples of how republicanism defeated the negative effects of the colonial legacy, other observations by Ancízar demonstrated the ways in which the colonial legacy endured, and dangerously so, among some popular sectors.

The sharp contrast Ancízar drew between the inhabitants of Charalá, a canton in the northeastern province of Socorro, and the slightly more remote canton of Soatá, located in the newly created province of Tundama, just over its border with Socorro, brings into focus Ancízar's evaluation of the colonial legacy, and prescriptions for eradicating it. Ancízar's description of Charalá as compared to that of Soatá illustrates a pattern prevalent throughout his writings concerning the relationship between civility, religiosity, hygiene, education, gender relations, and industry. Ancízar's analysis, although usually identified in the cannon of costumbrismo, offered what I would like to call a political ethnography of local populations around religious folkways. Through this form of political ethnography, Ancízar sought to identify the disparate ways the colonial legacy affected specific places, the extent to which republicanism was able to root that legacy out, and the responsibility of leading individuals, especially priests, to effect moral, republican transformations.

According to Ancízar, the Charalá inhabitants that the commission encountered exemplified the positive effects of republicanism. Ancízar often found himself comparing documents from the eighteenth century that described New Granada with what he encountered during his travels. The result was that Ancízar found many reasons to congratulate the work of republicanism in Charalá. Not only had the number of inhabitants increased overall; wealth had improved in encouraging ways since the eighteenth century. The most significant change was the improved "culture and civility of the people, and the development of a virile, honorable character that rural inhabitants display, the direct result of the different way in which these folks have been treated since the abolition of the oppressive colonial regime."[53] The hardworking, pious, and educated Charalá peasantry was completely different from the people described by Vicar Basilio Vicente de Oviedo in 1765 (197–98). Ancízar found Charalá residents sociable, resourceful, and easily approachable. In fact, as Ancízar pointed out, "From there several men have emerged prominently in politics and science given the education put within their reach by our system of public instruction" (197–98). As he had done for each town he visited, Ancízar noted the number of Charalá public schools and how many students attended. With a free public school for boys and four private schools for girls, and minor incidences of crime, Charalá exemplified the positive effects of republicanism and education in New Granada.

Despite Charalá's proximity to an idealized republican Bogotá capital in terms of the education of its citizens and their political engagement, Charalá nevertheless still proved a bit different from Bogotá when it came to religious celebrations. Ancízar anticipated his audience's repugnance of religious processions, considering them grotesque farces held over from the colonial period. A thinking Christian, according to Ancízar, "would like to see [processions] suppressed in order to restore the honor of a religion that has been ridiculed by those material and frequently absurd representations" (197). Nevertheless, Ancízar portrayed Charalá's procession in honor of San Isidro Labrador as one that the nation would do well to encourage among its peasantry. Ancízar explained to his audience that "San Isidro Labrador has for me a certain social signification that distinguishes and legitimates it." That was because, as the patron saint of agriculture, San Isidro represented the sanctification of productive agricultural labor. This saint allowed the church to give to its peasant followers a practical way of teaching the positive value of cultivating the land, and the honor with which such civilizing work needed to be held (197). Ancízar evocatively described how these lessons were not lost on Charalá residents (197–98). Charalá's most important religious procession was therefore morally acceptable given that local populations appropriated for themselves values sanctioned through the church, values that, in turn, were related to productivity and civility. These were key tenets espoused by elites that had formed the Instituto Caldas. Elite minds would be set at ease when it came time to expand political participation to these popular sectors in the northeast provinces.

Republican measures, embraced by Charalá residents, had improved their morality, civility, and dedication to hard work, and they had also seemed to help whiten a population already predisposed to whitening. According to Ancízar, "The pure indigenous race has completely disappeared, absorbed by the white race, leaving only a few families of mixed blood among whom some indigenous features can be found" (198–99). And yet Codazzi had surveyed and mapped the Guane indigenous resguardos only a few kilometers north of Charalá. Ancízar himself had quoted from Conquistador narratives that described the savagery of the original populations around this area. Ancízar recognized the inconsistency and pondered the possibility that the original inhabitants of Charalá were physically different from surrounding indigenous populations. There were civilizational effects to those supposed differences. Ancízar turned to the developing science of craniometrics to prove his point.

> The primitive bellicose and determined inhabitants were not of a miserable stature as were those who lived in the upper reaches of the Andes. The bones recently discovered in the caves of Coromor suggest they were of advantageous proportions: the high craniums and curious ceramic containers found in this ossuary make manifest the intelligence and hardworking nature of the aboriginal peoples, whose customs and civil regime are not described by the chronicles of conquest. (199)

Ancízar underscored the propensity of the specific indigenous population toward a republican whitening with a long footnote describing the history of independence and of civil wars fought by Charaleños. Fighting for the cause of independence and republicanism had just as an important effect on whitening and civilizing the Charalá population as race mixture, much like Acevedo y Tejada had explained in his geography primer from the 1820s. Warfare produced racial whitening because of the patriotism evinced by a region that, despite the marked presence of indigenous peoples, had nevertheless thrown its fortunes in with the national government centered in Bogotá, a move that left the shackles of the colonial period far behind. The seemingly more "advantaged" physiological dispositions of these indigenous groups as compared to their Andean highland brethren allowed Ancízar to suggest that the region's comparative whiteness was rooted in a past that reached back well before independence, yet independence was what had finally brought whiteness to the region.

Ancízar anxiously tried to convince his readers of the patriotism, bravery, hardworking nature, and moral religiosity of Charalá's whitened populations. This was not only to champion the positive inroads republicanism had made in rural areas far from Bogotá, but also because Ancízar wanted the nation to invest in roads to this area. Doing so would allow the nation, and especially Bogotá, to benefit from the vibrant textile production of the 26,500 inhabitants of the region, as well as several potentially rich salt, copper, iron, carbon, and sulfur mines (200). Moreover, Charalá offered a striking positive contrast. That was because Ancízar also spent considerable time describing towns that were not as civilized in their practices, towns that continued to suffer the effects of the colonial legacy and required targeted intervention from the republican enlightenment of Bogotá elites. Soatá, in the new province of Tundama, was one of these suffering places.[54]

From Ancízar's perspective, Soatá's immersion in the negative effects of the colonial legacy was a tragedy, especially because it enjoyed wealth in cattle, fertile agriculture production, and a healthy climate. An array of coal, iron, copper, sulfate, and salt mines abounded. The textile industry was vibrant. Commerce with neighboring towns of San Gil, Socorro, Santa Rosa, Sogamoso, Cocuí, Soto, and Santander all pointed to the assured prosperity and civilization of the villa. And yet Ancízar ominously pointed to evidence of the town's backwardness, suggesting that unwashed masses, poorly constructed housing, and lack of hospitality meant that "modern culture has not made a dent" among local populations (221). The fault did not lie with the people themselves. Ancízar observed how the majority of Soata residents were strong and of an "advantageous" stature, mostly white, with some mestizos and a few docile, generous Indians. Incidences of crime were negligible. Yet when these innocent populations came under the shadow of the "pretentious wealth and semi-enlightenment of the town's gamonales," that is, Soata's corrupt oligarchy, problems abounded. (223).

Soatá, in the early 1850s, when Ancízar passed through the town, was known as a Conservative Party stronghold. The treatment Ancízar received in Soatá indicated to him how Soatá's population clearly continued to suffer from the opprobrium of the colonial past, and how local elites perpetuated this backwardness. This diagnosis offered Ancízar a subtle way to assert that leading members of the Conservative Party imposed a colonial legacy on a peasantry that otherwise could offer vibrant contributions to culture and society.

The most alienating dimension of "backward" colonial practices in Soatá was made manifest for Ancízar in the strength and vitality of what he saw as exploitative and impious religious processions. As described above for Charalá, processions in general were something about which Ancízar was ambivalent, since they could potentially undermine moral church teachings and siphon time and resources away from more productive work. Charalá's San Isidro Labrador celebration of agricultural work and the moral, civilizing force that such labor produced among popular sectors was a notable exception. The Soatá celebration of the Octava de Corpus was completely different from that of Charalá, however. Ancízar rhetorically asked, "what moral teachings, what biblical lessons could be learned from this grotesque pantomime that perverts Christian ideas, and plants in their place idolatry and nonsense?" (223). The Octava de Corpus, as celebrated in Soatá, went directly against the values stated by the Instituto Caldas, and needed to be rooted out. But what did this celebration entail? The Octava de Corpus was, and is, a distinctly Spanish Catholic celebration that helps mark the passage of time for the faithful in terms of the resurrection of Jesus Christ. This holy day, or holy weekend, marks the end of a weeklong celebration of the transubstantiation of Christ's body into the Eucharist, the focus of the celebration of Corpus Christi. When celebrated, Octava de Corpus usually takes place about sixty days after Easter Sunday, the day that marks the resurrection of Christ. As celebrated in Soatá, this procession included elements that clearly troubled Ancízar. As described by Ancízar himself, some of those "troubling elements" suggest that Soatá was far more connected to global cultural trends and political changes than Ancízar would have liked to admit.

Ancízar derided the spiritual and physical preparations involved in Soatá's Octava de Corpus (222–25). Ancízar was especially puzzled by the surprising decorations. Pictures of young Parisian *grisetas*, or seamstresses, were included among the ornate ribbons, mirrors, and streamers. Ancízar remained speechless before strangely dressed statues, halls of mirrors, and paintings seemingly out of place. One such painting represented the dead and sensuous Atala from Chateaubriand's 1801 novel, who committed suicide so as to remain Christian and chaste rather than submit to her desire and love of the Indian Cháctas. Another prominently placed painting depicted Napoleon's exhumation in 1840, an effort by the French to restore the reputation of the July Monarchy. Ancízar does not stop to reflect on how Soateños seamlessly incorporated French authors and painters who had drawn on American themes into their celebration, as was the case of the Atala painting. Neither does he pause to consider the meaning of the July Monarchy and Napoleon for Soateño populations who may have been resentful of the deep Liberal transformations their province endured, including a new territorial division. Instead, Ancízar fell mute before the "courage of these innovations" that only managed to make the church "more akin to an Indian adoration site than a Christian temple" (222–23). To drive home the supposed barbarity and pagan undercurrents of the celebration, Ancízar cited his conversation with the local priest, who described how some folks

would reenact the crucifixion, encouraged with sips of the indigenous beverage *chicha*. Ancízar hoped that God would make such
practices cease, "for the decorum of religion and the honor of our
country" (225).

Despite the clear and surprisingly au courant ability of Soata
residents to plug into cultural and political developments that
crisscrossed the Atlantic, Ancízar argued such processions were
evidence of the continuation of the "barbarous centuries" among
the Soatanos. Overwhelmed, lazy priests sought profit from these
celebrations and, in doing so, improperly catechized their flock.
"That such practices from the barbarous centuries occurred among
small, remote populations of Indians as a source of wealth for bad
priests is conceivable, and lamentable. But that they still occur in
Soata is unforgivable" (225). The striking differences between the
Charalá procession and the Soatá procession lay, from Ancízar's perspective, primarily with differences in how parish priests assumed
their role within the republic. Charalá priests offered productive
ways to channel religious sentiments through San Isidro Labrador, a procession that engaged with the mission of the republic to
advance industry. The priests of Soatá, instead of correcting the supposed immoral displays of pagan-like rituals, profited from them
by collecting tithes from their flock that funded the processions.[55]

Ancízar's writings, unlike many of the maps, lithographs, and
botanical samples of the Chorographic Commission, did not remain
quietly tucked away collecting dust in the archives of the commission, but rather were immediately circulated via the national press.
By 1853 his travel narrative came out as a stand-alone volume. The
result was that Ancízar's scientific examination of the colonial legacy among the towns and villages northeast of Bogotá was widely
read. It had become an instrument of attributing honor to places
like Charalá while shaming the elite leadership and religious ministers who attended to popular sectors in places like Soatá. These
two towns were not the only ones to bear the brunt of Ancízar's
analysis. Elite leadership in some of these towns often tried to
contain the negative effects of Ancízar's writings. For instance,
Ancízar's description of Zipaquirá, the first town the commission
encountered on its way to the northeast provinces, upset local

elites for its suggestion that this salt-producing region was mired in a corrupt colonial legacy that placed a higher value on building a cathedral than in developing the local industry, schools, roads, and infrastructure.[56] Disgruntled Zipaquirá elites understood perfectly the impact that Ancízar's chorography of the colonial legacy could have on readers, especially government officials in Bogotá.

Ancízar's style of writing had a powerful hold on popular and official imaginaries of local populations. Local officials understood that these imaginaries could have concrete effects on how the national government would invest in local infrastructure. Ancízar, therefore, was by no means alone in the writing of political ethnographies of the everyday that could excise the colonial past in order to effectively establish republican-led progress. Ancízar operated in a polity that had made the ethnography of development into a veritable narrative art form. Now called "costumbrismo," ethnographic essays quickly became the tool of both Liberals and Conservatives who found radically different meanings in similar collective popular manifestations. It is to the political debates at stake in these ethnographic essays, especially those that offered a deep and biting criticism of Ancízar's *Peregrinación de Alpha*, that we now turn.

Eugenio Díaz Castro's *Manuela* as Political Ethnography

While some elites tried to defend their region through letters to the editor of the same newspaper that printed Ancízar's *Peregrinación*, others chose a more indirect, yet potentially more politically damaging way to challenge Ancízar and the condemnations and propositions he offered. This was the case of Eugenio Díaz Castro, whose novel *Manuela* offered, through fiction, a pointed ethnographic defense of the popular sectors that Ancízar described as suffering from the effects of a colonial legacy imposed upon them by elites. Díaz Castro, a champion of the Conservative political party, did not deny the possibility of a "colonial legacy" and its potential to block the progress and modernity that New Granada required. That "colonial legacy," however, was the fault of Liberal Party elites, not the Conservatives. Díaz Castro's fictionalized account launched a biting criticism of how Liberal elites, and especially Ancízar, had completely misread the creativity, industry, morality, and humor of popular sectors. Rather than posing an obstacle to modernity, these sectors offered a moral alternative to liberalism, republicanism, and modernity by grounding all of these transformations in pious, home-grown Catholicism. Díaz Castro transformed Ancízar into a conceited, cultural alien lost in his own hubris. As Liberals held the Conservative Party responsible for continuing colonial-era economies and individual behaviors, Conservatives such as Díaz Castro began to cast Liberals as elites alienated from popular culture and local realities because they were enamored of foreign models. For Díaz Castro, the problem lay with the neocolonial mentality of Liberal elites.

The very existence of Díaz Castro's *Manuela* points to how Ancízar's *Peregrinacion* was not an isolated text; it was simply the most elaborate, systematic, and well-known essay among an emerging body of ethnographic writings. Samples of these alternate examinations of folk life in the 1850s first emerged, much like Ancízar's *Peregrinación*, as installments in newspapers. The most active of these was *El Mosaico*, a cultural periodical, literary salon, and editorial house founded by Eugenio Díaz Castro and José María Vergara y Vergara in 1858, whose contributors, editors, and writers also included men who had been members of the Instituto Caldas.[57] Most notably, two founding members of the original Bogotá chapter, Lorenzo María Lleras and Rufino José Cuervo, as well as a member of the Mariquita provincial chapter of the institute, José María Samper, all were active participants in and contributors to *El Mosaico*, not to mention Manuel Ancízar himself.[58] In other words, *El Mosaico* brought together prominent contributors who had also signed on to the cultural project developed by a cross-party coalition of elites a decade prior, a cultural project whose mission was first articulated by Ancízar. Contributors to *El Mosaico*, even those with Conservative Party leanings, agreed with the founding mission of the Instituto Caldas. They also saw in Ancízar's ethnography a useful diagnostic tool rooted in science that could, in turn, extricate the colonial mentality from New Granada's soul. Ethnography would also allow government officials to determine which measures best suited development needs. And yet several of these ethnographic essays took the form of fiction, a narrative strategy that did not claim to be a factual eyewitness account, yet it was nevertheless held to be more evocative of popular sectors and embraced their spirit more fully. That was the point of costumbrismo literature for New Granada at midcentury.

Manuela fits squarely within the tradition scholars have called "costumbrismo." As Sergio Escobar argues, Díaz Castro adopted the method of costumbrismo to offer a deep reading of the customs of popular sectors from the point of view of popular sectors themselves, a move that did not sit comfortably later in the nineteenth century.[59] The overall significance of costumbrismo as a genre has been largely marginalized by scholars who have identified it as a nostalgic uncritical description of folk lifeways frozen in time, modeled on European literary trends, and deployed by the bourgeoisie to soothe a reading public eager to consume images of itself.[60] More recently some scholars have recognized the significance of the genre's rich description of national *typos*, or types, and as a result have examined costumbrista images and literature as a project of nation building through racialization.[61]

Despite these welcome approaches neither literary critics nor historians of Latin America's nineteenth century have paid sufficient attention to how the explosion of costumbrismo, and especially its ethnographic dimensions, represented the emergence of a new science of governance, one that would work through the transformation of public opinion through positive examples and through ridicule. This move was at the core of the Instituto Caldas mission in New Granada, and it was intended to engender the deep cultural revolution that republicanism required. This new science of governance did not work through institutions or laws as much as it needed to work through the printing press. Freedom of the press, and its expansion, would help shape public opinion in ways that would discipline self-governance among a broader sector of the population. Like the colonial ethnography of mendicant and Jesuit missionaries among Native Americans, the ethnographers of mid-nineteenth-century New Granada sought to pierce deep into the seemingly innocuous manifestations of the popular. Their mission was not to understand and interpret, but rather to excoriate, praise, or reform. It was in the folds and wrinkles of the mundane where one could identify the gripping power of the past. It was in the mundane too where future potential lay. The analysis and representation of popular culture became a diagnostic tool, an instrument to enact revolutionary sociopolitical reform. Ancízar and his peers understood that the ultimate locus of revolution lay in the radical transformation of everyday popular culture. Eugenio Díaz Castro's ingenious critique of Ancízar's interactions with popular sectors through the procession of the Octava de Corpus offered an alternative way of understanding just what was at stake in popular manifestations of religiosity for the future of the republic.

The novel's title character, Manuela, lived in "La Parroquia X," a warm-weather town about a day's travel down the slopes of Bogotá's mountainsides, much like warm-weather Soatá was about a day's travel from Bogotá. Díaz Castro dedicated an entire chapter of *Manuela* to the popular celebration of the "Octava de Corpus" in Parroquia X. Don Demóstones Bermúdez, an elite Liberal naturalist from Bogotá who was engaged in methodological scientific observations of the republic, visited this town. Díaz Castro narrates how Don Demóstenes observed the proceedings of the Octava the Corpus and reacted to them. Don Demóstenes, much like Ancízar, made no secret of his disdain for the procession or the decorations displayed throughout the town in celebration of it. In this way Díaz Castro sets up a fictional ethnographic narrative that allows readers to learn "what actually happened" when Ancízar had observed the Octava de Corpus procession in Soatá and then later wrote about his experiences. Soatá, as discussed above, was a noted Conservative Party stronghold within a largely Liberal Party–dominated region during the nineteenth century.[62] Since Díaz Castro could not offer a first-person eyewitness account of life in Soatá during the Octava de Corpus of 1850, as Ancízar had done, he instead assumed the voice of an omniscient narrator sympathetic to the creativity and humor of the town's popular sectors, noting the palpable benefits that Catholicism brought them. In this way Díaz Castro deployed Ancízar's method of ethnography of the everyday to launch a devastating critique of the ignorance and intolerance that elite Liberals such as Ancízar had for the religiosity and ingenious creativity of popular sectors.

Díaz Castro appealed Ancízar's negative ruling on Soatá's religious procession to the court of public opinion through print, offering instead a more thorough, in-depth understanding of popular sectors. Díaz Castro began by noting how "the Christian republic," that is, all New Granada towns, celebrated this holy day every year. Christianity and republicanism were inextricably tied; Christianity was what made a Spanish American republic moral. This argument flew in the face of the criticisms Ancízar had launched in his *Peregrinación* against religious processions. Díaz Castro then took aim at Ancízar by ridiculing the freedom of religion that the cosmopolitan essayist had so admired in the United States, by noting the disorder and disrespect that could result.[63] After chastising Ancízar for the religious pluralism he wished for New Granada based on the United States, Díaz Castro's chapter goes on to ridicule Ancízar and his elite urban Liberal clique's inability to understand—or be tolerant of—religious processions. Díaz Castro does so by demonstrating the irrational, laughable, yet demonstrably violent reaction that Don Demóstenes had to one particularly elaborate decoration. That decoration—unbeknownst to Don Demóstenes—was created by the novel's title character, the beautiful, young, intelligent, and chaste Manuela.

The decoration in question, titled, "Los Misterios de los gatos," appeared nowhere in Ancízar's original description of the Octava de Corpus, yet this fictionalized setting nevertheless carried a distinct message proper to the political dynamics of New Granada during the mid-1850s. A red cat, dressed in the typical style of dress by middling and lower sectors, a style that included a starched-collar shirt, vest, and ruana with *bayeta* lining and *alpargata* sandals on its paws, was wrapping up a young chicken in the official paper used to carry out the business of the national state. In turn, a well-dressed white cat, sporting boots that indicated his aristocratic status and a white overcoat and fashionable tie, was beginning to wrap the red cat with that same paper. Other young chickens were already wrapped up with pages taken from the *Recopilación*

Granadina. That book, which had been created by a founding member of Bogotá's Instituto Caldas, Lino de Pombo, offered a compilation of laws in force for the New Granada republic that circulated widely.[64] On this stage, however, the *Recopilación*'s pages offered a way for these Liberal cats to capture and trap the delectable chickens they would later devour. The white cat in the scene represented the winner (or most corrupt of the two Liberal cats on stage), for he got to wrap up the red cat and benefit from his labor of trapping the other chickens. While the aristocratic white cat represented elite Golgota Liberals like Ancízar, the red cat became a symbol for the Draconianos, or the more popular sector of the Liberal Party.[65] Don Demóstenes was infuriated by this display. He felt identified as the white, corrupting cat and could not bear the humiliating critique. Don Demóstones pulled out his gun and shot the red cat dead, daring the makers of the scene to face him. All the while, the appeals by local elites to Don Demóstones to respect popular rights to political expression through religious processions fell on deaf ears.

The humor directed against elite Liberals in general and Ancízar in particular through Don Demóstenes's unmeasured reaction to this popular display of religiosity is threefold. On the one hand, Díaz Castro ridicules Ancízar's inability to perceive or, at the very least, convey through his *Peregrinación* the complex political critiques woven into the Octava de Corpus decorations in Soatá. Ancízar's facile reading of the celebration missed the sophistication and wit that these expressions of popular religiosity offered their *aldeanos*. Beyond criticizing Ancízar, Díaz Castro's scene of violence by Don Demosténes also casts a wider net, ridiculing the hypocrisy of elite Liberal Party members more generally. These men vehemently defended the freedom of speech and supposed tolerance that came with it through the printing press, a medium they controlled. And yet, much like Don Demóstenes, these Golgota Liberals came down violently against those popular expressions of speech that challenged elite Liberal ideals. Finally, Díaz Castro also called attention to the "neocolonial" absurdity of adopting foreign models on New Granada realities, especially with respect to religious pluralism.

By simply cataloging Ancízar and Díaz Castro's essays within a broader genre of what literary critics and historians alike have termed "costumbrismo," a kind of elusive catch-all category that tends to emphasize the effort to freeze in time the customs of popular sectors, we would miss the rhetorical midcentury Conservative versus Liberal battle occurring in print in New Granada. Ancízar's writings as well as those of Díaz Castro offered forceful midcentury scientific explorations of picturesque folklife that would, through their ethnographic analyses and interpretations, shape public opinion in New Granada. Behind the conflict over interpretation of the Ocatava de Corpus, there lies a significant fact. Ancízar's chorography of the colonial legacy through ethnography was not exclusively a Liberal Party science. The same ethnographic chorography was also developed by Conservatives like Díaz Castro. Both Conservatives and Liberals deployed this form of political ethnography to identify the cultural bottlenecks slowing development. Popular religiosity became the most contentious arena for these analyses. Liberals like Ancízar identified these expressions of Catholic faith as dangerous obstacles to modernity, obstacles created by enduring, and negative, colonial legacies that Conservative Party leaders perpetuated. Conservatives like Díaz Castro saw in these expressions the unique way in which Spanish America could offer a moral path toward republican modernity. The negative effects of a colonial, or rather neocolonial, mentality were rooted elsewhere: among Liberal elites like Ancízar who supposedly sought to impose foreign models on local realities.

And yet both Díaz Castro and Ancízar fell speechless before the actual decorations that popular Soatanos developed for the Octava de Corpus. There is no record of there being cats in frocks in Soatá for the 1850 celebration of that holiday. This was decidedly a novelistic detail invented by Díaz Castro to drive home his point about detached, Liberal elites who refused to see the political engagement and sophistication of popular sectors. And yet Ancízar's travel narrative did note how Soateños displayed French images of literary figures like Atalah and Chactas and the burial of Napoleon. Ancízar had no words to interpret these representations by popular Soateños. Neither Ancízar nor Díaz Castro remarked how these displays suggested that Soateños were sensitive to global political and literary trends across the Atlantic. Much like elite Colegio Militar students like Manuel Peña had been. Instead, in Ancízar's hands, such decorations became akin to indigenous idolatry. Ancízar's framework of morality, industriousness, and education could not see popular Soateño expressions of religiosity otherwise. Díaz Castro, for his part, refused to see popular Soateño religious piety in any way connected to anything other than the high political stakes of local New Granada elections. The global dimensions of popular decorations went unmentioned. Díaz Castro's rendition of popular religiosity had no room for connected global trends.

The ideological project evinced by the political ethnography of costumbrismo was in line with the ideals of industry, education, and morality promoted by the bipartisanship of the Instituto Caldas. This is not to deny the deep fissures and potential for conflict that existed between Conservatives and Liberals. Rewards and punishments meted out to popular sectors on the printed page that were couched in the language of the colonial legacy were only one way that Liberal and Conservative elites battled each other. Territorial divisions occurring in the midst of political party formation proved an alternate, dramatically effective, and potentially violent way to do so as well. It is to those territorial transformations that we now turn.

Liberal and Conservative Divisions in the Instituto Caldas

Both Ancízar and Díaz Castro were trying to capture the souls of popular folk, assuming an expert witness stance to convey to readers what measures the New Granada republic needed to achieve progress. The risible conflict Díaz Castro portrayed in his novel was grounded in a far deeper class-based conflict ripping through New Granada, one that had its roots in the election of 1849. And yet Ancízar would have likely been bemused by Díaz Castro's character of Don Demóstenes, especially given Ancízar's own painstaking efforts to form interparty coalitions at the elite level. This cooperative purpose for the benefit of New Granada's development was at the core of the Instituto Caldas that Ancízar founded in 1847, one that rapidly expanded throughout the majority of existing provinces by 1848. Cross-party alliances at the national and provincial levels were what facilitated Ancízar's tours through the northeast provinces as official secretary for the Chorographic Commission.

And yet by 1849, just prior to the commission's inaugural expedition, political elections tested the resilience of the interparty and pan-provincial network created by the Instituto Caldas. The twenty-five provincial capitals existing at that time cast their votes for president. The electoral colleges for these provinces brought several different men as potential presidential candidates, including two Conservative-leaning Instituto Caldas members, José Joaquin Gori and Rufino Cuervo.[66] The plurality of provincial electoral votes, however, went to the Liberal Party's candidate, José Hilario López.[67] Since López did not obtain a clear majority, the national Congress was legally responsible for conducting final elections, which they did on 7 March 1849. Conservative Party congressional members later remembered these elections as verging on violent coercion, with the "March 7th knives" forcing the Conservative-majority Congress to cast their votes for the Liberal López.[68] Ancízar, by then clearly a member of the Liberal Party, nevertheless tried fortifying the cross-party alliances carefully created through the Instituto Caldas during the Mosquera administration in 1847 through his editorials in the *Neogranadino* in 1849. He employed the rhetoric of the colonial legacy to do so.

After the elections, which dealt an alarming blow to the Conservative Party, Ancízar shed light on the absurdity of the divisions between the two major parties. He underscored how republicanism, as opposed to monarchy, was the ideal toward which all New Granadians worked. He pointed to blurred political ideologies, with notable members of the Liberal Party defending supposedly "Conservative" measures and vice versa.[69] Despite common ground and political agendas, the political parties attacked one another as a result of the recent elections, most notably because some members of the Conservative Party resented losing their jobs to members of the Liberal Party.[70] Ancízar reminded those opposed to the election of General José Hilario López that he was "a recommendable citizen given his service to the cause of independence, to patriotic liberties, and for his genius in remaining detached [from partisan battles]."[71] Republican citizens needed to accept López's Liberal administration's naming of new people to government posts. This was a healthy measure that worked against a potential perpetuation of a colonial legacy where government posts were inherited rather than earned through demonstration of abilities.[72] To function effectively, democratic states needed to be the mirror opposite of the despicable stagnation suffered under Spanish rule. Liberals and Conservatives, needed to remember the republican mission New Granada had in the world.

Ancízar's analysis of the tensions between Liberals and Conservatives in 1849 was spot on, yet it did little to convince elite members of the Conservative Party that Liberal dominance in the Executive Branch was a positive reflection of republicanism shining its rational light over the darkness of the colonial period. Conservatives understood that as members of the Liberal Party enthusiastically assumed political posts in provincial and national government administrations, the influence of their own political network would dwindle. This Liberal threat to Conservative Party dominance grew ever more concrete as the Liberal López administration created more provinces, favoring Liberal Party leadership within them. Members of the Conservative Party recognized how these Liberal Party moves to reshape New Granada's territory, although they claimed to bring republicanism closer to the people, nevertheless effectively worked to undermine Conservative Party dominance in Congress and in provincial governments and legislatures. Conservatives did all they could to stop the Liberal Party threat to their control. The result, by 1851, was civil war.

The elite partisan dimensions of this conflict, including the territorial challenges to Conservative Party dominance that led up to it, can be best understood by viewing them through the looking glass of the provincial chapters of the Instituto Caldas together with the Chorographic Commission's work during 1850–1853. The Instituto Caldas was remarkably effective in identifying the most prominent local elite leaders of the provinces, no matter what party affiliation they espoused. This leadership could work across the party aisle in favor of development projects such as those proposed by the Chorographic Commission. As territorial divisions transformed the overall national political party balance in favor of Liberals to the detriment of Conservatives, this bipartisanship evaporated. Three provinces serve as a case in point. The first is Ocaña, carved out from the larger provinces of Mompox, Santander, and Pamplona as a separate province in 1849 by the Liberal López administration. The city of Ocaña became the provincial capital, and prominent city leaders welcomed their rise in status by immediately forming their own chapter of the Instituto Caldas. Several of members of Ocaña's Instituto Caldas, in turn, came to hold significant provincial government posts through 1853. The provinces of Antioquia and Buenaventura stand as Ocaña's mirror opposite in terms of how they received the new territorial divisions that the López administration dictated for Antioquia. Antioquia's capital city, Medellín, formed a chapter of the Instituto Caldas in 1848, as did the city of Buenaventura. When the López administration tried to carve out three provinces from the larger Antioquia starting in 1851, several Conservative Party members of the Instituto Caldas in Medellín and Buenaventura took up arms against the national government.

The fact that Ancízar and the Chorographic Commission went first to the northeastern provinces shortly after they were divided for their first two tours and then to the Antioquia region in 1853 in the wake of the 1851 Civil War was no coincidence. The Chorographic Commission offered the López administration a powerful way to solidify these new territorial divisions through the objective language of science. And yet the strategy of expanding the number of provinces while decentralizing national resources had the potential to undermine the work of the commission.[73] That is because most rents would devolve directly to the provinces rather than be concentrated at the national level, where funds for the Chorographic Commission came. The members of the commission nevertheless soldiered on. By the end of its tour of Antioquia, the political pendulum was beginning to swing back again toward an elite interparty coalition, one that would culminate in the reemergence of larger territorial units. The next chapter demonstrates how the commission once again aided in this territorial reconfiguration. For now, however, it is worth noting how the commission's most productive period occurred in the midst of violent disagreement between the two major parties that emerged precisely because of the newly created territorial divisions.

As suggested earlier, Ancízar was right to point out in the first paragraph to his *Peregrinación de Alpha* that no one prior to the Chorographic Commission had ever measured the counties he described in his travel narrative, at least not the provinces of Ocaña, Santander, Soto, or Tundama.[74] That is because prior to 1849 these specific provinces, as such, did not exist. From 1845 to 1853 the New Granada state had systematically broken up the twenty provinces that from 1831 to 1833 had joined to form the national state. While some of the new provinces emerged during the tail end of the Mosquera administration, the bulk of them were created during José Hilario López's presidency. In January 1850, when Codazzi and Ancízar set on their first mission, New Granada included twenty-four provincial governments. By the time the commission concluded its first two tours in December 1851, thirty-one provinces existed. Five more were created between January 1852 and May 1853 for a grand total of thirty-six provinces.[75] This multiplication of municipalities and provinces promoted by the Liberal elites tends to be elided in histories of Colombia, yet the process demands careful scrutiny. Given that political participation remained tied to spatial corporate rights, it is striking that the number of towns and provinces multiplied so rapidly. It signifies an acceleration of political participation, the arrival of mass politics within the polity that has yet to be fully understood.

One trend that can and should be noted is how traditional provincial capitals tended to resist this process of division while smaller cities that had been historically subordinated to provincial capitals saw value in the measure. By 1849 the national government in Bogotá, for the first time controlled by the Liberal Party under President José Hilario López, fomented political alliances with these smaller cities in the regions. Carving up large provinces into several smaller ones allowed the Liberal Party to continue to win even more seats in provincial and national assemblies. The larger provinces that supported the Lib-

ATLANTIC
OCEAN

*Territorio
de la Goajira*

PACIFIC
OCEAN

Territorio de San Martín

Territorio del Caquetá

Provinces in 1832	Added by 1853
1. Bogotá	20. Cauca
2. Tunja	21. Barbacoas
3. Antioquia	22. Túquerres
4. Cartagena	23. Tundama
5. Santa Martha	24. Chiriquí
6. Pamplona	25. Ocaña
7. Socorro	26. Azuero
8. Neiva	27. Valledupar
9. Mariquita	28. Soto
10. Mompós	29. Santander
11. Riohacha	30. Medellín
12. Vélez	31. Córdova
13. Pasto	32. Cundinamarca
14. Buenaventura	33. Zipaquirá
15. Panamá	34. Tequendama
16. Veraguas	35. Sabanilla
17. Chocó	36. García Róvira
18. Popayán	
19. Casanare	

—— 1832 border
------- 1853 border

0   100   200 mi

13. Changes in New Granada political divisions, 1835–1853. Map created by
Erin Greb.

eral Party understood the political advantages of breaking up into smaller units; the change would bring a greater overall Liberal control over local and national politics. Those dominated by Conservatives, however, were less than pleased given that their own political voice would be overwhelmed by the expanding network of Liberal-dominated provinces. At the same time the number of provincial governments grew, the central government experimented with decentralizing fiscal revenue back to provincial governments so they could assume the economic reigns of the region as promised. The effect, however, was that the overall budget the national government had at its disposal was significantly reduced.[76]

These two measures, increasing the number of provincial governments and decentralizing fiscal resources, directly impacted the logistics of the Chorographic Commission. One obvious issue for the commission was that the ground was shifting underneath its feet. The commission would have to continually revise its work as the number of provinces increased and internal territorial divisions changed. An even more complicated problem, however, was that the growing national need for the commission was met with a decreasing ability by that same national state to pay for the commission's work, given the shrinking national budget overall. Payments did not always come prior to each successive expedition, as promised. Neither could the national government fulfill its promise to supply the commission with all the instruments needed.[77] The Chorographic Commission dealt with the logistical implications of increasing the number of provinces while decentralizing national revenue by building on the network of like-minded elites into which commission members could tap through the Instituto Caldas. From Bogotá the commission connected with Instituto Caldas elites in provincial capitals, and those capitals, in turn, became the sites of knowledge assembly for the information gathered in the provinces.

The commission first traveled to the provinces of the northeast, precisely because these provinces had just been created by the López administration and needed to be mapped. Of these, Ocaña was the only one to form an Instituto Caldas. The Ocañeros who joined the institute clearly were among the most prominent; eight members of Ocaña's Instituto Caldas later held key positions in Ocaña's provincial government, as the bold names in Table 2 demonstrates.

Table 2. Founding Members of the Ocaña Province's Instituto Caldas 1849

Education Class	Charitable Aid Class	Development and Material Improvements Class	Roadways, Immigration, and Statistics Class
Sr. Manuel Lémus President of Ocaña Legislature 1853	Dr. José de Jesus Hóyos	**Sr. Fermin Lémus** Provincial Personero Signed Ocaña Constitution, 1853	Sr. José Antonio Jácome
Sr. Justo Lémus	Presb. Manuel de la Cruz Ribon	**Sr. Diego A Jácome** Governor of Ocaña 1853	Sr. Estéban Rodríguez
Sr. Ildefonso Quintero Ocaña Governor 1854	Presb. José de Jesus Conde	**Sr. Pedro Lémus** Signed Ocaña Constitution, 1853	Presb. Miguel Clavijo
Sr. Juan C. Pacheco Signed Ocaña Constitution, 1853	**Sr. José Rodríguez** Provincial Treasurer, 1849	Sr. Natividad Posada	Sr. Pedro Quintero Jácome
Dr. Miguel Araujo Signed Ocaña Constitution, 1853	Sr. Atanasio Roca	Sr. Joaquin Palacio	Sr. Andrés Lémus
Dr. Tomás de Andrés Tórres	Sr. José Antonio Quintero Monsalve	Sr. Gregorio González	Sr. Manuel Ibáñez
Sr. Federico Álvarez	Sr. Juan de la Peña	Sr. Eusebio González	Sr. Santiago Rizo

Source: Governor of Ocaña Province, Agustin Nuñez, and Secretary, Gabriel G. de Piñerez. *Gaceta Oficial*, # 1069, 26 August 1849, 391. Note: For Ocaña provincial elites, their role in passing the Ocaña Constitution of 1853, and their positions in government at that time, see Yebrail Haddad Linero, "Constituciónes Municipales de la Provincia de Ocaña," Cuento con Voz, 18 April 2015, http://www.cuentoconvoz.com/constituciones -municipales-de-la-provincia-de-ocana/.

Although Ocaña elites welcomed their new status, López faced a focused, principled push against his administration in 1851 from Antioquia Conservatives who declared that the new division of that province was cause for war. The López administration had divided Antioquia into three new provinces: Antioquia (capital Santa Fe de Antioquia), Córdova (Rionegro), and Medellin (Medellin).[78] These new divisions fomented popular political participation in ways that directly challenged the Conservative Party in the region. Several provincial members of the Instituto Caldas, who also ascribed to the Conservative Party, led the charge against what they perceived as a tyrannical Liberal-led move.

General Eusebio Borrero, originally from Buenaventura and a prominent member of Buenaventura's Instituto Caldas, invaded Antioquia in 1851 on the day the territorial division law was to take effect. Without bloodshed, he proclaimed himself civil and military governor of the province. His goal: abolish the new divisions and allow Antioquia to return to its former grandeur. Borrero then declared Antioquia a federal state, separating it off from New Granada, and issued a proclamation that invoked all Antioqueños to take up arms against the tyranny and immorality of General José Hilario López's regime.[79] Other Instituto Caldas members from Antioquia, such as Rafael M. Giraldo and Pedro Antonio Restrepo Escobar, took up Borrero's call. As noted above, Julio Arboleda, member of the Instituto Caldas in Popayán, was enraged by the expulsion of the Jesuits and the abolition of slavery. He launched a provincial rebellion against López's regime from Cauca. Colonel Francisco de Paula Diago and Mateo Viana, both members of Honda's Instituto Caldas, led the Conservative Party cause from Mariquita Province. Mariano Ospina, a founding member of the Bogotá Instituto Caldas chapter, wrote extensively in ways that fanned the Conservative Party flames against the López administration in 1851.[80] Despite the many regional leaders involved in the 1851 uprising, all of whom had pledged membership in the Instituto Caldas, President López denounced the rebellion by focusing on how it represented the worst of the colonial legacy, especially because, as he argued, the uprising threatened the republic with a return to monarchy.

López tapped into the language diagnosing the persistence of the colonial legacy and deployed it against Conservative dissidents. He noted how those who launched a rebellion against the emancipatory and liberating government he oversaw could only be people who wished to conserve and maintain old, worn-out privileges and fanaticisms from the colonial era.[81] López proved his point by citing diplomatic documents and a publicly circulating letter testifying to the fact that the dissidents had secret agreements with Great Britain. "And in this letter," López ominously warned, "a plan of monarchy is revealed, one secretly protected by foreign politics. Other facts confirm this plan, as sinister as it is serious."[82] López took specific aim at Conservative Antioqueños. These men had called for federalism, yet López argued his administration was doing just that: producing federalism. That was precisely the intention behind creating smaller provinces in Antioquia, a move that brought government administration closer to the citizen. Such a change was urgently needed in a province that was far too large and that had recently experienced an intense process of colonization of rural areas and population growth. Places that had formerly lacked political representation now required it, and López facilitated a solution. López concluded his remarks by signaling the lack of civility and republicanism of Antioqueño Conservative rebels. Their opposition to a simple territorial change in government administration could have easily been resolved through formal political channels; war was unnecessary and uncalled for. López's words were followed by military force. National armies in Antioquia led by Liberal general Tomás Herrera defeated the uprising within a few months' time. The rebellion was squelched. The Liberal Party's division of Antioquia was set in stone. Or at least so it seemed.

The Chorographic Commission offered a systematic survey of the three new Antioqueño provinces of Córdova, Medellín, and Antioquia in 1853 as an attempt to solidify the newly minted boundaries. These new boundaries also happened to expand popular participation in ways that enhanced the Liberal Party's political clout nationally and in the provinces. The commission offered a cross-section of these three provinces through its findings, but

Ancízar's Antioqueño travel narrative was not part of the corpus of information. Neither Ancízar, who by 1853 had left for Ecuador, nor Santiago Pérez, Ancízar's young replacement as secretary of the commission, traveled with the commission to these new provinces.[83] Despite missing an official secretary, the Chorographic Commission pushed on, and did so by connecting with the network of like-minded elites who supported the Instituto Caldas in the late 1840s. Several of the Antioqueño Conservative Party leaders who had been part of the Instituto Caldas were living in exile or imprisonment due to their leadership role in the civil war. The elites who welcomed Codazzi and the commission therefore were members of the Liberal Party who assumed political control of the province in the wake of the 1851 Civil War. They too had formed part of the Instituto Caldas.

Take, for instance, the governor of Medellín, José María Lince, who had formed part of the "Education" class for Antioquia's Instituto Caldas chapter in 1848.[84] In the wake of the 1851 Civil War, Liberal-leaning Lince became governor of Medellín, the province that had been most resistant to the new divisions. Lince organized an elaborate celebratory welcome for the commission's arrival in 1853.[85] Besides celebrating the commission's arrival, Lince also became an important informant for Codazzi and the commission. He offered a powerful narrative explanation for one of the deepest contradictions Codazzi found for Medellín and surrounding provinces: the region was rich in gold, yet poor in roads. The reason for such a puzzling enigma was simple, according to Lince. The "colonial legacy" explained the puzzle.

In the wake of the 1851 Civil War, the power of the "colonial legacy" went beyond demonizing Spanish colonization and came to be used to denounce the supposedly centralizing efforts of the party that had been in power prior to the Liberal López regime.

> The industrious sons of what had been the former Antioquia province had recognized the immense importance that short, easy, and secure roads would stamp on a country that was essentially commercial; yet the chains of the former regime maintained our arms and spirits under oppression. They forced the dispersed sections

of an immense territory to leave their luck abandoned to the languid movements that a central administration could offer them.[86]

Lince's words ambiguously referred to the "former," centralizing regime, one that could connote the colonial era as it could refer to the "centralizing" efforts of the ruling New Granada regime prior to that of José Hilario López. And yet Lince's words, however patriotically Liberal, also evoked the unity of purpose that all the sons of the "former" Antioquia, now divided in three, shared.

Despite the benefits that the division had brought to the Liberal Party at the national level, the division of Antioquia seemed to be hurting Antioquia's native sons. Lince, after all, pointed to how paralyzing was the centralizing morass of a "colonial legacy." Despite their efforts, safe, secure road building in their region had been impossible. Impossible, that is, until the commission arrived. Codazzi offered several road-building plans, and Lince dutifully presented these plans to Medellín's provincial legislature. Lince also requested a map from Codazzi that was not limited to the province of Medellín alone, but that contained the entire territory of the former Antioquia as well as the bordering sections of Chocó, Cartagena, Mompos, Mariquita, and Cauca. This would allow for planning communication routes and boundaries. Codazzi agreed with Lince. In his geographic report on the three provinces, Codazzi observed how Córdoba, Medellin, and Antioquia "will never form anything other than one single group, with identical characteristics, inclinations, and customs that are completely different than the other Provinces we have traveled through."[87] Antioquia, although divided in three by the López administration, would always be one, according to the Liberal Lince, and through Lince, Codazzi.

The meticulous and productive work of the Chorographic Commission during its first three tours suggests a somewhat seamless, rosy alliance between the Instituto Caldas, the commission, the national government, and the newly created provinces of New Granada. Provincial chapters of the Instituto Caldas that had emerged under the Mosquera administration in capital cities around New Granada allowed commission members to identify the people and cities most welcoming of their endeavor from 1847 through 1849. Elite leadership from both parties in Bogotá and in the overwhelming majority of provinces subscribed to the mission and purpose of the Instituto Caldas and the Chorographic Commission that emerged from it. The goal for both was to foment industry, morality, and education in ways that displayed the greatness of republicanism as opposed to the backwardness of monarchy. The language of the colonial legacy, developed by Liberal intellectuals such as Ancízar as a way to diagnose the obstacles to republicanism's progress, soon became a valuable political tool, especially for President López's administration.

Despite a shared ideological vision of progress among elites, as made manifest in the Instituto Caldas and the Chorographic Commission, dramatic changes in the balance of political influence between Liberals and Conservatives exploded with the election of Liberal candidate José Hilario López in 1849. His administration brought an intense round of new territorial divisions for New Granada. Ostensibly these new divisions were legitimated through discursive appeals to republicanism, especially the need to bring the government closer to the people, ideals integral to the founding mission of the Instituto Caldas. And yet these divisions also worked inordinately well to reshape political networks throughout New Granada in ways that favored the Liberal Party. Liberal-leaning cities, like Ocaña, were rewarded and became capital cities of entire provinces. The new territorial arrangement, under the existing constitutional framework, favored the Liberal Party's ability to control policy and government appointments at the national and provincial levels. Conservative-dominated provinces, in turn, were punished. The new divisions broke up Conservative bases of power. Conservative opposition came to be diagnosed by López as evidence of continued existence of the backwardness of the colonial legacy. The Chorographic Commission further legitimated López's territorial maneuvers by solidifying the new divisions scientifically, in ways that seemed to rise above party politics. And yet despite the López administration's efforts to carve out a stronger territorial presence for the Liberal Party, Liberals in Antioquia as well as Codazzi himself suggested to the national government that the new divisions might need to be reconsidered. The end of the López administration, and the rise of José María Obando and the popular sectors of the Draconianos, would bring this possibility back to the foreground.

Just as print culture began flourishing at midcentury in New Granada, the Chorographic Commission's findings became a central component of that culture. As Efraín Sánchez has noted, if one were to measure popularity by exposure through print, the year 1853 marked the apogee of the Chorographic Commission's popularity in New Granada.[88] Codazzi's assessments of provincial geographies were printed by installments in the official national paper, the *Gaceta Oficial*, and by 1853 Codazzi became the *Gaceta's* principle contributor. Botanist José Jerónimo Triana began publishing his findings on "New Granada's useful plants" through the *Neogranadino*. Ancízar's travel narrative, the *Peregrinación de Alpha*, also published by installments in newspapers from 1850 to 1852, emerged as a unified printed volume in 1853. Although Ancízar begrudgingly left the commission on a diplomatic assignment to Ecuador in 1853, his young replacement, Santiago Pérez, also managed to publish his travel narrative of trips he took with the commission in the *Neogranadino* late in 1853. Santiago Pérez had been far too young to form part of the Instituto Caldas in the late 1840s, but his teacher and mentor, Lorenzo María Lleras, had been a founding Bogotá member and in 1853 became incoming President Obando's secretary of international relations. Lleras's support for the commission included the publication of Santiago Pérez's materials in the press. This was not just because Lleras wanted his former student to succeed, but also because of popular demand. In September 1853 the newspaper *El Pasatiempo* pleaded with Secretary Lleras that he "send off to publication the works of Santiago Pérez in the Chorographic Commission. . . . We would be much obliged with Mr. Lleras if he were to satisfy our wishes."[89] This support in print resonated with the support the commission received from the national government, no matter who was in power. President Obando, a staunch member of the Liberal Party, initially offered significant support to the commission through his administration.

It increased the budget for the commission by 78 percent and also allocated an additional ten thousand pesos toward the formation and publication of maps of state-owned lands that could be used to offset New Granada's foreign debt.[90]

What was the origin of so much support and legitimacy? The connections between the bipartisan Instituto Caldas and the Chorographic Commission that this chapter has sought to elucidate are suggestive. On the one hand, these state-sponsored endeavors offered a vision of an integrated country of regions through a political economy of circulation and standardization. The systematic gathering of statistics and the chorographic study of the local and the regional sought to offer an integrated vision of the whole and mechanisms to hasten circulation and smash "colonial" bottlenecks. Sketching circulatory chorographies, however, was not the sole purpose of either. The institute and the commission were part of a larger public sphere of civic organizations, political parties, and newspapers. They were all determined to expunge the colonial from the mind of the public, or the neocolonial, depending on party affiliations. As part of this vibrant republican public sphere, the institute and the commission were also deeply enmeshed with traditional, corporate, spatial forms of political rights: municipalities. As the institute and the commission grew, so too did the number of towns and provinces, which in turn lent these institutions even greater support.

In other words, the Chorographic Commission seemed to be on a path toward continued success precisely because it could count on elite cross-party, pan-provincial, and print culture support in the early 1850s. This support allowed the commission to gather information in the provinces, begin to assemble it in provincial capitals, compile and integrate its findings in Bogotá, and disseminate them. And yet by 1854 the commission had suffered a serious disruption to its work and its Bogotá-centered network. These disruptions went far beyond the problems of fiscal decentralization. The midcentury transformations in New Granada territorial state formation that inspired the first three tours of the commission had created unprecedented political openings for popular sectors. These openings culminated in universal manhood suffrage through the Constitution of 1853. Civil war erupted once again. This time, however, the forces leading the side that challenged the national government were not like-minded elites who had socialized through organizations such as the Instituto Caldas. Popular sectors, especially middling and lower ranks of the military and urban artisans who increasingly found their own spaces of political socialization and assembly, joined with a few older Liberal leaders to challenge the Constitution of 1853. These popular sectors in Bogotá and several other provinces soon acted beyond the control of even these older Liberal elites. Commission members and the cross-party, pan-regional network of elites who supported the commission's work were called to the field of battle and to the halls of Congress to roll back the political openings created for popular sectors from 1847 to 1853. The legitimating reason these elites used to explain the rollback was clear: the negative effects of the colonial legacy continued to lead ignorant popular sectors astray. It is to these territorial-political transformations that we now turn.

CHAPTER 5

Constitutions and Political Geographies Harness Universal Manhood Suffrage

D ominant historiography on mid-nineteenth-century Colombia would have you read the two maps in figures 14 and 15 as radically different from each other. The first map was produced in 1847 by New Granada's native son, Joaquin Acosta, in Paris.[1] Acosta's map seems to reflect a historiographical truism, that New Granada's constitution of 1843 had a centralizing impulse. According to this narrative, New Granada during the 1840s saw the proto-Conservative political party, the Ministeriales, as still in charge of the national government administration. The Ministeriales developed favorable relations with key members of the Catholic Church, disdained popular political participation, rejected federalist tendencies, and were most suspicious of the emerging Liberal Party's efforts to gain political power.[2] It seems Acosta, a creature of this period of supposed Ministerial-led centralization, drew out that constitutional-territorial model of New Granada in 1847. Acosta's map includes no internal provincial boundaries. Instead, Bogotá emerges as the dominant capital of New Granada, surrounded by a network of twenty-two provincial capitals that in turn were linked to several hundred cities serving as heads of cantons, and to other cities and villas. The second map, printed by José María Samper in 1858, also if read in light of long-running historical narratives, reveals a radically different New Granada Republic. Samper's map displays a completely new constitutional territorial political project: federalism. The creation of the state of Panama in 1855 inaugurated the kind of federalism that was enshrined in the 1858 Constitution. This new charter was at the root of a radical Liberal project, one that championed the abolition of slavery, the expansion of suffrage, and a break between

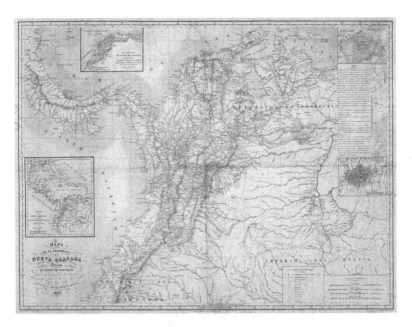

14. Mapa de la República de la Nueva Granada dedicado al Barón de Humboldt, á quien se deben los primeros conocimientos geográficos y geolojicos positivos de este vasto territorio, por el Coronel de Artilleria Joaquin Acosta," Paris, 1847. 60 x 81 cm on paper 70 x 88 cm. Scale 1:2,700,000. Biblioteca Nacional Mariano Moreno de la República Argentina.

church and state.[3] Clearly, Samper's 1858 New Granada, comprised of eight sovereign states, was a completely different republic than the one portrayed by Acosta in 1847.

But look at these two maps: they are the same! They are based off of the same topographical information. They include the same insets to illustrate significant aspects of New Granada's location, the navigability of the Caribbean ports of Sabanilla and Cartagena, and the urban space of Bogotá. They use the same scale, and the original printed versions are the same size. The reason for such striking similarities is simple. In 1858 José María Samper edited the same copper plates for the map that his father-in-law, Joaquin Acosta, had commissioned in 1847.[4] The second edition of Acosta's map helped illustrate Samper's 1857 *Ensayo aproximado* on the geography and statistics of the states that comprised New Granada. The edited copper plate itself now hangs

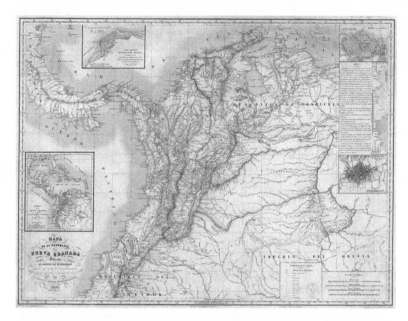

15. "Mapa de la República de la Nueva Granada dedicado al Barón de Humboldt, á quien se deben los primeros conocimientos geográficos y geolojicos positivos de este vasto territorio, por el Coronel de Artilleria Joaquin Acosta . . . Arreglado al Sistema federal de 1858 por J M Samper," Paris, 1858. 60 x 82 cm. Scale: 1:2,700,000. Bibliothèque nationale de France, département Cartes et plans, GE C-9813.

in the National Museum of Colombia, a gift to the nation from the woman who was Joaquin Acosta's daughter and José María Samper's wife, Soledad Acosta de Samper. These two printed maps are therefore intimately related to each other materially. The two maps emerge from the same copper plate. They are also genea-logically related in that the plate itself was produced and edited by close family relatives. The family connections and the material continuity shared by these two maps begin to point to something that historiographies on nineteenth-century Colombia reviewed above have missed.

The bases for the New Granada Republic reflected by Acosta's 1847 map and those embedded in Samper's 1858 map are, despite historiographical arguments to the contrary, one and the same. At the heart of those foundations was the desire to assure elite con-trol over the political process. This chapter demonstrates how constitutional and territorial changes implemented from 1847 to 1858 were done to salvage elite control over the republican project. Two episodes explain the formal differences that do exist between the two maps: the legal abolition of slavery in 1851 and universal manhood suffrage introduced by the 1853 Constitution. Both events together unleashed new forms of political participation that were not mediated through spatial corporate rights of municipalities and provinces. Individuals acquired political rights in ways that surpassed the political voice that provinces and municipalities had constitutionally enjoyed for decades under republicanism. This transformation in the franchise led to deepening partisan divisions in New Granada. Political strategies had to change. To win elected office, Liberals and Conservatives needed to mobilize popular sectors. Conservative networks, which built off of the Catholic Church, were far stronger than Liberal strategies for getting out the vote. One result was that popular votes in the 1850s largely favored the Conservative Party. Liberals who had politically benefited from the expansion of municipalities and provinces in the 1840s and early 1850s, and who ideologically supported emancipation and universal manhood suffrage, were stunned.

Results at the voting booth unleashed a long decade of civil war. Some Liberal elites argued that instead of following their own political self-interest by voting for the Liberal Party, the masses followed Conservatives whose defense of and alliance with the Catholic Church perpetuated colonial-era structures of subordination. Liberals this time could not limit themselves to liberating the populace from the manacles of colonialism via the public sphere. No amount of costumbrista irony would suffice in the short term. The stakes were simply too high to wait for the work of print culture to change minds. War offered a more expedient answer. The problem was that the newly found political position of popular sectors meant that war quickly spun out of the control of Liberal elites. Conservative elites, for their part, feared how Liberals had ignited massive armed popular mobilization throughout New Granada. Popular mobilization through war threatened the very institutions that both Liberal and Conservative elites had worked so hard to create for the Republic.

The "science" of constitutionalism worked in tandem with war in ways that allowed elite Liberals and Conservatives to negotiate their respective territorial strongholds, thereby reining in the political voice of popular sectors overall.

Constitutionalism became a "science" in the early 1850s as modernizing Liberal and Conservative elites grouped into the Instituto Caldas grew ever more comfortable with the idea of individual rights and sovereignty. After individual sovereignty was implemented, however, it had proven to be a mirage that benefited mostly the Conservative Party. The new constitutionalism that emerged in the mid- to late 1850s slowly began to play around with the notion that state sovereignty should supersede not only individual sovereignty but national sovereignty as well. This realization proved crucial in the emergence of a new, hard-won elite Liberal-Conservative consensus, one that was at the core of the reorganization of political territories from small provinces into sovereign states. Liberals asserted political control over some states, and Conservatives dominated others. In those states where the parties competed with each other for control, electoral fraud nevertheless served as the rallying cry for war. As territorialities were redrawn and civil wars subsided, competition lingered. New Granada became a nation of eight, then nine sovereign states in an attempt to restore elite consensus and control by the 1860s. But consensus came at a high cost. The balkanization of the national state into large sovereign states had the potential to delay, if not paralyze, the circulatory project of the 1840s. Elite leaders, Liberal and Conservative, began to worry that the threat of popular participation was much worse than allowing each state to assert a sovereign boundary. The circulatory project of the 1840s came to be maligned as a colonial-era holdover of "centralism." A new form of federalism, grounded in state sovereignty that overrode both individual and national sovereignty emerged.

The case of the two maps described above, Acosta's map of 1847 and Samper's revised edition from 1858, capture the essence of both the continuities and discontinuities between the elite national project of the 1840s and that of the late 1850s. Acosta and Samper both belonged to the same family and shared a common ideology. Yet their maps—or, rather, the single, changing map—reflect two different forms of territorialization and state administration. The first form of territorialization reflected in the 1847 map was organized around the principle of ever-greater mobilization of people and products within the national space, and the expansion of political rights to growing numbers of representative corporate bodies. This is the form of territorialization examined so far in this book. As chapter 4 notes, Joaquin Acosta's historical and scientific compilation work had been instrumental in the kind of emerging geographical, sociological, and anthropological work carried out by men such as Manuel Ancízar and members of the Instituto Caldas who focused on stimulating internal education, markets, and morality. Universal manhood suffrage and the war if unleashed forced the creation of a second form of terrirorialization and state administration. This new constitutional and territorial organization edited by Sampler is reflected in the second map. Samper, a member of the Mariquita chapter of the Instituto Caldas, joined Ancízar and other fellow Instituto Caldas members in a joint project to save the republican project displayed so clearly by Acosta back in 1847 through the radical constitutional territorial changes of 1858–1863. The second map reorganized New Granada space around sovereign states and did so in the wake of a tremendous political threat launched by politically and militarily mobilized popular sectors. This re-organization would have deep implications for the internal circulatory model offered by elites in the 1840s. But rather than open up internal markets, the new territorialization had in its sights the quelling of interparty strife while opening the future of New Granada to regional alliances and foreign investors. Rather than internal circulation, popular education, and morality, the new state form began to emphasize sovereign states, foreign investment, and trade.

Attention to the origins of mid-nineteenth-century civil wars and constitutions reveals a world of postcolonial theories about colonial legacies and the popular mind. Only through this kind of exploration can we better understand why a coalition of elites from both parties agreed to reorganize the national state from thirty-six provinces into eight or nine sovereign states in such a short period of time. This chapter traces how the coalition of elites who were first made notable throughout New Granada because of their membership in the Instituto Caldas in 1847, together with select members of the Chorographic Commission, played instrumental roles in the "scientific" territorial and constitutional changes occurring from 1853 through 1863. The chapter demonstrates how those changes were intended to preserve elite control over the republican project first envisioned in the 1840s by men like Acosta. By saving the republic from the popular mobilization that it had unleashed, these men sacrificed internal circulation.

The chapter is divided in four sections. The first examines the "science of constitutionalism" developed by José María Samper in 1852 in light of the explosion of constitutional thinking and writing that occurred nationally and provincially starting in 1853. This section argues that the Constitution of 1853 was not a "radical" Liberal invention, as historiography on Colombia often sustains. I show how the 1853 charter enjoyed wide support among the membership of the same regional elites who had created the Instituto Caldas and the Chorographic Commission, including Conservatives.

The second section examines the violent tensions growing between popular liberals and elite liberals made evident through the election of José María Obando in 1853, and the subsequent explosion of the 1854 Civil War. The section argues that the scale of the civil war reflected the very scale of the broad popular mobilization unleashed by the new constitutionalism based on individual rights and sovereignty. The Civil War of 1854 was not a one-off military coup focused in Bogotá, but a conflagration that engulfed most regions of the country. It began to make clear to all parties involved that emancipation and universal manhood suffrage had unleashed uncontrollable forces. Popular Liberals were defeated by a coalition of elites under the leadership former Instituto Caldas members and members of the Chorographic Commission, but constitutional changes were needed to avoid such uprisings in the future. With the war's end came a new round of constitutional reform. This tumultuous period marked the beginning of José María Samper's turn away from constitutionally enshrined individual suffrage to the establishment of sovereign state's rights within the national republic.

The third section examines how José María Samper and two of his fellow Instituto Caldas alumni, Manuel Ancízar and Justo Arosemena, revised the territorial and constitutional underpinnings of New Granada's constitution in the wake of the 1854 Civil War to save the republic from universal manhood suffrage. These efforts nevertheless erupted in war once again from 1859 to 1862. The section demonstrates that the entire reorganization of the territoriality of the republic into the sovereign states emerged as a legal technology from inside and outside of New Granada. Ancízar and Samper joined forces to create a new constitutional notion of sovereignty that privileged regional territories over individuals and over the national state. They did so as representatives of the Sovereign State of Panama. Prior to his representation of Panama in Congress, Ancízar had learned about new, "moderate" forms of constitutionalism during his travels through Ecuador and Chile as diplomatic representative of New Granada. It was in Chile that Ancízar was inspired by the moderate jurist, poet, and philologist Andrés Bello. Upon returning to New Granada via Panama, Ancízar and his brother-in-law, Samper, joined forces with Panamanian native son Justo Arosemena to introduce a radical new conception of the territorial state. The new arrangement was intended to address the peculiar concerns of the New Granada's Isthmus, which in 1855 was seeking ways of strengthening its position vis-à-vis the U.S. trans-isthmian railroad company, and to find better ways of disciplining the increasingly restless Afro-Panamanian populations. New Granada's constitutional turn away from universal manhood suffrage had as one of its central goals the strategic positioning of the country within continental geopolitics.

The final section centers on Felipe Pérez, a young man who joined the Chorographic Commission after Codazzi's death in 1859, and whose historical commentary on the 1859–1862 Civil War focused what he considered to be the legacy of Spanish colonialism squarely on corrupt practices of Conservative Party leaders. Felipe Pérez's take on the science of constitutionalism in the wake of this Civil War expanded a notion of the supposed false consciousness of popular sectors. He argued political mobilization needed to be reined in. The reterritorialization of the Grenadine Confederacy into the nine sovereign states of the United States of Colombia emerged out of efforts by regional elites, such as Pérez, to forbid the national state from deploying forces to the sovereign states in cases of electoral fraud. Pérez legitimated his new take on constitutionalism by arguing that electoral fraud was actually needed in a republic mired in a colonial legacy of Spanish Catholic corruption. Calculated fraud limited the extent to which popular sectors resisted secular and commercial modernity due to blind adherence to Catholic leaders in cahoots with the Conservative Party. Pérez was among the first to cast his new constitutionalism within a historical narrative of Conservative, retrograde centralism versus Liberal federalism, a trope that was to become canonical. "Radical Liberals" claimed "federalism's" victory as a Liberal victory, erasing the shared republican vision that a coalition of Liberals and Conservatives had fought so hard to rescue from the clutches of 1850s popular mobilization and from potential territorial invasions by the United States. Subsequent historiography, adopting Pérez's tantalizing narrative, occluded the vision of republicanism shared by Liberals and Conservatives and that was, at its very base, one inherited from the 1840s. A supposed Conservative Party centralism came to be pitted against a supposed Liberal federalism, and nothing else seemed to matter. This tension became the focus of several subsequent politicized historical narratives. The role universal manhood suffrage played in these conflicts came to be silenced as a side issue, if addressed at all. The same went for geopolitical positioning with respect to the United States and other countries in the region. In short, this chapter highlights the continuities and disjunctures between the republican project of the 1840s with that of the 1860s in ways that are sensitive to the emerging discourse of Liberal versus Conservative partisan conflict, and that carefully trace out the larger mid-century geopolitical context.

Sovereignty and Universal Manhood Suffrage

Before trying his hand at editing his father in law's cartography, José María Samper had proposed the development of a new science in New Granada: the science of constitutionalism.[5] As discussed below, Samper's constitutional and geographical thinking came to be increasingly intertwined in the wake of the Civil War of 1854. Samper had yet to fully integrate his understandings of climate, territory, and constitutional writing in 1852, however.[6] During his earlier career as a jurist, Samper devoted himself to developing a science that facilitated clear and principled constitutional writing. Samper was by no means the first person to posit that systematic scientific thinking would solve New Granada's social, political, or cultural problems. Much like Lorenzo María Lleras's adaptation of land surveys to the particularities of New Granada in the 1830s, Florentino Gonzalez's science of political administration from the 1840s, or Manuel Ancízar's contributions to ethnography in the 1850s, Samper articulated, adapted, and adopted what he called the science of constitutionalism to New Granada realities.[7] By 1852 Samper looked upon the expansion of popular political participation in New Granada with enthusiasm but argued it did not go far enough. His early science of constitutionalism offered clear methodological guidelines to facilitate true democracy by ensuring the practice of universal manhood suffrage.

This section explores the younger Samper's science of constitutionalism, which he envisioned as the method through which universal manhood suffrage would materialize in New Granada, putting that nation at the forefront of democratic republicanism in the world. The constitutional modeling work of Samper also helps shed light on the logic undergirding the explosion in constitutions at the national and provincial levels that occurred from 1851 to 1853. Within a decade's time, civil war demonstrated to Samper, and like-minded elites, the dangers that universal manhood suffrage posed to the kind of republic they had originally envisioned. In 1886, when Samper served as one of the drafters of Colombia's longest-lasting national constitution, Samper defined universal manhood suffrage as "one of the main causes originating our revolutions; the source of elements destructive of the social order."[8] But in 1852 Samper was a very different man, full of optimism and hope for radical liberal utopias.

Samper's thoughts on constitutional reform were inspired by the April 15, 1851, passage of a law facilitating constitutional reform for New Granada.[9] His "Notes on the cardinal principles of constitutional science" was intended to help law students understand and formulate constitutional projects.[10] For Samper, constitutional science had all the makings of an exact science for it offered a clear way for jurists to devise a logical framework of experimental truths regarding political organization that was based on concrete observations and on the deductive reasoning that came from them. The observational realm of constitutional science included all factors that influenced human organization, from the ways humans responded to governing laws and customs to the conditions of climate that shaped daily life.

Samper's entire science of constitutionalism rested on one essential universal principle: sovereignty resides in the people. Samper matter-of-factly reminded readers that there were limitations on how such sovereignty could be expressed in society. "Sovereignty *resides in all* because all are members of society; but only those society allows to exercise sovereignty do so. This is a matter of convenience because, just as the common interest is superior to individual interest, so too are social rights superior to individual rights."[11] Therefore, argued Samper, in order for suffrage to be truly universal, it could only be granted to those of a certain age who (unlike infants, women, criminals, or the mentally disabled) did not suffer from what he considered to be an objectively moral incapacity to conveniently exercise it. With these caveats in mind, constitutional science concerned itself only with those governmental forms that expressed sovereignty as residing in the people. "Any despotic or arbitrary Government," explained Samper, "falls outside constitutional science's sphere of action."[12]

Samper offered his readers a historical genealogy for constitutional science rooted in Christianity. He posited that, despite the existence of republics in antiquity, true constitutional science began the moment Christ proclaimed liberty, equality, and the sovereignty of people by rendering unto Caesar the things that were Caesar's.[13] Samper legitimated liberal democratic constitutional principles by alluding to Christ's teachings so frequently, and so evocatively, that more traditional political players ridiculed him. Most notably, Conservative party leader Mariano Ospina called

Samper and the younger generation of Radical Liberals "Golgotas," an allusion to Golgotha, or Cavalry, the place where Christ died on the cross.[14] The moniker stuck. It quickly expanded to embrace an entire swath of Liberal politicians in ways that eventually muddled the common purpose and origins that elite Liberals shared with fellow elite Conservatives from one generation to the next.

The radicalism of Samper's democratic ideals went beyond allusions to Christ, however. Although he acknowledged the role eighteenth-century French and German philosophers played in preparing the spirit of the people to triumph over absolutism, progress was most quickly made in the New World. Despite Old World developments, it was in the new American continent where "the science of constitutionalism, as with all other forms of knowledge, has made faster progress."[15] With these words, the young Samper placed Spanish America on the vanguard of the Atlantic World.[16] The legitimating effect that the negative legacy of Spanish colonialism had on Spanish American republicanism nevertheless drove Samper to silence the rich constitutional heritage from the colonial and early independence periods.[17] Samper instead decried the retrograde monarchical institutions that colonized Spanish America, arguing they gave too much power to church clergy and mired the early post-independence republics in a culture of militarism. Samper explained how, unlike the more enlightened English traditions that colonized North America, which had led to advances in constitutional principles, Spanish colonialism had limited the advancement of constitutional science. The forty-odd years since independence, however, had brought welcome and radical change. Samper proudly announced how "experience has given hard lessons to South American States and already the principles [of constitutional science] are invigorated and are consolidating towards definitively founding the liberties and rights of man."[18]

After defining the science of constitutionalism and its historical roots, Samper schooled his readers on concrete constitutional principles. In doing so, he critiqued existing tenets of New Granada's 1843 Constitution, while also targeting the deficiencies of republican constitutions in other parts of the world. For instance, since sovereignty resided in the will of the people, argued Samper, direct popular elections needed to be the primary way a nation decided what person would occupy which government post at every level. When popular elections did not directly appoint government representatives, then democratic governance was completely distorted.[19] Each branch of government needed to be completely independent of the others to ensure proper balance of power. Samper's observations pinpointed several examples demonstrating how New Granada's 1843 Constitution needed to be reformed, that is, if the principle of popular sovereignty was to be honored.[20] One of Samper's most significant critiques involved the territoriality of political representation and sovereignty. Samper argued direct, popular elections were the only way to consecrate sovereignty. This principle was degraded when suffrage depended on territorial divisions because territory became more politically significant than population.[21] Take, for instance, how a province large in size, yet small in population, such as Casanare, had the same political voice in determining who would be president, or a member of Congress, as a much more populated province such as Bogotá. If, indeed, the majority were to rule, a more populated province needed to have a larger representation in the national Congress than the smaller ones. Samper also recognized that government worked best when municipal power worked independently from the national government. The principle of federalism nevertheless meant municipalities could not act in contravention to the national constitution.[22] In short, for Samper, sovereignty emanated from individuals, not municipal or provincial governments, and those individuals belonged to a nation that could hold municipal and provincial governments in check. Samper's proposed reforms were so transformative that, if put into effect, New Granada would have been the most democratic republic existing on the planet.

Samper's words clearly had an impact. By 1853 the New Granada Congress had passed a new national constitution, and the popular Liberal incoming president, José María Obando, approved it. As we will see, that constitution adopts several of the core principles espoused by Samper in his "Notes." Samper had dedicated his notes on constitutional science to the Colegio de San Bartolomé, the place where he taught the science of constitutionalism. We therefore would expect that the young, budding liberal politicians and thinkers graduating from the school and whose constitutional fever ran high, were the primary avid readers of Samper's notes, and likely made up the core of the Congress that passed the new constitution. The 1853 Congress that introduced the new radical constitutional measure did include two graduates from the Colegio de San Bartolomé, Próspero Pereira Gamba and Januario Salgar.[23] The dominant number of representatives participating in the 1853 Congress was, nevertheless, Conservative.[24] Notably, several of the 1853 congressional representatives that passed the supposedly "radical" constitution had also formed part of the Instituto Caldas.

The signature page on the 1853 Constitution reveals that at least twenty-six members of the 1853 Congress, or about a third, had formed part of the cross-party, pan-regional elite group of Liberals and Conservatives that signed up for the Instituto Caldas under President Mosquera's administration between 1847 and 1849.[25] The Constitution of 1853 upheld the abolition of slavery and introduced universal manhood suffrage. These ideals were fully embraced by the same moderate, bipartisan constituency that had promoted the Instituto Caldas and the Chorographic Commission. These men had won congressional seats during a period when constitutional proposals abounded, including the draft for New Granada's 1853 Constitution. They shared the kind of constitutional thinking promoted by their fellow Instituto Caldas member from Mariquita, José María Samper. And yet, although their political leanings crossed the political party spectrum, historiography has painted the 1853 Congress as primarily "Golgota." Doing so erases the cross-party support and negotiations that went into the text of New Granada's 1853 Constitution. Both Conservative and Liberal elites, not just the "Golgotas," understood individual sovereignty and political rights similarly in 1853. The text of the constitution passed that year, seen in the context of the cross-party coalition that was the Instituto Caldas, helps us better understand both the constitution itself and the conflict that exploded a year after it was passed.

The most important change in the 1853 Constitution was that it made suffrage available to all adult male citizens, and their vote would directly count toward the election of the national president, members of Congress, the Supreme Court, and provincial governors and representatives. These male citizens included the individuals recently freed from slavery when the 1851 law took effect on January 1, 1852.[26] Universal manhood suffrage also determined the composition of provincial legislatures. Some national government checks on municipal government were put in place. For instance, the president could fire an elected provincial governor for cause. But as long as provincial constitutions did not contradict the national constitution, they could write their own legislative code. The republic also guaranteed a series of individual rights including the right to property, security, free expression of ideas, unarmed assembly, a jury trial, and freedom of worship.

The result was that New Granada's 1853 Constitution was among the most democratic charters existing on the planet. New Granada legislators expected their Spanish American neighbors to join them. The final article provided the mechanisms that would facilitate a reestablishment of the Colombian Union under a federal system that would bring New Granada together with Ecuador and Venezuela again. This stipulation in part suggests an elite convergence on transformative legislative initiatives toward republicanism for the former Gran Colombian republics. These initiatives included, most notably, the abolition of slavery. Venezuela and Ecuador both decreed the abolition of slavery by 1854.[27] Venezuela also adopted unrestricted universal manhood suffrage, at least for president and Congress in 1858.[28] Ecuador expanded suffrage in 1861 but insisted on a literacy requirement.[29]

Beyond inspiring converging democratic republican ripple effects among its immediate neighbors, New Granada's Constitution of 1853 also unleashed a wave of constitution writing within the republic unseen in the region since the period of independence. The thirty-six provinces existing in New Granada in 1853 each promulgated their own constitutions. By one historian's count, these documents totaled over sixty municipal constitutions in only three years.[30] That staggering number only takes into account constitutions that specific provinces adopted and amended. Judging by the dozens of national constitutional projects for New Granada that were drafted (but not adopted) between 1849 and 1853, the number of municipal constitutional projects was even higher.[31]

Samper's "Notes" identified a political, social, and scientific need in New Granada.[32] Elite government officials, lawyers, and intellectuals craved a systematic scientific approach to writing constitutions for a democratic republic. Samper's science of constitutionalism offered useful principles to republican constitution writers. And yet, despite this common constitutional ground, legislation passed by the 1853 Congress came to be the source of deep, divisive, and violent conflict, culminating in the Civil War of 1854.

Popular Mobilization and the Civil War of 1854

Traditional historiography has overwhelmingly treated the 1854 Civil War as a minor, urban-based military coup launched by one of Obando's underlings, José María Melo. Uribe de Hincapié and Lopez Lopera have offered a welcome corrective, demonstrating how this conflict was by all means a civil war, one that pitted popular sectors against elites in a way that had been truly revolutionary.[33] To contextualize the scope of the conflict for New Granada, consider how the War of the Supremes (1839–1842) encompassed thirteen battles in eight provinces. The 1851 Civil War, for its part, endured six battles in as many provinces. The Civil War of 1854, although short-lived, was intense: over forty-five battles were fought in eleven different provinces, and half of those battles occurred outside of Bogotá. The first step toward better understanding the conflict of 1854 therefore requires that we categorize it as a major civil war for New Granada, not just a one-off urban coup.[34] Contradictory alliances emerged, broke, and realigned during the lead up, explosion, and resolution of the 1854 Civil War. These patterns can still be as dizzyingly confusing now as they were then. This section takes another step toward better understanding this conflict by considering the social spaces that facilitated the formation of surprising alliances among political actors usually thought to be in direct opposition to each other.

One way to begin to clarify the complex patterns of alliance formation is to parse out class cleavages from political party divisions. The Constitution of 1853 laid bare growing class tensions among national leaders, especially those who belonged to the Liberal Party. In part this was due to the wholly new political strategies that needed to be adopted in the wake of the new constitution. As these intra-party tensions grew, Liberal elites sought out cross-party spaces of sociability that had their origins in the Instituto Caldas, the Chorographic Commission, and the halls of Congress. This cross-party coalition of elites attempted to assert control over popular sectors. Before coalition building, Liberal Party elites first tried to rein in the popular Liberal Sociedades Democráticas, or Democratic Societies, which supported President Obando. The problem was that the 1853 Congress, filled with Liberal and Conservative elites, passed legislation that directly and negatively affected artisans and lower-ranking military men. These attacks on popular sectors met significant resistance, and elite Liberal attempts to control the Sociedades Democráticas in ways that mirrored the Instituto Caldas's ways of functioning failed.

On April 17, 1854, José María Melo, one of the men appointed to lead efforts to control the Sociedades Democráticas, broke ranks and built on existing tensions within the Liberal Party to launch a coup in Bogotá that closed the halls of Congress. He tried transferring power to Obando and called for a new constitutional convention. Obando refused. Melo made himself president and pushed for constitutional reform to protect popular Liberal interests. Warfare ensued. Despite popular forces favoring the coup, military advantage lay with the self-proclaimed "constitutionalists," or the Liberal and Conservative coalition of elites opposed to Melo. Many members of the constitutionalist forces had either formed part of the Instituto Caldas in 1848 or had served in Congress in 1853, or both. This cross-party elite coalition counted on the military expertise of former president Tomás Cipriano de Mosquera and the kind of territorial knowledge his troops had accessed via the Chorographic Commission's members. Rather than trusting popular sectors, these traditional elite leaders placed their faith wholeheartedly in science and geography. In their minds the uneducated, illiterate popular forces supporting Melo threatened to undermine the republican political project on which these elites had worked for decades. It is to the unfolding of this complex conflict, its constitutional implications, and the historiographical misunderstandings it engendered that we now turn.

Historians of Colombia, taking note of growing tensions within the Liberal Party, have insisted that Obando openly resisted the 1853 charter.[35] They have pointed to Obando's inaugural presidential address, one that supposedly railed against key constitutional principles including federalism, the popular election of governors, or allowing provinces to write their own constitutions. While contemporary audiences, most notably historian José Manuel Restrepo, may have interpreted Obando in this way, the specific words President Obando articulated were strategically delivered. They did not openly challenge the tenets of the constitution or the constitution's writers. Nowhere in his inaugural address did Obando denounce the popular election of governors. On the contrary, he celebrated the constitution precisely because of universal manhood suffrage. Obando even nodded to José María Samper, openly praising the constitution, and its writers, for the practical and beneficial contribution that the document would make to Grenadians in particular and to the general "enrichment of constitutional science" more globally.[36]

Obando nevertheless did oppose absolute federalism. But so did the 1853 charter, as did José María Samper in 1852. Absolute federalism worked against universal manhood suffrage and the principles of individual sovereignty enshrined in the Constitution of 1853. Obando's words were emphatic: "The constitutional reform that will soon be our sacred code, object of our veneration, of our enthusiastic love, and of our decided support will prove to the world that absolute federated forms are not the essence of proper popular government."[37] Obando celebrated how the charter put universal manhood suffrage, and through it, individual sovereignty, over and above any other form of sovereignty, including the sovereignty of provinces or municipalities. Although tensions clearly existed between Congress and Obando, the president-elect supported constitutional order, as did Congress. One problem was that the new constitution, precisely because it embraced universal manhood suffrage, had transformed political calculations. To win elections, political party leaders had no choice but to mobilize popular sectors. Neither President Obando nor congressional leaders in 1853 foresaw just how far out of elite control popular political mobilization had moved.

A case in point: the Liberal Democratic Societies that had done so much to rally popular political support around Obando. The Liberal Democratic Societies and the Instituto Caldas had much in common. Both organizations were originally intended to help New Granada strengthen republicanism and democracy in ways that would decisively break with the colonial past.[38] As such, both societies were originally founded and led by elites, with their founding chapters launched from Bogotá in 1847 under the Mosquera administration. Provincial chapters of both societies also quickly emerged throughout New Granada. Unlike the Instituto Caldas, however, the Democratic Societies, which first emerged around the push to elect José Hilario López, were primarily organized to foment popular mobilization exclusively in favor of the emerging Liberal political party. Liberals led the way in creating these new spaces of sociability that fomented political socialization, yet Conservatives were not far behind. They too founded new societies, such as the Society for Popular Instruction and Christian Fraternity. As it turned out, the Conservative Party was even more adept than the Liberals in ably building on an already existing network of Catholic brotherhoods to boost Conservative victories in electoral polls.[39] Elections on the eve of the approval of the 1853 charter nevertheless meant that municipal bodies, rather than individuals, played an outsized role in determining the outcomes of elections. Obando's victory in 1853 defeated Conservative candidates. The problem was that Obando also defeated the candidates that elite Liberals preferred. Elite Liberals and Conservatives both were less than enthusiastic about Obando's victory, and these tensions were most clearly felt in Bogotá.

Obando's election in 1853 and the constitutional and legislative changes that ensued after his election brought class frictions to the foreground in Bogotá. The halls of Congress came to witness outright fights between elites and popular sectors. When a proposal to raise tariffs on imported textiles came under discussion in Congress in 1853, tensions ran high. Elite Liberals had long promised popular artisans that such protections would be put in place in order to mobilize voter turnout through the Democratic Societies.[40] Popular artisans, distrusting legislators, increased pressure on the representatives they voted into office by occupying the public arenas of Congress, as well as its neighboring streets. They chanted threats. When the desired protections on New Granada textiles failed to pass, elite legislators and popular artisans came to blows. Several people were hurt, and at least one artisan was killed in the scuffle.[41] Members of Congress blamed Obando and his second in command, Melo, for not acting against the popular artisans sooner, especially since the army barracks were so near to the uprising.

Class distinctions colored subsequent scuffles that ensued in Bogotá, and wardrobe and urban space mattered. Ruana-wearing men from the popular classes, also called "nieblunos" for the barrio of Las Nieves that Obando, Melo, and their followers inhabited, faced off against frock-coated elites in the streets of Bogotá. Festivals and public events provided the most tempting opportunities to engage in these fights. The "Corpus Christi" celebration, so much the subject of ethnographies by Liberal and Conservative elites, turned violent in Bogotá in 1853 as young, frock-coated youths attacked the popular procession. Artisans and other popular sectors responded blow by blow, launching an attack in the Rosa Blanca, a tavern frequented by young elites. Liberal elite leaders, notably Florentino González himself, were targeted. Former Instituto Caldas member José Manuel Restrepo later recalled how these attacks by popular sectors revealed that "it is very dangerous to declare sovereign an ignorant pueblo and to disseminate those ultrademocratic and socialist ideas among them."[42] These violent urban skirmishes convinced elites, Liberal and Conservative, that popular sectors were, indeed, out of control. Order was needed, but Obando, widely supported by popular sectors, and General Melo, who was next in command for ensuring order in the city and the nation, seemed to be on the side of the uneducated masses rather than on the side of governing elites.

In the midst of these conflicts, the split that had emerged within the Liberal Party had grown into a chasm. And yet, this split did not mean all Liberal elites opposed Obando and Melo. Some older elite Liberal leaders, especially Instituto Caldas member Lorenzo María Lleras, understood that universal manhood suffrage would ensure the Conservative Party's return to power at the local and national levels. In Bogotá this more resistant faction of traditional Liberal elites allied with disgruntled artisans and members of the military that stood to lose their jobs. This motley crew became the core of the so-called Draconianos. Given divergent interests, this political movement was riddled with internal tensions. A shared fear nevertheless brought them together: the 1853 Constitution guaranteeing universal manhood suffrage would bring Conservatives overwhelmingly to provincial and national government posts, threatening Liberal Party control. Their political calculations were correct.

September 1853 brought the first batch of results from elections conducted under universal manhood suffrage. An overwhelming number of Conservatives opposed to Obando's presidency, as well as some Liberals (many of whom also opposed Obando), were elected to provincial governors' offices, provincial assemblies, congressional seats, and Supreme Court positions.[43] Legitimate suspicions of fraud fueled inter- and intra-party tensions. In the neighboring province of Zipaquirá, for instance, the elected Liberal governor, Felipe Pérez, was formally accused of having falsified the electoral registers of the canton of La Palma. At nineteen, Pérez was Zipaquirá's youngest elected governor. The connections to influential Liberal elites that the young Felipe enjoyed were remarkable. His brother, Santiago Pérez, had been chosen to replace Manuel Ancízar as the Chorographic Commission's secretary in 1853, and both men had been students of Lorenzo María Lleras. Felipe Pérez would form a lasting bond with Lleras, marrying his daughter. Before becoming the governor of Zipaquirá, Felipe Pérez worked closely with Manuel Ancízar in 1852, not as a member of the Chorographic Commission, but rather as Ancízar's assistant to New Granada's diplomatic mission to Ecuador.[44] Felipe Pérez's ties to these influential figures and his own political trajectory would eventually bring him into the folds of the Chorographic Commission after Agustin Codazzi died in 1859. In 1853, however, the town of La Palma, which counted only a thousand inhabitants, had miraculously cast nine hundred votes in Pérez's favor.[45] Fraudulent elections that brought well-connected Liberal elites like Pérez to political posts had the effect of disenfranchising popular votes, and popular Democratic Societies, despite their supposed Liberal Party affiliation, mobilized protests against them.[46]

By January 1854, in the wake of popular Liberal protests to fraudulent local elections, a coalition of elite Liberals tried to produce a new national directorship for New Granada Democratic Societies. The plan was to create in Bogotá a Central Directive Junta that could bring back the "harmony and unity of action among all the grenadines who belong to the great liberal party, [and] communicate with all the Democratic Societies or Juntas [that the Directive Junta] believe[s] convenient for sustaining democratic institutions."[47] Elite Liberal leaders in Bogotá thought this coordinating body for the Democratic Societies would work much like what was intended for the founding Bogotá chapter of the Instituto Caldas a few years prior. One reason why this national coordination plan for the Democratic Societies resembled the Instituto Caldas so closely was because several members had themselves been members of either the Instituto Caldas or the Chorographic Commission that had emerged from it. Instituto Caldas veterans elected to the junta in January 1854 included Lorenzo María Lleras and Vicente Lombana. The two young brothers, Felipe Pérez and Santiago Pérez, also were elected. This tight-knit, like-minded group sought to impose an elite-led order over the widely dispersed and diverse 114 Democratic Societies that had cropped up in New Granada since 1847. Notably, General José María Melo, the man who would launch the coup against Congress soon thereafter, also formed part of this group.[48]

The stated cause that brought these men together to unite in leadership for the Democratic Societies was the electoral "triumph obtained through trickery and undignified maneuvers" by the Conservatives.[49] The fact that junta member and Zipaquirá governor Felipe Pérez was himself the subject of investigations regarding fraud in Zipaquirá fell by the wayside. These Liberals came together to argue that the Conservative Party only offered an "ultramontane reaction against democratic institutions ... [and their] ... proscriptions, the death penalty, and persecutions to perpetuate itself in power [allowed them to establish] a Government in which the rulers are everything and the pueblo nothing."[50] The rhetorical focus of the Liberal party became the need for a unified defense across provinces and classes against the colonial legacy, one embodied by the opposing political party, the Conservatives.

General José María Melo went further and took the call to unite against the Conservative Party to the battlefield. He rallied popular sectors of the military and artisans in Bogotá to force Congress to close. He issued a call to convoke a new constitutional convention that would, in part, roll back the universal manhood suffrage of the 1853 Constitution that had brought so many Conservatives to power. Melo then tried to turn the presidency over to the elected Liberal Party president, José María Obando, but Obando refused. These moves pointed to how Melo himself tried to enact measures that could be interpreted as constitutionally sound while also riding the support of a motley Liberal coalition for a military victory that could wrest control over Congress from elite Liberals and Conservatives. Melo's coalition placed the interests of popular members of the military and New Granada artisans at the front and center of his coup. Melo's ability to rally popular support in this way hurt efforts by elite members of the Liberal Party who wished to reduce the military and reduce tariffs on foreign textiles. Despite their best efforts to keep popular sectors under coordinated control from Bogotá, elite Liberals and Conservatives had lost control of popular sectors and popular mobilization. This was true not only within the city of Bogotá, but throughout New Granada. About half of the military action of the 1854 Civil War was concentrated in the capital city and in surrounding province of Bogotá, but other provinces, including Popayán, Soccorro, Tunja, Pamplona, Cauca, Buenaventura, Santa Marta, Tequendama, and Zipaquirá, also saw significant bloodshed on their battlefields.[51]

The artisan-military revolution of 1854 started as a war for the more effective inclusion of popular sectors in public life, and it morphed into a war for the restoration of institutional order led by the intellectual and scientific elite.[52] Melo launched the coup believing he could maintain continuous military and economic support from northeast artisans. The northeast region was historically the major center of rural artisan production of textiles and tobacco, as illustrated by the Chorographic Commission's lithographs and written accounts. Democratic Societies were also active in this region—so much so that some members of the Instituto Caldas in that region had also been members of the provincial Democratic Societies that effusively supported Obando.[53] Members of these overlapping political societies in the northeast were aware of how economic trade policies determined in Bogotá could negatively affect their interests, and they made their opinions known through social networks and the printing press.[54] Although many northeast artisans mobilized in support of the uprising, many others were distraught at the chaos unleashed by the coup. Elites in the northeast and in Bogotá believed that the best way to restore institutional order was by wresting the political and military power that popular sectors had gained. Elite Conservatives and Liberals had a distinct advantage over popular sectors: intimate geographic knowledge of key transportation networks from and to Bogotá. This was primarily because of the Chorographic Commission under the leadership of Agustín Codazzi.

Codazzi was fully aware of the instability in Bogotá and the support the northeast provinces could lend Melo's coup. Codazzi himself had suffered due to the disruptions. The Colegio Militar and the Astronomical Observatory in Bogotá, the places he conducted much of the assembly of the geographic data he gathered, came under siege late in 1853. The Chorographic Commission's laboratory and information assembly site was disrupted. Codazzi's home became a temporary laboratory. Given these extenuating circumstances, Codazzi agreed to join General Tomás Cipriano de Mosquera's war effort against the Melista forces in Pamplona, Ocaña, Santander, Socorro, Velez, and Soto. Codazzi's deep knowledge of these provinces from 1850 to 1852 proved critical for the success of Mosquera's military strategies. Botanist José Jerónimo Triana and Manuel María Paz, also members of the commission, joined Codazzi and Mosquera.[55] Armed with maps, situated knowledge, and portable bridges, Codazzi secured key river crossings for Mosquera's troops.

On December 4, 1854, Mosquera's *ejercito del norte,* which included Codazzi, outflanked the Melista forces. After cutting off reinforcements that could arrive in Bogotá from the north, Mosquera's army triumphantly marched into Bogotá, deposing Melo before he could convoke a new constitutional convention.[56] By then several elites formally associated with provincial chapters of the Instituto Caldas, many of whom had opposed each other during the war of 1851, joined forces against Melo. These men came together against what they denounced as an unconstitutional military coup. Consider how in Mariquita, for instance, Mateo Viana, one of the Conservative leaders of the 1851 rebellion from Honda against the Liberal José Hilario López regime, joined forces with young Honda Liberal Golgota leader José María Samper to defeat the Melistas. Both men had belonged to the Mariquita chapter of the Instituto Caldas.[57] The decisive defeat of popular sectors in 1854 allowed the cross-party, pan-regional coalition of elites who had originally come together in 1847 through the Instituto Caldas, but who had fought each other in 1851, to find common ground once again.

Liberal and Conservative elites later came to explain the 1854 Civil War as an uprising generated by the unfortunate continuation of the "colonial mentality" that bellicose artisans and popular military sectors suffered. The new elite republican mission was clear: the dangerous political openings created through popular political mobilization since 1849 needed to be rolled back, but in a way that met the political calculations of Liberal and Conservative Party leaders. It is to this transformative constitutional-territorial effort, one spearheaded by members of the Instituto Caldas and the Chorographic Commission, that we now turn.

Geopolitical Suppression of Universal Manhood Suffrage

As the dust settled from the Civil War of 1854, the "defenders" of constitutionalism returned from exile in Ibague to the congressional halls of Bogotá. Their first order of business: addressing the dramatic disorder that had nearly torn the republic apart in

1854. They also had to adjust to new political calculations. Liberal Party elites had expanded their presence in Congress and the presidency during 1849–1853 by carving out Liberal-friendly provinces. After universal manhood suffrage passed in 1853, provincial votes mattered less than individual votes by citizens, and the Conservative Party regained political strength. This strength was further evidenced by the fact that the first presidential elections under the new constitution occurred in 1856, and Conservative Party founder (and former Instituto Caldas member) Mariano Ospina Rodríguez was elected to presidential office via universal manhood suffrage. Conservatives clearly benefited from the popular political opening offered by the 1853 Constitution. Yet elite Conservatives were deeply concerned by the disorder and violence unleashed through popular mobilization that culminated in the 1854 Civil War.

During the decade following the 1854 Civil War, elite party leaders wrangled in the halls of Congress and on the battlefield to sort out how sovereignty and political power would balance out. They employed the science of constitutionalism, the science of geography, and strategic political calculations in their efforts. The most contentious arena became the process of shifting sovereignty from individual citizens to large territorial states. The thirty-six provinces of New Granada, each of which was constitutionally required to guarantee universal manhood suffrage in 1853, were stitched together into larger states from 1855 through 1858. The state of Panama was first, having been created through a constitutional amendment on February 27, 1855. This act set the precedent for other provinces to do the same. Liberal elites initially proposed these measures in Congress, and Conservatives, who held a congressional majority as well as the presidency, approved. These transformations brought forth a new national state, the Confederacion Granadina, or Grenadine Confederacy in 1858. During 1855–1858 elite Liberals and Conservatives marshaled in their expertise, political capital, and family kinship networks toward reshaping New Granada territorially and constitutionally. Their goal was to save the republic from itself. That is, they needed to recognize the value of democratic republicanism while at the same time rolling back the political power that popular sectors could enact on the state through elections or warfare.

Manuel Ancízar, whose ethnographic work for the Chorographic Commission is discussed in chapter 4, and José María Samper, whose expertise in the science of constitutionalism is discussed above, were the leading Liberal figures in these midcentury territorial and constitutional changes. They joined another Instituto Caldas member and Panamanian native son, Justo Arosemena, for this work. From 1855 through 1858 these men worked through Congress to stitch together larger states from smaller provinces. Their efforts culminated in the eight New Granada states that Samper etched out for national and international audiences on the copper plates originally designed in 1847 by his father-in-law, Joaquin Acosta. The goal became maintaining the kind of republic that elites had long had in mind, saving it from the worst excesses of the colonial legacy, that is, the excesses of universal manhood suffrage. The trigger for the distinct constitutional-territorial transformation launched by these men was the 1854 Civil War, but these constitutional changes also had geopolitically inspired roots.

Consider, for instance, the kind of constitutional influences Ancízar was exposed to on the eve of his partnership with Samper and Arosemena. During the buildup to and explosion of the 1854 Civil War, Manuel Ancízar was away from New Granada on a diplomatic mission. Ancízar had no desire to leave his work for the Chorographic Commission or his friend Codazzi, yet he nevertheless agreed to go.[58] As Loaiza Cano has argued, Ancízar likely was chosen for the diplomatic post not just because of his ample international experience and intellect, but also because of the expansive transnational social capital he had acquired as a founding member of the Star of Tequendama Masonic Lodge.[59] Ancízar's connection to the overarching American organization of the Masons facilitated his ability to identify scientists, geographers, and architects in Venezuela who subsequently arrived to work in New Granada under Mosquera late in the 1840s. Ancízar built on his Masonic connections during his diplomatic mission from 1852 to 1855. The original intended geopolitical impact of Ancízar's mission was to strengthen New Granada's relations with Great Britain. Most immediately Ancízar need to convince Peru to join with New Granada to pay off British loans that had helped finance the independence wars. Ancízar also needed to rescue hundreds of New Granada families who had been sold into slavery in Peru, in contravention to the spirit of abolition treaties signed by New Granada and Peru with Great Britain.[60] In practice Ancízar's mission came to encompass much more than New Granada relations with Peru to placate British allies. The "Pan-American" friendships Ancízar cultivated shed light on the kind of constitutional and political efforts in which he engaged after his return to New Granada in 1855.

From 1852 to 1855, Ancízar worked with several like-minded elite South American political players seeking to lay the foundations for an overarching federalized union of Spanish American republics. His diplomatic work took him from New Granada to Ecuador, then to Peru and Chile, and back. Ancízar came to understand the urgency of expanding republicanism on the continent by ensuring the end of slavery and weakening what he saw to be a powerful, and powerfully corrupt, clergy.[61] Ancízar expanded his view to include economic and political integration of the region in ways that could foment a radical republican project for the entire continent, one that not only would ameliorate New Granada's relations with Great Britain, but that would strengthen the region's global position overall, especially given recent territorial incursions by the United States in Mexico, and growing filibustering activities by U.S. nationals in Spanish America. Ancízar went directly to Chile from Ecuador to test out his ideas. Ancízar read and befriended Chilean radical liberals such as Francisco Bilbao, whose speech in Paris in 1856 that offered a tentative outline for a federal Latin American Congress of Republics and was among the first public statements to coin the term "latinoamerica."[62] Domingo Faustino Sarmiento and Ancízar also established a friendship in Chile, one founded upon a continental project to create an American library in South America. The cosmopolitan Andres Bello, originally from Venezuela, but who had a deep impact on Chilean politics and society, also became a close confidant of Ancízar. Bello helped Ancízar navigate Chile's rough political waters, as he also shared with Ancízar his writings, most notably his *Codigo Civil*.[63] This text, together with Ancízar's hemi-spheric experiences, would come to shape how Ancízar thought constitutionally upon his return to New Granada.

Ancízar's diplomatic travels allowed him to think continentally and geopolitically. By 1855 Ancízar realized the urgency with which sister republics in South America needed to come together to foment circulation and commerce with each other, not just within. As diplomat for New Granada, Ancízar proposed open navigation on the Amazon and called for similar measures for other major water transit routes. Free circulation among the different repub-lics would lead to prosperity for all. "These are neither fantasies nor exaggerations of the imagination," argued Ancízar. "They are the mere provisions of what will happen, that is, if we manage to escape the tiny circles of toxic politics, and finally occupy ourselves with laying down the bases for a grand and fertile Pan-American system."[64] This range of strategic mid-nineteenth-century "Pan-American" thinking informed Ancízar's diplomacy, not just with respect to New Granada's neighbors, but also in terms of the region's complicated relationship with the United States.

Ancízar's diplomacy could not lose sight of the fact that the Panama Railroad, funded by a private U.S. firm, had laid down its final rail in January 1855. The technological achievement occurred on New Granada soil, but through private capital and know-how from the United States. The railroad's inauguration occurred only weeks after New Granada's 1854 Civil War had been settled in favor of the Constitutionalists. As the young Manuel Peña had so cleverly conveyed in the imaginary landscape he drew as a Colegio Militar student, this situation had dire territorial conse-quences. Ancízar understood U.S.-based *filibusteros*, looking to assert complete control over a transit route connecting the Atlan-tic with the Pacific, eyed the railroad, and New Granada's unstable political situation, with interest. The 1854 Civil War threatened to undo even the little national control that local populations could extract from the railroad company. It was in the crossroads of post–civil war instability and geopolitical significance of the rail-road crossing the Isthmus that Panamanian representatives effec-tively convinced New Granada's Congress on February 27, 1855, to formally create the sovereign state of Panama out of the four isthmian provinces of Chiriqui, Veraguas, Panama, and Azuero.[65] Sovereignty would no longer be rooted in individuals; sovereign states would, in effect, come to overrule universal manhood suffrage. This would bring peace and attract foreign investment as well as aid the process of building coalitions with other Spanish American republics in the region.

With this geopolitical framework in mind, Ancízar finished his diplomatic work and left Lima on July 5, 1855, traveling to Bogotá via Panama. His passage through Panama allowed him to meet with the president of Panama's Constitutional Assembly, Mariano Arosemena. Ancízar learned the nuts and bolts of Panama's new state constitution from Arosemena. Impressed by Ancízar's own experience and potential influence back in Bogotá, Arosemena called on Ancízar to see through Panamanian interests in the New Granada Congress. "We trust that yourself, Samper, and Justo [Arosemena, Mariano's son] will be the three columns of the state [of Panama] in Congress. We need something from the railroad, even if it isn't everything."[66] Ancízar arrived in Bogotá on September 12, 1855. This was only days after the king of the filibusteros, William Walker, had scored military victories against the Nicaraguan national army. The fact that U.S. president Franklin Pierce recognized Walker's new regime in Nicaragua by May 1856 outraged Spanish American jurists, diplomats, and journalists.[67] Time was of the essence, and Ancízar knew he could not return to his beloved Chorographic Commission. Instead, he assumed a seat in Congress as a representative for Panama. The constitutional scientist and geographer José María Samper (whom Mariano Arosemena referenced in his letter) was at Ancízar's side. Neither had been popularly elected to Congress from Panama. Panama's State Assembly had instead directly appointed both men as congressional representatives. Geopolitical positioning with respect to the United States and Spanish America was too urgent to wait for universal manhood suffrage to come around to recognize Panamanian needs as national needs.

José María Samper's memoirs recalling his work for Panama in Congress during 1856–1857 mark a decisive shift in how Samper understood the fundamental principles of representative democracy as compared to his writings from 1852.[68] In the wake of the Civil War of 1854, universal manhood suffrage no longer served as the foundations of New Granada republicanism for Samper. As an able jurist, Samper shifted the balance of sovereignty from individuals toward territorial units, but carefully so. The first way we can detect Samper's shifting sovereignty balancing act is by contemplating the fact that he accepted the position of representative to Congress from Panama along with Ancízar, even though neither man was elected through universal manhood suffrage. Samper admitted in his memoirs how he was "totally unknown in Panama," having never set foot in that province.[69] The popular vote in Panama did not grant Samper's mandate as a congressional representative; it was the state government of Panama that did so. Just how Samper or Ancízar could divine the state's wants and desires without having run for office was easy: they only had to listen to the State Assembly president, Mariano Arosemena, with whom they had a close working relationship. By 1855 Samper's seat in Congress depended on a state government legislature controlled by a small number of select elite families, rather than majority rule through popular suffrage.

Samper may have self-servingly shifted away from his 1852 principle of individual sovereignty as expressed through popular suffrage, but as a jurist, he struck a careful balance when it came time to explain how sovereignty needed to work within a federated republic. After 1854 Samper declared himself a federalist, but he made an important distinction between different kinds of federalisms. Samper's preferred form of federalism held the nation as sovereign. That is, the weight of sovereignty no longer was born by individual citizens but rather by *one single pueblo comprised of the totality of the neo-grenadines, with the same rights and responsibilities within one common territory, and, as such, comprised one single sovereign nation.*[70] Samper's emphatic championing of the unified nation as sovereign made his brand of federalism one that rendered sovereignty indivisible. Sovereignty was derived from all the people of New Granada. This formula, argued Samper, would best allow New Granada to move even closer to the vanguard of democratic republicanism in the Atlantic world. Samper argued that his form of federalism stood in stark contrast to the kind of federalism called for by men such as Tomás Cipriano de Mosquera in 1860, in the midst of a civil war. Mosquera's brand of federalism was dangerous, argued Samper, for it placed the sovereignty of states over and above that of the national government. Despite Samper's best argumentative efforts, the sovereignty of states would eventually triumph over national and individual sovereignty.

In part this change came from elite consensus. Consider how, despite his effort to distinguish himself as different from Mosquera, Samper's preferred form of federalism required much larger states rather than the thirty-six small provinces that had existed in 1853. In this sense Samper's view on territorial divisions did not differ much from the kind of administrative organization of the national state that Tomás Cipriano de Mosquera proposed.[71] The thirty-six provinces that existed in 1853 were created ostensibly to bring state government closer to the people. Samper explained that the problem with so many provinces under the 1853 Constitution was that the charter had established an amply decentralized economic infrastructure, causing none of the provinces to have enough income for their administrative needs precisely because they were so small. Neither could they finance roadways nor find enough trained personnel to run local government. Samper pointed out that many provincial governments recognized the impotence that came with such small administrative units. Still, the majority of the newly created provincial governments, which had only begun to enjoy a measure of autonomy, were reluctant to be subsumed to the authority of larger neighboring towns. That, explained Samper, was the reason why the new category of state was invented. "Only the creation of federal States, by giving them a more significant political rank, could suppress among [the provinces] local sensibilities and inspire them to conform by sacrificing their rank and category of province."[72] Besides, added Samper, larger states more effectively reflected the overarching connections that made up the "natural" regions of New Granada.

Samper's role in helping establish and legitimate the state of Panama, followed by the state of Antioquia, inspired him to link his science of constitutionalism to his budding interests in the science of geography. In so doing he offered a significant constitutional-territorial contribution, one that worked to naturalize the ways that his midcentury elite cohort, most notably the men who participated in the Chorographic Commission, applied science to continue in the naturalization and racialization of New Granada regions.[73] Much of Samper's later writings, including his memoir, delved into the stark, long-standing differences in geography, culture, race, and temperament that he, his colleagues, and savants from the past, such as Caldas, had identified among New Granada regions.

Samper's writings in the wake of the 1854 Civil War eloquently convey his realization that federated states, rather than sovereign individuals in small provinces, offered a clearer path toward democratic republicanism. Rather than meditating on the significance of popular civil government and majority rule as he had done in 1852, Samper instead turned to how federalism was the most significant dimension of the republican project since the time of independence. According to Samper's narrative, New Granada clearly suffered through several civil wars that put a federalized republican idea to the test. The wars culminated in the happy resolution that was the Constitution of 1853, one that allowed individual provinces to write their own legal charters. The creation of the state of Panama through the constitutional amendment dated February 27, 1855 was simply a culmination of the 1853 charter, not a departure. The civil unrest that exploded in the wake of the passage of the 1853 Constitution went unmentioned. Instead, by Samper's pen, the creation of fewer, larger states starting in 1855 was simply a logical continuation of the 1853 Constitution.

Samper did his best to play down the significance of the 1854 Civil War. This was in part because the dynamic of the conflict, and the decision to shift sovereignty from universal manhood suffrage to states' rights directly challenged claims made by elites like Samper that they had the best interests of popular sectors in mind. Consider, for instance, the continued military dimensions of elite struggles with popular militias after the war. Once the larger states were forged, their forces helped squelch the still significant popular Liberal armies that continued to support Obando and Melo well after the end of the 1854 Civil War. Samper may have remained silent on this fact in 1857, but he did later observe in his memoirs how the creation of the larger states hammered down the nails on the coffin of the older brand of Liberalism.[74] That supposedly "older" brand of Liberalism had been brought to power through the creation of smaller provinces, and universal manhood suffrage began to undermine it. Popular mobilization through voting and war began to tear down dreams of a shared republican project that elites from both major parties had in mind since the 1840s. A new arrangement was needed to save the republic from itself by guaranteeing control to elites.

While Samper tried silencing the 1854 Civil War's significance for the creation of the federalized states, emphasizing instead the natural progression of federalism, Justo Arosemena approached the issue from an opposite direction. Arosemena openly blamed Melo's coup for delaying the creation of the state of Panama. Panama was on the cusp of creation thanks to the provisions granted by the 1853 Constitution, argued Arosemena. His treatise dedicated to legitimizing the creation of the state of Panama, first printed in 1855, offered the clearest argument in this regard. The first paragraph read: "Among the maladies caused by the pernicious uprising of April 17 [1854], we must include the paralyzing of several important legislative projects that were working their way through Congress. One of those projects was the constitutional reform establishing the State of Panama."[75]

Justo Arosemena had joined Samper and hundreds of other budding constitutional scientists in proposing a new constitutional project in 1852. Arosemena's proposal focused on bringing together the four provinces on the isthmus of Panama into one single "federal, sovereign State, but that is not independent from New Granada."[76] The proposed Panamanian state would depend on the New Granada national government for seven discrete items: all matters related to foreign relations; the organization and service of the army and navy; the national post office; the national debt; determining the contribution Panama owed for the national debt; the naturalization of foreigners; and the use of national symbols to represent the nation. On all other matters unrelated to these seven points, the state of Panama would be free to legislate as it saw fit. Arosemena's 1852 proposal also stipulated that all national property on the isthmus would become property of the state of Panama.

Arosemena recognized the boldness of his proposal, but he was confident that the New Granada Congress would consider it. Arosemena offered geographic and patriotic reasons making the four Panamanian provinces into a single Sovereign State loosely dependent of New Granada. Geographic isolation and difficulty with communications between the isthmus and Bogotá offered the most obvious justifications. Beyond this, however, Arosemena pointed out how, despite distances, Panama remained patriotically committed to defending the interests of New Granada. When New Granada called upon Panama to help put down the 1851 Civil War in Antioquia, the Panamanian provinces immediately complied. Had it not been for Panama, Arosemena argued, the government would have lost Antioquia, and perhaps would have suffered the toppling of José Hilario Lopez's regime.[77]

There is historical irony to Arosemena's justifications for his constitutional proposal for Panama given its "patriotism." The trigger for the 1851 Civil War in Antioquia was the national government's decision to carve three smaller provinces out of the larger province. As Arosemena was right to argue, Antioquia's rebellion failed because Panama sent forces to help the national government put down the rebel forces. Panama's contribution needed to be rewarded. The reward Arosemena's proposal sought: bring together Chiriqui, Veraguas, Panama, and Azuero, the four small provinces created under the Lopez regime, to create a single, sovereign state of Panama. Congress denied Arosemena's proposal in 1852.

In 1855 Arosemena did not discuss this denial nor mention historical ironies; he simply tried again. Arosemena contributed to José María Samper's line of argument: federalism was simply the next logical step given the institutional opening created by the 1853 Constitution. And yet the federalism that Samper, Arosemena, and Ancízar had together worked so hard to promote and put into motion was not, by any means, a mere natural progression of the

1853 Constitution. As we will see, allowing for the creation of sovereign states effectively rolled back universal manhood suffrage. Warfare riddled the entire existence of the Grenadine Confederation from 1858 to 1861. The major driving factor behind civil war was outrage at contested elections and accusations of fraud that came with them. As the section below demonstrates, such warfare culminated in each state having the right to develop their own constitution and define citizenship requirements however they saw fit, irrespective of the new national Constitution of 1863.

On the eve of this negotiation among elite party leaders, however, the larger overarching states had to be created. Panama was first in line to receive this concession, and it won sovereignty as a larger state within New Granada, with Panama City as its capital.[78] The driving reason for Panamanian autonomy was rooted in the geopolitical significance of the isthmus for New Granada interests vis-à-vis the United States. Antioquia was not far behind Panama, and it too was erected as a sovereign state out of the smaller divisions that had driven Antioqueños to war in 1851. With these two states created by February 1856, Ancízar and Samper together proposed their version of a new constitution to replace that of 1853, one informed by Andrés Bello.[79] By 1858 congressional representatives, Liberal and Conservative, eventually agreed with Ancízar, Samper, and Arosemena: only a new constitution could bring the emerging, larger states into coordination as a national state that could potentially work in concert with other republics in the region.

The constitution passed in 1858 drew significantly from the project that Samper and Ancízar proposed in 1856.[80] Ancízar and Samper's project included a list of the nine basic rights upon which no state could infringe. The Constitution of 1858 also included a similar listing, expanding the number of inalienable rights to twelve. Both constitutional arrangements maintained and upheld the kind of individual rights enshrined in the 1853 Constitution that had been equally supported by elite Conservatives and Liberals.[81] The Conservative Party still dominated Congress in 1858, and yet they welcomed the changes that Samper and Ancízar, already well-known Liberals, proposed. In part this may have been because the creation of larger states undermined the kind of territorial organization that had given Liberals a major political opening from 1849 to 1853. Within a period of three years, a total of eight states were created, and the 1858 Constitution, drawing on Ancízar's proposals, also allowed for the creation of more states when necessary.[82] Yet by 1859, despite these clear federalizing provisions, the question of sovereignty of the states nevertheless still remained unresolved. Sovereignty would be foregrounded in yet another civil war. It is that war, as seen through the historical narrative of Felipe Pérez, compiler of Chorographic Commission geographic texts, that ends this chapter.

Inventing the Colonial Legacy of the Conservative Party

Felipe Pérez, who had worked closely with Ancízar during his diplomatic mission in South America in 1852, who had served as the youngest elected Zipaquirá governor, and who had also served the Liberal Party on the (failed) Directive Junta for the Sociedades Democraticas in 1854, decided to try his hand at historical writing. He penned an influential historical account of the civil war that had erupted in 1859. That same year, Agustín Codazzi died. His death brought dissemination of the Chorographic Commission's work to a standstill. After toppling President Mariano Ospina from office, General Tomás Cipriano de Mosquera, who had played a key role in launching the commission more than a decade prior, urgently sought a replacement for Codazzi. Felipe Pérez set his sights on assuming that role. Pérez's biting account of the Civil War that exploded in 1859 placed blame squarely on the Conservative Party. Doing so, he hoped, would place him in the good graces of Mosquera.

Felipe Pérez argued that one of the triggers for the 1859 Civil War had been the rampant fraud that had occurred in Santander and Cauca. President Mariano Ospina (a Conservative and founding member of Bogotá chapter of the Instituto Caldas), sent in national troops to ensure proper electoral procedures, bringing on a vicious response from local militias loyal to the Liberal Party. Pérez's historical account framed Mariano Ospina's actions as dangerous legacies from the colonial era because they constituted centralizing moves that attacked federalism and the sovereignty of the states. Pérez's writings demonstrated his unwavering loyalty to Tomás Cipriano de Mosquera, who had led the war against Ospina from Cauca. After toppling Ospina and establishing a new provisional government in Bogotá, Mosquera immediately hired Pérez in 1861 to compile, edit, and publish the geographic information gathered by the Chorographic Commission. Mosquera, who had been behind the inauguration of the commission since his first presidential administration (1845–1849), understood that the work of the commission urgently was needed to naturalize and stabilize the new territorial-constitutional order of the nine sovereign states that had replaced the thirty-six provinces of 1853. Mosquera believed Pérez's loyalty would place a positive spin on the geographic depictions he would produce. Pérez's work for the commission needs to be read in light of his support for Mosquera but, more importantly, in terms of the ways he had denounced the Mariano Ospina regime as a colonial-era holdover because it threatened state sovereignty. Pérez's criticisms of Ospina played a critical role fashioning an eventually triumphant narrative about Liberal federalism over Conservative centralism in ways that construed Conservatives as perpetuators of the negative effects of the colonial legacy. Pérez's colonial legacy criticisms of Ospina had gone so far, that Pérez himself denounced his Spanish Catholic origins, a move that even Mosquera would not tolerate.

Felipe Pérez assumed his position with the Chorographic Commission after the commission's project needed radical transformations in the wake of the constitutional and territorial changes that followed the Civil War of 1854. Consider how in 1853 the Liberal regime sent the maps Codazzi had drawn between 1850 and 1853 for publication in Europe. The purpose was to solidify cartographically the kind of provincial divisions that the Liberal Party had fought so hard to create. Still, Codazzi himself had disapproved of the early printing of those maps before he concluded the entire commission. The national government, as it turned toward a Conservative presidential administration, agreed with Codazzi. In part that was because the territorial divisions Codazzi had employed from 1850 to 1853 were no longer in operation. By June 1857 the official government box containing Codazzi's maps returned to Bogotá after a four-year stint in Paris and London. The maps contained inside were not published as had been the intended purpose of the voyage.[83]

As the unpublished Chorographic Commission manuscript maps made their way back to Bogotá, New Granada elites worked tirelessly to reshape political institutions in ways that allowed them to find some common ground. In the wake of the Civil War of 1854, an interim presidency under Conservative Manuel María Mallarino helped calm the waters starting in 1855. Felipe Pérez remembered the period of the Mallarino presidency fondly. Pérez reminisced about the cross-party alliance that had been forged between elites during and immediately in the wake of the Civil War. "It was a transitional government that allowed the Republic to enjoy very beautiful days of peace," recalled Pérez, "during which the political parties were lulled under the shade of respected laws, under which it was believed that the future would bring more of the same since the parties had been corrected in their passions, and their hatreds attenuated."[84] From Pérez's perspective the peace and rule of law that followed the Civil War of 1854 under Mallarino's transitional rule created the conditions for the cross-party acceptance of the commonsense cause of "federalism." Although Pérez did not mention the Instituto Caldas as a key space of elite sociability that allowed for elite cross-party alliances since the 1840s, Pérez's memory of Mallarino's presidency echoed the pro-federalist sentiments of Instituto Caldas alumni, including Samper, Ancízar, and Arosemena. Pérez noted how all elites, no matter what party, generally agreed that federalism was the best way to ensure republican institutions.

Much like Samper, Pérez argued that since the time of independence, New Granada men had gained many valuable lessons in the practice of republican governance, lessons that helped them surpass the obstacles of the legacy of Spanish colonialism.

No longer was that wrong-headed idea proper to the times of General Nariño, during which each province of the Viceroyalty dreamed with making itself into a powerful and sovereign State, even though [the provinces] lacked income, education, respectability, and what is worse, the fact that each lacked men of State with political schooling.[85]

The political misfiring committed during the early part of the nineteenth century was over. Knowledgeable men had focused their efforts on making federalism "a form of rational and realizable thought." Pérez echoed Ancízar's earlier efforts to point out the common ground shared by Liberals and Conservatives. When it came to federalism, neither party "emerged on the scene as the owner of the idea. After all, there were federalist conservatives and anti-federalist liberals."[86] Pérez underscored federalism as emerging from a longer-term, rational, informed process of debate and governance since the time of independence. Since members from both parties agreed with federalism, both parties would be responsible for federalism's effects. "For if it is true that the more ideologically advanced portion of the Liberal party was federalist in its totality, it is also true that the Congress that sanctioned the federation through its most recent and solemn act was Conservative in its majority."[87] The shared ideals of federalism across parties allowed Felipe Pérez to then set his sights on Mariano Ospina, the man whom Pérez accused of fomenting the most negative effects of the colonial legacy, especially among popular sectors.

Felipe Pérez underscored the long-term, cross-party consensus built around the question of federalism in order to launch a devastating critique against the first president to be elected through universal manhood suffrage, Mariano Ospina. Pérez cast Ospina's presidential maneuvers as primarily anti-federalist policies. Proving the anti-federalism of Mariano Ospina was no easy task. Ospina had himself approved the "federalizing" Constitution of 1858. To prove his invectives against Ospina, Pérez colored each and every pro-federalist decision made by the president as evidence of Ospina's dark, underhanded plan to undermine federalism and assert centralism. Pérez argued that Ospina "became party to the federation in theory, so he could bastardize it and betray it later in practice."[88] Ospina first gave signals that he intended to "bastardize" the principle of federalism by calling for the strengthening of the national army and expanding the national government's coffers. Pérez dismissed Ospina's arguments that a strong army and a strong central government were both needed in light of a potential invasion by the United States. And yet the threat of just such an invasion lurked on the horizon. Already William Walker's invasion of Nicaragua had been recognized by U.S. president Franklin Pierce. The Watermelon Slice Incident of April 15, 1856, threatened potential invasion by the United States as well.[89] Pérez was so focused on tearing down Ospina's judgment and character that, unlike several of his elite contemporaries, Pérez played down the Watermelon Incident's significance for New Granada.

The incident was, nevertheless, significant. It involved José Manuel Luna, a fruit vendor and person of color, who was approached by a small group of drunken travelers from the United States.[90] One traveler grabbed a watermelon slice, tasted it, and threw it on the ground. After Luna demanded payment, the traveler responded with vulgarity and pulled a gun on Luna; a scuffle began. A bystander disarmed the traveler, but the scuffle escalated into a full-blown riot. According to official reports, seventeen people were killed, including two Panamanians and fifteen foreigners. Buildings and property belonging to the U.S.-owned Panama Railroad Company were also damaged. The incident had made headlines in Panama, and its diplomatic fallout circulated throughout New Granada. Ospina justified the expansion of the national army in light of the possibility that the United States, in defense of the U.S.-owned railroad company, might invade. Pérez acknowledged that U.S. "Southern filibustering annexationists had screamed for an invasion through the organ of the press controlled by [William] Walker and his pirate comrades."[91] Several folks throughout New Granada and in the rest of the Spanish America, especially diplomats, understood the very real potential for just such an invasion.[92] Spanish America needed to band together to resist. These pro-Pan-American elites were mentors of Pérez, including Manuel Ancízar, José María Samper, and Justo Arosemena. And yet Pérez assured his readers that the threat of a U.S. invasion was simply "smoke, and nothing more."[93] Pérez was less interested in forging Pan-American ties with his continental neighbors than he was in tearing down Ospina. What about Ospina's policies had made Pérez so politically irate?

Pérez reserved his most scathing critiques of Ospina for how he chose to enforce the electoral process within the Grenadine Confederacy's shifting territorial divisions. Pérez agreed with Ospina, Samper, and his other more senior mentors that the legitimate source of federal power was universal manhood suffrage.[94] Unlike his mentors, Pérez did not present the Grenadine Confederacy as a model of democratic republicanism that should be emulated throughout the world. Instead Pérez argued fraud was an inevitable reality that came with democracy. He rhetorically interrogated his readers, looking to assert the reality and inevitability of electoral fraud: "what society exists in the world where an electoral corporation is exempt from the spirit of a political party? When has it not occurred that an individual or a corporation, which would first cut off his or her own hand before falsifying a private document, would not flinch before falsifying an electoral register?"[95] Pérez, as noted above, had himself been charged with committing fraud in Zipaquirá elections at the tender age of nineteen. Fraud won him that province's governorship, a move that added fuel to the fire that had spurred Melo and other Draconianos to launch a civil war in 1854. Perhaps for this reason Pérez had no qualms underscoring fraud as a normal part of the democratic process. Pérez dismissed any and all efforts by Ospina to counter fraud as a thinly veiled attempt to win overwhelming political power for the Conservative Party. Fraud was needed, he argued, to keep in check the ignorant masses that blindly followed the Catholic Church due to the long term effects of the colonial legacy.

Pérez's critical, and politically charged, analysis of Ospina's speeches and writings not only allowed him to discount the president's calls for strengthening the military and efforts to ameliorate fraud in popular elections, but it also facilitated blame. Pérez placed blame for the civil war that exploded in 1859 squarely on Ospina and his Conservative Party's shoulders. The Ospina administration passed electoral reform and defended it with military force. Pérez argued that Opsina's electoral reform measures seeking to ensure universal manhood suffrage rights were unconstitutional because they threatened the sovereignty of the states. The national state had no business intervening in elections held within the states. According to Pérez, those reforms became "one of the most powerful motives driving the bloodied situation in which the Republic found itself."[96] When several local municipalities in Cauca and Santander were suspected of engaging in fraudulent elections, Ospina sent in troops to defend the electoral will of universal manhood suffrage. The problem was that both of these states tended toward the Liberal Party. Conservative opposition was nevertheless robust. The suspected fraud committed at the local municipal levels favored the Liberal Party by suppressing Conservative votes. Pérez's narrative helped frame Ospina's actions as a politically motivated invasion targeted to defend the Conservative Party's control over the national government by expanding its control over Liberal-dominated states. This narrative of Ospina as the Conservative "anti-federalist" helped excuse Mosquera's toppling of the first president to ever be elected through direct universal manhood suffrage in New Granada.

Mosquera toppled Ospina, took control of Bogotá in 1861, and set up a provisional government. Pérez's influential *Anales de la Revolución* was clearly an ode to Mosquera's rebellion against Ospina. Mosquera would also have known of Felipe Pérez through Ancízar, whom Mosquera trusted since his first presidential administration (1845–1849), as well as Felipe Pérez's work as an editor for *El Tiempo* alongside José María Samper and Manuel Murillo Toro. After Agustin Codazzi's death in 1859, and after gaining control of the national government in Bogotá in 1861, among Mosquera's first order of business was disseminating the Chorographic Commission's work. He hired Pérez to help disseminate among popular audiences the new territorial-constitutional order then emerging: The United States of Colombia. That political order placed sovereignty squarely in the power of the states that joined together to form a significantly weakened national government of Colombia. This constitutional-territorial change was intended to save the republican political project that a coalition of elites had envisioned since the 1840s from the destabilizing effects universal manhood suffrage had on elite control.

After skewering Ospina in his historical narrative of the war, Felipe Pérez worked assiduously to freeze the new territorial configuration of the United States of Colombia's nine sovereign states through his geographic treatises.[97] Pérez's geographic writings were decidedly less colorful than his historical meanderings, yet they invited the ire and spite of Tomás Cipriano de Mosquera, the very patron Pérez had worked so hard to please.[98] The dispute between these men had to do with reputation, both in terms of their individual professional standing as well as the international reputation of Colombia in the world. But Mosquera was not only concerned about building his own international standing as a geographer; he also worried about how international audiences would read Colombia given Pérez's representations of it. At the core of the disagreement between Mosquera and Pérez was a disagreement between the two men concerning what effects the period of Spanish colonialism had on Colombia.

In a published 1866 letter critiquing Pérez's geography, Mosquera accused Pérez of launching a "polemic against the Spaniards."[99] Mosquera insisted that "we Colombians are Spanish, and the son should be just."[100] Mosquera, much like Samper, had argued that what had placed Colombia on the vanguard of democratic republicanism was the fact that it had been the product of three hundred years of Spanish colonialism, a history that made early republicanism a struggle, but that had also avoided the pitfalls of the structural racism and exclusion inherent to Spanish America's Anglo-Saxon neighbor to the north. Despite Samper's later admonitions of Mosquera, the fact remained that, much like Samper, Mosquera tried to save Colombia's international reputation through geography. Pérez took a radical departure from these two men. Pérez refused to acknowledge that the colonial legacy, especially what he saw as the nefarious influence of the church clergy over popular sectors, could in any way be interpreted positively. According to Pérez, his own Spanish ancestry was a "disgrace."[101] Pérez eschewed Samper and Mosquera's efforts to portray the positive elements of the "colonial legacy" narrative.

For all their disagreements over the details of geographic measurements and the way geographic representations needed to present Colombia to the world, a fundamental agreement did undergird the work of Pérez, the work of other members of the Chorographic Commission, and Mosquera's own political goals. Pérez in the early 1860s left for Paris to join two former Colegio Militar students and disciples of Codazzi's, Manuel Ponce de Leon and Manuel María Paz, to publish the commission's manuscript maps. The resulting printed maps are strikingly different from the manuscript maps drawn by Codazzi a decade earlier. Yet these differences, much like the 1858 changes Samper had engraved upon the copper plates first produced by Acosta in 1847, do evince important continuities.

That is because the large states they depict reveal the project that elites of all political stripes envisioned for their republic since the 1840s, when the commission was in its planning stages. The problem was that popular political participation, from the point of view of Liberals like Felipe Pérez, had unleashed the turbulent effects of a popular consciousness that still blindly followed Catholic teachings. Since the Conservative Party supported the Catholic Church, and popular sectors simply voted according to what their priests told them to do, the entire exercise in democracy failed the true aims of liberalism and federalism. A new territorial-constitutional order needed to bring back institutional order. Even though members of the Instituto Caldas generation, such as Mosquera and Samper, may have cringed when hearing the ways younger Liberals like Pérez characterized the legacy of Spanish Catholicism, they nevertheless pragmatically recognized that elite political calculations could not solely depend on popular suffrage. It is true that the creation of larger "sovereign" states in 1863 included the constitutionally enshrined right to respect the rights of the individual.[102] And yet the sovereignty granted to these states within the United States of Colombia had the ultimate effect of undermining universal manhood suffrage at the state level.

Consider, for instance the most immediate result of granting sovereignty to the states, rather than to individuals: a total disparity among the states concerning who qualified as an "active" citizen, that is, who had the right to vote and be elected.[103] The one state that guaranteed suffrage rights most expansively was Cauca, the state that also happened to be Mosquera's main source of political and military support. There, all men who had been married at any age, or who were at least eighteen years old, were active citizens. This level of enfranchisement surpassed even the Constitution of 1853, which granted active citizenship to men over the age of twenty-one. Popular liberals forced republican bargains out of elites in the Cauca, and in return they delivered victories, including Mosquera's victory over Ospina in the 1860s.[104] This dynamic explains why the Cauca state legislature most openly embraced universal manhood suffrage. The state of Magdalena came next, granting active citizenship to all men over the age of eighteen, yet that state did not offer active citizenship to younger married men. We start to see growing restrictions on suffrage among other states. Santander and Tolima, for instance, both granted suffrage rights to men who were married or eighteen years old, but both states restricted suffrage with literacy requirements. The states of Bolívar, Panama, and Cundinamarca did not impose a literacy restriction on suffrage. These three states nevertheless did maintain the active citizenship age at twenty-one years (or married) rather than eighteen as in Cauca, Magdalena, Santander, and Tolima. Literacy restrictions were included in Antioquia's state constitution, as was the twenty-one-year age requirement for voting or holding office. Antioquia thereby became the most restrictive of all the new Colombian states when it came time to define active citizenship.

Beyond age, marriage, or literacy restrictions, the constitutional details regulating how state officials could be elected to their respective office in each state also varied considerably. These variations represented the subtler ways the new states restricted individual suffrage as had been originally guaranteed in the 1853 Constitution. The state of Boyaca stands out most in this regard, and not only because it oddly was the only state to set the active citizenship age at twenty years (or married).[105] Universal manhood suffrage in Boyaca allowed for the election of a local Cabildo. The Cabildo, not direct suffrage, elected the municipal mayor.

Universal manhood suffrage elected members to the state legislature. But the legislature, not universal manhood suffrage, elected state Supreme Court justices. Boyacá's district prefects, or municipal authorities, were not elected but were named by the state president. In short, with sovereignty devolving to each of the nine states that made up the United States of Colombia, the expansive political power that had been granted to individuals through universal manhood suffrage in 1853 had begun to dissolve a decade later.

This chapter has demonstrated how the supposed dichotomy that pitted mid-nineteenth century Conservatives against Liberals on the question of "federalism" is a false one. Building on previous chapters, it has shown how elites from the newly forming Conservative and Liberal political parties shared spaces of sociability and governance. Starting with the first Mosquera presidential administration, a generation of elites either met or knew of each other through membership in the Instituto Caldas. This network of literate men committed to morality, industry, and education facilitated the work of the Chorographic Commission, no matter what political party held national political power. These men also fought each other in the field of battle and in the field of politics. They nevertheless negotiated with each other in the halls of Congress. These spaces of sociability allowed elites, regardless of party affiliation or regional origins, to work together toward ensuring continuity for the modernizing project elites envisioned for New Granada since the 1840s.

Changes in the way the "science of constitutionalism" needed to be applied in the wake of emancipation, universal manhood suffrage, and the civil wars they unleashed, together with how histories about these conflicts were written, shifted the narrative away from consensus in elite spaces like the Instituto Caldas toward interparty conflict. Men such as Ancízar, Samper, Arosemena, and Mosquera, all committed republicans, nevertheless produced a new kind of federalism targeted toward bringing universal manhood suffrage under elite control. Pérez took his historical writings on the conflicts that emerged from constitutional changes one step further. He transformed the Civil War of 1859–1862 from a conflict over ensuring the constitutional expression of universal manhood suffrage into a struggle over two completely different models of state formation: Conservative-backed centralism that evidenced the most negative effects of the Spanish colonial legacy versus Liberal Party federalism that pointed toward modernity and republicanism. Liberals alone supposedly wanted federalism. Conservatives supposedly wanted centralism. Attempts by the Instituto Caldas generation to rein in the younger, maverick Liberal Pérezes of Colombia from representing Colombia to the world as a place mired in a Spanish colonial legacy of ignorance and corruption did not work very well. Those narratives tended to stick in the minds of international audiences and audiences of later generations.

Despite deep disagreements over the nature of Spanish colonial legacies, a consensus did emerge over the kind of national state that would best serve the interests of polarized elites. Both Liberals and Conservatives preferred larger states that would allow each party to territorialize their site of political dominance. The Chorographic Commission's work at midcentury was redeployed to legitimate the new constitutional-territorial project that emerged as a result of conflicts and negotiations spurred on by universal manhood suffrage. Consider the original manuscript maps Codazzi had drawn during his first two tours to New Granada's northeast provinces in 1850–1851, and how they compare to the printed maps that Pérez devised for what had become the state of Boyacá by 1863.

These maps are so different from each other that it seems they depict entirely different places. And yet, what we have here is the 1860s incarnation of the Chorographic Commission. Codazzi's maps from the early 1850s were stitched together to create the overarching map for the sovereign state of Boyacá. Gone are the detailed charts that organized information on what had been the smaller province according to cantons. Cantons were the key location for municipal governance prior to 1853. That was the unit of territorial analysis for Codazzi, and all information on topography, resources, population, vegetation, cattle, trade, state lands,

16. Mapa corográfico de la Provincia de Tundama (Boyacá), levantado por orden del gobierno por Agustín Codazzi, 1850. 66 x 63 cm. Bogotá as meridian. Scale: 1:345,000. SMP 6, Ref. 19. Archivo General de la Nación, Bogotá.

and more was organized canton by canton. But cantons, after 1853, had begun to disappear. These cantons not only disappeared from the national constitution; they also disappeared from the Chorographic Commission's cartography.

This new incarnation of the commission had, under the Mosquera administration, the funding it needed to print maps, atlases, and travel narratives intended to teach future generations of the Colombian territory. It was under Mosquera's first presidential administration, after all, that the Chorographic Commission had originally been hatched through the Instituto Caldas formed in

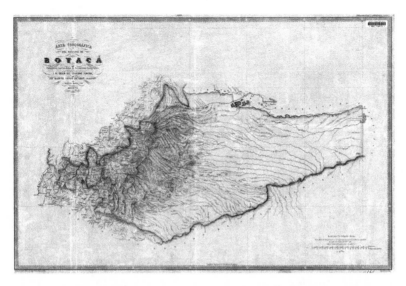

17. Estado de Boyacá, París, 1864. 58 x 90 cm. Bogotá as meridian. SMP 6, Ref. 2. Archivo General de la Nación, Bogotá.

Bogotá in 1847. And yet, for Mosquera in the 1860s, Codazzi's complex statistical tables, which offered detailed information on population, including the number of men available to bear arms, travel distances between towns, trading patterns among localities, and much more, were erased. Such detailed information, so important to a nation that was embarking on a project toward universal manhood suffrage and internal circulation from 1850 to 1853, no longer mattered much for the United States of Colombia a decade later, where sovereignty resided in the states, not individual citizens. What was needed instead were printed maps that could be hung in primary schools so young Colombian citizens could begin to imagine their political affiliations. Rather than local municipal government, students needed to pledge allegiance to the sovereign states and the national state. As the next chapter argues, allegiance to the state also needed to surpass the strong support local populations had for the Catholic Church, and these printed maps of the Chorographic Commission were intended to aid that effort.

CHAPTER 6

Civic Religion vs. the Catholic Church and the Ending of a Republican Project

Tomás Cipriano de Mosquera, military general, former president of the New Granada Republic and avid geography enthusiast, seized power during the Civil War of 1860 to 1862, became president of the Grenadine Confederacy from 1861 to 1863, served as the first president of the United States of Colombia from 1863 to 1864, and again from 1866 to 1867. In January 1862, as civil war raged and the outcome still hung in the balance, Mosquera wrote a letter to Pope Pius IX, the first pope to have personal experience living in Latin America.[1] Mosquera's letter justified Colombia's larger long-term goal of inheriting the church-granted right of *patronato* that formerly had been wielded by the Spanish Crown in the New World.[2] The reason was simple. He explained to the pope how vacancies in important Catholic Church positions had been filled by men who dishonored the church's role in Colombia through scandalous conduct, including actively fanning the flames of civil war by mobilizing popular sectors at the pulpit and taking up arms themselves.[3] Unfit priests and prelates had also unlawfully disposed of church assets in Colombia. Colombia therefore ordered the disentailment of properties held in mortmain by the church. The Colombian government needed to take control of church assets to ensure the proper functioning of the church throughout the national territory. Mosquera pleaded with Pope Pius IX to ensure that church functionaries complied with the Colombian government's decrees on disentailment.

In the wake of independence, republican elites, no matter their political stripe, believed they had the right to inherit the colonial-era church-state relationship of patronato. By the 1860s the question was not so clear. Conservatives like Mariano Ospina, for instance, were very much in favor of the liberal principle separating church and state, arguing that "a sincerely Catholic Government, with a free Church, would know how to live in harmony with her, but on the contrary, an anti-Christian power (directed by enemies of the Faith and under the obedience of Francomasonry) would turn even the best concordato into a formidable arm against Catholicism."[4] Whatever their stance on church-state relations, elite Liberals and Conservatives nevertheless both came to see the value of disentailing church lands held in mortmain by the church. This liberal policy had long been championed by Spanish American republicans, but not until the 1860s was the national state in a position of carrying it to fruition. As this chapter demonstrates, Mosquera and the *Olimpo Radical*, or the Liberal Radical Olympus that dominated national Colombian politics from the 1860s through the 1880s, enacted the disentailment of church property in each of Colombia's sovereign states. The success of this policy was not just because the Liberal Party was in power, but, more significantly, because members of the Conservative Party agreed to implement the policy in the states they controlled. A measure of consensus elite returned to governance after popular moderization had been reined in by the 1860s.

Mosquera and the Radical Olympus had as their ultimate goal breaking into the Catholic Church's vast economic and political resources. This story of Mosquera, the Liberals, and the church is intimately related to the story told in previous chapters. Radical Liberals had come to see how a church independent of state control had induced the supposedly innocent masses to the voting booth or on the battlefield to support the Conservative Party under the guise of defending Catholicism. Universal manhood suffrage subsequently produced results that led to violence and deep constitutional crises. A coalition of elites offered a solution that enshrined the rights of states over the rights of individuals through the United States of Colombia. Liberals and Conservatives tenuously agreed to carve out political territories, with Liberals dominating some states and Conservatives others. Each state wrote up its own constitution that defined citizenship in the ways each saw fit. This brokered agreement was not enough for Mosquera or the Radical Liberals, however. The separation of church and state, a hallowed liberal principle enshrined in the Constitution of 1853, became the principle obstacle to republican progress precisely because the Catholic Church was a corporate body that controlled the bulk of the landed wealth of the nation, sequestering it from free circulation. Insidiously, it was that wealth that supported Catholic priests who preached outside the control of the republican state that Liberals dominated.

Mosquera and the Radical Liberal Olympus therefore pushed forward policies of disentailment, seeking a longer-term goal of patronato. The Liberal policy of disentailment, from the 1860s through the 1880s, was intended to set off a chain reaction. First, by breaking the power of the church over land markets, internal markets would flourish. Second, disentailment would liberate economic resources needed to finance and broaden popular education. Third, the national system of public instruction that would emerge through the funding that came from disentailed church properties would weaken the cultural and political power Catholic clergy enjoyed over popular sectors through the pulpit. Public education would create an alternate cultural broker: the school teacher. Teachers trained in *escuelas normales*, or normal schools, would introduce the populace to secular ideas that would lead individuals to responsible citizenship and support of the republic. Schooling would encourage virtue and morality among popular sectors, inoculating them from supposedly corrupt priests suspicious of a modernity that harmed their economic interests. The Liberal Party was, in a way, setting the scene for a cultural and political reformation that would bring church power under state control. Mosquera's solution to ensure republican modernity by asserting state control over the Catholic Church not only was a modern form of reformation, it also paradoxically brought back a central way the Spanish Crown had legitimized itself during the period of monarchical rule: through the patronato real.

But by the late 1880s and into the early twentieth century, the relationship between church and state in Colombia could not be farther from that envisioned by Mosquera and the Radical Liberal Olympus. Rather than achieving the right of patronato, which would have given the civic state government the right to participate in the creation of a dioceses and designate its leadership, Colombia had signed a *concordato* with the Vatican. This concordato transformed the church into an autonomous body in the nation that would conduct business as if it were the diplomatic representative of a foreign state, and rejected interference by the civil government in clerical matters, giving greater maneuvering room to the Catholic Church. By the early twentieth century, the church also gained absolute authority to govern, police, educate, and control indigenous populations in Colombia's peripheral regions via the religious orders chosen by the Vatican.[5] Although these regions were not heavily populated, they did amount to approximately 65 percent of the national territory. Within the more populated Andean and Caribbean areas of Colombia, the church also gained significant cultural power in the wake of the new constitution of 1886. The church gained control over the secular national education system, originally developed by the Radical Olympus with funds generated by the disentailment of church properties held in mortmain. The question of disentailment was also addressed. The Catholic Church, unsurprisingly, sought reparations. And yet the supposedly staunch pro-church Conservatives in power did not cede much. Recognizing the significance of disentailed properties for the wealth and stability of the state, Conservatives did not dismantle the work carried out by Radical Liberals.[6]

This final chapter offers perspective on how these dramatic changes and notable continuities in church-state relations emerged in Colombia during the second half of the nineteenth century. It builds on studies centered on church-state relations in Spanish America that show how several republics in the region tried to enact the policy of disentailment during the early nineteenth century by building on Bourbon-era reforms and by sharing legal models and approaches with each other.[7] What emerges from these studies is that the longer historical trajectory of disentailment's implementation was originally a project that all republicans from across the political spectrum supported, at least in theory. By midcentury, as Matthew Butler is right to argue, states with larger churches, such as Mexico and Colombia, were experiencing a seismic shift in church-state relations.[8] Several scholars of Colombian history have suggested that the mid-nineteenth-century shift was rooted in partisanship sparked by the disentailment policies enacted under the Radical Liberal Olympus.[9] There are legitimate reasons for the emergence of this partisan take on Colombian history, especially given the deep Conservative bent of many Catholic priests as Mosquera's letter to Pope Pius IX suggests. This chapter nevertheless nuances this partisan narrative.

The chapter demonstrates how Mosquera's proposal to expropriate church wealth did not prove controversial for either Liberal or Conservative republicans. All considered landed wealth sequestered by the church and kept out of circulation was a negative legacy of the colonial period that needed to be addressed. Many elite members from both parties also agreed that the state needed to expand its public education system, and the property of the Catholic Church offered the best untapped resource to finance it. The chapter argues that when partisanship did begin to divide folks, it was when it came time to define the content of public school education. Significantly, the rallying cry for civil war was less over disentailment, then it was over who would be hired to teach future generations, and what content those public school teachers needed to teach.

Notably, the national government under Mosquera made a priority out of publishing a series of large-scale images of the United States of Colombia and each of the sovereign states that comprised it for the purposes of public instruction. These maps were based on the Chorographic Commission but were heavily edited. The dozens of provinces that had made up New Granada were stitched together to form the nine "sovereign" states that had emerged from warfare on the field of battle and in the field of politics. The heart of Codazzi's chorographic maps—the detailed statistics tables with information on population, trade, distances between major towns, the number of hectares of "baldio" state-owned lands, men available for war, heads of cattle, and more—was cut out. That is because the printed maps no longer served the bipartisan project that the Instituto Caldas had envisioned for the Chorographic Commission's cartography. Rather than serve as placeholders for sensitive state-building statistics, the printed maps would serve as a technol-

18. "Carta Geográfica de Los Estados Unidos de Colombia," Paris, 1864. Scale: 1:1,350,000. 150 x 165 cm. SMP 3, Ref. 12. Archivo General de la Nación, Bogotá.

ogy that could facilitate indoctrination and belonging in the United States of Colombia through public education. Conservatives began to chafe when these strikingly large maps replaced crucifixes on walls of school classrooms and when geography primers based on the commission's findings found a place in every classroom, but bibles less so. Still, geography was important. What neither Conservatives nor, for that matter, many Liberals could take was the hiring of German Protestant teachers by the Liberal regime to educate future cadres of teachers in state-sponsored normal schools.

Liberal efforts to introduce a new system to uproot what they perceived to be the "colonial legacy" of Catholicism from individual minds led ultimately to the undoing of the last shreds of elite consensus this book has sought to identify. For some fifty years elites across the political spectrum had produced a remarkable consensus around the need to identify the many ways the colonial past got in the way of a republican future. Elites agreed on the need to accelerate the circulation of objects, peoples, and ideas in a polity that had been artificially fragmented by geography and a colonial past. Elites from all provinces came together to create a capital city in Bogotá where resources and training could circulate outward and back. They also created a political economy that established rules and mechanisms to foment circulation across locals and regions. They created ways to incorporate the republican "indíjena" into the markets of land and labor after centuries of discrimination and unequal land distribution. In short, elites promoted a national market of internal consumers and producers. Elites came together to promote virtue, morality, and science as embodied in the ideals articulated through the founding of the Instituto Caldas. Elites agreed on the need to stimulate a public sphere of newspapers that would help identify the behaviors that got in the way of republican virtue. After devastating warfare, elites agreed that the expansion of the franchise through universal manhood suffrage needed to be administered state by state via a reorganization of political geography. Increasingly divided by political party affiliation, elites nevertheless still agreed in the 1860s and 1870s that the church's unequal share in the wealth of the nation blocked the creation and growth of agrarian markets and that that wealth could and should be reoriented toward the creation of a national public school system.

However, when Liberals used the new public school system to launch the equivalent of a religious Reformation by offering an alternative civic religion that worshipped the nation, and when the Liberals substituted the Catholic priestly bureaucracies with Protestant teachers, the system of consensus collapsed. A furious backlash ensued spearheaded by local resistance and civil war. As noted in the last chapter, the creation of the sovereign states began dismantling the project of circulation. Liberals attempted to revive circulation through the networked system of public education that was funded by disentailment. Their aim to carry out a religious Reformation failed. The church aided by Conservatives emerged triumphant in a wave of counterreformation and reconfessionalization. The church lacked the immense landed wealth that it had enjoyed prior to the 1860s, but by the early twentieth century with Conservatives and moderate Liberals firmly in control, it came back to take control of the national school system and administered through missions nearly 65 percent of Colombia's national territory. This change, ultimately, marked a dramatic surrender of the postcolonial state to an institution that had played a fundamental role in the success of the Spanish monarchical regime during the colonial period. This time, however, the church avoided subordination to civil authorities via the age-old patronato. Instead the church declared itself part of a transnational, sovereign body whose foreign status the state was forced to recognize via the concordato. The triumph of a renewed ultramontane church was accompanied by a new constitution, the reorganization of political geography, and reterritorialization of authority within the national territory. This triumph also marked a turning point in the political economy of circulation for internal markets. The priority of the state thereafter became insertion into global markets through plantation economies and agrarian exports. The crafting of a republic for the world as envisioned through the Instituto Caldas came undone. A new elite of Catholic transnationals emerged to do battle against crass, immoral liberalism and the scientific racism spearheaded by the growing Protestant imperial behemoth of the United States that was to take over Panama in the early twentieth century. Hispanism, pan-Latinism, and positivism eventually came to replace the ideas of the Instituto Caldas.

The chapter begins by showing how difficult it was for the radical Liberals to actually enact the twin policies of disentailment and national public education without the help of the Conservative Party. The first section recounts the long-term republican consensus on disentailment, demonstrating how the policy was not a Liberal Party policy alone. The second section, drawing on surveying records and reports from local officials, shows how resistance to disentailment tended to come from local folks with distinct material or political interests in the specific properties to be expropriated. Despite local resistance, each of the nine Colombian states did enact the policy of disentailment because, no matter the political party affiliation of the leaders of each state, all recognized how state coffers would benefit. The third section turns to the inauguration and functioning of the national public education system, which was largely funded through or housed in disentailed church properties. The section points to how the Radical Liberal Olympus's plan for national education uncannily resembled earlier 1840s ideals for circulation of morality, education, and development. The fourth section turns to how members of the Conservative Party together with members of the church, infuriated by the Protestant normal school educators hired to train future Colombian teachers, launched a civil war. The final section highlights how the civil war from 1876 to 1877 eventually drove the Radical Liberals from power, opening the opportunity for a new constitutional order for Colombia in 1886. Bringing in the historical writings of José Manuel Groot helps underscore the points of convergence among moderate Liberals and Conservatives on the role of the Catholic Church should play in Spanish American Republics repudiating radical Liberal excess. By the 1880s that new order returned the Catholic Church to a position of authority by building on the national public education system developed under the Radical Olympus, yet the new state nevertheless maintained the financial stability that came from the disentailment of church properties.

Consensus on Church-State Relations

Historians of Colombia wisely and repeatedly caution against generalizing about Liberal versus Conservative Party makeup and party platforms.[10] They have noted, and rightly so, how adherence to a particular party by any one individual was conditioned by a variety of factors including social class, regional origins, family, kinship and patronage networks, race, and ethnic background, not to mention access to education. Government officials from both parties supported many similar political and fiscal policies, including the liberal policy of disentailment of Catholic Church properties, at least during the late colonial and early republican periods. These disclaimers, however, nevertheless do not apply to the 1860s in Colombia. Historians have simply taken for granted that by the 1860s political platforms had consolidated, and party politics and political violence from then on became an integral part of nation-state formation. This book so far has argued that in the mid-nineteenth century political parties were in a loose process of formation, with elites generally coalescing around common projects for republicanism and modernization during the first half of the nineteenth century, and popular sectors tended to force one or another political party's hand. This section offers an overview of the ways elite spaces of agreement carried over to the question of disentailment of landed church properties though the 1870s, even despite polarization given mid-nineteenth century civil wars.

During the period of the Spanish Monarchy, the Catholic Church, which served a powerful legitimating arm of the monarchy in the New World, had acquired vast amounts of landed wealth from people who donated their earthly possessions to religious orders and the church. Catholic individuals bequeathed their possessions to the church for several reasons. Some, seeking spiritual redemption in the hereafter, willed their property to the church in return for prayers that would release the benefactors' souls from purgatory. The income the church received from these properties was also intended to foment the propagation of the faith and to support charitable works.[11] In other instances, property that belonged to those who died without leaving behind heirs or a will automatically went to the church. The church and secular orders also acted as the principal moneylenders both in the Spanish colonies and in Spain during the colonial period. Seeking loans, people mortgaged their landed property to the church or a religious order. The church repossessed the mortgaged land of those who did not repay their loan within a specified period. Other sources of property for the church included the dowries paid to convents when a woman was interned in a nunnery. In general, these properties were highly valued precisely because they were located near heavily populated areas or close to accessible communication routes, allowing their agricultural products to easily supply population centers.

Early republican government leaders in the wake of independence had long contemplated plans to disentail properties held in mortmain by the church and religious orders, yet they were tentative about implementing *desamortización*.[12] They worried it would antagonize public opinion. One of the first Gran Colombian republicans to try was Finance Secretary José María del Castillo y Rada, who considered that the abolition of property held in mortmain was necessary both to encourage the free circulation of wealth and to increase productivity.[13] Some initial measures were passed, but implementation occurred only with difficulty. The national state was too weak to challenge the strong position of the church. From the time of independence the Catholic Church was clearly a dominant force in Colombian politics and society. According to the 1825 census, there was approximately one representative of the Catholic Church for every seven hundred Gran Colombians, and the church was overwhelmingly responsible for education.[14] Therefore, despite legislative and political agreement around the need for disentailment during these early years, implementation proved difficult at best.

The emerging Liberal Party renewed efforts to implement ideologically liberal policies, including those that targeted the Catholic Church. The most dramatic changes began under the first Liberal president elected into office, President Hilario López. Starting in 1849 the Liberal-led regime dismantled the *fuero ecclesiastico*, or church tribunal, allowing priests to be subjected to civil justice, taking control over the fates of church members out of the hands of the church hierarchy. Lopez's regime also expelled the Jesuit order from the country and took away the church's right to compulsory tithes. During these years the national state also renewed its efforts to enact legislative reforms that would disentail church property, but the measures still had yet to be carried out. Liberals explained the delays in implementation of disentailment on the significant sway that the church as a religious institution had over the population since the colonial period.[15] The supposedly corrupt church sought to exploit popular sectors by holding on to its landed wealth. Liberals also argued that the Catholic Church retaliated against modernizing policies by overwhelmingly preaching support for the Conservative Party. Such preaching had direct political effects starting in 1853, with the inauguration of universal manhood suffrage. Liberals may have had a point. Conservatives overwhelmingly were voted into office at the local and national levels immediately in the wake of the inauguration of universal manhood suffrage.

Liberals were not alone in their efforts to disentail church properties, however. Between 1853 and 1861, when the Conservative Party dominated Congress and the presidency, three laws were issued on property held in mortmain. The most significant of these, passed in 1855, dictated that Catholic neighbors could, after twenty-five years of residence, dispose of all the property of the religious diocese on which they lived, including the parish temples.[16] This law allowed the national state to define who could have the right to claim and sell church properties. Members of the Catholic Church resented this legislative move, arguing the Executive Power did not have the right to define who was a member of the Catholic community.[17] The law itself caused conflicts between the church and the neighbors who sought to appropriate religious community property.[18] Though threatening, these new laws nevertheless left intact the church's basic structures of economic and social power.[19] The Catholic Church continued to enjoy wealth from property it held in mortmain and ideological power over popular sectors through its control over education.

From the 1850s and into the 1870s, politicians from the Liberal and Conservative parties increasingly positioned themselves strategically against each other with respect to the church in order to maintain or gain political ground—and offices. As we saw with their costumbrista ethnographic explorations into the souls of popular sectors, Conservative elites articulated the value of Catholic morality among popular sectors as the much-needed contribution that New Granada could offer the world. They did so increasingly as a targeted attack on Liberal-leaning ethnographies that critiqued the corruption among members of the clergy and the ways some had exploited popular sectors in part by forcing ignorance upon them.

Popular participation at the voting booth overwhelmingly supported the Conservative Party and its defense of Catholic morality. The perception that Conservatives were allied with the Catholic Church against the Liberals began with the electoral results that brought the Conservative Party overwhelmingly to political office in the wake of the Constitution of 1853 and reached its peak in the Civil War of 1859–1862, which culminated in the overthrow of Conservative president Mariano Opsina by Tomás Cipriano de Mosquera. Mosquera, as Butler and others have argued, had become deeply anticlerical during his 1861–1864 administration.[20] This period saw Mosquera issue the *tuición de cultos* decree, which imposed state licenses on clergy, and the disentailment of church properties decree that Mosquera described in his letter to Pope Pius IX. Mosquera also passed the Constitution of 1863, which enshrined freedom of worship, prohibited the clergy from assuming any political post, and prohibited the clergy from owning property. This new constitution, however, also allowed for quite a bit of autonomy for each of the sovereign states that made up the United States of Colombia. This maneuvering room meant that despite the fact that Liberals dominated the national government, Conservatives quickly asserted control of political offices in states dominated by their party, thereby strengthening and consolidating regional strongholds.[21] This tentative agreement opened up space for peace within the newly established United States of Colombia.

Mosquera, the able politician, understood that Liberals and Conservatives, at least the moderate elite members of both parties, would be amenable to reining in the Catholic Church under the control of Colombia's civil government. Conservatives firmly defended the church as a valuable and modern cultural institution, and several Liberals, including Mosquera, did not completely disagree. Conservatives, like Liberals, also held republicanism dear. Members of both parties valued the morality that Catholicism could bring to popular sectors. By the 1860s, some elite Conservatives could not fully embrace a church that was undergoing a radical ultramontane revolution by connecting itself firmly to Rome. Therefore, despite the many differences pitting Liberals against Conservatives, those elite party leaders whose interests were not deeply tied to church economic interests pragmatically agreed to share the church's material spoils, regardless of party affiliation. Mosquera's ability to finally enact the disentailment of church property enjoyed not only Liberal Party support. Elite members of the Conservative Party also quietly embraced the measure. States dominated by the Conservative Party nevertheless did prove difficult to bend to the ostensibly Liberal Party policy of disentailment.

Table 3. Revenue from Disentailed Property (in pesos)

Place	Real Estate	Debt on Property Owed to Church	Movable Goods and Cattle	Totals
Bogotá (Capital)	$3,352,463	$1,208,253	$92,012	$4,652,738
Cauca	$547,970	$1,198,397	$14,936	$1,761,304
Boyacá	$517,395	$528,468	$5,938	$1,051,801
Santander	$498,230	$528,468	$8,402	$1,035,101
Cundinamarca	$262,694	$354,420	$13,386	$630,501
Bolívar	$256,590	$522,367	$4,996	$783,954
Panamá	$188,964	$443, 850	$6,727	$639,542
Tolima	$160,267	$344,362	$108,469	$613,099
Antioquia	$87,407	$701,899	$202	$789,509
Magdalena	$9,056	$72,345	$8,402	$85,962
Total	$5,881,048	$5,902,832	$259,632	$12,043,513

Source: Miguel Salgar, *Ajencia General de Bienes Desamortizados. Informe al Secretario del Tesoro*, 1870. See also Jorge Villegas, *Colombia: Enfrentamiento iglesia-estado, 1819–1887* (Bogotá: La Carreta, 1977), 83.

In Antioquia, for instance, where the Conservative Party dominated political control, government officials openly resisted the disentailment of church lands. Consider how national agent for disentailment J. Herrera characterized the process in Antioquia. "There, the functionaries of the State are all so opposed to such an extent that it borders on resistance," argued Herrera. "Judges and functionaries openly refuse to offer their services in the business of disentailment because, they say, it is repugnant to their conscience. In this way they forget that by accepting their post as government functionaries for the State *and for* the Nation, they cannot refuse to comply with the obligations that the latter demands from them."[22] Antioquia, a Conservative Party stronghold, resisted national policies of desamortización in ways that seemed to solidify the ties between the church and Antioquia as a state. Conservative Antioqueño government functionaries were not only concerned about their conscience as Catholics if desamortización was allowed to occur; they also were worried about questions of political power. And yet, despite resistance, expropriation of church lands occurred in Antioquia anyway. If we leave aside the tremendously successful implementation of disentailment in the capital city of Bogotá, Antioquia generated $789,509 pesos worth of revenue from disentailed properties. As can be seen from Table 3, this was a significant sum that placed Antioquia fourth among the nine sovereign states, all of which implemented the policy to a significant extent.

Resistance to the disentailment of church properties therefore did not block the process, not even in the states dominated by the Conservative Party. Ruling elites in each state, regardless of political party affiliation, supported the measure. This is not to say resistance did not occur. As the next section shows, those most opposed to disentailment tended to be popular sectors with close ties to church leaders. These men often were behind direct challenges to disentailment on the ground. Despite these challenges from below, disentailment nevertheless eventually won out.

Everyday Resistance to Disentailment on the Ground

Delving into archives that testify to the process of disentailment in different states allows for an on-the-ground perspective on the extent of politicization around the expropriation of church properties. The case of Boyacá offers an illustrative case in point. Dominated by Conservatives during the 1859–1862 Civil War, Mosquera nevertheless successfully supported the mobilized Liberals in that state. Armed Liberals in Boyacá helped score a Liberal military victory in Bogotá.[23] Liberals predictably came to control Boyacá in the wake of the Civil War, yet Conservatives maintained some political control at the local level. When it came time to implement the policy of disentailment in Boyacá, the available historical record does not suggest resistance to the measure was primarily a Conservative Party cause, however. Resistance and delays seemed to be related more to how timing could impact local real estate interests. This is not to say resistance to disentailment of church properties was completely depoliticized. There were cases in Boyacá where popular resistance to the policy had developed clear associations with national-level ideas linked to Conservative Party identities. And yet even these encounters were eventually solved in favor of the measure.

Consider the early processes of disentailment in Boyacá. In 1866 Rufino Chaparro, the state of Tunja's agent for enacting the disentailment of church properties, wrote to the national chapter of the Bienes Desamortizados office. He explained that despite the direct orders he received from his superior in Bogotá, he was simply unable to move forward in Tunja, the capital city of Boyacá. Chaparro's efforts found an overwhelming number of obstacles, especially with respect to the property named Hato Grande in the district of Chiquinquirá. Hato Grande was under the control of the Concepción monastery. One reason for the delay in measuring this hacienda was that the surveying engineer hired to appraise the property, draw the map, and divide the property into lots had yet to appear. Only after the surveyor showed up could work proceed. Chaparro hoped the general agent of Bienes Desamortizados in Bogotá could encourage the named engineering surveyor to fulfill the duties of his job.[24] The reasons for the surveyor's absenteeism in the case of Hato Grande went unexplained. Perhaps the taboo of surveying church properties for the purposes of expropriation was one problem, but this was never explicitly mentioned. The sources instead point to the kind of local interests existing in Chiquinquirá over the increasingly valuable plots of Hato Grande lands. The delays and obstacles identified by the Tunja agent of Bienes Desamortizados were less about partisan conflict or ideological opposition to disentailment, at least in 1866. Instead, the Tunja agent described specific local circumstances that had caused frustrating delays.

The Bienes Desamortizados office in Tunja was frustrated time and again in its attempts to assert control over the hacienda of Hato Grande. By 1868, presumably after a surveyor finally was assigned to the hacienda, the local cabildo of Chiquinquirá occupied Hato Grande and refused to allow the local Bienes Desamortizados agent entry. Their occupation barred even a basic appraisal of the property. This kept the national government from collecting even the comparatively small penalty payments from the Concepción monastery for refusing to comply with the law.[25] The desamortización agent in charge of Chiquinquirá noted how the cabildo's resistance to survey Hato Grande was due to profit margins, not ideology. Local populations knew that a new road was being planned to connect Hato Grande with larger population centers. Agricultural goods produced on Hato Grande lands would more easily get to market, but only after the road was finished. The problem, then, was not that the Concepción monastery resisted disentailment. Rather, the monastery wanted to hold off on the appraisal and survey of the lands so that the value would more accurately reflect the newly constructed road. The Chiquinquirá cabildo supported the monastery's argument for barring the immediate survey of Hato Grande. Given that he could not get information on the hacienda through a direct inspection, the Bienes Desamortizados agent interviewed the nearby populations of the neighboring town of Simijaca for their interest in the lands. Several folks from this neighboring town wished to purchase Hato Grande lands and wished to do so as soon as possible, before the price of Hato Grande land parcels increased.

The Concepción monastery had the political and logistical support of the Chiquinquirá cabildo to resist the implementation of desamortización, at least through the 1860s. This was while agents in other areas of Boyacá were increasingly successful in disentailing church properties. With over one million pesos in revenue coming into the national state from disentailed properties over the course of a decade, Boyacá represented the third most effective state in implementing the policy.[26] Yet it seems this success was causing problems. Incidents of more direct, and in some cases violent, resistance to disentailment, especially from people whose interests were tied to the church's wealth increasingly came to the fore in Boyacá.

Disagreements over expropriation on the ground became so virulent that by the 1870s parts of the Altiplano were inaccessible to the government officials working to have these lands surveyed. Early resistance to disentailment could be couched in face-saving nonpartisan terms that emphasized delays intended to maximize the value of a specific land, as was the case of Hato Grande. But by the 1870s local resistance to disentailment increasingly intertwined with political party platforms. That was because those individuals or groups resisting the measure, by calling themselves Conservatives, counted on members of the Conservative Party in other parts of Boyacá and other states to come to their aid. The state agents of disentailment nevertheless had ample resources to combat local resistance, no matter how partisan resistance claimed to be.

On August 31, 1872, Miguel Cortés, the subaltern agent of Bienes Desamortizados in Fumeque, another city in Boyacá, appealed to both the executive power of the state and to the national head of Bienes Desamortizados for help to fulfill his task.[27] His report on the progress of sales of disentailed lands in the parish of Úmbita explained how a *cuadrilla de malhechores,* or a band of evildoers whom he referred to as the Molino gang, was impeding the survey of disentailed lands that legally belonged to Bienes Desamortizados. Cortés explained that there were many people interested in participating in an auction of these lands, but the Molino gang refused to vacate them. No one showed up at the auction as a result. In Úmbita there were several other properties that also legally belonged to the government's branch of Bienes Desamortizados, but the terror instilled by the Molino gang had blocked surveys, registration, and the land parcel auction. Miguel Cortes emphasized how the Molino gang identified themselves as belonging to the Conservative Party. Just going by that name had been enough for folks to know that the Molino gang would block any use of the lands that would be sold at auction by Bienes Desamortizados.[28]

As Miguel Cortes's statement suggests, some local populations violently resisted the work of the Bienes Desamortizados office and claimed affiliation with the Conservative Party to gain greater legitimacy. Reading this second case after the Hato Grande case nevertheless is suggestive. The desire to delay or impede disentailment likely had direct material reasons rather than pure ideological ones. By calling themselves Conservatives, folks whose economic interests would be negatively affected by the timing or sale of church properties could call upon Conservative Party members in other areas as allies that would further intimidate and resist desamortización.[29] Such a move heightened tensions, and officials of the Bienes Desamortizados office had legal tools at their disposal to counter even these violent self-proclaimed Conservative Party gangs.

Cortes's description of the Conservative Molina group in Fumeque specifically as a "cuadra de malhechores" was neither arbitrary nor innocent. Beginning in 1837 the national penal code defined "cuadrillas de malhechores" as an association that perpetrated a crime against society and that was subject to severe criminal penalties.[30] The people in the Molina group may have sought legitimacy by announcing their affiliation to the Conservative Party, yet their tactics, from Miguel Cortes's perspective, were clearly illegal. As an official for the Bienes Desamortizados office, Cortes petitioned the government. He pleaded that it help put an end to the harm the Molina gang had caused by "granting him all the resources necessary to allow me to recognize the necessary boundaries and appraisals."[31] In short, Cortes needed the help of the national government to combat the Molino cuadrilla in Fumeque and proceed with his task, even if (or precisely because) the Molinos claimed to belong to the Conservative Party. The Molinos perhaps counted on Conservative Party support to help prevent the sale of the *fincas*, or farms, that the government claimed in Umbita and its outlying areas. The Liberal-dominated national government in Bogotá therefore needed to come to the aid of an agent trying to enact that government's policies by giving him full national military support.

This explains why, despite surveyor absenteeism, competing economic interests, occasionally violent local resistance, and attempts at local collusion to resist the measure by government officials, the national policy of desamortización had remarkable success. By December 31, 1869, the national state had disentailed the equivalent of $12,043,513.85 Colombian pesos of church property. Table 3 above details the real estate, movable goods and cattle, and individual debts on property that were transferred to the national state by way of disentailment from 1861 to December 31, 1869.[32] The cost of implementing the measure had been approximately $1 million pesos. Most of the disentailed property was in and around the city of Bogotá. These second most effective process of disentailment occurred in the state of Cauca, followed closely by Boyacá. By the 1870s the most attractive properties had already been sold at auction by the government.[33] The $13 million pesos that the national government generated through desamortización—the bulk of which was amassed from 1861 to 1869—was significant, especially considering that the net revenue typically generated by the Colombian government in one year was about $3.3 million pesos.[34] The question remains, then, if disentailment was contentious at the local level, how come it became so successful during this period. Jorge Villegas Arango has suggested that some individual Conservative Party members in Antioquia, for instance, may have supported the disentailment of church property for personal gain.[35] Personal profit among a few Conservatives in Antioquia, however, does not fully explain the necessary cooperation among state-level authorities and the national government to implement disentailment in each and every state of Colombia. As the next section demonstrates, housing national public education in disentailed properties formerly owned by the church offered Liberals a way to build consensus with Conservatives in different states over the question of state sovereignty over former church properties.

Expropriate the Church to House Public Instruction

The Radical Liberal regime that held national power effectively carried out the disentailment of church property during the 1860s and 1870s and also implemented another, related measure: a national public education system that reached each and every state within the United States of Colombia. To do so, the Olimpo Radical used newly acquired church wealth largely to fund the normal school public education system. In many cases, the expropriated buildings from the church or religious orders often served to house public instruction. Before the Liberal regime at the national level could implement their plan to use disentailed properties for the benefit of a national public education system, they needed the help of key Conservatives, especially in Conservative-dominated states, or those states where the Liberal Party had only a tenuous hold on power.

Tracing out the strategic forms of negotiation between Liberals and Conservatives at the state level underscores, on the one hand, the ways that Conservatives, even within a supposedly Radical Liberal regime, bought into a measure that ultimately strengthened the sovereignty of the states over and above both the national state and the Catholic Church. On the other, tracing out the dimensions of the national public instruction network also reveals the ways in which the Radical Liberal regime adopted models from the first presidential administration under Mosquera in the 1840s. The supposedly federalizing effort of the Liberals, when seen through the national network of public instruction that it created and the materiality of the educational materials that circulated through it, can be better understood as a political system that was less about state's rights to autonomy than it was reminiscent of an earlier effort to improve circulation of people and ideas in ways that put Bogotá at its center.

Before we turn to the national-level vision of the Radical Liberal project, let us return to Boyacá and Hato Grande, the valuable landed property controlled by the Concepción monastery in the town of Chiquinquirá during the 1860s. How this property eventually came to be expropriated from that monastery underscores the connection between disentailment policies and the effort to place public instruction buildings on the sites formally occupied by the church. The earlier discussion of this property showed that the local desamortización agent had noted how folks in the neighboring town of Simijaca wished to purchase lands from Hato Grande, whereas the Chiquinquirá cabildo wanted to hold off on the surveying and parceling out of that monastery's property until a road was completed nearby. This would allow the surveyor to most accurately calculate the value of the land. An earlier surveyor's absenteeism, together with these stalling tactics, would suggest that local members of the population were resisting efforts to expropriate it. The archival record further supports this possible explanation given that as late as 1872 the Concepción monastery still controlled Hato Grande.[36]

The process of expropriation of that particular monastery was further complicated by the fact that the *Bienes Desamortizados* office no longer had a subaltern agent present in Chiquinquirá to oversee the process of disentailment. The principal agent of Tunja in 1872 reported that the reason the Chiquinquirá office had closed was because "the properties that exist in it are totally insignificant and so for this reason no one could be found to take charge of that subaltern agency."[37] That explanation rings somewhat false given the interviews the Tunja agent's predecessor conducted only a few years earlier evidencing interest among Chiquinquira and Simijaca residents regarding the sale price of Hato Grande lands. A decade later, however, a government agent for a different branch of the Liberal regime, the director of public instruction, reported how the property known previously as the "monasterio de concepción" had become property of the state as a result of congressional Law 90 of July 3, 1870.[38]

Law 90 of 1870 allowed the national state to transfer control over disentailed properties from the church to each of the sovereign states. Each state could then subsequently rent out these properties to produce revenue. The case of Hato Grande is instructive. The director of public instruction calculated the value of the land at $16,000 pesos and reported that the national government paid the state of Boyacá $400 annually for rent. The national government had finally expropriated the Concepcion monastery, after over a decade of resistance from the Chiquinquirá cabildo. That it could do so had much to do with Law 90, which finally passed in 1870. The national government, after expropriating the monastery, turned over control of that land and property to the state of Boyacá, where the monastery was located. The national government then guaranteed an income for the state of Boyacá by renting the property for the purposes of national public instruction. That this law was passed and implemented in places like Hato Grande and the Concepción monastery suggests the effective negotiations the Liberal regime carried out with resistant sectors in order to disentail church properties so as to use them for the purposes of public instruction.

Consider how, by May 5, 1875, a normal public school for women opened where the Monastery of the Concepción used to be. The state of Boyacá saw a clear benefit: the national government promised to pay rent on the building to use it for public instruction. Resistance to disentailment melted away.[39] During its first few years this women's school was awash in resources, infrastructural and educational. The national state endowed the school with textbooks, maps, and atlases much like it had done with other recently established normal schools in the capitals of the other *estados soberanos*.[40] Materials included colossal printed maps and atlases based on information by the Chorographic Commission. A school needed substantial wall space to accommodate these images. The largest map was, of course, of Colombia itself, which measured 154 x 172 centimeters. The other maps were not far behind in size; the majority of the state maps measured 73 x 55 centimeters. Children and not a few teachers would be dwarfed when confronted with the sheer size of Colombia and its states. The purpose of these maps was precisely that: to patriotically educate Colombia's schoolchildren with a stable image of the national and state territories, much like Caldas had called for in 1808.

In order to make feasible a nationally sponsored public education system teeming with expensive educational materials, the national state needed to ensure that each individual state was as invested in this program as the national state. The Radical Liberals also knew that for the program to work in the way they wanted, the national state needed to outspend the sovereign states in public education. It should therefore not be surprising that during the 1870s the amount of money the national state dedicated to public instruction was roughly equal to the combined expenditures of all nine states in education.[41] A combination of national, state, and municipal resources funded the national public education system, and funds made available through the disentailment of church lands became most useful for the funding and logistical functioning of public instruction. Law 45 of May 22, 1865, for example, allocated the use of 6 percent of the total amount of revenue generated by disentailment for this purpose. Five years later, the percentage of disentailed funds used toward public instruction dramatically increased to almost 100 percent. By 1870 the national government invested 4 percent of its yearly budget in public education, close to $200,000 pesos, which was roughly the same amount as all funds generated by disentailment that year.[42] With effective disentailment of church properties, the national state was able to increasingly fund public instruction, while also asserting control over the Catholic Church.

Still, there were folks who resisted disentailment, and so the national state tried enticing even Conservative-dominated states to comply. The enticement: each state's sovereignty would be respected and enhanced vis-à-vis disentailed properties. The national state would not control these properties or the rents generated from them. Instead, the states would control this potential source of revenue. The national state further sweetened the deal by guaranteeing each state that it would pay annual rent to each sovereign state on these properties in order to house public instruction within them.

This dynamic allowed the radical Liberal regime to secure the disentailment of church properties despite Conservative Party hostility. Several sovereign states, such as Boyacá, had important pockets of Conservative Party resistance to disentailment. Other states, like Antioquia, were more openly resistant within the very government institutions of the state. Once it became clear that each state could find a potential source of revenue through these disentailed properties, however, such resistance started to dissipate. Fears that funds would directly strengthen the Liberal Party's hold on political power abated, at least somewhat. That was because funds would flow directly into the coffers of each sovereign state, regardless of what political party held control of which state. In turn, the Liberal regime made the logistics of housing public schooling appealing to the sovereign states by guaranteeing an annual rent on these disentailed properties. This was the reason why the national government finally was able to disentail the Monasterio de la Concepción in Boyacá, after a long period of wrangling with the cabildo in Chiquinquirá. The national state then ceded it to the Boyacá state for administration. The national government proceeded to rent the property from the Boyacá state to house the normal school for women.[43] The national government established a similar arrangement with the state of Boyacá over the former monastery of Santa Clara in Boyacá for the normal school for men.[44]

These arrangements proved mutually beneficial for the national government and the sovereign states. The national government housed public instruction in ways that allowed each state to have a new source of revenue as well as access to education. The sectors most resistant to disentailment in the sovereign states accepted, finally, as in Boyacá, the disentailment of prominent church properties that had been a source of resistance and discord. Still, conducting public schooling within the physical space of disentailed church properties sent a strong message to local populations about state power: the government was in control both of church property and a traditionally church-dominated function—education.

Celebrations related to school events went beyond the classroom, crossing into public, political space, and these celebrations excised Catholic imagery. Instead of religious figurines born on the shoulders of the pious and led by Catholic clergy, the pageantry and music in these celebrations served to foreground the significance of government officials as the ministers attending to the educational achievements of students. The annual school examinations in Bogotá became nationally recognized public spectacles, attended by the president, members of the diplomatic corps, city officials, and the commander of the Colombian Guard.[45] Consider how the inauguration of public education in regions far from the capital inspired patriotic celebrations. Jane Meyer Loy has recounted how the opening of a public school in Banco, Magdalena, brought out most of the residents as well as the town band in celebration. "When the *Alcalde* presented the students to their new teacher, he confidently predicted that the school would transform the district into one of the most important localities on the coast."[46] The circulation of ideas, people, and material culture would finally come to Banco, Magdalena, precisely because a public school, connected to a national network of public education, had opened. Properties formerly owned by the Catholic Church facilitated the secular state's ability to expand the public education system in this way. The opening of public schools in each of the sovereign states also had the effect of administratively and imaginatively strengthening the territorial organization of the United States of Colombia.

Consider, for instance, how the legal underpinnings of a national education program intended to strengthen both the territorial organization and the legitimacy of the United States of Colombia. The Organic Decree of 1870 regulating primary education stipulated that the territory of each of the nine states would be subdivided into departments and districts of public instruction.[47] "The territorial demarcations of these Departments and territories will be the same as those that the States have established for their internal political and municipal organization."[48] The state's decision to locate and run the public instruction system according to departmental and district divisions strengthened the meaning of these demarcations and how they functioned, as did setting up normal schools in each capital of every state. This move responded to the political territorial configuration of Colombia that had been consolidated by the Rionegro Constitution of 1863. The national state, under a Liberal regime, thereby expanded its presence among popular sectors beyond what the church had previously accomplished and did so with the help of a new ideological tool they had at their disposal: printed cartographies and geographies.

The director of instruction in Bogotá systematically collected school statistics, encouraged the production of textbooks for school instruction, and supplied schools with the textbooks and materials it deemed appropriate. In 1872 alone the national directorship of public instruction distributed 87,000 books and 8,000 maps throughout the school system.[49] These materials supported an intensive and rigorous academic schedule for normal school students that ran from seven o'clock in the morning to six in the evening, Monday through Saturday. The elementary schools that were annexed to the normal schools had a lighter load: seven o'clock to two in the afternoon, Monday through Saturday. Geography dominated all other subjects. In Boyacá, for instance, the amount of time allotted just to the discipline of studying geography was four times the amount of time dedicated to teaching students history. Students also spent more time learning geography than they did learning how to read, write, or do math.[50]

It should not be surprising that this period became the most active for the popularization of geographic knowledge among

Colombians in the nineteenth century. State inventories of educational materials further reveal that nationally produced geographies and maps were the critical basis for this overwhelmingly significant component of their education.[51] Within the normal schools for men, twenty-four of the forty-six maps available to students were of Colombia and its nine states. The school also possessed "a geography collection of the Sates and the general geography of Colombia by Codazzy."[52] The inventory also counted several geographic dictionaries produced by T. C. Mosquera and other Colombian geographers, all of which emphasized the territorial composition of Colombia. Though the normal school for women had fewer maps, it did possess two maps of Colombia, two globes, several world maps produced in Europe, and a small atlas of the United States of Colombia. The women's school also had forty geography textbooks for learning about the physical and political geography of Colombia as recommended by the general direction of public instruction in Bogotá.[53] The national system of public education thereby further underscored the legal territorial reality of the nine states of the United States of Colombia through the printed images of the newly formed states. The maps that were used in public instruction were the maps that the Radical Liberals, especially under Mosquera, had printed in the 1860s. These maps, of course, drew on (and reshaped) the manuscript provincial maps originally drawn by the Chorographic Commission in the 1850s.

Normal school students in the 1870s learned world geography through these maps of Colombia that finally had been printed in Europe, despite the long, tedious delays that had prevented printed dissemination of the Chorographic Commission's work during the 1850s. This was because the Liberal regime in the 1860s, once again under Mosquera's presidential administration, wasted no time in printing the work of the commission. Gone from those maps, however, are the detailed charts that inform the map reader of the distances between major towns, the supplies traded, the populations ready to bear arms, or the number of beasts of burden. The municipal significance of the cantons was also obliterated. Codazzi's detailed mappings became large, overarching images of the sovereign states to which all students in each state needed to pledge allegiance. Although each state was different, the images conveyed a puzzle-piece quality to them that rendered them all part and parcel of the United States of Colombia. And, as geography textbooks filled school libraries, Bibles were noticeably absent from official school inventories. Printed maps dominated classroom wall space, taking the place of crucifixes.

From the national-level perspective, then, the materiality of the instruction materials that circulated through the newly established normal school system is suggestive of the kind of model that Radical Liberals had in mind for development. Read in light of the circulatory federalizing ideals of the 1840s and 1850s described in chapter 2, the Radical Liberal regime's national public school system of the 1870s and early 1880s is uncannily familiar. The mid-century model, developed during Mosquera's first presidential administration during 1845–1849, acknowledged the flexibility of federalism to address local needs and concerns, as it also allowed for the efficient flow of people and ideas throughout each of the nine individual states, with Bogotá, as the capital city, facilitating and coordinating these flows. This coordinated pattern of federalism centered on Bogotá is reflected in the Radical Olympus's laws regulating public instruction, in the properties and buildings used to finance and house public instruction, and in the texts that circulated within public instruction to support educational activities. These continuities would finally begin to facilitate a generational transformation. From an elite perspective, the deeply entrenched "colonial legacy" would be obliterated from the minds of popular sectors since the Catholic Church would no longer be the only effective educator in the country. Furthermore, only individuals approved by the secular government could teach in this national education system. But when Catholic Church teachings were increasingly and purposefully sidelined, the tenuous consensus agreements struck by national government authorities and state officials were strained to the breaking point.

Ultimately, the success of a secular national education system would prove to be partly responsible for its unraveling. Conservative Party members began to fear how the new cadre of normal school educators would owe their loyalties to the Liberal national regime. The national government, controlled by the Liberal Party, had, after all, funded their training. Those folks loyal to the Liberal Party would in turn work to educate young minds. This reality, together with elite Liberal decisions to hire German Protestant teachers to lead the process of normal school education, sparked the first civil war the United States of Colombia had seen since its constitutional inception of 1863. Although the Liberal Party emerged militarily victorious, financially the Olimpo Radical was in dire straits, putting the national education system in jeopardy. It is to the civil war unleashed by secularization and its effects on the national public instruction system and the Olimpo Radical that we now turn.

Partisan Conflict over Educational Content and Hirings

Radical Liberals carefully negotiated with state officials, regardless of political party affiliation, to win acceptance of the national network of public instruction they wished to open. The shape of that network, together with the distribution of recently printed geographies and maps, lent the newly created United States of Colombia a tangible, imaginable geographic space within students' minds. In order for this network of public instruction to properly function, however, it needed properly trained teachers.

To best understand the significance of public education as a state building effort, we must carefully reconstruct the major contours of the national education network that Radical Liberals had developed in the 1870s. The *escuelas normales*, or teachers colleges, were the cornerstone of the Radical Liberal plan for public education. The July 2 Law of 1870 authorized the national Executive Power to exercise complete control over setting up normal schools in the capitals of each state.[54] That "complete control" was nevertheless negotiated within each state through the disentailed properties that had originally belonged to the church. As previously described, the Executive Power ceded control over the disentailed properties to each state government. Folks resistant to disentailment in different states, such as Boyacá and Antioquia, thereafter warmed to the measure. The national government sweetened the deal even more by guaranteeing to pay state governments rents on these disentailed properties. These properties would, in turn, house normal schools in each state. Therefore, even though the 1870 organic decree on education authorized the federal government to organize, direct, and inspect public primary education in the national territories and states, state governments could nevertheless wield significant power when it came time to housing the normal schools.[55]

One of the key ways the national government tried to support the educational activities of normal school teachers was through the *sociedad de institutores*, or society of instructors. The general director of public instruction, based in Bogotá, decreed the organization and establishment of this society. The chapters of this society supported the activities of normal school teachers in each state. This kind of network implicit in the society of instructors bore striking similarities with societies like the Instituto Caldas considered earlier in this book. The society of instructors brought together the directors and subdirectors of all the public schools in each state including the male and female normal schools. It included members of the public instruction council and the commissions of vigilance, organizations that oversaw school discipline and educational programs. The national state also welcomed all "friends of education" and students of the school deemed worthy of forming part of the committee. This heterogeneous group spanned regional, age, class, and gender differences. The organic decree proposed this support network for teachers so it would "help public instructors keep alive the spirit of their vocation, and through this society they will continue their own instruction through regular meetings, classes, select lessons, consultations, conversations, and written theses."[56] In practice, state directors of public instruction had ample power in naming who participated in several of these organizations and could expel members from the chapters of this society at will. The states, however, had only limited input on the hiring of state directors of public instruction. The director of public instruction in Bogotá named them. But if the state education director gave the state governor any reason to question the newly appointed director's "moral rectitude," this could spell trouble for the functioning of public schools in the state.

Beyond setting up chapters of the society of instructors closely overseen by trusted directors of public instruction, the national government in Bogotá also established clear lines of communication from Bogotá to every publicly supported school in each state. The biweekly official newspaper of public instruction, *La Escuela Normal*, became a principle means for that communication. The periodical, run by the national director of public instruction, was intended as a "true normal school that can help complete instruction for teachers, giving them all kinds of instructions related to their profession."[57] The national government widened readership of *La Escuela* through accessibility. The periodical was free for public schools, artisan guilds, libraries, and scientific and literary societies. Federal and state postal workers were incentivized to distribute the magazine, earning a 10 percent share of the subscriptions that they managed to sell to people they encountered along their routes. The general director of public instruction in Bogotá, who answered directly to the president, controlled the overall content and distribution of the magazine.

Still, it was the directors of normal schools in each state who were the most significant agents of education for the national state. Each director oversaw the hiring and firing of schoolteachers and suggested names of candidates to public instruction councils, where decisions were made about issues specific to local schools. These directors could also remove people from the education councils at will.[58] The national executive power, according to the 1870 decree, again was solely responsible for hiring directors of normal schools. Still, this did not mean that state government officials had no voice in the matter. State governors could suspend the nationally appointed director of public instruction in their state for cause. To do so the governors needed to prove the directors "lacked care and consecration to the carrying out of their duties, or do not demonstrate the intelligence, instructional rigor, firmness of character, and other aptitudes required for the exercising of their important functions."[59] This brokered agreement meant that even though the national government had ample maneuvering room when it came time to determine who would be in charge of public instruction, it nevertheless needed to be careful.

The broad geographic network of public instruction, the negotiations Liberals needed to make with Conservatives to set them up, and the educational societies established to support the training of public school teachers suggest a cross-party effort to enact public education in Colombia. Still, Radical Liberals clearly preferred a kind of training for teachers that would challenge the ideological authority of the Catholic Church and, less explicitly, the Conservative Party. Consider, for instance, Eustacio Santamaría, one of the most articulate expositors of the kind of educational ideals that the Radical Liberal program for public instruction would bring to fruition in Colombia. Santamaría championed German pedagogical methods.[60] He wrote textbooks that provided a holistic approach to education based on German pedagogical styles and adapted these techniques for the needs of Colombian children.[61] Santamaría's idea was to go beyond the mere teaching of reading and writing skills. He wished to "awaken in the minds of children the practical spirit of observation, analysis and investigation, and fix it in their nature in an endurable manner that would make it an integral part of them, giving people from their most tender age the means by which to think with clarity and integrity, that is, to make good use of their intellectual faculties in all circumstances of life."[62] The Catholic spirit was subtly replaced in Santamaría's vision by the spirit of observation, analysis, and investigation. This would be the pedagogical movement that would end the dark colonial legacy of Spanish colonial-era obscurantism that had supposedly been fomented by the Catholic Church. Textbooks adapted for Colombian children were not enough, however. Santamaría proposed to the Colombian government the hiring of Protestant directors to run the normal schools that would teach teachers how to be teachers in Colombia. These Protestant leaders in normal schools would ensure moral rectitude. They would also extirpate any remaining corrupt educational practices lingering through Catholicism. President Eustorgio Salgar, a Radical Liberal, approved Santamaría's proposal.[63] The significance of hiring German Protestant normal school directors cannot be underestimated.

The question remains as to why Santamaría's plan to hire foreign school directors was needed in the first place. According to the decree of 1870, the directors of normal schools would be Colombians trained in the Escuela Central, or Central School in Bogotá. The Central School was designed to be the major center for training the future directors of the escuelas normales in each state.[64] The national government offered four-year government-sponsored fellowships for Escuela Central students. The organic decree ensured meritocracy by stipulating that no other consideration besides intelligence, energy, good character, morality, and vocation would be considered for the award of the fellowships.[65] To receive a fellowship, the students only had to prove

> that they will attend classes at the Central School, dutifully fulfill the assignments stipulated by the requirements, and that upon passing these courses, graduates will serve for at least six years as teachers to the schools that they are appointed to work in. They must dutifully comply with the obligations required of them by the Director or Subdirector [of public instruction], and they if they fail to meet any of these conditions, they must return the total amount of their tuition in addition with six percent interest.[66]

With their education paid for by the government, Escuela Central graduates did not incur debt and could count on guaranteed employment for at least six years with stable wages, also paid for by the government. These students would embark on an adventure, for the government was free to appoint graduates to work at schools wherever they saw fit. As Colombians, presumably Catholic, these directors would not raise the ire of state government officials in any state.

But directors and instructors for normal schools were urgently needed in each state given the spectacular growth of public schools that followed the 1870 organic decree. The problem was, at least as Eustacio Santamaría explained, the government had to wait at least four years for the first graduating class from Escuela Central to produce enough normal school directors for a rapidly expanding network of public instruction. The state director of public instruction for Cundinamarca documented that in 1872 there were 3,594 public school students enrolled. The following year, that number increased to 16,489.[67] Primary public school enrollment overall had increased from the record high of 8.6 percent of the school-age population in 1837 to 18 percent in 1875.[68] From 1873 to 1881 public school enrollments more than tripled nationwide from 23,418 to 71,070.[69] Normal schools were up and running, and demands for public education were at an all-time high. By 1875 twenty normal schools were in operation throughout Colombia, one for each gender in each state in addition to the two Central Schools in Bogotá.[70] That was why the directors of these schools were imported from Europe as per Santamaría's plan. Local populations did not always welcome these Protestant German directors, to say the least. Not only did few of the directors speak Spanish, but their religious beliefs inflamed passions against Protestantism in defense of Catholicism.[71] Furthermore, the growing network of folks who would be loyal to the Liberal Party that provided educators with training and employment threatened to indoctrinate younger populations to support the Liberals rather than Conservatives, even in states controlled by Conservative Party. Civil war loomed.

Devastating civil unrest broke out in Cauca and Tolima in July 1876. Historians have indicated that public education was merely an emotional, superficial issue, albeit a useful one that rallied Conservative forces to fight this war.[72] By framing the causes for the 1876–1877 Civil War in this way—arguably the most violent war during the Olimpo Radical—historians have underestimated the key role that public education actually did play in territorial national state formation during the second half of the nineteenth century. A substantial amount of revenue and resources went into the new education system. To make it work, significant negotiation between the national and state governments ensued. These negotiations went beyond the fiscal revenue that the national government granted state administrations by paying rent on school buildings. The national state also conceded changes in the public school curriculum—in some cases including religious instruction—in order to appease Conservative-dominated states. The problem was that Protestant school directors of normal schools significantly shifted the delicate balance between national and state power. Conservative leaders exploited the move, leading to the explosion of the civil war in 1876–1877. Though the Radical Liberals emerged victorious, they were severely crippled by the blow. The most serious destruction came to the delicate network of public instruction that the Radical Liberals tried to broker with state officials.

Consider how, by 1883, the material conditions for Boyacá's normal school for women set up in the former Concepción Monastery, which had been awash in educational materials and resources in 1875, had changed for the worse. Inoncencia Nariño, in her eighth year of running the school, pleaded with the state director of public instruction. The school was in dire need of reform. Sewing classes were underfunded and lackluster, the school facilities were falling apart, and enrolled students were performing poorly because class sizes were far too large. If Boyacá wanted to successfully train a greater number of women to be teachers, then adequate resources to train them were needed. The school needed either to reduce the number of students or to increase personnel and reduce the number of grade levels for which the current teachers were responsible. Otherwise the school risked training future teachers inadequately.[73] Nariño signed off her yearly report to Boyacá's director signaling the most egregious problem: salaries were paid with "too much informality."[74] Boyacá owed its enthusiastic, dedicated, and hard-working teachers and administrators a total of three months' salary by October of 1883.

As Innocencia Nariño's pleas suggest, by 1883 the Liberal regime's carefully planned national public instruction network was in utter disarray, largely due to the costs of the Civil War. The case of Boyacá is again instructive. The newly inducted director of public instruction for Boyacá complained that most of his time was absorbed in trying to reestablish good working relations with Boyacá's Executive Power.[75] Part of his problem arose from the fact that with the decline in resources due to the war, public instruction necessarily became increasingly dependent on the good will of the state of Boyacá. Furthermore, the national government could no longer support the printing of *La Escuela Normal*, a fact that destroyed national communication among public school functionaries. One way to make up for the loss of this essential teaching aid was trying to convince each state to put state-owned printing presses to work for public education by producing a local version of the paper. This measure was implemented in Boyacá, where the Executive Power ceded the government paper *El Boyacense* to the state director of public instruction for the communication of education-related activities to even the most remote regions of the state. Despite this demonstration of goodwill, tensions mounted between the state governor and the state director of public instruction.

A major problem that arose from the weakened condition of the federal state was that it became difficult if not impossible for Boyacá's state director of public instruction to execute one of his most critical functions: the hiring of public school personnel. In Boyacá a new ordinance signed in 1882 required the state director to consult with the state governor concerning the staffing of schools with inspectors and teachers. The Boyacá governor refused to consult with the director of public instruction and instead hired people of his own choosing, directly challenging federal power coming into the states through public education. The state director complained that as a result popular education was not moving forward as quickly as the national executive power desired.[76] This administrative struggle for control over who got to appoint people to public school posts did not provoke a violent clash. The Boyacá director of public schools instead recommended a workaround. The president of Colombia needed to reassert control over education in Boyacá by bringing in national inspectors to his state. The national director of public instruction would name them, with approval of the executive power. Without this provision, the Boyacá director warned, school inspectors would serve as agents for the state government that named them rather than as representatives for the national public education system.[77]

Catholicism, Education, and Colombian Regeneration

In the 1860s President Mosquera understood the appeal that bringing the Catholic Church under state control would have for Liberals and Conservatives alike. At the very least, the appeal lay with the fiscal revenue that could come from expropriating church landed wealth. Although there were people claiming to be members of the Conservative Party who resisted efforts by the national state to expropriate church lands, all of the nine balkanized states in

Colombia nevertheless did carry out this measure to some extent. That is because under Mosquera, the Colombian government struck deals with each state, allowing them to charge rents on properties expropriated from the Catholic Church. Income from those rents was guaranteed since expropriated church buildings were destined to house the new national education system.

Despite some cross-party support for disentailment of church properties, the nature of the relationship between church and state concerning popular education was a sensitive issue. Liberal leaders understood that the institutional church shaped the minds of the populace in schools and parishes. Liberals were especially keen on replacing Catholic piety with a civic religion organized around the body of the nation, literally. President Mosquera understood how printed maps could help vividly represent the national body to popular sectors. To have huge canvases in schools blanketing the walls made perfect sense. The circulation of such materials within state-sponsored public education, together with a growing cadre of secular teachers, would weaken church control over education and, in doing so, challenge a resilient base of Conservative Party support. Members of the Conservative Party understood this and reacted violently against the growing secular education in schools, unleashing one of the few civil wars fought during the Radical Liberal Olympus.

As a result of conflict during this period of Colombian history, we have a dominant narrative of partisan division as rooted in the nature of church-state relations. There were of course several historical actors who themselves facilitated this partisan narrative regarding the church. For instance, chapter 5 showed how Radical Liberals, like Felipe Pérez, saw the Catholic Church as an obscurantist force in the republic that needed to be excised. And yet there were more moderate Conservatives who understood the Catholic Church as the very foundation of republican virtue and modernity. One such Conservative Party thinker and historian was José Manuel Groot. As it turned out, the overwhelming number of political elites from both the Liberal and Conservative parties hewed closer to Groot's ideas about the Catholic Church's role in the republic than they did toward Felipe Pérez.

This explains why by the 1880s José María Samper, the same jurist and former member of the Instituto Caldas who developed New Granada's science of constitutionalism in the 1850s, wrote an enthusiastic, glowing review of José Manuel Groot's life and his works. Recently deceased in 1878, Conservative thinker Groot had been Samper's life-long friend and teacher. Samper recounted differences in political leanings over the course of their lives, but these differences had been bridged by their shared passion for poetry, art, literature—especially costumbrismo—and the science of historical writing. Samper dedicated special attention to Groot's three-volume *Historia eclesiastica y civil de Nueva Granada* (1869).[78] Samper noted how, in contrast to existing works at the time, including that of his father-in-law, Joaquin Acosta, and one that he himself had written, Groot single-handedly filled a gaping lacuna. "Don José Manuel Groot," explained Samper, "has made manifest that all of the civilization of this country was the work of the Catholic clergy in its diverse branches. . . . His integrity and his historical science have guided him in such a way that have led him to actually write a true national history."[79] The science of history became, by Groot's pen, the foremost way through which New Granada elites, Liberal and Conservative, came to a consensus on the unique role that the Catholic Church played in fostering a national republican identity.

Groot had begun to write his history in 1856. This was in the wake of the 1854 Civil War and in the midst of the rise of a new territorial order that was coupled with increasing Liberal Party anticlerical attacks looking to undermine popular support for the Conservative Party. These attacks were especially colorful when it came time to paint the Catholic Church in a negative light, as a holdover from the obscurantism of Spanish colonialism. Groot's inspiration for his study on the church came as a reaction to these negative portrayals. By 1856 he considered that it was "dishonorable for a Catholic and civilized country to lack the history of its church, especially when its clergy has been so unjustly slandered by some national writers of our times, who have presented [the clergy] to the new generations as the enemy of lights and hostile to the cause of American independence."[80] Groot rescued historical archives on the church from the dangers of oblivion, documenting its long history in Spanish America in order to show how Catholicism had been the "vital element of its civilization and progress."[81]

Groot's turn toward a scientific history of the church brought him head-to-head against those who had invented a negative colonial legacy for Catholicism. He explained how,

> either because of a misunderstood patriotism, or because of fashion, or because of bad intentions, or because of ignorance of the facts, they have stubbornly slandered the former Spanish government, and, lacking any consideration or even criteria, they have attributed to [Spain] an infamous political position towards its colonies in America.[82]

Although Groot's historical study seems to fit a pattern occurring throughout the Spanish Atlantic world that leaned toward an embrace of Spanish culture and history at the end of the nineteenth century with the U.S. defeat of the Spanish in 1898, Groot's 1869 history was a generation ahead of this trend. Groot sought to offer a scientifically documented history that put the Catholic Church as a marker of a Spanish identity that was at the center of the republican civilization that had emerged in Colombia. "Who is responsible for our presence in America?" Groot rhetorically asked. His answer: "We are not Indians. We are sons of the Spanish, and it is because of them that we have the societies that have allowed us to make a republic."[83]

As Mark Thurner and others have shown, the commissioning of historical writings by Spanish American states in the nineteenth century offered a scientific way of establishing a civilized, national identity that could foment patriotic sentiment.[84] These historical writings also could have a consensus-building effect, especially among elites divided over the cultural meaning and historical identity of the nation. Samper's literary eulogy of Groot came during efforts by the Colombian state to assert control over the Catholic Church by disentailing church properties held in mortmain and then using those funds and properties to support the expansion of a national public education system. President Mosquera's 1860s administrations tried bringing the Catholic Church to heel by to reasserting the patronato, or national state control over naming Catholic Church leadership. Not surprisingly, several leading Conservatives joined the church in championing the liberal principle that called for the separation of church from state precisely because of the negative effects that a national patronato had on church power.[85] And yet, as detailed above, there were some Conservatives in the 1860s and 1870s who saw a clear benefit to, at the very least, disentailing church wealth so that state coffers could expand along with public instruction.

Radical Liberals understood how the precarious place of the public education network in each state reflected their own tenuous hold on political power through client networks. In the wake of the Civil War of 1876 to 1877, political rivalries and factionalism within the Liberal Party contributed to the breakdown of Liberal control over the national government. A split emerged in the Liberal Party between Radicals and Independents. These Liberal Independents began to ally with Conservative Party members who backed Rafael Nuñez for the presidency against Radical Liberal candidate Aquileo Parra. The Radical regime's fate was sealed with the death of their longtime leader, Manuel Murillo Toro, in 1880.[86] That same year Nuñez was elected to his first term as president and initiated the beginnings of a new, more centralized political system. Termed the Regeneración, or Regeneration, this new political regime brandished the Radical Liberal political efforts at state building as too intolerant of Catholic piety, too violent, and ultimately obsolete. The careful negotiations struck by the Liberal Party regime and members of the Conservative Party in each state during the 1860s and 1870s, which served as the basis for cross-party coalitions at the national government level, came to be rendered invisible. In part this was because, contrary to the Mosquera administration's targeted attack on the autonomy and political power of the Catholic Church in Colombia, the Regeneración underscored the importance of popular religiosity as expressed through Catholicism for the purposes of cultural integration and social cohesion.

Radical Liberals made one last desperate attempt at rebellion against the Regeneración and the Catholic Church in 1885, only to be defeated by the Regeneración's national reserve army. After the defeat of the Radical Liberals, Nuñez declared the death of the 1863 Rionegro Constitution and inaugurated a new constitutional process. The Constitution of 1886 sought political stability by centralizing political power in the national state, restoring the alliance between the state and the Catholic Church, and weakening the political power of the states. The new political organization fundamentally changed the relationship between the national government and the new territorial entities into which it was divided, now termed "departments."

The 1888 approval of the signed Concordat between Colombia and the Catholic Church restored full privileges to the Catholic Church including a legal monopoly on marriage, territorial control over missions in Colombia that spanned approximately 65 percent of the national territory, and, notably, control over the public education system developed by the Radical Liberals largely with funds from disentailment of church properties. The eventual defeat of the ideological underpinnings behind the Radical Liberal program for public education was made legally manifest in the 1886 Constitution that explicitly linked public education to Catholicism. And yet the incoming Regeneración regime did not dismantle the work of the Radicals. They realized the utility of having national presence in the states via public schools. The subsequent regime simply maintained and furthered the infrastructure set up under the Olimpo Radical for public instruction, but strengthened their relationship with the Catholic Church by handing over control of public education to the church. The process was not an easy one, especially since the War of 1876 had severely disrupted education and destroyed many school facilities. Nevertheless, by 1918 a program of public school instruction flourished that was supported by the state but controlled by the Catholic Church.[87] Many Liberals, incensed at these measures because they weakened the effects of liberal secularization, continued to rebel against the Regeneración, which by then was a largely Conservative Party regime.[88] Despite these measures and continued conflict with some Liberal Party members, the Conservative Party was not so pro–Catholic Church that it would return to that institution the vast wealth that it had lost though disentailment. Instead, Colombia simply placed itself in debt with the church for only 13 percent of the total value of the wealth that the Colombian state had expropriated during the previous decades.[89]

Political wrangling and civil war over the role that the church needed to play in the nation eventually gave way, once again, to consensus. Enough elites from across the political spectrum agreed the church was a central component of Colombian identity. The constitutional transformation of the 1880s reflected this agreement. José María Samper emerged once again as a principle framer of that constitution. By then Samper had turned away from the Liberal political party and joined the Conservatives. Also by then José Manuel Groot and his science of history helped articulate for elites like Samper the kind consensual ideal that the church historically played, and should play, in the Colombian Republic's national identity.

This chapter has shown Liberal and Conservative party elites who had little direct connection to Catholic Church wealth largely agreed on the policy of disentailment. That is because such a policy was rooted in a larger republican goal: asserting the right of patronato over the Catholic Church, much like the Spanish monarchy had done prior to independence. Church resistance to the measure nevertheless was strong throughout the early nineteenth century. We saw how national government representatives in different states reported on the difficulties of implementing an unpopular measure in states like Boyacá, whose roving bands of Conservatives threatened retaliation. Implementing disentailment in Conservative Party–dominated states like Antioquia also proved challenging, to say the least. And yet, disentailment did occur in each of the nine states that made up the United States of Colombia. By the 1860s a Liberal-dominated national regime engaged state government officials strategically, winning over even Conservative Party officials to the policy of disentailment by ceding national control over properties expropriated from the Catholic Church to state governments. The negotiations and wrangling over control over disentailed land translated quickly into the emergence of the national public education system, precisely because funds and infrastructure disentailed from the church were used to fund and house the public education network that Liberals had in mind.

State sovereignty finally came to overrule even the Catholic Church's claims to wealth and doctrinal power through education. The common ground of state sovereignty allowed the Radical Liberals to expand a system of normal school education they wished would reform Colombia's national community, state by sovereign state. Printed maps and school geographies would be disseminated to schools led by moral normal school teachers who would extricate from young minds the most negative effects of the colonial legacy that had been perpetuated by immoral Catholic priests. At least that was the Radical Liberals' hope. Running such an education program would be expensive, and so the national government dedicated a significant portion of the monies and properties gathered through the disentailment of church lands to this end.

The national network of public instruction the regime set up was impressive. The seats of teacher-training normal schools occupied former church properties and were located in the capital cities of each sovereign state. The smaller schools in which normal school graduates would work were located in the capital cities of each district in each state. The Radical Liberal regime supported the work of normal school teachers through an education society modeled closely on the Instituto Caldas from a generation prior. This society also had chapters in several major cities within each state. The different chapters communicated with each other via an education newspaper. The national state supported these spaces of education sociability and through them distributed newly printed maps, geography primers, atlases, and lesson plans to schools that taught students about the connection between humans and the earth through geography and natural sciences. President Mosquera himself had the maps of the Chorographic Commission transformed into large canvasses to reflect the new territorial reorganization of the country into states. The maps were no longer meant as archives and placeholders for commercial data, resource availability, and population statistics of municipalities and provinces. The maps instead became useful as pedagogical tools to mold the minds of the youth as pliable clay, but significantly, young minds could no longer be vessels for the values of clericalism and the Catholic Church. No longer would the Catholic Church serve as a unifying cultural force that would promote republican entrepreneurship and virtue within a large master plan of internal markets and circulation. That was because some leaders of the Liberal Party came to see the Catholic Church as an institution that firmly backed the Conservative Party and so needed to be controlled by the Liberal Party dominated national state.

The new network of schools and education societies not only afforded hundreds of people, men and women, a greater measure of education as well as spatial and social mobility; it also threatened to extirpate the (misguided, in Liberal minds, and moral, in Conservative minds) Catholic piety who had undergirded so much of the political support popular sectors had given to the Conservative Party starting in the 1850s. That was the point. The territorial presence and potential influence of the public school system developed by the Radical Liberal regime from the 1860s to the 1880s had made it both a threat and an object of desire for the Conservative Party and the Catholic Church. Moreover, this centralized network of public schools set up throughout the national territory underscores how the Radical Liberal regime implemented measures that offered continuity with the kind of state-building models developed through consensus by elites during the 1840s under Mosquera's first presidential administration. The form the state needed to take through public education, at least as evidenced by the measures taken by the historical actors themselves, was less about federalism versus centralism in the 1860s; it was about implementing a kind of national network that facilitated the flow of ideas, people, and material goods throughout the nation. This model came to be heavily criticized by Conservatives under threat. When it came time to decide the role of the Catholic Church in popular education, violent conflict erupted.

Historical narratives that emerged in the wake of civil conflict tended to erase the critical sites of consensus that Liberal and

Conservative party elites shared, even with respect to the role the Catholic Church should play in the republic. Both Conservatives and Liberals agreed in the 1860s and 1870s that the republic should assert control over the church. That was because Conservative and Liberal party elites all benefited, state by sovereign state in the United States of Colombia. By the late 1870s through the 1880s the national secular public education system expanded in ways uncannily similar to the circulatory model of the 1840s. This networked expansion, however, threatened to challenge the Conservative Party within the states they controlled. When German Protestant teachers were hired to teach teachers how to be teachers, civil war erupted. Parallel to this conflict came new narratives of the Catholic Church as foundational to Spanish American republicanism. José Manuel Groot's history of the church became the cultural rallying cry that brought consensus to elites once again. Rather than controlling and extirpating the church, the path forward became placing Catholicism at the center of Colombian republican identity.

Conclusion

*A Continental Postcolonial Colombia
Challenges the Latin Race Idea*

José Manuel Groot's death in 1878 marked a decisive moment for José María Samper. Samper poured his intellect into writing an eloquent elegy of Groot and his life's works. Samper emphasized the notable contribution Groot had made to the science of history, given Groot's impressive volumes on the history of the Catholic Church. By doing so, Samper, the noted liberal thinker, geographer, and jurist, signaled a significant political shift within New Granada. The deep rupture that had emerged among elite party leaders was just starting to move toward consensus once again. This book has underscored the theme of consensus among elite political leaders throughout the nineteenth century. This is not to say conflict did not occur. Tensions between the newly formed Liberal and Conservative parties exploded in the wake of the early 1850s constitutional republican experiment to abolish slavery and establish universal manhood suffrage. As each party expended significant efforts to mobilize popular sectors toward its own cause, Liberal elites came to resent the ability of the Conservative Party to build their base off of the influence of the Catholic Church. From the late 1850s and throughout the 1860s and 1870s, Liberal Party leaders, spearheaded by Tomás Cipriano de Mosquera, launched targeted attacks against the Catholic Church. More radical Liberals, such as Felipe Pérez, lambasted the church as the last bastion and example of the continuing and negative effects of the colonial legacy. More centrist Liberals and Conservatives who had come out of the Instituto Caldas generation nevertheless understood that the wealth held by the church in mortmain impeded circulation of land and property through free markets. While some more centrist Liberals like Ancízar argued corrupt church leaders impeded a proper, liberal, and secular education for New Granada citizens, they did not go as far to reject the Catholic Church altogether. Groot's history of the Catholic Church in Spanish America helped bring ideas about consensus over the cultural and moral value of the church back to the forefront of national identity. New Granada republicans, Liberal and Conservative, were not alone in their efforts to grapple with respect to the place of the Catholic Church in the newly founded states; several Spanish American republics launched similar criticisms and policies against the Catholic Church.[1]

By the 1870s, however, New Granada republicans like Samper began to see the Catholic Church in New Granada in a different light. Samper approved of Groot's championing of the Catholic Church, precisely because Groot had managed to document a history of Catholicism that proved the church to be an essential institutional component of modernity, rather than an obstacle to modernity. Samper was ready to praise Groot's assessments precisely because he had long attributed the origins of constitutional democracy to Jesus Christ, earning himself and other elite Liberals the moniker Gólgotas. But Liberals were not alone in their belief in the positive impact of the Catholic Church on Spanish American republics. Samper's embrace of Catholicism for modern republics emerges most clearly in the writings he produced while traveling with his newly wedded wife, Soledad Acosta de Samper, through Europe from 1858 to 1862.[2] Samper's conversion to Conservatism, then, was not a radical departure from the core foundational premises of the Instituto Caldas in the 1840s to which he had ascribed. President Mosquera himself, for instance, did not go as far as Felipe Pérez in lambasting the totality of Spanish cultural heritage in Spanish America. Samper, like many other former members of the Instituto Caldas, were open to, and willing to embrace, the positive influence the Catholic Church brought to Spanish American republics.

The Samper family's travels through Europe allowed them respite from the worst of the battles between New Granada Liberals and Conservatives over the colonial legacy, especially the most egregious legacies that had been invented for the Catholic Church. The

Samper family nevertheless did encounter other Spanish Americans in Europe who held firm beliefs about the Catholic Church as a negative holdover from the colonial period. These ideas circulated widely through midcentury periodicals.

From Europe the Samper family also came to witness a larger, related ideological battle. The ire of Spanish Americans throughout the continent was directed against the imperial moves made by the United States of America. Not only had the United States expanded territorially in the wake of the U.S.-Mexican War, but by 1856 William Walker's filibustering expedition to Nicaragua had toppled the legitimate government. Insultingly, pro-South, Democratic U.S. president Franklin Pierce formally recognized Walker's regime, one that had reinstituted slavery in Nicaragua. The autonomy and sovereignty of all Spanish American polities in the region were coming under attack, as was their commitment to the abolishment of slavery. Unity would be the only way to counter these incursions. Such unity required the emergence of a new identity for the postcolonial world that Spain begot in the continent. For many, "Latin" America seemed an appealing term for it emphasized a modern "Latin" race, one that could downplay ties to the former colonial power of Spain while highlighting links with France, a clearly modern force in the world. This supposed Latin race could formidably oppose "Anglo-Saxon" expansionist designs from the United States. Upon his arrival in London in 1858, José María Samper reflected on the term "Latin America." Unlike his contemporaries, however, Samper found the Latin race to be an unfortunate term at best, and a scientifically vapid one at that.

Several scholars, including Michel Gobat, Aims McGuiness, Arturo Ardao, and Miguel Rojas Mix have shown how the term "Latin America" had been in circulation as early as 1856, in the wake of the U.S. recognition of William Walker's "piratical" regime in Nicaragua.[3] The Radical Liberal and Chilean Francisco Bilbao notably used the concept of "Latin America" as a way to differentiate the "Latin" race of peoples occupying America from those "Anglo-Saxons" launching attacks from the United States. Bilbao's concept did double duty, for it also differentiated "America" from the monarchical imperial designs that Europe, especially France and Spain, had projected onto the New World in the wake of the repression that followed Europe's democratic republican spring of 1848. Speaking to an audience in Paris, Bilbao underscored the significance, and modernity, of a "Latin" race that was at once far more democratic than the monarchical regimes of Europe and far more advanced than the racist, expansionist, and individualistic characteristics that made up the Anglo-Saxon "race" in the United States.[4]

José María Samper also spoke to Spanish-speaking audiences on these themes while in Europe at around roughly the same time, but he did so from a different perspective. Samper agreed that a distinction between the United States and the rest of the region was urgently called for, but he notably disagreed with Bilbao's assertions regarding the genealogical determinism that a Latin "race" implied.[5] Samper also demurred from the term "Hispanic America" as a way to connote the transference of inherited, unchangeable traits from one generation to the next. Neither "Latin" nor "Hispanic," in Samper's opinion, would effectively mark off parts of America as different from—and a counter to—the looming imperialism of the United States. Instead, Samper preferred a term that had been out of circulation since Venezuela and Ecuador had seceded away from New Granada in 1830: Colombia.

By 1858 Samper revived the name "Colombia" to evoke a continental ideal, one first imagined by Francisco de Miranda and later taken up by Bolívar.[6] This continental Colombia would bring together all Spain's possessions in America under one united republican name. Samper's justifications for "Colombia" as a term were rooted in a fundamentally different take on "race" than that held by Radical Liberal thinkers like Bilbao and other intellectuals and scientists in Europe and across the Atlantic World. Samper, writing the same year Franz Boaz was born, produced an uncannily similar argument in 1858 to the one that the German-Jewish newborn would later pen in 1911 as an anthropologist.[7] Samper directly challenged the idea of the genealogical determinism implied by the racial descriptor "Latin" or "Hispanic" as applied to the former domains of Spain in America. His reflections bear repeating at length:

The Latin race does not exist in Colombia. Neither does the indigenous race, nor the African race, which was unfortunately brought with slavery. Within the great majority of Colombia, we find the modern race of democratic republicanism. . . . That which unites or differentiates the pueblos is not their genealogy, but instead their civilization. That is to say, differences lie with the kind of principles that move the pueblos towards improvement versus those principles that force pueblos to stagnate and weaken.[8]

Samper did not deny the existence of distinct human races in 1858; given the latest trends in scientific and intellectual writings, especially in Europe, it was impossible for him to do so. Yet although he used "race" to describe differences among human groups, Samper argued the word "race" needed to be replaced by the concept of "civilization."[9] Climate and institutions played a much more important role in producing differences among human groups than any inherited, biological trait. Well before the Latin American eugenicists of the early twentieth century, Samper emphasized the malleability of human groups when placed in different institutional and natural climates.[10] Samper further suggested that the driving force behind arguments championing either the "Latin" or the "Anglo" race were reflective of a deep conflict that pitted Roman Catholic Spain against anti-Catholic England, a conflict that had been transplanted to the Western Hemisphere, influencing the development of institutions there.[11]

Samper went further and ridiculed the idea of a purely Spanish or "Latin" race. He argued that it was the "crossing" of the European, the indigenous, and the African peoples, together with the social, economic, and historical impact of this mixing, that had most impacted development in the New World. Spanish America was not the only place to endure such transformations. For thousands of years the population of Spain had itself long been the product of mixture given the several different bloodlines that had traversed the Iberian Peninsula precisely because of its geographic location on the Mediterranean crossroads.[12] The liberal revolutions experienced in continental Colombia were as deep and wide-ranging as the kind of liberal transformations that Spain endured in the wake of the dissolution of its Atlantic Empire—so much so that Samper believed stitching Spain and Spanish America back together was not only possible but also necessary. This complex reweaving would be made possible by the moral threads of Catholicism that historically shaped life for people on both sides of the Atlantic.

The Catholicism Samper had in mind was not the Catholicism of the colonial period, however. The current-day Spanish Catholicism that Samper witnessed was vibrant and modern, wholly adapted and adaptable to the political modernity emerging in America and in Spain. Material and spiritual unity was the only logical conclusion:

> A civilization that is exclusively based on materiality is as impossible as one that is based exclusively on morality. The world lives off of the harmony between the spirit and the material, Rome and Carthage have made their alliance during this century, and poetry, arts, and sciences prosper wherever industry develops and vice versa.[13]

Spain and Colombia together would be strengthened through the circulation of both moral ideals and material goods in an era of civilized modernity.

Samper's midcentury vision for a united Hispano-Colombia came much earlier than most scholars might expect. As oligarchic republics strengthened their hold on the region in the 1880s, several Spanish American elites warmed up to the idea of forging closer cultural, spiritual, and material ties to Spain. The quadricentennial celebration of Columbus's voyage to the Americas in 1892 further inspired cultural and diplomatic ties. These ties were consolidated in the wake of the dramatic loss by Spain of Cuba, Puerto Rico, Guam, and the Philippines to the United States in 1898.[14] The political and economic transformations ushered in by the "Regeneration" regimes sprouting up throughout the region and across the Atlantic were, in turn, reflective of this new moment of unity, one that rejected popular republicanism in favor of a much more oligarchic strain.[15] As Betancourt-Medieta has demonstrated, however, José María Samper made significant contributions to the idea of an Hispano-American unity facilitated from Spain much earlier than the Hispano-Americanism that came into vogue during the late nineteenth century.[16]

In the late 1850s José María Samper saw unity based on cultural and institutional commonalities—rather than on inherent racial traits—as the best way to mount an effective challenge to the United States and its growing territorial hunger. The liberalism and Catholicism shared by a continental Colombia with Spain offered a strong, moral, and modernizing counter to the imperialistic designs of the rapacious and indivisible United States. At least that was Samper's hope. In the late 1850s through the early 1860s, however, audiences and intellectuals in Spain were reluctant to take up Samper's call. Spanish Americans, for their part, could not ignore the fact that Spain continued to hold colonies in the Caribbean that maintained exploitative slave regimes, no matter how liberal Spanish rule over those colonies claimed to be. To make matters worse, in December 1861 Spain collaborated with France and Britain to invade Mexico, eventually bringing Maximilian I to power as Mexico's second emperor.[17] These dramatic changes and long-term continuities ultimately shaped opinions on both sides of the Atlantic in ways that rendered Samper's proposals moot. The kind of Hispano-Colombia Samper envisioned was not to be.

Samper's ideas, however much they came to be ignored, are nevertheless remarkable. Samper was very much part of a world where the "science" of race was in its infancy, a moment that allowed Samper to directly challenge the notion that racial traits were inherited and unchangeable. In so doing, he sought to liberate both Spain and Spanish America from a racial destiny that forever would condemn these places to an indelible inherited "racial" stain that could never be erased. The obscurantist and exploitative institutions of the colonial period were not inherently Spanish, argued Samper. Instead, they were rooted in the kind of exploitative institutions of colonialism as they played out from the fifteenth through the eighteenth centuries. In other words, Samper limited the "colonial legacy" to the colonial period. Even so, not all institutions from the colonial period were tainted with this legacy. The Catholic Church was the light of spiritual modernity that tempered the negative effects of unfortunate colonial institutions.

As a "Latin" race idea vied for dominance in the mid-nineteenth century and was working its way toward offering a new name for the former Spanish colonies, Samper forcefully argued against it. He offered the "Colombian" label as a way to identify a continent that had unchained itself from a "colonial" matrix only to struggle for decades to erase the negative effects of these "colonial" legacies. There was nothing innately or genealogically "Spanish" about those legacies. It is this remarkable ability of men like Samper to step out of the narrow restraints of all dominant discursive structures that has been the focus of this book.

This book takes the innovative and unique intellectual creativity of men like Samper seriously. It highlights the myriad forms of geographic and territorial sciences that these men reworked and created anew for the complex needs of New Granada during the nineteenth century. By doing so, this book seeks to do for Colombia's nineteenth century what Samper had sought to do for Spain and Hispano-Colombia's colonial period. Scholars have repeatedly called into question the false divide between federalizing Liberals and centralizing Conservatives. Yet overwhelming numbers of studies nevertheless continue to reify these shorthand distinctions in order to make sense of an admittedly complex period. Rather than strict partisan divisions, at least at the elite level, what this book has found is an overwhelming republican consensus around the need to modernize politically and economically, and to do so morally. Doing so would allow elite republicans to diagnose and root out what they believed to be the negative effects of the "colonial legacy."

The book has traced out how, from the period of independence, republican leaders invented a series of "colonial" legacies that legitimated independent republican rule. With the emergence of the first Colombian Republic, remembered as Gran Colombia, men such as Secretary of the Interior José Manuel Restrepo drew on the lights produced by late eighteenth-century wise men and shone them on the barbarity of the Spanish monarchy. They did so precisely because during the wars of independence the Crown had so viciously executed enlightened men like Francisco José de Caldas. In that early period Caldas and his geographic writings offered

Gran Colombia officials the kind of descriptions they needed to legitimate a fledgling if gargantuan republic that encompassed most of northern South America. The barbarity and obscurantism that executed Caldas was projected back onto all of the three hundred years that the Spanish monarchy had ruled over Spanish America, legitimating claims to independence. One result was that the original loyalty to the Crown that Francisco José de Caldas had expressed as late as 1808 was easily erased. Caldas's own words supplicating the Crown to support greater research into the geography of the Kingdom of New Granada by signaling that "geography was in its infancy" served the subsequent republican regime's efforts to point to the ignorance that the Crown had spread in Spanish America. These reinterpretations of Caldas also helped bolster the "Black Legend" of Spanish colonialism perpetuated outside the monarchy's dominions, especially in the Anglophone world. Although these reinterpretations may have helped legitimate Spanish American independence, they also insidiously erased the deep and long cartographic and geographic tradition created by agents and officials working in the name of the Spanish Crown throughout the period of monarchical rule.[18]

In the wake of the dissolution of Gran Colombia, elites from across the political spectrum saw in scientific innovation all that was moral, innovative, and enlightened about New Granada. Provincial elite leadership organized around the first presidential administration of Tomás Cipirano de Mosquera, forging a consensus on the meaning of the colonial legacy. All agreed that for the national project to work, New Granada needed to break its many barriers to circulation. Problems to circulation abounded. Measuring systems, currencies, and grammars varied widely. Travel over land and sea was onerous, long, and often life threatening. Each region had different ideas about what policies would foment development and progress. This unevenness was at the core of interregional conflict. By midcentury, and with help from Mosquera's administration, Bogotá emerged as the hub for the homogenization and circulation of know-how, resources, educational institutions, expertise, grammars, laws, and political communication. This 1840s project, articulated best by the founders of the Instituto Caldas, was "federalist" in nature, bipartisan in political consensus, and it became the blueprint for the rest of the century.

One of the driving inspirations behind the innovation and creativity of the new scientific developments unleashed by folks affiliated with the Instituto Caldas was how these men sought to dismantle a supposed "colonial legacy." But much like the new sciences developed during this period, the colonial legacy was itself a nineteenth-century republican invention. The result was that ever more sophisticated sciences were intended to root out the negative effects of an ever more elusive and intractable colonial legacy from the New Granada republic.

The science of political economy, for instance, allowed for an early recognition of a consensual path to modernity that supposedly led away from the colonial period and toward the recognition of regional differences, comparative advantage, and circulation. This kind of political economy was at the heart of the Chorographic Commission. Similarly the training of young elite men from various New Granada provinces in a cartographic language that identified valuable resources, agricultural lands, rivers, and roads would help foment the circulation that would tackle the legacy of colonial "lethargy" that blocked development.

The training Colegio Militar students received also plugged into a longer effort at perfecting land surveys, especially the survey of indigenous resguardo lands. New Granada land survey training focused on indigenous resguardos in an effort to perfect a utopian calculus of equality. This was a science designed to turn the colonial "Indio" into the national "indigena" that then could be made into a New Granada citizen like all others—that is, once communal resguardo lands were abolished. Drawing on the popular model developed first by Bolívar, the New Granada legislature idealized a form of abolishment of resguardos that would give equal parcels of land to each individual, deserving indigena family. This move entailed a radical agrarian reform, one that never worked. It was buried by the minutia of a calculus seeking to define value for lands in different microclimates, while also trying to identify who actually was a deserving "indigena." The complexities in calculations and census taking opened up several fronts of litigation and challenges. No matter how well trained the land surveyor, no matter how refined the sciences in which the surveyor trained, challenges and lawsuits abounded.

This failed experiment in the science of agrarian equality, however, strengthened the republican state. The fragmentation and decentralization of legal authority favored drawn-out litigation and counter appeals. In a world of constant civil wars and radical agrarian reform, New Granada, unlike Mexico, did not witness large-scale armed violence over disputed indigenous land ownership during this period. The nineteenth-century aspiring modern republic built the state on the back of the legal pluralisms that had first emerged during the colonial period. Ironically, this was a very effective way of legitimating the state because it was the essence of the monarchical state during the colonial period. The Spanish monarchy proved resilient precisely because it inserted itself as the legitimate arbiter of conflict. And yet this palpable "legacy" did not factor into nineteenth-century ideas about what the "colonial legacy" was. Instead, nineteenth-century courtrooms, governor's offices, legislative sessions, and on-the-ground field work by surveyors allowed folks across the political and ethnic spectrum to invent the miserable indigena as a holdover from the colonial period, one who either refused the benefits of modernity or who had been exploited by those claiming to bring those benefits of modernity to the indigenas.

The book turned from the fieldwork of Colegio Militar graduates trained by Chorographic Commission members to the lives and times of the Chorographic Commission itself. The book underscored how the commission emerged from the consensus among elites seeking modernity and republicanism through science in the late 1840s. This explains why, despite profound schisms that emerged between Liberal and Conservative elite leaders, the commission continued to receive national support, no matter which party held power. Building on the deep and rich work that has recently emerged on the Chorographic Commission, I underscore the way commission members helped launch a new form of scientific writing: political ethnography. I gave this term to a type of literature that historians and literary scholars have called "costumbrismo." Rather than dismiss this form of writing as "nostalgic and hardly ever critical," I have teased out how this form of narrative description constituted a science of the minute that revealed larger cultural worlds of the self.[19] That is because, of all the information gathered and organized by the commission, the narrative description by Manuel Ancízar as secretary of the Chorographic Commission, was the most widely read at the time. The commission was not alone in developing this science as a way of working out the "colonial" through the analysis of the quotidian. Political ethnography was the discourse articulated though reports printed in an immense network of short-lived newspapers that appeared in almost every middle-class household, particularly in Bogotá, but not exclusively. It was a world of publications that has been barely understood. This kind of political ethnography sought to change the individual from within, through collective reading of self-recognition that could ridicule and shame as much as it could honor and venerate popular religiosity and popular culture.

By midcentury, however, cross-party consensus over where the colonial legacy lay, how its effects played out, and what was needed to extirpate it had vanished. This was especially true when it came time to evaluate its manifestations in the mundane. As New Granada's republican vanguard splintered into viciously opposed political parties, popular mobilization came to shape elite party leaders' strategies to win political power and elected posts. Elites drew sharp, reifying lines between themselves and the opposing political party. Liberal and Conservative forms of self-identification emerged among popular sectors as well. By 1853, sweeping political transformations tied to popular mobilization led to the abolition of slavery and the inauguration of universal manhood suffrage. One result was that competition between the two parties for political posts at the national and provincial levels became the basis for the radical territorial reorganization that New Granada witnessed from the 1840s into the 1860s. The original twenty provinces of New Granada from 1832 mushroomed into thirty-six by 1853, only to rework themselves into nine sovereign states by the 1860s. Liberals in the early 1850s followed a territorial strategy to expand the number of provinces by carving out Liberal-friendly political spaces. Universal manhood suffrage transformed the political outcome for Liberals given the ways the Conservative Party had effectively come to identify itself with the Catholic Church. This despite the fact that many Conservative elites agreed with Liberals that the church needed to be under the control of the republican state. Civil war erupted. For elites across the political spectrum the quandary lay not with constitutions, or liberal ideas, but with the long-term impact of the colonial legacy on unprepared citizens.

For Liberals and Conservatives alike, popular participation seemed to unleash the cultural forces of the "colonial legacy." Liberals worried that members of the Catholic Church who either were hostile to the Liberal-led government or were corrupt morally could easily manipulate and mobilize the superstitious, uneducated, and misinformed population due to their power at the pulpit. This form of manipulation not only hurt popular sectors, but it would drag down the vanguard republic, or at the very least keep the Liberal Party out of office. Conservatives, for their part, championed the sophistication of popular religiosity. Its manifestations were themselves a form of political discourse that challenged the immoral Liberal elites, who had distanced themselves from the Catholic Church. These Liberals, from the point of view of elite Conservative writings, were far too blinded by the draw of foreign models. Their "neocolonial" mentality (avant la lettre) meant elite Liberals could not appreciate the ingenuity of popular sectors or how popular sectors rejected the immoralities of foreign liberalism. As these ethnographies of the everyday did battle in the public sphere to win popular hearts and minds to one or another cause, civil war erupted again. More extreme Liberals like Felipe Pérez blamed the Conservative Party and the corrupting power of the church for creating popular hostility toward the Liberal Party. By the end of the conflict, the first president to be elected through universal manhood suffrage in Colombia, Conservative Party founder Mariano Ospina, was deposed from office by former president and general Tomás Cipriano de Mosquera. Nine sovereign states emerged as the United States of Colombia. Although at the national level control was in the hands of the Liberal Party, the Conservative Party did manage to carve out political control over key sovereign states. One result was that universal manhood suffrage, though not uniformly repealed by the Constitution of 1863, was either significantly curtailed or expanded, depending on what party held power in which state, and on the kind of republican bargains party leaders had struck with popular sectors.

The science of constitutionalism came to be at the heart of these dramatic political and territorial changes that radically altered Liberal and Conservative discourses and practices regarding sovereignty. José María Samper himself, who had championed the location of sovereignty in the individual, had a change of heart by the end of the nineteenth century. In the wake of the 1854 Civil War, it became clear to most elites, including Samper, that sovereignty needed to lie with the territorial state, not individuals. To curtail the unpleasant outcome of universal manhood suffrage, the new constitutionalists claimed the right of states to limit the franchise, to engage in electoral fraud, and even to dismiss electoral results. Each state within the United States of Colombia created its own constitution. The territorially of the national state changed, as did the constitutional makeup of the nation. But these transformations were precisely what allowed the project of vanguard modernity from the 1840s to be saved, or at least it seemed that way.

The final chapter considered how efforts by the republican state to control the church were deeply paradoxical. Liberals were especially keen to excise a supposed colonial legacy of corruption by immoral church clergy by reinstating an arrangement of state control over the Catholic Church not seen since the period of Spanish monarchical rule. In the wake of the civil wars of the 1850s, extreme Radical Liberals like Felipe Pérez rejected the Catholic Church outright as a corrupt institution held over from the colonial period. Property held in mortmain by the church had supposedly blocked circulation through the monopolization of agrarian and urban property and credit, creating benighted individuals who could not become autonomous and entrepreneurial enough to be good, modern citizens. Even more problematic, as explained by President Mosquera in his letter to Pope Pius IX, immoral men had assumed positions of power within Colombia's church hierarchy and tried to influence popular sectors at the voting booth, incited them to war against the constitutional government, and often took up arms themselves. This was why, instead of supporting a liberal measure that ensured the absolute separation of church and state, Radical Liberals called for state control over the church, beginning with disentailment of church properties held in mortmain. And yet many Conservatives ideologically were very much in favor of a republican state that held the rights of patronato over the church. Several Conservatives also supported disentailment of church properties as long as such expropriation enhanced state coffers dominated by the Conservative Party. Much like the republican state took the place of the monarchy as the principle arbiter of innumerable conflicts engendered by resguardo privatization, republicans, Liberal and Conservative, tried to build the state by asserting control over the church as the Spanish monarchy had done prior to independence. Partisan conflict over the role of the church in the Colombian state emerged elsewhere: when it came time to determine what popular sectors were taught and who taught them.

Beyond controlling the church, Radical Liberals in power wanted to assure popular sectors received a proper, secular education that would pry them away from their loyalties to the church and the Conservative Party. Public school education, largely funded through the disentailment of church properties, promised a more comprehensive way of transforming the individual that went beyond printing political ethnography intended to extirpate the colonial legacy through self-recognition in reading. Normal school education increasingly succeeded in educating greater numbers of teachers and students, and it was carried out through catechisms on geography rather than on Catholic doctrine. Oversized printed maps and geographies based on information produced by the Chorographic Commission tried displacing crucifixes and Bibles. Secular public education controlled by entrepreneurial German Protestant female teachers hired by Radical Liberal politicians became the ideal vehicle for shaping individual and collective behavior. Even though the public school system developed under the Radical Liberals was controlled by the national state, Liberals were not all powerful in their ability to determine content within the public school system, or who could teach within it. Liberals constantly had to negotiate with Conservatives, especially in Conservative-dominated states. Civil war broke out again precisely because Conservatives disagreed with secular public instruction. The Radical Liberal regime was ultimately defeated, yet the Colombian Republic that emerged in its wake had nevertheless effectively brought in the Catholic Church as a partner in governance and public instruction by the early twentieth century, not unlike the church had lent legitimacy to the Crown during the period of monarchical rule.

Conservatives together with some Liberals emerge from this story as the leading radical republicans who claimed the church was essential for the making of modernity—a moral modernity. Ecclesiological histories of Colombia, like those of Groot, found in the church the original impulse to science, modernization, entrepreneurship, and national community. For them, this history was as true for the colonial period as it was for the wars of independence and throughout the young history of the republic. By the early 1880s a moral, Catholic critique of disorderly popular republicanism, one that got in the way of modernity and engagement with external markets, waxed triumphant.

It is worth stopping to note how late nineteenth- and early twentieth-century dynamics have blinded us to the innovative and creative sciences developed by men like Samper, Mosquera, Ancízar, Groot, and Díaz Castro in Spanish America, and especially in New Granada during the middle of the nineteenth century. Only recently have scholars begun to explore the kind of experiments with republicanism occurring at midcentury as evidence of how Spanish America was, indeed, on the vanguard of democracy in the Atlantic world.[20] This book has uncovered how these creative political experiments were undergirded by scientific innovations that could work to bolster and expand republicanism. José María Samper, for instance, was amazingly innovative and creative in his effort to contribute to the sciences of geography, constitutionalism, and history, yet not until now have we been able to see the merits of his contributions and those of his fellow New Granadians from the time of independence into the mid-nineteenth century. The historiographical blinders imposed by the late nineteenth and early twentieth century suggest the reasons why.

Much like the historical actors of the nineteenth century ascribed a negative "colonial legacy" to the period before independence, historical actors of the nineteenth and twentieth centuries ascribed a negative legacy of chaos, violence, and caudillos to the early to mid-nineteenth-century Spanish American republics.[21] More recently, in the wake of the bicentenary of independence, scholars have examined much more deeply the liberal thinking that went into both the Constitution of Cadiz of 1812 and the liberalism of concurrent constitutions emerging in Spanish America.[22] Studies that have deepened our understanding of nineteenth-century cartography and science in the region have allowed us to begin to rethink this period, and this study builds on these works, as well as those that have allowed us to see the political sophistication and experimentation that early republican leaders engaged in during this period.[23]

This book has sought to delve into the sciences of a republican vanguard. It has done so to challenge historiographical interpretations that have enjoyed remarkable staying power in their ability to shape the kinds of questions historians of Latin America ask of this period. Rather than reaffirm the long-standing trope of Liberal federalists challenging Conservative centralists, this study has shown instead how everyone, at least at the elite level, was a democratic, Catholic, and moral republican who championed popular education. Elites shared republican values rooted in Catholic morality and believed that for the nation to succeed, it needed to foment circulation of ideas, people, and material goods. The conundrum these elites faced, however, was that to be a modern vanguard in the world, the backward (and constantly shifting) "colonial legacy" needed to be identified and eliminated from within. If they managed to do so, these men believed they would succeed in crafting a republic for the world; one poised between the aristocratic, monarchical regimes of Europe and the democratic—yet structurally racist—world of the antebellum United States.

Notes

Introduction

1. Consider, for instance, the sheer volume of influential monographs and undergraduate history textbooks that emphasize the persistence of Latin America's "colonial legacies." These legacies, we are told, joined the contradictions inherent to elite adoptions of foreign nineteenth-century ideas like liberalism and produced entrenched patterns of underdevelopment and dependency. Works in that line include Stein and Stein, *Colonial Heritage of Latin America*; Viotti da Costa, *Brazilian Empire*; Schwartz and Bulmer-Thomas, *Economic History of Latin America*; Williams, *Columbia Guide to the Latin American Novel*; Wright, *Latin America since Independence*; Eakin, *History of Latin America*; Cardoso and Faletto, *Dependencia y desarrollo en América Latina*; Grosfoguel, "Developmentalism, Modernity, and Dependency Theory in Latin America." The result of this literature has culminated in a "Poverty of Progress" that implicitly suggests a "Poverty of Theory" among nineteenth-century historical actors. See Burns, *Poverty of Progress*.

2. Racist readings of Latin American republics as incapable of democratic institutions due to Iberian colonial heritage emerged in the United States in the 1930s. The only solution this scholarship offered was intervention by the United States. See Chapman, "Age of the Caudillos." This period was also marked by vigorous efforts by Latin American states to force the United States to act more like a good citizen of the American hemisphere and stop military interventions. See Grandin, "Your Americanism and Mine." And yet, more current readings still take for granted the supposed resilience of colonial legacies in ways that ignore the critical role nineteenth-century actors played in their invention. See Adelman, *Colonial Legacies*; Quijano, "América Latina en la economía mundial; Quijano, "Coloniality of Power"; Larson, *Trials of Nation Making*.

3. For similar readings challenging postcolonial dichotomies see Cooper, *Colonialism in Question*. See also Thurner, *History's Peru*.

4. Gobat, "Invention of Latin America."

5. Sanders, *Vanguard of the Atlantic World*.

6. A growing body of literature by historians of science and medicine has underscored the "craft" of scientific discoveries. See Seth, *Crafting the Quantum*; Fujimura, *Crafting Science*; Kroker, Keelan, and Mazumdar, *Crafting Immunity*.

7. Safford, *Ideal of the Practical*; Sánchez, *Gobierno y geografía*; Loaiza Cano, *Manuel Ancízar y su época*; Obregón Torres, "La sociedad de naturalists neogranadinos."

8. Restrepo, *Historia de la Nueva Granada*.

9. López-Alves, *State Formation and Democracy*; Peloso and Tenenbaum, *Liberals, Politics, and Power*; Dore and Molyneux, *Hidden Histories of Gender*; Hosbawm, "La revolución"; Safford and Palacios, *Colombia*.

10. Sanders, *Contentious Republicans*.

11. Halperín Donghi, *Contemporary History of Latin America*; Wiarda and Kline, *Latin American Politics and Development*; Schneider, *Comparative Latin American Politics*.

12. Harding, *Postcolonial Science and Technology Studies Reader*; Arnold, *Colonizing the Body*; Prakash, *Another Reason*.

13. Chakrabarty, *Provincializing Europe*; Bhabha, *Location of Culture*.

14. Cooper, *Colonialism in Question*.

15. The center-periphery model for Latin American history of science was offered by scholars such as Basalla, "Spread of Western Science". For critiques see Chambers, "Locality and Science."

16. Shapin, "Invisible Technician."

17. Latour, *Science in Action*.

18. Gootenberg, "Forgotten Case of 'Scientific Excellence'"; Cueto, *Excellence in the Periphery*.

19. Portuondo, "Constructing a Narrative"; Sanders, *Vanguard of the Atlantic World*; Saldaña, "Science and Freedom."

20. Paquette, "Dissolution of the Spanish Atlantic Monarchy."

21. Ruiz Gutierrez, "La génesis del federalismo."

22. Safford and Palacios, *Colombia*; Bushnell, *Making of Modern Colombia*.

23. McGreevey, *Economic History of Colombia*; Palacios, *Coffee in Colombia*; Ocampo, *Café, industria y macroeconomía*; Palacios, *Between Legitimacy and Violence*; Berquist, *Coffee and Conflict in Colombia*; LeGrand, *Frontier Expansion and Peasant Protest*; Rausch, *Colombia*; Sánchez Torres, Fazio Vargas, and López-Uribe, "Land Conflict, Property Rights."

24. Rosenthal, *Salt and the Colombian State*; López-Bejarano, *Un estado a crédito*; Bonilla, "Consequencias económicas de la independencia."

25. Oslender, *Geographies of Social Movements*.

26. Safford and Palacios, *Colombia*.

27. García-Mejia, *Transformation of the Indian Communities*; Díaz Díaz, "Estado, iglesia y desamortización," in *Manual de historia de Colombia*, vol. 2: 413–16.

28. McGraw, *Work of Recognition*; Tovar Mora and Tovar Pinzón, *El oscuro camino de la libertad*.

29. Sowell, *Early Colombian Labor Movement*.

30. Martínez Garnica, "La acción de los liberales panameños."

31. McGuiness, *Path of Empire*.

32. Earle, *Return of the Native*. See also Jaramillo Uribe, *El pensamiento colombiano en el siglo XIX*.

33. Earle, "Information and Disinformation."

34. Cummins et al., *Manuscript Cultures of Colonial Mexico*.

35. Anderson, *Imagined Communities*; Trouillot, *Silencing the Past*.

36. Bleichmar, *Visible Empire*; Craib, "Cartography and Power"; Cañizares-Esguerra, *How to Write the History*; Safier, *Measuring the New World*; Pimentel, *La física de la monarquía*.

37. Paquette, "Dissolution of the Spanish Atlantic Monarchy;" Dym, *From Sovereign Villages to National States*; Morelli, *Territorio o nación*; J. Rodríguez, *Independence of Spanish America*.

38. My approach for reading this period is informed by Bell, *Cult of the Nation in France.*

39. De la Vega, *La federación en Colombia*; Gilmore, *El federalismo en Colombia*; Pérez Aguirre, *25 años de historia colombiana*; Camargo, "La federación en Colombia"; Stoller, "Ironías del federalismo"; Borja, *Espacio y guerra*; Palacios and Safford, *Colombia.* For an excellent historiographical discussion of these texts, see Ruiz Gutierrez, "La genesis del federalismo."

40. Bassi and Múnera show how the early national period sought to erase connections to the Caribbean in the nineteenth century to try to define Colombia as an Andean nation and in doing so erase Afro-Colombia. See Bassi, *Aqueous Territory*; Múnera, *Fronteras Imaginadas.* There was a turn away from the Atlantic during the early republic. However, here I argue that the reason was less due to a deliberate effort to erase the Afro-Colombian elements of the nation as much as it was an effort to reorient national markets toward the interior.

41. Torget, *Seeds of Empire*; Beckert, *Empire of Cotton*; Johnson, *River of Dark Dreams.*

42. Bachelard, *Poetics of Space*; Bourdieu, "Social Space and Symbolic Power"; Lefebvre, *Production of Space*; Warf and Arias, *Spatial Turn*; Stock and Vöhringer, *Spatial Practices*; Arias, "Rethinking Space."

43. The literature on nineteenth-century communal land privatization is extensive. Some key works include Gotkowitz, *Revolution for Our Rights*; Gould, *To Die in This Way*; Rappaport, *Politics of Memory*; Grandin, *Blood of Guatemala.*

44. Craib, *Cartographic Mexico.*

45. Quijano, "Coloniality of Power"; Stein and Stein, *Colonial Heritage of Latin America*; Larson, *Trials of Nation Making*; Safford, "Race, Integration, and Progress."

46. Yannakakis, "Beyond Jurisdictions"; Owensby, *Empire of Law and Indian Justice*; Herzog, *Frontiers of Possession.*

47. Dym, *From Sovereign Villages to National States.*

48. Sánchez, *Gobierno y geografía*: Restrepo Forero, "La Comisión Corografica"; Appelbaum, *Mapping the Country of Regions.*

49. For dismissal of costumbrismo, see Sommer, *Foundational Fictions.* For studies that take costumbrismo seriously, see Escobar, "*Manuela,* by Eugenio Díaz Castro."

50. Fanon, *Wretched of the Earth*; Memmi, *Colonizer and the Colonized*; Césaire, *Discourse on Colonialism.*

51. Thurner, *History's Peru.*

52. Vargas Martínez, *Colombia 1854*; Gómez Picón, *El golpe militar*; Bushnell, *Making of Modern Colombia.*

53. Sanders, *Contentious Republicans.*

54. Rodríguez Piñeres, *El olimpo radical.*

55. Mijangos, *The Lawyer of the Church.*

56. Samper, "La cuestión de las razas." In this sense my reading of Samper challenges scholarship that sees the European-styled racism of disconnected elites as foundational for national culture. See, for instance, Martínez Pinzón, *Una cultura de invernadero*; Castro Gómez, *La hybris del punto cero.* This is not to say Samper did not engage in any form of race-based exclusion or discrimination. Rather, his thoughts on race formation echo the mid-nineteenth-century implications of the myths of racial harmony examined by Lasso in *Myths of Harmony.*

1. Gran Colombian Print Culture

1. Pohl Valero, *¡Soy Caldas!*

2. Nieto Olarte, *La obra cartográfica*.

3. Hobsbawm and Ranger, *Invention of Tradition*. Obregón Torres, *Sociedades científicas en Colombia*.

4. Livingstone, *Geographical Tradition*; Pickles, *History of Spaces*; Harley and Woodward, *History of Cartography*; Wood, *Power of Maps*; Monmonier, *How to Lie with Maps*; MacEachren, *How Maps Work*; Tyner, "Mapping Women."

5. Vila, "Caldas y los origenes eurocriollos," 16–20; Silva, *Los ilustrados*; Nieto Olarte, *Orden natural*; Múnera, *Fronteras imaginadas*.

6. Harley, *New Nature of Maps*, x. Recent works include Appelbaum, *Mapping the Country of Regions*; Safier, *Measuring the New World*; Bleichmar, *Visible Empire*. For work that emphasizes individual mapmakers during the nineteenth century, see Carrera, *Traveling from New Spain to Mexico*; Kingston, "Trading Places"; Nieto Olarte, *La obra cartográfica*.

7. Mejía, *La Revolución en Letras*.

8. AGN, SR, EOR, Caja 186 Serie Poblaciones carpeta 685; AGN, SR, Min Rel Ext, tomo 111, AGN, SR, Neg. Adm., vols. 1–12.

9. Restrepo, *Historia de la revolución*, atlas.

10. Acevedo y Tejada. *Noticia*.

11. Anderson, *Imagined Communities*; Castro-Klarén and Chasteen, *Beyond Imagined Communities*.

12. Steele, *Flowers for the King*.

13. Mundy, *Mapping of New Spain*; Scott, *Contested Territory*.

14. Berquist Soule, *Bishop's Utopia*; Mendoza Vargas and Lois, *Historias de la cartografía de Iberoamérica*; Nieto Olarte, *Remedios para el imperio*; Pimentel, *La física de la monarquía*; Bleichmar et al., *Science in the Spanish and Portuguese Empires*; Afanador, "Political Economy, Geographical Imagination, and Territory."

15. Bleichmar, *Visible Empire*, 197.

16. Nieto Olarte, *Orden natural*.

17. Caldas, *Semanario del Nuevo Reyno*, 3 September 1809, 254–56.

18. Nieto Olarte, Castano, and Ojeda, "Ilustracion y orden social."

19. Artola, *Los afrancesados*.

20. Carrillo Rocha, "Comienzos de una desilusion."

21. Nieto Olarte, *Orden natural*, 375.

22. Paquette, "Dissolution of the Spanish Atlantic Monarchy," 175–212.

23. One of the most notable examples of these eighteenth-century struggles by New Granada population centers to gain official city status with a cabildo, or municipal government, was reflected in the tensions between Socorro, San Gil, and Vélez that culminated in the Comunero Rebellion. See Phelan, *People and the King*. For formation of juntas in Spanish America see J. Rodríguez, *Independence of Spanish America*.

24. Quintero and Almarza, "Dos proyectos," 55–70.

25. Nieto Olarte, *Orden natural*, 104.

26. *Semanario del Nuevo Reyno de Granada*, 1808.

27. Soto Arango, *Recepción y difusión de la producción*. Participants included Jorge Tadeo Lozano, Pedro Fermín de Vargas, Camilo Torres, Francisco José de Caldas, Simón Bolívar, Sinforoso Mutis, José María Cabal, Francisco Antonio Zea, and others. Those who published in the *Semanario* included José Manuel Restrepo (1781–1861), Jorge Tadeo Lozano (1771–1816), José María Salazar (1785–1828), Joaquín Camacho (1766–1816), José

María Cabal (1770–1816), Sinforoso Mutis (1773–1822), and Nicolás Tanco (1774–1865), among others. Nieto Olarte, *Orden natural*.

28. Caldas, *Semanario del Nuevo Reyno de Granada*, issue 4, Santafé (Bogotá), 24 January 1808, 29n1.

29. Cited in Bateman, *Obras completas de Francisco José de Caldas*, 213.

30. Cited in Bateman, *Obras completas de Francisco José de Caldas*, 213.

31. See "Mapa de la provincia de Antioquia, en la República de Colombia, por José Manuel Restrepo, año de 1819," AGN, SMP 6, ref. 53.

32. Withers, "Social Nature of Map Making."

33. Caldas, *Semanario del Nuevo Reyno de Granada*, issue 4, Santafé (Bogotá), 24 January 1808, p. 29n1.

34. Restrepo, *Ensayo sobre la geografía*.

35. Caldas, "Estado de Geografía," in *Semanario del Nuevo Reyno de Granada*, issues 1–6, Santafé, 3 January 1808–7 February 1808. The following discussion of Caldas's *Semanario* all draw citations from these six issues of the periodical..

36. Caldas, "Estado de Geografía." A *legua* was approximately 20,842 feet, or 6,353 meters (6.3 kilometers). Two inches per league meant each inch represented approximately 3.176 kilometers.

37. Caldas, "Estado de Geografía."

38. Caldas, "Estado de Geografía."

39. Caldas, "Estado de Geografía."

40. For the extensive network of elite Spanish American contributors to the *Semanario*, see Nieto Olarte, *Orden natural*.

41. Palacio Fajardo, *Outline of the Revolution*, 100.

42. The same publication emerged in 1817 through a New York press, James Eastburn and Co., Literary Rooms, Broadway, Clayton & Kingsland, Printers. The 1818 edition of the *American Monthly Magazine and Critical Review* reported this news.

43. *El Correo del Orinoco*, nos. 4–5 (18 and 25 July 1818).

44. "Ley Fundamental de la república de Colombia (17 December 1819)," in Uribe Vargas, *Las constituciones de Colombia*, 2:699–702.

45. *Constitucón de Cucuta*, 6 October 1821, Articulo 191, Titulo X.

46. Decreto 1 of 11 October 1821.

47. Articulo 150, Titulo VII de la organizacion interior de la República, *Constitución de Cucuta*.

48. Eight hundred copies of the *Gaceta* were issued regularly. The government paid for distribution of the paper to the main government offices within Colombia. The official post office delivered the *Gaceta* from Bogotá to Antioquia (discontinued after issue 13), Soledad (Cartagena Province), Santa Marta, Caracas, Citará (Chocó), Maracaibo (Venezuela), Popayán, Cartagena, Panamá, and Medellín. Not until after 25 August 1822 did the *Gaceta* reach Quito, later appearing in Cumaná (Venezuela) and Guayaquil. After November 1825 the *Gaceta* could be purchased in all national post offices in each of the provincial capitals of the republic. One issue was given reciprocally to each editor of contemporary papers within Colombia and outside it. Some 330 issues were sent abroad. The paper sold originally for 2.5 reales and eventually lowered its price. The government nevertheless ran the paper at a continual loss. See Torres Cendales, "Gazeta [Gaceta] de Colombia (1821–1826)."

49. Bushnell, "El desarrolllo de la prensa," 29.

50. "Respuesta de José Manuel Resterpo a la solicitud de . . . Vicente Azuero al cargo de redactor de la Gaceta de Colombia," in Hernandez de Alba, *Documentos sobre el doctor Vicente Azuero*, 83.

51. AGN, Sección Asuntos Criminales. Legajo 42, Folio 240r.

52. "Geografía" in *Gaceta de Colombia*, no. 24, 31 March 1822, 2.

53. "Geografía" in *Gaceta de Colombia*, no. 24, 31 March 1822, 2.

54. For a review of key works in the history of cartography and exploration for colonial Mexico, see Craib, "Cartography and Power."

55. De Leon Pinelo, *El paraiso en el Nuevo Mundo*.

56. Cañizares-Esguerra, *Nature, Empire and Nation*, 117–19.

57. The *Gaceta de Colombia* republished Caldas, "Estado de Geografía." See *Gaceta de Colombia*, nos. 24, 25, 26, 27, 29.

58. Caldas, *Semanario del Nuevo Reyno de Granada*, January 1808.

59. *Gaceta de Colombia*, no. 24, 31 March 1822, 2.

60. *Gaceta de Colombia*, no. 24, 31 March 1822.

61. *Gaceta de Colombia*, no. 24, 31 March 1822.

62. *Gaceta de Colombia*, no. 58, 24 November 1822.

63. *Gaceta de Colombia*, no. 58, 24 November 1822.

64. *Gaceta de Colombia*, no. 58, 24 November 1822.

65. Simón Bolívar, "Reply of a South American to a Gentleman of This Island [Jamaica]," Kingston, Jamaica, 6 September 1815, in Bolívar, *Selected Writings of Bolívar*.

66. Rodríguez Prada, *Le musée national de Colombia*; Lucena Giraldo, *Historia de un cosmopolita*.

67. Restrepo, *Historia de la revolución*.

68. *Gaceta de Colombia*, no. 24, 31 March 1822.

69. Earle, "Information and Disinformation."

70. Soto Arango, *Francisco Antonio Zea*.

71. Francisco Antonio Zea to Pedro Gual, 14 November 1821, AGN, SR, FGM, tomo 18-2.

72. Rodríguez Prada, *Le musée national de Colombie*.

73. *Gaceta de Colombia*, no. 112, 7 December 1823..

74. See AGN, SR, FMRE, tomo 111. See also AGN, EOR, Caja 186 Serie Poblaciones, Carpeta 685; AGN EOR, caja 69, "División provincias, informes, empadronamientos, 1821–1830."

75. AGN, FNA, vols. 1, 2, 4, 7, 8, 10.

76. José Manuel Restrepo, "Text page: Historia de Colombia, Atlas," *Historia de la revolución*, 6–7.

77. Del Castillo, "Colombian Cartography."

78. Restrepo, "Text page," 6–7.

79. Restrepo, "Text page," 6–7.

80. Restrepo, "Text page," 6–7.

81. Restrepo, *Historia de la revolución*, Atlas. See also Lucena Giraldo, *Historia de un cosmopolita*.

82. Restrepo, *Exposición que el secretario de Estado*, 8.

83. Sánchez, *Gobierno y geografía*, 213.

84. Romero, *El héroe niño de la independencia*.

85. Acevedo y Tejada, *Noticia*, 101–8.

86. "Ley orgánica de instrucción pública," *Gaceta de Colombia*, no. 266, 18 March 1826. See also Romero, *El héroe niño*, 61.

87. Acevedo y Tejada, *Noticia*, 5.

88. Acevedo y Tejada, *Noticia*, 9.

89. Acevedo y Tejada, *Noticia*, 9, emphasis added.

90. Acevedo y Tejada, *Noticia*, 9.

91. Acevedo y Tejada, *Noticia*, 9.

92. Acevedo y Tejada, *Noticia*, 9.

93. Acevedo y Tejada, *Noticia*, 10

94. Acevedo y Tejada, *Noticia*, 10.

95. Earle, "Creole Patriotism and the Myth"; Earle, "Indian Rebellion and Bourbon Reform."

96. Silva, *Los ilustrados*, 23, 39, 58–60; Elliott, *Spain, Europe and the Wider World*.

97. Brown, *Struggle for Power*.

98. Sánchez, *Gobierno y geografía*, 138–41.

99. Acosta, *Compendio histórico*, 1.

100. "Mapa de la República de la Nueva Granada (1847), AGN, SMP. 2, ref. 1275.

101. "Observaciones que hace un granadino . . . ," *Gaceta Oficial* (GO), 28 May 1848, 335–36, continued 9 July 1848, 426–27.

2. A Political Economy of Circulation

1. For Bogotá's midcentury nomenclature, see Pérez, *Geografía general*, 416–20.

2. Mosquera, *Memoria sobre la geografía*, 54–58.

3. Mosquera, *Memoria sobre la geografía*, 54–58, 61–63.

4. Sánchez, *Gobierno y geografía*, 218–26, 660–65.

5. Safford, *Ideal of the Practical*; Sánchez, *Gobierno y geografía*; Soto Arango, "Aproximacion historica a la universidad Colombiana"; Helguera, "First Mosquera Administration."

6. Saldarriaga Roa, Ortiz Crespo, and Pinzón Rivera, *En busca de Thomas Reed*.

7. GO no. 961, 9 March 1848, 160.

8. Members of the Class of Education: Alejandro Osorio, José Manuel Restrepo, Ulipiano Gonzalez, Lorenzo M. Lleras, José M. Triana, Pedro Fernandez Madrid, Miguel Bracho. The Class of Development and Material Improvement: Rufino Cuervo, Mariano Ospina, Eladio Urisarri, Juan Manuel Arrubla, Manuel Ancízar, Tomás Reed, Antonio Silva. The Class of Philanthropy: Archbishop M. J. de Mosquera, Joaquin Gori, Joaquin Barriga, José Ignacio Paris, Urbano Pradilla, Guillermo Iribarren, Justo Arosemena. The Class of Roads, Immigration, and Statistics: Florentino Gonzalez, Lino de Pombo, Raimundo Santamaría, Antonio Poncet, José Eusebio Caro, Vicente Lombana, Jian Antonio Marroquin. Ancízar, *Instituto Caldas*, 6.

9. Ancízar, *Instituto Caldas*; Ancízar, "Instituto Caldas" in GO no. 942, 2 January 1848.

10. GO no. 951, 3 February 1848, 80.

11. Of the twenty-two provinces existing in 1848, Instituto Caldas chapters were set up in fourteen: Bogotá on 2 January 1848 (GO no. 942); Antioquia on 20 January 1848, with 25 members (GO no. 954, 13 February 1848); Santa Marta on 10 February 1848 with 34 members; Mompos on 2 March 1848 with 23 members; (GO no. 972, 16 April 1848); Tunja on 17 February 1848 with 25 members (GO no. 984, 1 June 1848); Choco on 8 March 1848 with 13 members (GO no. 966, 26 March 1848); Neiva on 16 March 1848 with

27 members; Popayán on 21 March 1848 with 28 members; Buenaventura on 23 March 1848 with 24 members; Socorro on 2 April 1848 with 24 members (GO no. 973, 23 April 1848); Cartagena on 21 March 1848 with 34 members (GO no. 974, 27 April 1848); Riohacha on 9 May 1848 with 10 members (GO no. 987, 11 June 1848); Pamplona subsumed its school for the weaving of jipijapa hats (Panama hats) to the Instituto Caldas on 22 February 1848 (GO no. 962, 12 March 1848); Mariquita on 20 July 1848 with 20 members (GO no. 997, 30 July 1848). Several new provinces were created in New Granada between 1843 and 1848, and not all of these new provinces gave notice of an Instituto Caldas. The more traditional ones that did not respond: Panama, Pasto, and Casanare. The new provinces that did not respond: Cauca; Velez, Barbacoas, and Tuquerres. By 24 July 1849, the newly created province of Ocana formed an Instituto Caldas with 27 members (GO no. 1069, 26 August 1849).

12. Safford, *Ideal of the Practical*, 69.

13. Manuel Ancízar, "Circular Sobre las Secciones Corresponsales del Instituto," GO no. 942, 2 January 1848, 5.

14. "Catecismo del obrero," GO no. 999, 13 August 1848, 468.

15. GO no. 979, 14 Mayo 1848, 303.

16. Restrepo, *Historia de la Nueva Granada*, vol. 2, 71–72, cited in Sánchez, *Gobierno y geografía*, 176.

17. Mosquera, *Memoria sobre la geografía*, 63.

18. GO, no. 1062, 15 July 1849, 337.

19. Students in the Universidad del Primer Distrito in Bogotá also took classes with Colegio Students under Bergueron. Sanchez, *Gobierno y geografía*, 222; Albis Gonzalez, "A falta de una iconografia."

20. José Vejarano from Cauca (GO no. 969, 6 April 1848), Antonio Rivera from Antioquia (GO no. 973, 23 April 1848), José Antonio Osorio from Neiva (GO no. 999, 13 August 1848). See also "Cuadro de los jovenes aprendices en la escuela practica de arquitectura que estan a mi cargo, por Tomás Reed 31 august 1848," GO no. 1003, 10 September 1848: Candido Arenas and Miguel Ignacio Bautista from Socorro, Bartolome Monroi from Tunja, Jorge and Lorenzo Torres from Bogotá, José Salcedo from Neiva, Gregorio Vidal from Popayán, José Antonio Rivera from Pamplona, Francisco Ruiz from Pasto, Ramon Betancur from Casanare, Vicente Alderete and Joaquin Fajardo from Buenaventura, Pascual Morales from Mariquita, Joaquin Mosquera from Choco, José Antonio Rincon from Tunja.

21. Earlier in the 1840s, a national university system divided education according to districts: Bogotá was the first district, Cartagena was the second, and Popayán was the third. See Soto Arango, "Aproximacion historica a la universidad Colombiana." On Thomas Reed and apprenticeship training, see Saldarriaga Roa, Ortiz Crespo, and Pizón Rivera, *En busca de Thomas Reed*.

22. Lei 1 de junio de 1847, GNG, no. 866. For underestimations of regional participation in the Instituto Caldas, see Safford, *Ideal of the Practical*, 175; Helguera, "First Mosquera Administration."

23. Sánchez, *Gobierno y geografía*.

24. Loaiza Cano, *Manuel Ancízar y su época*, 55, 59, 88–100.

25. Loaiza Cano, *Manuel Ancízar y su época*, 100–104, 121–56.

26. Corradine Angulo and Mora de Corradine, *Historia de la arquitectura colombiana*, vol. 2, 59–60. The students who came to study architecture in Bogotá came from several different New Granada provinces. See GO, no. 948–78 from year 1848: Candido

Arenas and Miguel Ignacio Bautista from Socorro; Manuel Olarte Angulo and Ricardo Olarte Ricaurte from Velez; Valeriano Acosta and Martolome Monroy from Tunja; Jorge Torres and Lorenzo Torres from Bogotá; Luciano Garcia from Casanare; Francisco Garcia and José María Salcedo from Neiva; Gregorio Vidal, Martin Buenaventura, Vicente Alderete, and José Joaquin Fajardo from Buenaventura; Francisco Ruiz from Pasto; Antonio Pineda from Pamplona.

27. *El Neogranadino*, Bogotá no. 50, 23 June 1849, 210. See also Sanchez, *Gobierno y geografía*, 224. For Ancízar's control of El Neogranadino, see Loaiza Cano, *Manuel Anciízar y su época*, 182–83.

28. J. Ospina, *Diccionario biografico y bibliografico de Colombia*, vol. 3, 997–99.

29. The origins of Colegio Militar students are available in Orjuela, *Edda, la bogotana*, 28–29. See also AGN SMP 1, ref. 67, SMP 1, ref. 69, and SMP 2, ref. 1246.

30. GO no. 1028, 25 January 1849, 62–64. See also Sanchez, *Gobierno y geografía*, 223.

31. For cartographic literacy see MacEachren, *How Maps Work*, 1–6. See also Winichakul, *Siam Mapped*, 51–56.

32. For language and map comprehension see MacEachren, *How Maps Work*, 320; Wood, *Power of Maps*, 96–101; for propositional knowledge representation (PKR) see Matthews, "Measure of Mind," 131–46.

33. For examples of nineteenth-century map cartouches as expressions of mapmakers' ideology see Edney, *Mapping an Empire*, 13–16.

34. AGN, SMP 2, ref. 1-21, "Bogotá y sus alrededores," 1849.

35. AGN, SMP 6, ref. 59. "Rio Magdalena, 1849."

36. AGN, SMP 2, ref. 1-21, "Bogotá y sus alrededores," 1849.

37. Esquiasqui 1797, modificado 1816 by Morillo, "Plano geometrico de la ciudad de Santafé de Bogotá, capital del Nuevo Reino de Granada. . . ." For Cabrer's map and reproductions of it by Colegio students, see AGN, SMP 6, ref. 142, "Bogotá y sus alredededores, 1797;" SMP 1, ref. 143, "Bogotá" Plano topografico copiado por Indalecio Lievano; and SMP 6, ref. 142.

38. *El Neo Granadino* (Bogotá), 23 June 1849, 210.

39. Sanchez, *Gobierno y geografía*, 224–25.

40. Múnera, *Fronteras imaginadas*, 33.

41. AGN, SMP 1, ref. 67; SMP 1, ref. 69; SMP 1, ref. 143; SMP 2, ref. 1246; SMP 2, ref. 1–21; SMP 6, ref, 142; SMP 6, ref. 246; SMP 6, ref. 242bis.

42. AGN, SMP 6, ref. 246, "Topografía 1852, Planos humorísticos de Manuel J. Peña."

43. Agustín Blanco, history of cartography lecture, 16 September 2004, Pontificia Universidad Javeriana. See "Plano topográfico, copiado por Indalecio Liévano," 1797, AGN, SMP 1, ref. 143.

44. Although not as numerically overwhelming as compared to the thousands of immigrants that poured into the temperate regions of North and South America in the late nineteenth and early twentieth centuries, there nevertheless were significant numbers of people not born in New Granada who flowed in during, and in the wake of, independence. For foreign adventurers who decided to stay in Colombia after the wars of independence, see Brown, *Adventuring through Spanish Colonies*, 42, 176–86. For examples of how foreign arrivals were reported see "Colonisación," *Gaceta de Colombia* 223 (22 January 1826). For correspondence between diplomats stationed in the exterior and the ministry of foreign relations to bring in colonists during the 1820s, see Salazar to Gual, AGN, SR, FMRE, DT2, 130, 134, 137. See also Gutierrez Ardila, *El reconocimiento de Colombia*.

45. "Rio Magdalena, 1849: Carta Corográfica del curso del río Magdalena en la parte que puede ser navegada por buques de vapor . . . ," AGN, SMP 6, ref. 59.

46. Laurent, *Contrabando en Colombia*, 413–17.

47. AGN, SMP 1, ref. 67 and 69.

48. AGN, SMP 2, ref. 1246.

49. Múnera, *Fronteras imaginadas*, 16.

50. Safford, *Ideal of the Practical*.

51. Peña, *Geometría práctica*.

52. MacEachren, *How Maps Work*, 342–45.

53. Monmonier, *How to Lie with Maps*.

54. Borges, "Del rigor de la ciencia."

55. Safford and Palacios, *Colombia*, 211.

56. See "Informe del Secretario de Guerra de la Nueva Granada al Congreso consitucional de 1850," GO (Bogotá) 24 March 1850, 124–28.

57. Restrepo Forrero, "Comisión Corográfica," 37; Helguera, "First Mosquera Administration," 183–91.

58. Safford, *Ideal of the Practical*, 110–11.

59. Lei 1 de abril de 1847 sobre establecimiento de un colegio militar, aprobada 1 de junio de 1847. *Gaceta de la Nueva Granada* (GNG, Bogotá, 13 de Junio de 1847 no. 886.

60. Enrolled students included José Cornelio Borda, Alejandro Sarmiento, Manuel Ponce de Leon, Alejandro Ortega, Antonio Dussan, Nepomuceno Gonzalez Vasquez, Indalecio Lievano, Manuel H. Pena, Joaquin Barriga, Nepomuceno Santamaría, Nicolas Caicedo D'Eluyar, Tomás Cuenca, Ignacio Ortega, and Rafael Pombo. José Cornelio Borda and Alejandro Sarmiento graduated as military engineers. The rest graduated as civil engineers.

61. GO, 17, 29 March, 2, 15 April 1853.

62. Safford, *Ideal of the Practical*, 175–76.

63. Safford, *Ideal of the Practical*.

64. GO, 7 April 1854.

65. Samper, *Historia de un alma*, 133.

3. Calculating Equality

1. GO no. 1435, 18 October 1852, 701.

2. Rafael Reyes Prieto, president of Colombia, 1904–1909, and nephew of Joaquin Solano, later recalled in his memoirs the deep technical knowledge regarding land surveys that his uncle lovingly imparted during a ten-day tour of their home region of Boyacá. Reyes, *Memorias de Rafael Reyes*, 91.

3. GO no. 1336, 7 April 1852, 246.

4. "Contrata," *El Constitucional* (Bogotá), 14 February 1852, 27–28.

5. GO no. 1435, 18 October 1852, 701.

6. "Contrata," *El Constitucional* (Bogotá), 14 February 1852, 27–28.

7. García, Jiménez, and Ochoa, "Indigenismo."

8. Garcia-Mejia, "Transformation of the Indian Communities," 112.

9. GO no. 1435, 18 October 1852, 703.

10. Safford, "Race, Integration, and Progress, 1–33; Sanders, "Belonging to the Great Granadan Family," 56–86; Irurozqui, "Las paradojas de la tributación," 705–40; Brienen, "Clamor for Schools," 616–49; Mallon, *Peasant and Nation*; Thurner, *From Two Republics to One Divided*; Gould, *To Die in This Way*; Reeves, *Ladinos with Ladinos*.

11. Craib, *Cartographic Mexico*, 91–126; Lauria-Santiago, *Agrarian Republic.*

12. Curry, "The Disappearance of the Resguardo Indígenas of Cundinamarca, Colombia." Tovar Pinzón, *La formación social chibcha;* and Friede, *El indio en la lucha por la tierra.* See also Larson, *Trials of Nation Making*, 81–90, 266.

13. Garcia-Mejia, "Transformation of the Indian Communities," 35.

14. Bolívar, "Mediante un decreto expedido en el Rosario de Cúcuta, el 20 de mayo de 1820, el Libertador dicta normas para restablecer en sus derechos a los indígenas y para fomentar su progreso económico y su educación," in *Doctrina del Libertador*, http://www.cervantesvirtual.com/obra-visor/doctrina-del-libertador--0/html/ff6f5f94-82b1-11df-acc7-002185ce6064_29.html#I_38_.

15. Echeverri, *Indian and Slave Royalists.*

16. Bolívar, "Decreto 20 de Mayo 1820," Article 15.

17. Bolívar, "Decreto 20 de Mayo 1820," Article 9.

18. Bolívar, "Decreto 20 de Mayo 1820," Article 16.

19. Congreso general de Colombia, "Ley sobre estincion de los tributos de los indíjenas, distribución de sus resguardos, y esenciones que se les concenden," in *Cuerpo de leyes de la República de Colombia*, 174–77.

20. Congreso general de Colombia, "Ley sobre estincion," in *Cuerpo de leyes de la República de Colombia*, 174–77.

21. Congreso general de Colombia, "Ley sobre estincion," in *Cuerpo de leyes de la República de Colombia*, 174–77.

22. Congreso general de Colombia, "Ley sobre estincion," in *Cuerpo de leyes de la República de Colombia*, 174–77. For the liberalism of the Cortes de Cadiz, see Chust, *La cuestión nacional americana;* Anna, *Fall of the Royal Government in Peru;* Peralta Ruiz, "El impacto de las cortes de Cadiz en el Peru," 67–96.

23. Slatta and Lucas De Grummond, *Simón Bolívar's Quest for Glory*, 74.

24. Congreso general de Colombia, "Ley sobre estincion," in *Cuerpo de leyes de la República*, 174–77.

25. Congreso general de Colombia, "Ley sobre estincion," in *Cuerpo de leyes de la República*, 174–77.

26. "Parte Oficial . . . de los jefes políticos municipales," *Gaceta de Colombia*, no. 181, 3 April 1825, trimester 14.

27. *Gaceta de Colombia*, no. 178, 13 March 1825, trimester 14.

28. Congreso general de Colombia, "Ley sobre estincion," in *Cuerpo de leyes de la República*, 174–77.

29. Suplemento a la *Gaceta de Colombia*, no. 284, 5 March 1827.

30. "Juntas Provinciales" *Gaceta de Colombia*, no. 218, 18 December 1825, trimester 18.

31. *Gaceta de Colombia*, no. 324, 30 December 1827.

32. "Decretando los medios de civilizar los indios salvajes," *Gaceta de Colombia*, no. 148, 15 August 1824, trimester 11.

33. "Decreto del Gobierno," *Gaceta de Colombia*, no. 156, 31 October 1824, trimester 12.

34. Helg, *Liberty and Equality in Caribbean Colombia*, 173.

35. *Gaceta de Colombia*, nos. 226–28, 1824.

36. "Decreto del Poder Ejecutivo," *Gaceta de Colombia*, no. 379, 19 December 1828, trimester 30.

37. "Titulo V. de los resguardos o tierras de los indíjenas," *Gaceta de Colombia*, no. 379, 19 December, 1828, trimester 30.

38. "Decreto del Poder Ejecutivo," *Gaceta de Colombia*, no. 379, 19 December 1828, trimester 30.

39. Arana, *Bolívar*, 435.

40. "Tesoreria departamental de Cundinamarca," *Gaceta de Colombia*, no. 545, 16 October 1831, trimester 43; "Tesoreria de Bogotá," GNG, no. 11, 5 February 1832, trimester 1; "Nombramientos en el ramo de hacienda . . . ," GNG, no. 15, 19 February 1832.

41. Gaceta de Colombia, no. 530, 21 August 1831, trimester 42.

42. GNG, no. 9, 29 January 1832, trimester 1.

43. Article 6 of "La convención del estado de la Nueva Granada decreta . . . ," GNG, no. 21, 11 March 1832, trimester I.

44. "Decreto del Poder Ejecutivo," GNG, no. 29, 15 April 1832, trimester 2.

45. "Ministerio de Hacienda," GNG, no. 25, 25 March 1831, trimester 1.

46. "Lei adicional a la de 6 de marzo de 1832 sobre repartimiento de resguardos de indíjenas," GNG, no. 145, 6 July 1834, trimester 11.

47. Article 5, "Lei Adicional a la de 6 de marzo de 1832 sobre repartimiento de resguardos de indígenas," GNG, no. 145, 6 July 1834, trimester 11.

48. Article 4, "Lei Adicional . . . ," GNG, no. 145, 6 July 1834, trimester 11.

49. Artículo 146, Capitulo 21 of "Concluye la ley que fija los derechos que corresponden a los jueces . . . ," *Gaceta de Colombia*, no. 164, 5 December 1824, trimester 13.

50. Lleras, *Catecismo*.

51. Lleras, *Catecismo*.

52. Lorenzo María Lleras was active in education starting in the 1840s, and by the 1860s he was appointed director of the Colegio Militar, reopened under the Mosquera presidency. See Uribe-Uran, *Honorable Lives*,193; Torres Sánchez and Salazar Hurtado, *Introducción a la historia*, 194.

53. Colegio Nacional de San Bartolomé, *Colección de asertos de las materias que se defenderán en certámenes públicos en el Colejio de San Bartolome* . . . (Bogotá: Imprenta de la Universidad, 1835), 16, Biblioteca Nacional de Colombia [BNC]), FPineda_887_pza45.

54. Lleras, *Catechismo*, 21.

55. For Jeremy Bentham's texts in schools, see Safford and Palacios, *Colombia*, 246, 265, 291–309.

56. Lleras, *Catecismo*, 29.

57. Lleras, *Catecismo*, 30.

58. Lleras, *Catecismo*, 30.

59. Lleras, *Catecismo*, 30.

60. Mantilla, *Esposición*, 17–18.

61. Mantilla, *Esposición*, 17–19.

62. Mantilla, *Esposición*, 17–19.

63. Villoría, "Estracto de la esposición," pza 1.

64. "Decreto adicional a los despedidos sobre resguardos (28 September 1838)." Bogotá (Provincia) Cámara. Colección de todos los decretos de interés general, expedidos por la Honorable Cámara de la Provincia de Bogotá desde 1832, en que principió sus funciones hasta 1843/formada por el gobernador de la provincia Alfonso Arcevedo Tejada (Bogotá: Imprenta de Nicolás Gómez, 1844), BNC, FQuijsno_310_pza1.

65. Pombo, "Esposición del secretario de estado . . . 1834," 45.

66. Pombo, "Esposición del secretario de estado . . . 1834," 45.

67. Pombo, "Esposición de secretario de estado . . . 1835," 58; Pombo, "Esposición del secretario de estado . . . 1836," 71; Pombo, "Esposición de secretario de estado . . . 1838," 59.

68. Pombo, "Esposición de secretario de estado . . . 1838," 59.

69. Alcántara Herrán, "Esposision del secretario de estado . . . 1839," 49–51.

70. Diario del Debates de la Camara del Senado en sus sesiones de 1840, 1–2, BNC, FPineda_365_pza1.

71. Ospina, *Memoria del secretario de Estado*, 70.

72. Acevedo, "Memoria del Gobernador de Bogotá."

73. "Ordenanza 47 (de 5 de Octubre de 1848)," in Bogotá (Provincia). Cámara, Ordenanzas dictadas por la Cámara Provincial de Bogotá en sus sesiones de 1848 (Bogotá: Imprenata de Mariano Sánchez Caicedo, 1849). BNC, Pineda_203_pza7.

74. Vicente Lombana, "Informe del Gobernador de Bogotá a la Cámara de Provincia en su reunión ordinaria de 1849," BNC, *F. Antiguo*, VFDUI-438 pza. 5, 14–15.

75. Hand-written dedication on the top of BLAA, *F. Hemeroteca*, no. Topográfico: 32819 ed, *El Constitucional de Cundinamarca* (Bogotá), 24 September 1849.

76. Lleras, *Catechismo*.

77. L. C. Arboleda, "Introducción del Sistema Métrico Decimal," 73–86.

78. Agustín Codazzi, "No official. Colejio Militar," GO (Bogotá), 25 February 1849, 62–64.

79. Tomás Cipriano de Mosquera, "Mensaje del Presidente de la República al Congreso de 1849," GO, no. 1029, 4 March 1849.

80. Safford, *Ideal of the Practical*, 172.

81. Lino de Pombo, "Secretaria de Hacienda: Estado general de despachos de la Corte de Cuentas," GO, no. 1027, 18 February 1849.

82. "1853. Proyecto de ley sobre establecimiento de escuelas especiales para agrimensores, ingenieros civiles y militares," in AGN, SR, FC, f. 364–67. For General José María Melo's coup and its effects on the Colegio Militar, see Sánchez, *Gobierno y geografía*, 226–27. See also Arias De Greiff and Sánchez, *La Universidad Nacional*, 15.

83. Manuel Ponce, "Representación," *El Constitucional de Cundinamarca* (Bogotá), 22 November 1851, 201.

84. Januario Salgar, "Invitación," *El Constitucional* (Bogotá), 3 January 1852, 4.

85. "Contrata," *El Constitucional* (Bogotá), 14 February 1852, 27–28.

86. "Provincia de Bogotá: Informe del gobernador de la cámara provincial, Indígenas," GO no. 1435, 18 October 1852, 701.

87. Secretario de Guerra, "Informe sobre los exámenes del colegio militar," in GO no. 1336, 7 April 1852, 246.

88. GO no. 1435, 18 October 1852, 701.

89. "Provincia de Bogotá: Informe del gobernador de la cámara provincial, Indígenas" GO no. 1435, 18 October 1852,701.

90. El Repertorio, no. 3 (1853), cited in Garcia-Mejia, "Transformation of the Indian Communities," 101n76.

91. J. Miguel Acevedo, "Provincia de Cipaquira: Informe del Gobernador a la Camara Provincial," GO no. 1435, 18 October 1852, 703.

92. AGN, SR, FGB, vol. 34: 314r-315v, "Request from the Indijenas of Suba and Cota to the Provincial Chamber, 1854," cited in Garcia-Mejia, "Transformation of the Indian Communities," 102n77.

93. GO no. 1507, 28 April 1853.

94. "Así viven los muiscas que sobreviven en Suba," *El Tiempo* (Bogotá), 7 February 2014.

95. José Juan Leiva Millán, *El Neogranadino* (Bogotá), 1 December 1853, 441.

96. En cumplimiento del art 7 del decreto ejecutivo de 31 de Oct de 1861 sobre "formación de padrones," AGN Notarías, Notaría 4a/1888 f.161rv.

97. "Copia del Padrón de indigenas comuneros en el Resguardo del Distrito de Suba Año de 1877," AGN Notarías, Notaría 4a/1888 f. 189r-200rv.

98. Craib, *Cartographic Mexico*, 115. See also Nuijten, "Family Property"; Van Mejil and Benda-Beckman, *Property Rights and Economic Development*.

99. *Constitucional de Cundinamarca* (Bogotá), 6 November 1836, 195–96.

100. See Craib, *Cartographic Mexico*; Ducey, "Liberal Theory and Peasant Practice" in Jackson ed., *Liberals, the Church and Indian Peasants*, 65–94.

4. Political Ethnography

1. Sánchez, *Gobierno y geografía*, 249–442.

2. Ancízar, *Peregrinación*, 6.

3. López-Alves, *State Formation and Democracy*; Peloso and Tenenbaum, *Liberals, Politics, and Power*; Dore and Molyneux, *Hidden Histories of Gender*; Hosbawm, "La revolución"; Safford and Palacios, *Colombia*.

4. Peloso and Tenenbaum, *Liberals, Politics and Power*.

5. Acosta, *Compendio histórico*.

6. José Manuel Restrepo set off this narrative trend on the Instituto Caldas through his *Historia de la Nueva Granada*, 71–72. See also Safford, *Ideal of the Practical*, 65–68; Sanchez, *Gobierno y geografía*, 175–77.

7. Mariano Ospina Rodríguez y José Eusebio Caro, "Declaratoria Política," in *La Civilización*, 4 October 1849.

8. Otto Morales Benitez, "Florentino González."

9. For Vicente Lombana and the Golgota founding of the Escuela Republicana, see Sowell, *Early Colombian Labor Movement*, 63.

10. For Lleras as leader of the Draconianos faction, see Sowell, *Early Colombian Labor Movement*, 61–62.

11. Loaiza Cano, *Manuel Ancízar y su época*.

12. Loaiza Cano, "Manuel Ancízar y sus *Lecciones*," 43–60.

13. Other spaces of elite sociability, most notably Masonic Lodges, also played a key cross-party role. Salvador Camacho Roldán later recalled how he met with Manuel Ancízar and Miguel Bracho, as well as with several noted elites, in Bogotá's Masonic Lodge. Camacho Roldan, "Capitulo XX: Otros Asuntos del Año 1850," *Mis Memorias*. Every president of New Granada from 1846 to 1854 was a member of a Masonic Lodge: Tomás Cipriano de Mosquera, José Hilario López, José María Obando, and José María Melo. Manuel Murillo Toro, second president of the United States of Colombia after Mosquera, was also a Mason. See Brown, *Struggle for Power*, 164.

14. Ancízar, *Instituto Caldas*, 1, original emphasis.

15. Ancízar, *Instituto Caldas*, 1.

16. Ancízar, *Instituto Caldas*, 1.

17. Ancízar, *Instituto Caldas*, 3.

18. Triana was botanist for the Chorographic Commission. See Sanchez, *Gobierno y geografía*, 25–35. Miguel Bracho was a Venezuelan artist who taught drawing at the Colegio Militar, engraved the first map of New Granada printed on a New Granada

press, and assisted Codazzi with the 1849 map of New Granada. Sánchez, *Gobierno y geografía*, 187, 221, 236.

19. Sánchez, *Gobierno y geografía*, 170.

20. Lombana subsequently was elected president of the House of Representatives in 1853, suggesting he would continue to support the endeavor from Congress. GO no. 1483, 1 March 1853, 141.

21. Cited in Sánchez, *Gobierno y geografía*, 278.

22. Camacho Roldán, "Capítulo XII: Costumbres políticas," in *Mis Memorias*. For Codazzi and the commission's contract renewal under Mallarino, see A. Codazzi, *Informe sobre los trabajos corogáficos y propuesta que pone a la consideración del gobierno respecto a nuevos términos para su contrato* (Bogotá, 27 January 1855) in AGN, EOR, box no. 66. and Pastor Ospina, Resolución (Bogotá, 2 February 1855) in AGN, EOR, box no. 66.

23. Thomas Reed was the architect hired by Mosquera to design the national Capitol Building; Raimundo Santamaría with Francisco Montoya founded a steamship navigation company that sailed from Santa Marta up the Magdalena River until the rapids known as the "Salto de Honda" with two steamships built in the United States. Poncet, in turn, was hired in France to direct roadway commissions, and in 1848 he explored the route from Bogotá to Honda, which would connect the capital city to steamboat navigation from the Caribbean up the Magdalena to Honda. See Sánchez, *Gobierno y geografía*, 187–88. Juan Manuel Arrubla was hired in 1847 to construct the national Capitol Building. Antonio M. Silva was on the commission to inspect if Arrubla followed through on his construction contract. GO no. 1406, 21 July 1852, 550.

24. GO 2 January 1848, no. 942, 5.

25. The five "original" provinces of 1832 that did not establish an Instituto Caldas were Riohacha, Velez, Pasto, Panama, and Casanare. Cauca (established in 1833) also did not found a chapter. New Granada's "original" provinces that did establish a chapter in 1848 were (in order of date of founding of their Instituto Caldas chapter): Bogotá, Antioquia, Pamplona, Tunja, Mompós, Santa Martha, Chocó, Popayán, Buenaventura, Cartagena, Neiva, Socorro, Mariquita, and Veraguas (part of Panamanian isthmus). See 1848 *Gaceta Oficial*, assorted issues on pages 80, 143, 144, 166, 167, 187, 246, 251, 262, 295, 452.

26. In addition to the money that members themselves contributed to the Instituto Caldas and patriotic donations by others, Mosquera assigned 16,000 reales for introducing new machinery, 16,000 for immigration plans, 8,000 for roadways, 2,000 for lazaretos, 2,000 for prisons, and 8,000 for vaccinations and supplies for primary public schools. The total: $52,000 reales. See GO 2 January 1848, no. 942, 5.

27. Chapter 1; Nieto-Olarte, *Orden natural*.

28. GO, 23 April 1848, no. 973, 251–52.

29. GO, no. 984, 1 June 1848, 341.

30. J. M Villarreal, "Puente de Sanjil," in GO no. 113, 20 July 1850, 292.

31. Sánchez, *Gobierno y geografía*; Restrepo-Forero, "La Comisión Corografica"; Appelbaum, *Mapping the Country of Regions*; Jagdmann, "Del Poder y la geografía"; Duque Muñoz, "La representación limítrofe."

32. M. Ancízar, "Agustín Codazzi," *El Mosaico*, Bogotá, no. 1–8, 13 January to 5 March 1864; Luis G. Rivas, "D. José Triana," in Papel Periodico Ilustrado, Bogotá, no. 40, 1883, 251.

33. Sánchez, *Gobierno y geografía*; Restrepo Forero, "La Comisión Corografica."

34. Appelbaum, *Mapping the Country of Regions*. See also Appelbaum, "Reading the Past."

35. See de Plaza, *Lecciones de estadistica*. Plaza's textbook on statistics defined it as "the science of social actions, expressed in numerical terms. The object of statistics is to obtain a profound understanding of society, considered in its elements, in its economy, in its location and circumstances, and in its movements" (1). As early as 1840, Instituto Caldas member Florentino Gonzales also offered a treatise on statistics as related to government administration, suggesting centralism was the colonial regime's way and republicanism required another method that gives importance to the regions. See Fl. Gonzalez, *Elementos de ciencia administrativa*. See also Lleras, *Catecismo*, considered in chapter 3.

36. Ancízar, *Instituto Caldas*, 4–5.

37. Joaquin Acosta's expertise would have made him an excellent candidate to lead a systematic geographic expedition to study New Granada. His fragile health and advanced age culminated in his death in 1852, making it impossible for him to lead the Chorographic Commission, which was not launched until 1850. Sánchez, *Gobierno y geografía*, 70–85.

38. Upon his arrival to New Granada in 1849, Acosta was encouraged by the Instituto Caldas especially after the failed effort to hire Jean-Baptiste Coraboeuf to lead a trigonometric survey. see Sanchez, *Gobierno y geografía*, 86; Jagdmann, "Del Poder y la geografía," 35-116. Acosta proposed the legislation that had led Coraboeuf to issue his proposal. Acosta translated Coraboeuf's proposal for New Granada audiences. See GNG, no. 904, 19 August 1847.

39. Lasserre, *Semanario de la Nueva Granada*.

40. Figueroa Cancino, "La formación intelectual de Joaquín Acosta," 181–216.

41. Acosta, *Compendio histórico*, 439–43. The most significant of the unpublished accounts that Acosta used were Fray Aguado and the two unpublished parts of the mammoth *Noticia historial* and Fray Pedro Simon, who had only published part 1 in Cuenca, Spain, in 1627.

42. Vélez Barrientos, "Notice sur les Antiquités." Vélez Barrientos made his discovery known through a letter he sent to Jean Baptiste Boussingault, who, in turn, published the letter in the *Bulletin de la Société de Géographie de Paris* in 1847. See Botero, "Construction of the Pre-Hispanic Past," 61. This exchange with Boussingault occurred just as Acosta was engaging in deep discussions with that French naturalist, culminating in the translation and publication of Boussingault and Roulin's articles in 1848. Ancízar too was current on Vélez Barrientos's "discovery." See Ancízar, *Peregrinación*, 336.

43. Acosta, "Ruines découvertes pres de Tunja."

44. Acosta, *Compendio histórico*, vii.

45. De la Espada, after accompanying the Scientific Commission to the Pacific between 1862 and 1865, became a noted historian of the colonial period in the Americas and promoted knowledge about the region during the second half of the nineteenth century by publishing manuscript chronicles of conquest. See López-Océn, "Objetos, imágenes y textos de Jiménez."

46. Figueroa Cancino, "La formacón intelectual de Joaquin Acosta."

47. Acosta, *Compendio histórico*, ix.

48. Jomard, "Rapport a la Société de Géographie;" Jomard, "Expliocacion d'une planche; Jomard, "Sure la angue des muyscas ou la langue chibcha."

49. Acosta, *Compendio histórico*, ix.

50. Ancízar, *Peregrinacion*, 16.

51. Ancízar, *Peregrinacion*, 16.

52. Afanador, "Political Economy, Geographical Imagination, and Territory."

53. Ancízar, *Peregrinación*, 197–99. All subsequent citations for this section discussing Charalá come from Ancízar, *Peregrinación*, 197–225. Specific page numbers are indicated parenthetically in the text.

54. All citations about Soatá come from Ancízar, *Peregrinación*, 220–25. Specific page numbers are indicated in the text.

55. Ancízar cited the example of Presbítero Felipe Salgar, which had taught women in Jirón to weave jipijapa hats, bringing industry to the region. Ancízar also offered concrete solutions such as retirement plans and greater involvement by the state in appointing priests to regions in need. Ancízar, *Peregrinación*, 397–98, 439–40.

56. Ancízar, *Peregrinación*, 12.

57. Biblioteca de "El Mosaico," *Museo de cuadros de costumbres,* 2 vols.

58. Escobar, "*Manuela*, by Eugenio Díaz Castro," 73n28.

59. Escobar, "*Manuela*, by Eugenio Díaz Castro," 7.

60. Doris Sommer dismissed costumbrismo, citing how Eduardo Camacho Guizado, among others, characterized the genre as "almost always nostalgic and hardly ever socially critical." Sommer, *Foundational Fictions*, 369n8. Camacho Guizado, *Sobre la literatura colombiana e hispanoamericana*. For costumbrismo in Spain, see Kirkpatrick, "Ideology of Costumbrismo," 37; Pérez Carrera, *Periodismo y costumbrismo*.

61. Poole, *Vision, Race, and Modernity*; Péres Salas, *Costumbrismo y litografía en México*; Kennedy-Troya, *Escenarios para una patria*; Appelbaum, *Mapping the Country of Regions*; Dominguez, "Ethnografía, literatura, y proyectos nacionales." A study that engages with the Liberal versus Conservative Party agendas evident in costumbrismo in nineteenth-century Colombia is Ruiz, "El discurso costumbrista colombiano."

62. Casas Aguilar, *La Violencia en los Llanos Orientales*, 24.

63. Díaz Castro, *Manuela*.

64. Nueva Granada, *Recopilación de leyes de la Nueva Granada*.

65. Díaz Castro, *Manuela*.

66. Safford and Palacios, *Colombia*, 381.

67. José Hilario López obtained 725 votes, José Joaquin Gori obtained 384, Rufino Cuervo 304, and the remaining 275 votes went to other candidates. Safford and Palacios, *Colombia*, 381.

68. Uribe de Hincapié and López Lopera, *Las Palabras de la guerra*, 272–300.

69. Ancízar, *Editoriales del Neogranadino*, 90–92.

70. Ancízar, *Editoriales del Neogranadino*, 132.

71. Ancízar, *Editoriales del Neogranadino*, 150.

72. Ancízar, *Editoriales del Neogranadino*, 120–21.

73. Ruiz Gutierrez, "La Génesis del federalismo en la Nueva Granada."

74. Ancízar, *Peregrinación de Alpha*, 6.

75. See SR, Fondo Gobernaciones, Catalogo Documental Tomo 1, Archivo General de la Nación, Bogotá, and *Gaceta Oficial* laws as according to the following dates creating provinces and territories: Territorio de Bocas del Toro (from Veraguas), 3 June 1843; Territorio de San Martín, 2 June 1846 (from Bogotá); Territorio de la Goajira, 19 May 1846 (from Rio del Hacha); Territorio de Darién, 2 June 1846 (from Panama); Provincia Barbacoas, 8 June 1846 (from Pasto y Buenaventura); Provincia de Tuquerres (from Pasto central), 8 June 1846; Provincia Tundama (with Santa Rosa, Soata, Cocuy, Sogamoso de Tunja), 7 May 1849; Provincia de Chiriqui, 26 May 1849; Provincia Ocaña (from Mompox), 29 May 1849; Provincia de Azuero (from Panama y Veraguas), 8 April 1850; Pro-

vincia de Valledupar (from Santa Marta), 15 April 1850; Provincia de Soto (from Giron, Piedecuesta, y Bucaramanga from Pamplona), 17 April 1850; Provincia de Santander (from San José de Cucuta, Villa del Rosario, Salazar de Pamplona), 17 April 1850; Provincia de Medellín (from central canton of Antioquia), 16 May 1851; Provincia de Cordova (from southern Antioquia cantons), 16 May 1851; Provincia de Cundinamarca, Provincia de Zipaquirá, and Provincia de Tequendama (from Bogotá), 6 May 1852; Provincia de Sabanilla (with Barranquilla, Soledad, and Sabanalarga of Cartagena), 22 May 1852; Provincia de Garcia Rovira (with cantons of Malaga, Concepcion, and Fortuol/San Andres from Pamplona), 9 May 1853.

76. Ruiz Gutierrez, "La Génesis del federalismo."

77. Sánchez, *Gobierno y geografía*, 174–75.

78. Uribe de Hincapié and López Lopera, *Las Palabras de la guerra*, 224–29.

79. "Eusebio Borrero Gobernador civil y military de la provincial de Antioquia, a los habitantes del Estado federal," Medellín, Imprenta Jacobo Lince, 7 July 1851, in Hojas sueltas, Colección de Patrimonio documental, Universidad de Antioquia.

80. Mariano Ospina was a founding member of the Instituto Caldas chapter in Bogotá; see Table 2. For Eusebio Borrero's membership in the Buenaventura chapter Instituto Caldas, and for Julio Arboleda's membership in the Popayán chapter, see GO, 23 March 1848, no. 973, 251. For Rafael M. Giraldo and Pedro Antonio Restrepo's membership in the Antioquia chapter of the Instituto Caldas, see GO, 2 March 1848, no. 959, 143. For Colonel Francisco de Paula Diago and Mateo Viana's membership in the Mariquita Province, see GO, 25 May 1848, no. 982, 324. For the Conservative Party leadership of the 1851 Civil War, see Decreto del 22 de octubre de 1851 and Decreto de 8 de noviembre de 1851, Codificacion nacional de todas las leyes de Colombia, tomo X, 662, 672. Leaders included Mariano Ospina, Pastor Ospina, Mateo Viana, Colonel Francisco de Paula Diago, General Eusebio Borrero, Rafael María Giraldo, and Pedro Antonio Restrepo Escobar. See also Uribe de Hincapie and López Lopera, *Palabras de Guerra*, 314–17.

81. López, "Proclama del presidente de la República."

82. Nueva Granada Presidente López, "Mensaje del Poder Ejecutivo a las Cámaras Lejislativas" (Bogotá: Imprenta del Neo-Granadino, 1852). BNC, FPineda_786_pza4, pte 1.

83. *Neogranadino*, Bogotá, no. 191, 9 January 1852, 14; Plata, *Informe del secretario de estado*, 33.

84. "Instituto Caldas," in GO no. 959, 2 March 1848, 143.

85. Codazzi a su esposa, Medellín, 18 May 1852, in Soriano Lleras, *Itinerario de la Comisión Corográfica*, 59–60.

86. GO no. 1451, 26 November 1852.

87. GO no 1681, 17 February 1854, 138.

88. Sanchez, *Gobierno y geografía*, 339–40.

89. *El Pasatiempo*, Bogotá, no. 117, 3 September 1853, 121.

90. GO no. 1763, 10 March 1855, 591.

5. Constitutions and Political Geographies

1. Duque Muñoz, "La representación limítrofe y fronteriza."

2. Bushnell, *Making of Modern Colombia*, 92–104; Safford and Palacios, *Colombia*, 309–14, 381–83. See also De la Vega, *La federación en Colombia*; Gilmore, *El federalismo en Colombia*; Pérez Aguirre, *25 Años de historia colombiana*; Cruz Santos, *Federalismo y centralismo*; Camargo, "La federación en Colombia."

3. Delpar, *Red against Blue*, 10–17; Safford and Palacios, *Colombia*, 411–26; Bushnell, *Making of Modern Colombia*, 115–17.

4. Samper, "La historia de una alma," 465. See also Samper, *Ensayo Aproximado*.

5. Samper, "Cuaderno."

6. José María Samper argued political parties needed to recognize the role of climate and institutions on human social and political organization in his *Ensayo aproximado*.

7. Lleras, *Catecismo de agrimensura*; Ancízar, *Peregrinación de Alpha*, Fl. González, *Elementos de ciencia administrativa*.

8. Gargarelia, *Latin American Constitutionalism*, 29.

9. Ruiz, "La Génesis del federalismo en la Nueva Granada."

10. Samper, "Cuaderno."

11. Samper, "Cuaderno," 5–6.

12. Samper, "Cuaderno," 8.

13. Samper, "Cuaderno," 2.

14. Camacho Roldán, "Chapter 21: Los Golgotas," in *Mis Memorias*.

15. Samper, "Cuaderno," 3.

16. Sanders, *Vanguard of the Atlantic World*.

17. J. Rodríguez, *Divine Charter*.

18. Samper, "Cuaderno," 4.

19. Samper, "Cuaderno," 14–15.

20. Samper, "Cuaderno," 14–15.

21. Samper, "Cuaderno," 16–17.

22. Samper, "Cuaderno," 9.

23. Delpar, *Red against Blue*, 49. For graduates of San Bartolomé during this period, see Camacho Roldán, *Mis Memorias*.

24. Bushnell, *Making of Modern Colombia*, 101–39.

25. The 1853 constitution signers who were also IC members were IC Bogotá: Vicente Lombana, J. J. Gori, Antonio María Silva, Florentino González; Justo Arosemena; IC Antioquia: Jorje Gutierrez de Lara, Julian Vázquez, Nicolas F. Villa; IC Chocó: Ramon Argáez; IC Neiva: Eujenio Castillo; IC Mompox: Nicomédes Flórez; IC Ocaña: José de J. Hóyos, Manuel Lémus; IC Popayán: Manuel Antonio Bueno, Joaquin Valencia; IC Riohacha: Nicolas Prieto (he had been the governor who installed the Riohacha IC), Miguel Macaya; IC Socorro: Francisco Vega, Gonzalo A. Tavera, Ricardo Roldan; IC Tunja: Hilario Gómez, Luis Reyes, Segundo del Castellblanco; IC Veraguas: Francisco Fábrega; and IC Santamarta: Julian Ponce. Nueva Granada, *Constitución política de la Nueva Granada*, 34–39.

26. McGraw, *Work of Recognition*.

27. Venezuela abolished slavery under President José Gregorio Monagas on March 24, 1854; see Appaiah and Gates, *Africana*, 311. Ecuador's abolition of slavery began in Esmeraldas, with the Urbina Decree signed on July 25, 1851, which was ratified by the Convention of Guayaquil on September 18, 1852. National abolition did not happen until 1854. See Appaiah and Gates, *Africana*, 554; Henderson, *Gabriel García Moreno*, 26.

28. For universal manhood suffrage in Venezuela with no literacy requirement, see Zahler, *Ambitious Rebels*, 57; Bushnell, "La evolución del derecho del sufragio," 202.

29. Henderson, *Gabriel Garcia Moreno*, 26.

30. Restrepo Piedrahita, *Constituciones de la primera República liberal*.

31. Projects for national constitutions during this period in New Granada included Rafael Pombo, "Proyecto de reforma de la constitución política de la Confederación Gra-

nadina," BNC, FPombo_9; Arosemena, *Proyecto de acto reformatorio de la constitución*; Fl. Gonzalez, *Proyecto de Constitución*; Vanégas, *Proyecto de Constitución*, Vanégas drafted the Vélez province constitution granting women suffrage in 1853, a move that was struck down by the New Granada Supreme Court.

32. Samper, "Cuaderno," 27.

33. Uribe de Hincapié and López Lopera, *Las Palabras de la guerra*, 339–474.

34. Uribe de Hincapié and López Lopera, *Las Palabras de la guerra*, 486–88.

35. Gómez Picón, *El Golpe militar*, 101. See also José Manuel Restrepo's interpretation of the speech in *Diario político y militar*, tomo IV, 281.

36. *Constitución política de . . . 1853*, 47.

37. *GO* no. 1496, 2 April 1853, 245.

38. Molina, *Las ideas liberales*, 1–127; Jaramillo Uribe, *El pensamiento colombiano*, 173–80.

39. Arboleda, *Historia contemporanea de Colombia*, tomo V, 57.

40. Uribe Hincapié and López Lopera, *Las palabras de la guerra*, 360.

41. Cordovez Moure, *Reminiscencias*, 222.

42. Restrepo, *Diario político y militar*, tomo IV, 31.

43. Elected officials hostile to Obando's regime included Bogotá governor Pastor Ospina and Medellín governor Mariano Ospina. Even Obandista strongholds were lost to conservatives, including Buenaventura to Manuel María Mallarino, and Córdoba (Rionegro) to Valencia Restrepo. Pasto, Tequendama, and Mariquita also became conservative strongholds. Golgotas came to power in García Rovira, Moniquirá, Neiva, Ocaña, El Socoro, Tundama, Vélez, and, of course, Zipaquirá. Gómez Pinzón, *El Golpe Militar*, 127.

44. Loaiza Cano, *Manuel Ancízar y su época*, 215–16.

45. Restrepo, *Diario político y militar*, tomo IV, 311.

46. Ortiz, *Historia de la revolución*, 47; Valencia Llano, *La revolución de Melo*, 75–77; Uribe de Hincapie and López Lopera, *Las Palabras de Guerra*, 366–67.

47. "Numero 697. República de la Nueva Granada.–Libertad-Igualdad-Fraternidad.–Presidencia de la Junta Central Directiva.–Bogotá, 25 de enero 1854," in Cámara de Representantes, *Causa de Responsabilidad*, 70–71.

48. Ancízar, *Anarquia i rojismo en Nueva Granada*.

49. "Numero 697. República de la Nueva Granada," Cámara de Representantes, *Causa de Responsabilidad*, 70–71.

50. "Numero 697. República de la Nueva Granada," Cámara de Representantes, *Causa de Responsabilidad*, 70–71.

51. Uribe Hincapié and López Lopera, *Las Palabras de la guerra*, 488–89.

52. Uribe Hincapié and López Lopera, *Las Palabras de la guerra*, 355.

53. José María Villareal, a member of the provincial chapter of Socorro Province, vehemently defended Obando and Socorro's Sociedades Democraticas in his *Al criterio público*. See also *GO* no. 973, 23 April 1848, 251–52.

54. Gutierrez, *Santander y sus municipios*, vol. 1, 202–8.

55. Sánchez, *Gobierno y geografía*, 386.

56. Gutierrez, *Santander y sus municipios*, 221.

57. For the common participation of Viana and Samper in the Mariquita Chapter of the Instituto Caldas, see *GO* no. 997, 30 July 1848, 452. For their joint Conservative-Liberal leadership of the Honda flank against Melista forces, see Ortiz, *Historia de la revolución*, 67–79; Samper, "La historia de un alma," 363–368.

58. Loaiza Cano, *Manuel Ancízar y su época*, 213.

59. Loaiza Cano, *Manuel Ancízar y su época,* 211–91.

60. Loaiza Cano, *Manuel Ancízar y su época,* 214. See also Kitchens, "New Granadan-Peruvian Slave Trade," 205–14.

61. Loaiza Cano, *Manuel Ancízar y su época,* 226–27.

62. Bilbao, "Iniciativa de la America."

63. Bello, *Obras Completas.*

64. Letter by Ancízar to secretary of exterior relations of New Granada, Lima, 11 March 1855, AFA.

65. Januario Salgar, *Memoria del Secretario de Hacienda i Fomento, dirijida al ciudadano Presidente de los Estados Unidos de Colombia para el Congreso de 1870,* 188. BNC, FPineda_331_pza1.

66. Carta de Mariano Arosemena a Manuel Ancízar, Panama, 24 November, 1855, AFA.

67. Gobat, "Invention of Latin America."

68. Samper, "La historia de un alma."

69. Samper, "La historia de un alma," 400.

70. Samper, "La historia de un alma," 401, original emphasis.

71. Mosquera's presidential address, 1849; Mosquera, *Memoria sobre la geografía.*

72. Samper, "Ensayo aproximado," 4.

73. Appelbaum, *Mapping the Country of Regions.*

74. Samper, "La historia de un alma," 403.

75. Arosemena, *El Estado federal de Panamá,* 1.

76. Arosemena, *Proyecto de acto reformatorio de la constitución,* 1.

77. Arosemena, *Proyecto de acto reformatorio de la constitución,* 7.

78. Article 1 of "Acto Adicional de la Constitución creando el Estado de Panama," in Panama, *Disposiciones Lejislativas i ejecutivas.*

79. Ancízar and Samper, "Proyecto de constitución para la federacion neo-granadina."

80. Ancízar and Samper, "Proyecto de constitución para la federacion neo-granadina." For the text of the 1858 Constitution see http://www.alcaldiabogota.gov.co/sisjur/normas /Normal.jsp?i=13697.

81. Nueva Granada, *Constitución política de la Neuva Granada . . . 1853.*

82. Article 69 Constitución of 1858.

83. Secretario de Relaciones Exteriores a secretario de Gobierno (Bogotá, 13 de Junio de 1857), AGN, EOR, caja No 66.

84. Pérez, *Anales de la revolución 1857–1861,* 5.

85. Pérez, *Anales de la revolución 1857–1861,* 6.

86. Pérez, *Anales de la revolución 1857–1861.* 6.

87. Pérez, *Anales de la revolución 1857–1861,* 7.

88. Pérez, *Anales de la revolución 1857–1861,* 10.

89. McGuiness, "Searching for 'Latin America.'" See also *Gaceta de Estado,* 26 April 1856. For the official report that circulated throughout New Granada, see New Granada, *Final controversia diplomatica.* See also Chen Daley, "Watermelon Riot," 85–108.

90. McGuinness, "Searching for 'Latin America.'"

91. Pérez, *Anales de la revolución 1857–1861,* 33.

92. Gobat, "Invention of Latin America," 1345–75.

93. Pérez, *Anales de la revolución 1857–1861,* 32.

94. Pérez, *Anales de la revolución 1857–1861,* 116.

95. Pérez, *Anales de la revolución 1857–1861,* 119.

96. Pérez, *Anales de la revolución 1857–1861*, 122.

97. The geographies of Felipe Pérez first came out in installments through newspapers. For his collected printed geographies, see Pérez, *Compendio de jeografía jeneral*; Pérez, *Geografía general*; Pérez, *Jeografía física i política*; Pérez, *Jeografía jeneral de los Estados Unidos de Colombia*.

98. Appelbaum, *Mapping the Country of Regions*, 188–92; Sanchez, *Gobierno y geografía*, 443–53.

99. Cited in Appelbaum, *Mapping the Country of Regions*, 198–99.

100. Cited in Appelbaum, *Mapping the Country of Regions*, 198–99.

101. Cited in Appelbaum, *Mapping the Country of Regions*, 198–99.

102. Uribe de Hincapie and Lópes Lopera, *La Guerra por las soberanias*.

103. The following comes from the different state constitutions issued in 1863–1864. See Antioquia (Estado: Confederado), *Constitución política*; Bolívar (Estado: Confederado), *Constitución i leyes*; Cauca (Estado: Confederado), *Constitución política*; Cundinamarca (Estado: Confederado), *Recopilacion de leyes*; Magdalena (Estado: Confederado), *Constitución Política del Estado*; Panamá (Estado: Confederado), *Disposiciones lejislativas*; Santander (Columbia: Department), *Codigos Lejislativos*.

104. Sanders, *Contentious Republicans*.

105. Constitución y leyes espedidas por la Asamblea Constituyente del Estado de Boyacá en sus sesiones de 1857 (Bogotá: Imprenta de la Nación, 1857), HathiTrust, http://hdl.handle.net/2027/mdp.35112102361641.

6. Civic Religion vs. the Catholic Church

1. Calm, *El Chile de Pio XI*.

2. During the period of monarchical rule, the papal bulls that had guaranteed the Spanish Crown's rights to patronato meant that church wealth was inextricably linked to the Spanish Crown's control over the Catholic Church in the New World. The monarchy appointed all bishops, archbishops, cathedral chapter members, and parish priests. The Crown also had the right to license construction of churches and chapels, determine the territorial limits of dioceses and parishes, approve and convene all canons and decrees of local synods and councils, and regulate the travel of clerics to and from the New World. See Shiels, *King and Church*; Fariss, *Crown and Clergy*; Schwaller, *Church and Clergy*.

3. Mosquera, "Carta autógrafa," 3–5.

4. Ospina, cited in Gómez Barrientos, *Don Mariano Ospina*, 262–63.

5. Rausch, "Church-State Relations."

6. Jaramillo and Meisel Roca, "Más allá de la retórica."

7. For a collection of essays on church-state relations in Mexico, Guatemala, Peru, and Bolivia see Jackson, *Liberals, the Church, and Indian Peasants*. For Colombia, see Villegas, *Colombia*; Díaz Díaz, *La desamortización de bienes eclesiásticos*; Díaz Díaz, "Estado, iglesia y desamortización"; Parra de Avellaneda and Muñoz Patiño, "Aspectos de la agricultura y la desamortización"; Cascavita Mora, "La desamortizacón en Colombia"; De la Cruz Vergara, "Remates y ventas de bienes desamortizados"; Fazio Vargas and Sánchez Torres, "Educational Effects of 19th Century Disentailment," 441–67.

8. Butler, "Liberalism, Anticlericalism, and Antireligious Currents," 261.

9. Rodríguez Piñeres, *El olimpo radical*; Bermúdez, *El bello sexo*; Fe. González, "Iglesia y estado desde la convención," 91–163; Gaitan Ammann, "Recordando a los Uribe," 125–46.

10. Sanders, *Contentious Republicans*, 20; Bushnell, *Making of Modern Colombia*; Delpar, *Red against Blue*, 1–59; Dix, *Colombia*.

11. For the growth of church wealth in Spanish America and efforts to disentail it, see Herr, *Rural Change and Royal Finance*; López Garavito, *Historia de la hacienda*. For studies on Mexico see Knowlton, "Church Property"; Bazant, *Alienation of Church Wealth*; Juárez, *Reclaiming Church Wealth*. For Bolivia, see Millington, *Debt Politics*.

12. Message of May 20, 1824, in AGN, *Archivo del Congreso, Senado*, vol. 6, no. 54.

13. Bushnell, *Santander Regime in Gran Colombia*, 223–24.

14. Cited in Cobo Borda, *Manual de Historia*, vol. 2, 357.

15. Díaz Díaz, "Estado, Iglesia y Desamortización," 413–19.

16. Executive Power Decree of July 29, 1853, Article 8, quoted in Restrepo, *Iglesia y Estado*, 376.

17. Restrepo, *Iglesia y Estado*, 376.

18. Restrepo, *Iglesia y Estado*, 376.

19. Bushnell, *Colombia*, 120.

20. Butler, "Liberalism, Anticlericalism, and Antireligious Currents," 263.

21. Safford and Palacios, *Colombia*, 221–24; Helg, *La educación en Colombia*, 17–35; Uribe Urán, *Honorable Lives*, 120–37; Bushnell, *Colombia*, 92–94. These analyses draw largely from an argument posed by Frank Safford. See Safford, "Social Aspects of Politics," 344–370.

22. Herrera, *Informe del Ajente Jeneral*, 10, emphasis added.

23. Rosenthal, *Salt and the Colombian State*, 116–18.

24. "Al Señor Ajente general," in AGN, SR, Fondo B/D, tomo 6, folio 117.

25. AGN SR, Fondo B/D, tomo 6, folio 320 r.

26. See Table 3.

27. AGN, SR, B/D, tomo. 6, folio 675r.

28. AGN, SR, B/D, tomo 6, folio 675v.

29. López-Alves, *State Formation and Democracy*, 96–139.

30. New Granada, "De las cuadrillas de malhechores," in *Recopilación de leyes de la Nueva Granada*.

31. AGN, SR, B/D, vol. 6, f. 675v.

32. Villegas, *Colombia: Enfrentamiento*, 83.

33. Cobo Borda, *Manual de Historia*, 462.

34. Revenue for 1874 cited in Safford and Palacios, *Colombia*, 227.

35. See Villegas, *Colombia: Enfrentamiento*, 35–37, 41.

36. AGN SR, Fondo B/D, tomo 6, folio 688.

37. AGN SR, Fondo B/D, tomo 6, folio 688.

38. Barreto, *Informe annual del Director*, 40.

39. Barreto, *Informe annual del Director*, 40.

40. *Escuela Normal* (Bogotá), 18 January 1872, 15.

41. Safford and Palacios, *Colombia*, 227.

42. Helg, *La educación en Colombia*, 23–24. See also Fals Borda, *La educación en Colombia*, 20; Jaramillo Uribe, "El proceso de la educación," 274.

43. Barreto, *Informe anual del Director*, 40.

44. Barreto, *Informe anual del Director*, 41.

45. Dámaso Zapata, *Tercer informe annual del Director de Instrucción Primaria del E.S. de Cundinamarca* (Bogotá, 1874), cited in Meyer Loy, "Primary Education," 288.

46. See Meyer Loy, "Primary Education," 288–89.

47. Meyer Loy, "Primary Education," 275–94.

48. "Decreto Orgánico de la instrucción pública primaria," *La Escuela Normal* (Bogotá), 7 January 1871, 2, BNC, Microfilm 546.

49. *Escuela Normal* (Bogotá), 18 January 1872, 15.

50. Barreto, *Informe anual del Director*, 15–16.

51. Barreto, *Informe anual del Director*, 18–21, 37–40.

52. Barreto, *Informe anual del Director*, 18–21, 37–40.

53. Barreto, *Informe anual del Director*, 18–21, 37–40.

54. See "Lei de 2 de Julio que autoriza al Poder Ejecutivo para organizar la Instrucción pública primaria a cargo de la Unión," in *La Escuela Normal* (Bogotá), 7 January 1871, 1, BNC.

55. "Circular" and "Decreto orgánico de la Instrucción pública primaria," in *La Escuela Normal* (Bogotá), 7 January 1871, 1, BNC.

56. Decreto Orgánico," *La Escuela Normal* (Bogotá), 14 January 1871, BNC.

57. Decreto Orgánico," *La Escuela Normal* (Bogotá), 14 January 1871, BNC, 3.

58. "Circular" and "Decreto orgánico de la Instrucción pública primaria," in *La Escuela Normal* (Bogotá), 7 January 1871, 1, BNC, 9.

59. "Circular" and "Decreto orgánico de la Instrucción pública primaria," in *La Escuela Normal* (Bogotá), 7 January 1871, 1, BNC, 4.

60. Meyer Loy, "Primary Education," 286.

61. Santamaría, *Primer Libro de instrucción objetiva.*

62. Santamaría, *Primer Libro de instrucción objetiva.*

63. Rodríguez Plata, *La inmigración Alemana al Estado Soberano*, 12.

64. "Decreto orgánico de la Instrucción pública primaria," *La Escuela Normal* (Bogotá), 14 January 1871.

65. "Decreto orgánico de la Instrucción pública primaria," *La Escuela Normal* (Bogotá), 14 January 1871.

66. "Decreto orgánico de la Instrucción pública primaria," *La Escuela Normal* (Bogotá), 14 January 1871.

67. Ramón Zapata, *Damáso Zapata o la reforma educativa en Colombia* (Bogotá, 1961), 205, cited in Helg, *La educación en Colombia*, 25.

68. Safford, *Ideal of the Practical*, 53.

69. See Helg, *La educación en Colombia*, 27. See also Urrutia, *50 años de desarrollo económico colombiano*, 138–39; H. Arboleda, *Estadística general de la República de Colombia.*

70. Meyer Loy, "Primary Education," 286–87.

71. Helg, *La educación en Colombia*, 26.

72. Meyer Loy, "Primary Education," 290; Helg, *La educación en Colombia*, 26.

73. Inocencia Nariño, "Estados Unidos de Colombia—Estado de Boyacá-Dirección de la Escuela Normal de Institutoras.–Numero 117. Tunja 4 de Octubre de 1883," in Barreto, *Informe annual del Director*, 28–29.

74. Nariño, "Estados Unidos de Colombia."

75. Barreto, *Informe anual del Director.*

76. Barreto, *Informe anual del Director.*

77. Barreto, *Informe anual del Director.*

78. Barreto, *Informe anual del Director.*

79. Samper, "Don José Manuel Groot," in *Cuadros de Costumbres*, 17–18.

80. Groot, *Historia eclesiastica y civil*, i.

81. Groot, *Historia eclesiastica y civil,* ii.

82. Groot, *Historia eclesiastica y civil,* ii.

83. Groot, *Historia eclesiastica y civil,* ii.

84. Thurner, "Peruvian Geneologies of History and Nation." See also Earle, *Return of the Native.*

85. Similar trends existed in Mexico and Ecuador. See Mijangos y González, *Lawyer of the Church;* Henderson, *Gabriel García Moreno.*

86. Safford and Palacios, *Colombia,* 224.

87. Helg, *La educación en Colombia.*

88. For more on Rafael Nuñez and the Regeneration see Safford and Palacios, *Colombia,* 243-51; Bergquist, *Coffee and Conflict in Colombia;* Park, *Rafael Nuñez;* Delpar, *Red against Blue,* 110-58.

89. Jaramillo and Meisel Roca, "Más allá de la retórica," 51.

Conclusion

1. Butler, "Liberalism, Anticlericalism, and Antireligious Currents."

2. For the impact of Soledad Acosta de Samper on José María de Samper's political leanings see Alzate, "Soledad Acosta de Samper."

3. Gobat, "Invention of Latin America"; Ardao, *Génesis de la idea y el nombre*; Rojas Mix, "Bilbao y el hallazgo de América Latina"; McGuiness, "Searching for 'Latin America,'" 87-107. The Spanish-American War also inspired a retrospective on the Latin American origins of "Latin America." See Estrade, "Del Invento de 'América Latina,'" 179-88; and Quijada, "Sobre el origen y difusión del nombre," 595-616.

4. Bilbao, "Iniciativa de la América."

5. For the early emergence of Hispanism in the 1860s and Samper's role in it, see Betancourt-Mendieta, "Una mirada al hispanoamericanismo," 111-45.

6. Del Castillo, "Colombian Cartography."

7. Boas, "Instability of Human Types," 99-103.

8. Samper, "La cuestión de las razas," 2.

9. Samper, "España y Colombia," 4.

10. Leys-Stepan, *Hour of Eugenics.*

11. Samper, "España y Colombia," 2-4.

12. Samper, "La cuestión de las razas," 2-3.

13. Samper, "España y Colombia," 4.

14. Betancourt-Mendieta, "Una mirada al hispanoamericanismo."

15. Capello, *City at the Center of the World;* Earle, *Return of the Native;* Sanders, "Vanguard of the Atlantic World,"104-27.

16. Betancourt-Mendieta, "Una mirada al hispanoamericanismo."

17. For Spanish and British collaboration on the French Invasion, see Topik, "When Mexico had the Blues."

18. Mundy, *Mapping of New Spain;* Arias and Meléndez, *Mapping Colonial Spanish America;* Herzog, *Frontiers of Possession;* Portuondo, *Secret Science.*

19. Sommer, *Foundational Fictions,* 369n8, citing Camacho Guizado, *Sobre la literatura colombiana.*

20. Sanders, "Vanguard of the Atlantic World."

21. The most famous of these was Domingo F. Sarmiento, whose original "Civilización i barbarie: Vida de Facundo Quiroga, aspecto físico, costumbres, i abitos de la república

Argentina," published in Chile in 1845, became an international sensation. See Fishburn, "Concept of 'Civilization and Barbarism,'" 301–308. In the early twentieth century, U.S. historians drew on the barbarism described by Sarmiento to develop their own narratives about Hispanic America that disparaged their ability for autonomous, republican governance that was not dominated by dictators. See Chapman, "Age of the Caudillos," 286–92. Caudillos have been a point of fascination for several scholars thereafter, and these studies help elucidate shifting historiographical methodologies precisely because they address these familiar, charismatic figures. See Wolf and Hansen, "Caudillo Politics"; Chasteen, *Heroes on Horseback*; De la Fuente, *Children of Facundo*.

22. Eastman and Sobrevilla Perea, *Rise of Constitutional Government*.

23. Appelbaum, *Mapping the Country of Regions*; Capello, *City at the Center of the World*; Craib, *Cartographic Mexico*; Sanders, "Vanguard of the Atlantic World"; Nieto-Olarte, *Orden natural*; Cañizares-Esguerra, *Nature, Empire, and Nation*.

Bibliography

Archives

Ancízar Family Archive (AFA)
Archivo General de la Nación (AGN)
  Notarías: Notaría 4a
  Seccion Asuntos Criminales
  Seccion Mapas y Planos (SMP)
  Sección República (SR)
    Fondo Congreso (FC)
    Fondo Negocios Administrativos (FNA)
    Fondo Guerra y Marina (FGM)
    Fondo Ministerio de Relaciones Exteriores (FMRE)
    Fondo Bienes Desamortizados (B/D)
    Fondo Gobernación de Bogotá (FGB)
  Sección Negocios Administrativos (NA)
  Enrique Ortega Ricaurte (EOR)
Biblioteca Nacional de Colombia (BNC)
Fondo Antiguo (FA)
Fondo (F.)
Biblioteca Luis Angel Arango, Libros Raros y Manuscritos (BLAA, LRM)
Instituto Geográfico Agustín Codazzi (IGAC)
University of Miami Archives and Special Collections (UM ASC)

Published Works

Acevedo, Alfonso. "Memoria del Gobernador de Bogotá a la Camara Provincial en sus sesiones de 1843." Bogotá, 1843. BNC, FPineda_733_pza9.

Acevedo y Tejada, Pedro. *Noticia sobre la geografía política de Colombia.* Imprenta Española de M. Calero, 1825.

Acosta, Joaquin. *Compendio histórico del descubrimiento y colonización de la Nueva Granada en el siglo décimo sexto.* Paris: Imprenta de Beau en San German en Laye, 1848.

———. "Ruines découvertes pres de Tunja dans l'Americque Centrale." *Bulletin de la Société de Géographie* 13.73–78 (1850): 299–303.

Adelman, Jeremy, ed. *Colonial Legacies: The Problem of Persistence in Latin American History.* New York: Routledge, 1999.

Afanador, María José. "Political Economy, Geographical Imagination, and Territory in the Making and Unmaking of New Granada, 1739–1830." PhD diss., University of Texas at Austin, 2016.

Albis Gonzalez, Victor. "A falta de una iconografia de Aime Bergeron." *Revista de la Academia Colombiana de Ciencias Exactas, Físicas, y Naturales* 22, no. 85 (1998): 587–90.

Alcantara Herran, Pedro. *Esposisión del secretario . . . 1839*. Bogotá: Nicomedes Lora, 1839. BNC F. Vergara 264 pza 3.

Alzate, Carolina. "Soledad Acosta de Samper: Mujer y escritura en el siglo XIX colombiano." *Voces y silencios, Soledad Acosta de Samper, 100 años*. Bogotá: Ministerio de Cultura, 2013.

Ancízar, Manuel. *Anarquia i rojismo en Nueva Granda*. Santiago: Impr. De Julio Belin, 1853.

———. *Editoriales del Neo-Granadino*. 3rd ed. Selección Samper Ortega de Literatura Colombiana, Periodismo, no. 63. Bogotá: Editorial Minerva, 1967.

———. *Instituto Caldas*. Bogotá: Losada, 1848. BNC, FPineda_248_pza43.

———. *Peregrinación de Alpha por las provincias del Norte de la Nueva Granada, en 1850 i 1851*. Bogotá: Imprenta de Echeverría Hermanos, 1853.

Ancízar, Manuel, and José María Samper. "Proyecto de constitución para la federacion neo-granadina." Bogotá: Imprenta del Estado, 1856. BNC, FPineda_223_pza15.

Anderson, Benedict. *Imagined Communities: Reflections on the Origin and Spread of Nationalism*. London: Verso, 1983.

Anna, Timothy. *The Fall of the Royal Government in Peru*. Lincoln: University of Nebraska Press, 1979.

Annino, Antonio, and François-Xavier Guerra. *Inventando la nación: Iberoamérica siglo XIX*. Mexico City: Fondo de Cultura Económica, 2003.

Annino, Antonio, and Marcela Ternavasio, eds. *El laboratorio constitucional Iberoamericano: 1807/1808–1830*. Madrid: Asociación de Historiadores Latinoamericanos Europeos, 2012.

Antioquia (Estado: Confederado). *Constitución política del estado soberano de Antioquia, 1863*. Medellín: Impreso por Silvestre Balcázar, 1863. BNC, FPineda_478_pza5.

Appaiah, Kwame Anthony, and Henry Louis Gates Jr., eds. *Africana: The Encyclopedia of the African and African American Experience*. 2nd ed. Oxford: Oxford University Press, 2005.

Appelbaum, Nancy. *Mapping the Country of Regions: The Chorographic Commission of Nineteenth-Century Colombia*. Chapel Hill: University of North Carolina Press, 2015.

———. *Muddied Waters: Race, Region, and Local History in Colombia, 1846–1948*. Durham NC: Duke University Press, 2003.

———. "Reading the Past on the Mountainsides of Colombia: Mid-Nineteenth-Century Patriotic Geology, Archaeology and Historiography." *Hispanic American Historical Review* 93, no. 3 (August 2013): 347–376.

Arana, Marie. *Bolívar: American Liberator*. New York: Simon and Schuster, 2013.

Arboleda, Gustavo. *Historia contemporanea de Colombia (desde la disolución de la antigua república de ese nombre hasta la época presente)*. 6 vols. Bogotá: Arboleda & Valencia, 1919–1935.

Arboleda, Henrique. *Estadística general de la República de Colombia*. Bogotá: Imprenta Nacional, 1905.

Arboleda, Luis Carlos. "Introducción del sistema métrico decimal en Colombia a mediados del siglo XIX." *Cuadernos de investigación y formación en educación matemática* 9, no. 12 (2014): 73–86.

Ardao, Arturo. *Génesis de la idea y el nombre de América latina*. Caracas: Centro de Estudios latinoamericanos, 1980.

Arias, Santa. "Rethinking Space: An Outsider's View of the Spatial Turn." *GeoJournal* 75 (2010): 29–41.

Arias, Santa, and Mariselle Meléndez, eds. *Mapping Colonial Spanish America: Places and Commonplaces of Identity, Culture, and Experience*. Lewisburg PA: Bucknell University Press, 2002.

Arias De Greiff, Jorge, and Clara Helena Sánchez. *La Universidad Nacional en el siglo XIX, Documentos para su historia: escuela de ingeniería*. Bogotá: Facultad de Ciencias Humanas UN Colección CES, 2004.

Arnold, David. *Colonizing the Body: State Medicine and Epidemic Disease in Nineteenth-Century India*. Berkeley: University of California Press, 1993.

Arosemena, Justo. *El Estado Federal de Panamá*. Panamá: Editora Panameña, SA, 1965.

——. *Proyecto de acto reformatorio de la constitución*. Bogotá: Imprenta de Echeverría Hermanos, 1852. BNC, FPineda_937_pza3.

Arriquibar, Nicolás. *Recreación política: Reflexiones sobre el amigo de los hombres en su tratado de población, considerando con respecto a nuestros intereses. Primera Parte: Obra póstuma de Don Nicolás de Arriquibar, natural y del comercio de la villa de Bilbao, e individuo con los títulos de Mérito y Benemérito de la Real Sociedad Bascongada*. Tomás de Robles y Navarro: Impresor de la misma Real Sociedad, 1779.

Artola, Miguel. *Los afrancesados*. Madrid: Alianza, 2008.

Bachelard, Gaston. *The Poetics of Space*. New York: Penguin Books, 1964.

Barreto, Isidro. *Informe anual del director de la instrucción pública del estado de Boyacá al señor secretario de la Instrucción Pública Nacional*. Tunja, 1883. UM ASC, Eder Collection.

Barriga, Joaquin. *Informe del secretario de guerra de la Nueva Granada al Congreso Constitucional de 1848*. Bogotá: Imprenta de M. Sánchez Caicedo, 1848.

Basalla, George. "The Spread of Western Science." *Science*, no. 156 (1967): 611–22.

Bassi, Ernesto. *An Aqueous Territory: Sailor Geographies and New Granada's Transimperial Greater Caribbean World*. Durham NC: Duke University Press, 2017.

Bateman, Alfredo, ed. *Obras completas de Francisco José de Caldas: Publicadas por la Universidad Nacional de Colombia como homenaje con motivo del sesquicentenario de su muerte*. Bogotá: Imprenta Nacional, 1966.

Bazant, Jan. *Alienation of Church Wealth in Mexico: Social and Economic Aspects of the Liberal Revolution, 1856–1875*. Edited and translated by Michael Costeloe. Cambridge: Cambridge University Press, 1971.

Beckert, Sven. *Empire of Cotton: A Global History*. New York: Vintage Books, 2014.

Bell, David. *The Cult of the Nation in France: Inventing Nationalism, 1680–1800*. Cambridge MA: Harvard University Press, 2001.

Bello, Andres. *Obras completas: Código civil de la república de Chile. Introducción y notas de Pedro L Urquieta*. 2 vols. Caracas: Ediciones del Ministerio de Educación, 1954.

Bermúdez, Suzy. *El bello sexo: La mujer y la familia durante el Olimpo Radical*. Bogotá: Ediciones Uniandes, 1993.

Bergquist, Charles. *Coffee and Conflict in Colombia, 1886–1910*. Durham NC: Duke University Press, 1978.

Berquist Soule, Emily. *The Bishop's Utopia: Envisioning Improvement in Colonial Peru*. Philadelphia: University of Pennsylvania Press, 2014.

Bertomeu Sanchez, J.R., and A. Garcia Belmar. *La revolución en química: Entre la historia y la memoria*. Valencia: Universitat de Valencia, 2006.

Betancourt-Mendieta, Alexander. "Una mirada al hispanoamericanismo en el siglo XIX: Las observaciones de José María Samper." *Canadian Journal of Latin American and Caribbean Studies/Revue canadienne des etudes latino-américaines et caraibes* 32, no. 63 (2007): 111–45.

Bhabha, Homi. *The Location of Culture*. New York: Routledge, 1994.

Biblioteca de "El Mosaico." *Museo de cuadros de costumbres*. Bogotá: Impreso por Focion Mantilla, 1866. 2 vols.

Bilbao, Francisco. "Iniciativa de la América: Idea de un congreso federal de las repúblicas." *Latinoamerica: Cuadernos de cultura latinoamericana* 3 (1978): 5–27.

Bleichmar, Daniela. *Visible Empire: Botanical Expeditions and Visual Culture in the Hispanic Enlightenment*. Chicago: University of Chicago Press, 2012.

Bleichmar, Daniela, Paula de Vos, Kristin Huffine, and Kevin Sheehan, eds. *Science in the Spanish and Portuguese Empires, 1500–1800*. Stanford: Stanford University Press, 2009.

Boas, Franz. "The Instability of Human Types," *Papers on Interracial Problems Communicated to the First Universal Races Congress Held at the University of London*, July 26–29, 1911. Edited by Gustav Spiller. Boston: Ginn, 1912.

Bolívar (Estado: Confederado) Asamblea Legislativa. *Constitución i leyes espedidas por la asamblea lejislativa del Estado Soberano del Bolívar en las sesiones estraordinarias de 1863*. Cartagena: Imp. De Ruiz e Hijo, 1864. BNC, FPineda_795_pza8.

Bolívar, Simón. *Doctrína del Libertador*. Compilation, notes, and chronology by Manuel Pérez Vila. Caracas: Ayacucho, 1985.

——— . *Selected Writings of Bolívar*. Translated by Lewis Bertrand. New York: Colonial Press, 1951.

Bonilla, Heraclio. "Consequencias económicas de la independencia en hispanoamérica." *Economía* 9, no. 22 (December 1988): 133-146.

Bonnet, Diana. *Tierra y comunidad un problema irresuelto. El caso del altiplano cundiboyacense (Virreinato de Nueva Granada) 1750–1800*. Bogotá: Instituto Colombiano de Antropología e Historia, 2002.

Borda, Ignacio. *Monumentos patrióticos de Bogotá: Su historia y descripción*. Bogotá: Imprenta La Luz, 1892.

Borges, Jorge Luis. "Del rigor de la ciencia." In *Collected Fictions*, translated by Andrew Hurley. London: Penguin, 1999.

Borja, Miguel. *Espacio y guerra: Colombia federal, 1858–1885*. Bogotá: Universidad Nacional de Colombia, IEPRI, 2010.

Botero, Clara Isabel. "The Construction of the Pre-Hispanic Past of Colombia: Collections, Museums, and Early Archaeology, 1823–1941." PhD diss. University of Oxford, 2001, 61.

Bourdieu, Pierre. "Social Space and Symbolic Power." *Sociological Theory* 7 (1989): 14–25.

Brading, David. *Mineros y comerciantes en el México Borbónico*. Mexico City: FCE, 1975.

Brienen, Marten. "The Clamor for Schools: Rural Education and the Development of State-Community Contact in Highland Bolivia, 1930–1952." *Revista de Indias* 62, no. 226 (2002): 616–49.

Brower, Benjamin. *A Desert Named Peace: The Violence of France's Empire in the Algerian Sahara, 1844–1902*. New York: Columbia University Press, 2009.

Brown, Matthew. *Adventuring through Spanish Colonies: Simón Bolívar, Foreign Mercenaries and the Birth of New Nations*. Liverpool: Liverpool Latin American Studies, 2006.

———. *The Struggle for Power in Post-Independence Colombia and Venezuela*. New York: Palgrave Macmillan, 2012.

Brunnschweiler, Dieter. *The Llanos Frontier of Colombia: Environment and Changing Land Use in Meta*. East Lansing: Michigan State University Press, 1972.

Burns, E. Bradford. *The Poverty of Progress: Latin America in the Nineteenth Century*. Berkeley: University of California Press, 1980.

Bury, J. P. T., ed. *The New Cambridge Modern History*. Vol. 10, *The Zenith of European Power, 1830–1870*. Cambridge: Cambridge University Press, 1971.

Bushnell, David. "El desarrollo de la prensa en la Gran Colombia." In *Ensayos de historia política de Colombia siglos XIX y XIX*. Medellín, Colombia: La Carreta Editores, 2006.

Bushnell, David. "La evolución del derecho del sufragio en Venezuela." *Boletín histórico*, no. 29 (1972): 202.

———. *The Making of Modern Colombia: A Nation in Spite of Itself*. Berkeley: University of California Press, 1993.

———. *The Santander Regime in Gran Colombia*. Newark: University of Delaware Press, 1954.

Butler, Mathew. "Liberalism, Anticlericalism, and Antireligious Currents in the Nineteenth Century." In *The Cambridge History of Religions in Latin America*, edited by Virginia Garrard-Burnett, Paul Freston, and Stephen Dove. Cambridge: Cambridge University Press, 2016.

Caldas, F. J. *Semanario de la Nueva Granada: Miscelánea de ciencias, literatura, artes é industria publicada por una sociedad de patriotas granadinos, bajo la dirección de Francisco José de Caldas*. Edited by J. Acosta. Paris: Lassere, 1849.

Calm, Lillian. *El Chile de Pio IX: 1824*. Santiago: Editorial Andres Bello, 1987.

Camacho Guizado, Eduardo. *Sobre la literatura colombiana e hispanoamericana*. Bogotá: Instituto Colombiano de Cultura, 1978.

Camacho Roldán, Salvador. *Mis memorias*. Bogotá: Cromos. 1923.

Cámara de Representantes. *Causa de responsabilidad contra el Ciudadano Presidente de la República i los señores secretarios del despacho*. Bogotá: Imprenta del Neo-granadino, 1855. BNC, FPineda_503_pt1.

Camargo, Pedro Pablo. "La federación en Colombia." In *Los sistemas federales del continente americano*. México City: FCE, UNAM, 1972.

Cañizares-Esguerra, Jorge. *How to Write the History of the New World: Historiographies, Epistemologies, and Identities in the Eighteenth-Century Atlantic World*. Stanford: Stanford University Press, 2001.

———. *Nature, Empire and Nation: Explorations of the History of Science in the Iberian World*. Stanford: Stanford University Press, 2006.

Capello, Ernesto. *City at the Center of the World: Space, History and Modernity in Quito*. Pittsburgh: University of Pittsburgh Press, 2011.

Cardoso, Fernando Henrique, and Enzo Faletto. *Dependencia y desarrollo en América Latina*. Mexico City: Siglo XXI, 1969.

Carrera, Magali. *Traveling from New Spain to Mexico: Mapping Practices of Nineteenth-Century Mexico*. Durham NC: Duke University Press, 2011.

Carrillo Rocha, Magali. "Comienzos de una desilusion: Noticias publicas y lealismo. Nueva Granada, 1808." *Historia y sociedad*, no. 21 (July—December 2011): 95–115.

Casas Aguilar, Justo. *La violencia en los llanos orientales: Comando hermanos Bautista*. Bogotá: ECOE, 1986.

Cascavita Mora, Juan David. *La desamortizacón en Colombia, 1861–1865: Primeros Años, el caso de los censos, tesis*. Bogotá: Universidad Nacional de Colombia, 2013.

Castrillon Arboleda, Diego. *Tomás Cipriano de Mosquera*. Bogotá: Planeta, 1994.

Castro-Gómez, Santiago. *La hybris del punto cero: Ciencia, raza e ilustración en la Nueva Granada (1750–1816)*. Bogotá: Editorial Pontificia Universidad Javeriana, 2005.

Castro-Klarén, Sara, and John Charles Chasteeen, eds. *Beyond Imagined Communities: Reading and Writing the Nation in Nineteenth-Century Latin America*. Baltimore: Johns Hopkins University Press, 2003.

Cauca (Estado: Confederado). *Constitución política del Estado Soberano del Cauca, 1863*. Bogotá: Imprenta de la Nacíon, 1863. BNC, FPineda_749_pza7.

Césaire, Aimé. *Discourse on Colonialism*. Translated by Joan Pinkham. New York: Monthly Review Press, 1972, 2000.

Chakrabarty, Dipesh. *Provincializing Europe: Postcolonial Thought and Historical Difference*. Princeton: Princeton University Press, 2000.

Chambers, David Wade. "Locality and Science: Myths of Centre and Periphery." In *Mundialización de la ciencia y cultura nacional*, edited by Antonio Lafuente, Alberto Elena, and María Luisa Ortega, 605–18. Madrid: Ediciones Doce Calles, 1993.

Chapman, Charles E. "The Age of the Caudillos: A Chapter in Hispanic American History." *Hispanic American Research Review* 12, no. 2 (May 1932): 286–92.

Chasteen, John Charles. *Heroes on Horseback: A Life and Times of the Last Gaucho Caudillos (Dialogos)*. Albuquerque: University of New Mexico Press, 1995.

Chen Daley, Mercedes. "The Watermelon Riot: Cultural Encounters in Panama City, 15 April 1856." *Hispanic American Historical Review* 70, no. 1 (February 1990): 85–108.

Chiaramonte, José Carlos. *Ciudades, provincias, estados: Orígenes de la nación Argentina: 1800–1846*. Buenos Aires: Compañia Editora Espasa Calpe, Ariel, 1997.

Chust, Manuel. *La cuestión nacional americana en las Cortes de Cádiz*. Valencia: Fundación Instituto Historia Social y Universidad Nacional Autónoma de México, 1999.

Cobo Borda, Juan Gustavo, and Santiago Mutis Durán, eds. *Manual de historia de Colombia*. Vol. 2. Bogotá: Circulo de Lectores, 1979.

Colombia. *Codificacion nacional de todas las leyes de Colombia desde el año de 1821: Hecha conforme a la ley 13 de 1912*. Vol. 10: *1843–1844*. Bogotá: Imprenta Nacional, 1924–.

Congreso general de Colombia. *Cuerpo de leyes de la República de Colombia: Comprende la Constitución y leyes sancionadas por el primer congreso jeneral en las sesiones que celebro desde 6 de mayo hasta 14 de octubre de 1821*. Bogotá: Imprenta de B. Espinosa, 1822. BNC, FPineda_154_pza1.

Cooper, Frederick. *Colonialism in Question: Theory, Knowledge, History*. Berkeley: University of California Press, 2005.

Coraboeuf, Jean-Baptiste. *Memoire sur les operations geodesiques des Pyrenees et la comparaison du niveau des deux mers*. Paris: Impr. Royale, 1831.

Cordovez Moure, José María. *Reminiscencias: Santafé y Bogotá*. Vol. 1. Imp. de "El telegrama," 1893.

Cormack, Lesley B. "Chorography: Geography Writ Small." In *Charting an Empire: Geography at the English Universities, 1582–1620*, 163–202. Chicago: University of Chicago Press, 1997.

Corradine Angulo, Alberto, and Helga Mora de Corradine. *Historia de la arquitectura colombiana*. Vol. 2. Bogotá: Universidad Nacional de Colombia, 1989.

Cowie, Helen. *Conquering Nature in Spain and Its Empire, 1750–1850*. Studies in Imperialism. Manchester: Manchester University Press, 2011.

Craib, Raymond. *Cartographic Mexico: A History of State Fixations and Fugitive Landscapes*. Durham NC: Duke University Press, 2004.

Craib, Raymond. "Cartography and Power in the Conquest and Creation of New Spain." *Latin American Research Review* 35, no. 1 (2000): 7–36.

Crawford, Matthew. *The Andean Wonder Drug: Cinchona Bark and Imperia Science in the Spanish Atlantic, 1630–1800*. Pittsburgh: University of Pittsburgh Press, 2016.

Cruz Santos, Abel. *Federalismo y centralismo*. Bogotá: Banco de la República, 1979.

Cueto, Marcos. *Excellence in the Periphery: Scientific Activities and Biomedical Sciences in Peru*. New York: Columbia University Press, 1988.

Cummins, Thomas B. F., Emily A. Engel, Barbara Anderson, and Juan M. Ossio, eds. *Manuscript Cultures of Colonial Mexico and Peru: New Questions and Approaches*. Los Angeles: Getty Research Institute, 2014.

Cundinamarca (Estado: Confederado). *Recopilacion de leyes i decretos del estado soberano de Cundinamarca*. Bogotá: Departamento de Cundinamarca, 1868. HathiTrust, http://hdl.handle.net/2027/coo.31924011914508.

Curry, Glen. "The Disappearance of the Resguardo Indígenas of Cundinamarca, Colombia, 1800-1863." PhD diss., Vanderbilt University, 1981.

Dávila Ortiz, Alfonso. *Minifundio rural: Latifundio urbano; un enfoque liberal sobre las reformas agraria y urbana*. Bogotá: Editorial Revista Colombiana, 1971.

De la Cruz Vergara, Maribel. "Remates y ventas de bienes desamortizados en Colombia. El caso del Estado Soberano de Bolívar, 1861–1875." *América Latina en la historia económica* 21, no. 1 (January/April 2014).

De la Fuente, Ariel. *Children of Facundo: Caudillo and Gaucho Insurgency during the Argentine State-Formation Process (La Rioja, 1853–1870)*. Durham NC: Duke University Press, 2000.

De la Vega, José. *La federación en Colombia, 1810–1912*. Madrid: Editorial América, 1940.

Del Castillo, Lina. "Colombian Cartography in the Production (and Silencing) of Independence History, 1807–1827." In *Decolonizing the Map*, edited by Jim Akerman. Chicago: University of Chicago Press, 2017.

De Leon Pinelo, Antonio. *El paraiso en el Nuevo Mundo (1645–50)*. Edited by Raul Porras Barrenechea. Lima: Imprenta Torres Aguirre, 1943.

Delpar, Helen. *Red against Blue: The Liberal Party in Colombian Politics, 1863–1899*. University: Alabama University Press, 1981.

De Luna, Frederick A. *The French Republic under Cavaignac, 1848*. Princeton: Princeton University Press, 1969.

De Plaza, José Antonio. *Lecciones de estadística, o testo de enseñanza para la clase de esta ciencia en el colejio nacional de Bogotá*. Bogotá: Imp. De Morales y Compañía, 1851. BNC, FPineda_13_pza5.

Díaz Castro, Eugenio. *Manuela: Novela de costumbres Colombianas*. Paris: Librería Española de Garnier Hermanos, 1889.

Díaz Díaz, Fernando. "Estado, Iglesia y Desamortización." In *Manual de historia de Colombia, tomo 2*, 413–16. Bogotá: Instituto Colombiano de Cultura, 1979.

———. *La desamortización de bienes eclesiásticos en Boyacá*. Tunja: Universidad Pedagógica y Tecnológica de Colombia, 1977.

Dix, Robert. *Colombia: The Political Dimensions of Change.* New Haven: Yale University Press, 1967.

Dominguez, Daylet. "Etnografía, literatura, y proyectos nacionales en el Caribe insular hispánico." PhD diss., Princeton University, 2014.

Dominguez Ossa, Camilo, Agusto Gómez López, and Guido Barona Becerra, eds. *Obras completas de la Comisión Corográfica: Geografía física y política de la Confederación Granadina.* 7 vols. Bogotá: Lerner, 1996–2005.

Dore, Elizabeth, and Maxine Molyneux. *Hidden Histories of Gender and the State in Latin America.* Durham NC: Duke University Press, 2000.

Ducey, Michael. "Liberal Theory and Peasant Practice." In *Liberals, the Church, and Indian Peasants: Corporate Lands and the Challenge of Reform in Nineteenth-Century Spanish America*, edited by Robert H., Jackson, 65–95. Albuquerque: University of New Mexico Press, 1997.

Duque Muñoz, Lucia. "La representación limítrofe y fronteriza en el 'Mapa de la República de la Nueva Granada' (1847) de Joaquin Acosta y su incidencia sobre la cartografía colombiana de mediados del siglo XIX." Anais do XXVI Simpósio Nacional de História–ANPUH (Associação Nacional de História), Sao Paulo, June 2011.

Dym, Jordana. *From Sovereign Villages to National States: City, State, and Federation in Central America, 1759–1839.* Albuquerque: University of New Mexico Press, 2006.

Eakin, Marshall. *The History of Latin America: Collision of Cultures.* New York: St. Martin's Griffin, 2007.

Earle, Rebecca. "Creole Patriotism and the Myth of the Loyal Indian." *Past & Present* 172 (2001): 125–45.

———. "Indian Rebellion and Bourbon Reform in New Granada: Riots in Pasto, 1780–1800." *Hispanic American Historical Review* 73, no.1 (1993): 99–124.

———. "Information and Disinformation in Late Colonial New Granada." *Americas* 54, no. 2 (1997): 167–84.

———. *The Return of the Native: Indians and Myth-Making in Spanish America, 1810–1930.* Durham NC: Duke University Press, 2007.

———. *Spain and the Independence of Colombia, 1808–1825.* Liverpool: Liverpool University Press, 2000.

Eastman, Scott, and Natalia Sobrevilla Perea, eds. *The Rise of Constitutional Government in the Iberian Atlantic World: The Impact of the Cádiz Constitution of 1812.* Tuscaloosa: University of Alabama Press, 2015.

Echeverri, Marcela. *Indian and Slave Royalists in the Age of Revolution.* Cambridge: Cambridge University Press, 2016.

Edney, Matthew. *Mapping an Empire: The Geographical Construction of British India, 1765–1843.* Chicago: University of Chicago Press, 1997.

Elliott, John H. *Spain, Europe and the Wider World, 1500–1800.* New Haven: Yale University Press, 2009.

Escobar, Sergio. "*Manuela*, by Eugenio Díaz Castro, The Novel about the Colombian Foundational Impasse." PhD diss., University of Michigan, 2009.

Escobedo Delgado, Martín. *El debate de las ideas: Propaganda política en la Nueva España, 1792–1814.* Zacatecas: Universidad Autonoma de Zacatecas, 2008.

Estrade, Paul. "Del Invento de 'América Latina.'" In *París y el mundo ibérico e iberoamericano: Actas del xxviii Congreso de la Sociedad de Hispanistas Franceses (S.H.F.), (Paris, 21 22, y 23 de marzo de 1997)*, 179–88. Paris, 1998.

Fals Borda, Orlando. *La educación en Colombia, bases para su integración sociológica.* Bogotá, 1962.

Fanon, Frantz. *The Wretched of the Earth.* New York: Grove Press, 1968.

Farriss, Nancy. *Crown and Clergy in Colonial Mexico, 1759–1812.* London: Athlone, 1968.

Fazio Vargas, Antonella, and Fabio Sánchez Torres. "The Educational Effects of 19th Century Disentailment of Catholic Church Land in Colombia." *Revista de Historia Económica, Journal of Iberian and Latin American Economic History* 28, no. 3 (2010): 441–67.

Figueroa Cancino, Juan David. "La formación intelectual de Joaquín Acosta y el Compendio histórico del descubrimiento y colonización de la Nueva Granada (1848)." *Anuario Colombiano de Historia Social y de la Cultura* 38, no. 2 (July/December 2011): 181–216.

Fishburn, Evelyn. "The Concept of 'Civilization and Barbarism' in Sarmiento's "Facundo"–A Reappraisal." *Ibero-amerikanisches Archiv Neue Folge* 5, no. 4 (1979): 301–308.

Flores López, Carlos A. *Constituciones Municipales de Santander, Siglo XIX.* Bogotá: Universidad Cooperative de Colombia, 1997.

Friede, Juan. *El indio en la lucha por la tierra.* Bogotá: Ediciones La Chispa, 1972.

Fujimura, Joan F. *Crafting Science: A Sociohistory of the Quest for the Genetics of Cancer.* Cambridge MA: Harvard University Press, 1996.

Gaitan Ammann, Felipe. "Recordando a los Uribe: Memorias de hygiene y de templanza en la Bogotá del Olimpo Radical (1870–1880)." *Revista de antropologia y arqueologia (Bogotá)* 13 (2001–2002): 125–46.

García, Antonio, Edith Jiménez, and Blanca Ochoa. "Indigenismo: Resguardo indígena de Tocancipá. Informe del Instituto Indigenista de Colombia, en visita a dicho resguardo en el año de 1943." *Boletín de Arqueología* 1, no. 1 (1945): 609–24. Ministerio de Cultura, Instituto Colombiano de Antropologia e Historia (ICANH). http://www.icanh.gov.co/index.php?idcategoria=8201.

García-Bryce, Iñigo. *Crafting the Republic: Lima's Artisans and Nation Building in Peru, 1821–1879.* Albuquerque: University of New Mexico Press, 2004.

Garcia-Mejia, Aydée. "The Transformation of the Indian Communities of the Bogotá Sabana during the Nineteenth Century Colombian Republic." PhD diss., New School for Social Research, 1989.

Gargarelia, Roberto. *Latin American Constitutionalism, 1810–2010: The Engine Room of the Constitution.* Oxford: Oxford University Press, 2013.

Gilmore, Robert. *El federalismo en Colombia, 1810–1858.* 2 vols. Bogotá: Universidad del Externado de Colombia, Sociedad Santanderista de Colombia, 1995.

Gobat, Michel. "The Invention of Latin America: A Transnational History of Anti-Imperialism, Democracy, and Race." *American Historical Review* 118, no. 5 (2013) 1345–75.

Gómez Barrientos, Estanislao. *Don Mariano Ospina y su época.* Medellín: Imprenta editorial, 1913.

Gómez Picón, Alirio. *El Golpe militar del 17 de abril de 1854.* Bogotá: Editorial Kelly, 1972.

González, Fernán. "Iglesia y estado desde la convención de Rionegro hasta el Olimpo Radical, 1863–1878." *Anuario Colombiano de historia social y de la cultura,* no. 15 (1987): 91–163.

———. *Para leer la política: Ensayos de historia política Colombiana.* 2 vols. Bogotá: CINEP, 1997.

Gonzalez, Florentino. *Elementos de ciencia administrativa: Comprende el bosquejo de un sistema de administración pública para un estado republicano.* Bogotá: Imprenta de J.A. Cualla, 1840. BNC, FPineda_247_pza5.

———. *Proyecto de Constitución para la Confederación Colombiana, formada de las provincias que actualmente compone la Nueva Granada.* Bogotá: Imprenta del Neo-Granadino, 1853. BLAA LRM Misceláneas.

Gootenberg, Paul. "A Forgotten Case of 'Scientific Excellence on the Periphery': The National Cocaine Science of Alfredo Bignon, 1884–1887." *Comparative Studies in Society and History* 49, no. 1 (January 2007): 202–32.

Gotkowitz, Laura. *A Revolution for Our Rights: Indigenous Struggles for Land and Justice in Bolivia, 1880–1952.* Durham NC: Duke University Press, 2007.

Gould, Jeffrey. *To Die in This Way: Nicaraguan Indians and the Myth of Mestizaje, 1880–1965.* Durham NC: Duke University Press, 1998.

Grandin, Greg. *The Blood of Guatemala: A History of Race and Nation.* Durham NC: Duke University Press, 2000.

———. "Your Americanism and Mine: Americanism and Anti-Americanism in the Americas." *American Historical Review* 111, no. 4 (2006): 1042–66.

Groot, José Manuel. *Cuadros de costumbres.* Bogotá: Fundación Editorial Epígrafe, 2006.

———. *Historia eclesiastica y civil de la Nueva Granada escrita sobre documentos autenticos.* Bogotá: Imprenta a Cargo de Focion Mantilla, 1869.

Grosfoguel, Ramón. "Developmentalism, Modernity, and Dependency Theory in Latin America." *Nepantla: Views from South* 1, no. 2 (2000): 347–374.

Guerra, François-Xavier. *Modernidad e independencias: Ensayos sobre las revoluciones hispánicas.* Madrid: Encuentro, 2009.

Guhl, Ernesto. *Utilización de la tierra en Colombia.* Bogotá: ESAP, 1963.

Gutierrez, José Fulgencio, ed. *Santander y sus municipios.* Vol. 1: *Reseña Historica del Pueblo de Santander (1529–1940).* Bucaramanga, Colombia: Imprenta del Departamento, 1940.

Gutierrez Ardila, Daniel. *El reconocimiento de Colombia: Diplomacia y propaganda en la coyuntura de las restauraciones (1819–1931).* Bogotá: Universidad Externado de Colombia, 2012.

———. *Un nuevo reino: Geografía política, pactismo, y diplomacia durante el interregno en Nueva Granada, 1808–1816.* Bogotá: Universidad Externado de Colombia, 2010.

Halperín Donghi, Tulio. *The Contemporary History of Latin America.* Edited and translated by John Charles Chasteen. Durham NC: Duke University Press, 1993.

Harding, Sandra, ed. *The Postcolonial Science and Technology Studies Reader.* Durham NC: Duke University Press, 2011.

Harley, J. B. *The New Nature of Maps: Essays in the History of Cartography.* Baltimore: Johns Hopkins University Press, 2001.

Harley, J. B., and David Woodward, eds. *The History of Cartography.* Chicago: University of Chicago Press, 1992.

Helg, Aline. *La educación en Colombia, 1918–1957: Una historia social, economica y política.* Bogotá: Cerec, 1984.

———. *Liberty and Equality in Caribbean Colombia, 1770–1835.* Chapel Hill: University of North Carolina Press, 2004.

Helguera, Joséph León. "The First Mosquera Administration in New Granada, 1845–1849." Ph.D. diss., University of North Carolina, 1958.

Helmsing, A. H. *Firms, Farms, and the State in Colombia: A Study of Rural, Urban, and Regional Dimensions of Change.* Boston: Allen & Unwin, 1986.

Henao, Jesús María, and Gerardo Arrubla. *Historia de Colombia para la enseñanza secundaria.* 2 vols. Bogotá: Escuela Tipográfica Salesiana, 1911-1912. BNC, FSuaerez_205_v1, 206_v2.

Henderson, Peter. *Gabriel García Moreno and Conservative State Formation in the Andes.* Austin: University of Texas Press, 2008.

Hernandez de Alba, Guillermo. *Documentos sobre el doctor Vicente Azuero.* Bogotá: Academia Colombiana de Historia, 1944.

Herr, Richard. *Rural Change and Royal Finance in Spain at the End of the Old Regime.* Berkeley: University of California Press, 1989. BNC.

Herrera, Julián. *Informe del Ajente Jeneral de Bienes Desamortizados [1872].* Bogotá: Imprenta de Gaitán, 1873. BNC, FPineda_868_pza3.

Herzog, Tamar. *Frontiers of Possession: Spain and Portugal in Europe and the Americas.* Cambridge MA: Harvard University Press, 2015.

Hilario López, José. "Proclama del presidente de la República a sus conciudadanos." Bogotá: Imprenta del Neo-Granadino, por Rubinat i Ovalles, 1851. BNC, FPineda_1065_pza9. Microfilm VFDU1-3411.

Hobsbawm, Eric. "La revolución." In *La revolución en la historia*, edited by R. Porter and M. Teich, 16-70. Barcelona: Editorial Crítica, 1990.

Hobsbawm, Eric, and Terence Ranger, eds. *The Invention of Tradition.* Cambridge: Cambridge University Press, 1983.

Informe del Ajente Jeneral de Bienes Desamortizados, 1866. Bogotá, Imprenta de Gaitan, 1866. BNC, FPineda_pza23.

Instituto Geográfico. "Agustín Codazzi." In *Origen y desarrollo y realizaciones, 1935-1985.* Bogotá: IGAC.

Iriarte, I. *Bienes comunales y capitalismo agrario en Navarra, 1855-1935.* Madrid: Ministerio de Agricultura, Pesca y Alimentación, 1996.

Irurozqui, Martha. "Las paradojas de la tributación: Ciudadanía y política estatal indígena en Bolivia, 1825-1900." *Revista de Indias* 59, no. 217 (1999): 705-40.

Jackson, Robert H., ed. *Liberals, the Church, and Indian Peasants: Corporate Lands and the Challenge of Reform in Nineteenth-Century Spanish America.* Albuquerque: University of New Mexico Press, 1997.

Jagdmann, Anna-Telse. "Del poder y la geografía como fuente de legitimacion en Colombia." PhD diss., Freie Universitat Berlin, 2006.

Jaramillo, Roberto Luis, and Adolfo Meisel Roca. "Más allá de la retórica de la reacción, análisis económico de la desamortización en Colombia, 1861-1888." *Cuadernos de Historia Económica y Empresarial.* Centro de Estudios Económicos Regionales (CEER) no. 22, December 2008. Cartagena, Colombia: Banco de la República.

Jaramillo Uribe, Jaime. *El pensamiento colombiano en el siglo XIX.* Bogotá: Editorial Ternis, 1964.

———. "El proceso de la educación, del virreinato a la época contemporánea." In *Manual de Historia de Colombia*, vol. 3., edited by Cobo Borda. Bogotá: Procultura, 1992.

Johnson, Walter. *River of Dark Dreams: Slavery and Empire in the Cotton Kingdom.* Cambridge MA: Harvard University Press, 2013.

Jomard, Edme. "Expliocacion d'une planche relative au monument de Tunja et aux figures gravées sur des rochers (nouvelle Grenade)." *Bulletin de la Société de Géographie* 14, nos. 79-84 (1850): 425-28.

Jomard, Edme. "Rapport a la Société de Géographie sur la carte de la Nouvelle-Grenade de M. le Colonel Acosta." *Bulletin de la Société de Géographie* 9, nos. 49–54 (1848): 239–45.

Jomard. Edme. "Sure la angue des muyscas ou la langue chibcha." *Bulletin de la Société de Géographie* 8, nos. 43–48 (1847): 85–88.

Jones Shafer, Robert. *The Economic Societies in the Spanish World, 1763–1821.* Syracuse: Syracuse University Press, 1958.

Juárez, José Roberto. *Reclaiming Church Wealth: The Recovery of Church Property after Expropriation in the Archdiocese of Guadalajara, 1860–1911.* Albuquerque: New Mexico University Press, 2004.

Kennedy-Troya, Alexandra, coord. *Escenarios para una patria. Paisajismo ecuatoriano 1850–1930.* Serie Documentos 12. Quito: Museo de la Ciudad, 2008.

Kingston, Ralph. "Trading Places: Accumulation as Mediation in French Ministry Map Depots, 1798–1810." *History of Science* 52, no. 3 (September 2014): 247–76.

Kirkpatrick, Susan. "The Ideology of Costumbrismo." *Ideologies and Literature* 2, no. 7 (1978): 28–44.

Kitchens, John W. "The New Granadan–Peruvian Slave Trade." *Journal of Negro History* 64, no. 3 (1979): 205–14.

Knowlton, Robert. "Church Property and the Mexican Reform, 1856–1910." In *The Origins of Modern Mexico,* edited by Laurens Ballard Perry. DeKalb: Northern Illinois University Press, 1976.

Kroker, Kenton, Jennifer Keelan, and Pauline M. H. Mazumdar, editors. *Crafting Immunity: Working Histories of Clinical Immunology.* Farnham, UK: Ashgate, 2008.

Larson, Brooke. *Trials of Nation Making: Liberalism, Race and Ethnicity in the Andes, 1810–1910.* New York: Cambridge University Press, 2004.

Lasserre, A., ed. *Semanario de la Nueva Granada: Miscelánea de ciencias, literatura, artes, e industria publicada por una sociedad de patriotas Granadinos bajo la dirección de Francisco José de Caldas.* Nueva Edición Corregida, Aumentada con varios opúsculos inéditos de F. J Caldas. Paris: Librería Castellana, 1849.

Lasso, Marixa. *Myths of Harmony: Race and Republicanism during the Age of Revolution, Colombia, 1795–1831.* Pittsburgh: University of Pittsburgh Press, 2007.

——. "Race, War, and Nation in Caribbean Gran Colombia, Cartagena, 1810–1832." *American Historical Review* 111, no. 2 (April 2006): 336–361.

Latour, Bruno. *Science in Action: How to Follow Scientists and Engineers through Society.* Cambridge MA: Harvard University Press, 1987.

Laurent, Muriel. *Contrabando en Colombia en el Siglo XIX: Prácticas y discursos de resistencia y reproducción.* Bogotá: Uniandes-CESO, Departamento de Historia, 2008.

Lauria-Santiago, Aldo. *An Agrarian Republic: Commercial Agriculture and the Politics of Peasant Communities in El Salvador, 1824–1918.* Pittsburgh: University of Pittsburgh Press, 1999.

Lefebvre, Henri. *The Production of Space.* Translated by Donald Nicholson-Smith. Oxford: Blackwell, 1991.

Le Grand, Catherine. *Frontier Expansion and Peasant Protest in Colombia, 1850–1936.* Albuquerque: University of New Mexico Press, 1986.

Leyes espedidas por la Asamblea Lejislativa del Estado Soberano de Panama, 1856.

Leyes y decretos expedidos por la Asamblea Legislativa del Estado Soberano de Boyacá, en sus sesiones de 1865, 1866, 1867. Bogotá: Imprenta Torres y Hermanos, 1867.

Leys-Stepan, Nancy. *The Hour of Eugenics: Race, Gender, and Nation in Latin America.* Ithaca: Cornell University Press, 1991.

Livingstone, David N. *The Geographical Tradition: Episodes in the History of a Contested Enterprise.* Oxford: Blackwell, 1992.

———. *Putting Science in Its Place: Geographies of Scientific Knowledge.* Chicago: University of Chicago Press, 2003.

Livingstone, David N., and Charles W. J. Withers. *Geography and Revolution.* Chicago: University of Chicago Press, 2005.

Lleras, Lorenzo María. *Catecismo de agrimensura, apropiado al uso de los granadinos.* Bogotá: Imprenta de la Universidad, 1834.

Loaiza Cano, Gilberto. *Manuel Ancízar y su época: Biografía de un político hispanoamericano del siglo XIX.* Medellín: Fondo Editorial Universidad EAFIT, 2004.

———. "Manuel Ancízar y sus *Lecciones de psicolojia moral.*" *Historia Crítica* no. 13 (July–December 1996): 43–60.

López-Alves, Fernando. *State Formation and Democracy in Latin America, 1810–1900.* Durham NC: Duke University Press, 2000.

López-Bejarano, Pilar. *Un estado a crédito: Deudas y configuración estatal de la Nueva Granada en la primera mitad del siglo XIX.* Bogotá: Editorial Pontifica Universidad Javeriana, 2015.

López Garavito, Luis Fernando. *Historia de la Hacienda y el Tesoro en Colombia, 1821–1900.* Bogotá: Banco de la República, 1992.

López-Ocón, Leoncio. "Objetos, imágenes y textos de Jiménez de la Espada como tecnologías de apropiación del saber." In *Entre textos e imágenes: Representaciones antropológicas de la América indígena,* edited by Fermín del Pino-Díaz, Pascal Riviale, and Juan J. R. Villarías-Robles, 39–52. Madrid: Consejo Superior de Investigaciones Científicas (CSIC), 2009.

Lucena Giraldo, Manuel. *Historia de un cosmopolita: José María de Lanz y la fundación de la ingeniería de caminos en España y América.* Madrid: Colegio de Ingenieros de Caminos, Canales, y Puertos, 2005.

MacEachren, Alan M. *How Maps Work: Representation, Visualization, and Design.* New York: Guilford Press, 1995.

Magdalena (Estado: Confederado). *Constitución Política del Estado Soberano del Magdalena, sancionada 1863.* Santa Marta: Imprenta del Estado, 1863. BNC, F. Pineda, 359 pza 9.

Mallon, Florencia. *Peasant and Nation: The Making of Postcolonial Mexico and Peru.* Berkeley: University of California Press, 1995.

Mantilla, José María. *Esposición que el Jeneral José María Mantilla, Gobernador Interino de la Provincia de Bogotá Presenta a la Camara de la Misma en sus sesiones de 1835.* Bogotá: Nicomedes Lora, 1835. bnc, F. Pineda_242_pza 1.

Martínez Garnica, Armando. "La acción de los liberales panameños en la determinación de las políticas del Estado de la Nueva Granada, 1848–1855." *Procesos históricos: Revista de historia y ciencias sociales* 1, no. 2 (July 2002): 1–52.

Martínez Pinzón, Felipe. *Una cultura de invernadero: Tropico y civilización en Colombia (1808–1928).* Madrid: Iberoamericana Vervuert, 2016.

Martínez Pinzón, Felipe. "Una geografía para la Guerra: Narrativas del cerco en Francisco José de Caldas." *Revista Estudios Sociales* no. 38 (January/April 2011).

Matthews, Robert J. "The Measure of Mind." *Mind,* new series, 103, no. 410 (April 1994): 131–46.

Mayhew, Robert J. "The Character of English Geography c. 1660–1800: A Textual Approach." *Journal of Historical Geography* 24 (1988): 385–412.

Mayhew, Robert J. "Geography Books and the Character of Georgian Politics." In *Georgian Geographies: Essays on Space, Place and Landscape in the 18th Century,* edited by Miles Ogborn and Charles W. Withers, 192–211. Manchester: Manchester University Press, 2004.

McGraw, Jason. *The Work of Recognition: Caribbean Colombia and the Post-Emancipation Struggle for Citizenship.* Chapel Hill: University of North Carolina Press, 2014.

McGreevey, William Paul. *An Economic History of Colombia, 1845–1930.* New York: Cambridge University Press, 2008.

McGuiness, Aims. *Path of Empire: Panama and the California Gold Rush.* Ithaca: Cornell University Press, 2008.

McGuiness, Aims. "Searching for 'Latin America': Race and Sovereignty in the Americas in the 1850s." In *Race and Nation in Modern Latin America,* edited by Nancy P. Appelbaum, Anne S. Macpherson, and Karin Alejandra Rosemblatt, 87–107. Chapel Hill: University of North Carolina Press, 2003.

Mejía Pavony, Germán Rodrigo. *Los años de cambio: Historia urbana de Bogotá, 1820–1910.* Bogotá: Pontificia Universidad Javeriana, 2000.

Mejía, Sergio. *La revolución en letras: La historia de la revolución de Colombia de José Manuel Restrepo (1781–1863).* Bogotá: Universidad de los Andes, Facultad de Ciencias Sociales, Departamento de Historia, Centro de Estudios Socioculturales e Internacionales (CESO), Universidad EAFIT, 2007.

Memmi, Albert. *The Colonizer and the Colonized.* Boston: Beacon Press, 1965.

Mendoza Vargas, Héctor, and Carla Lois. *Historias de la cartografía de Iberoamerica: Nuevos caminos, viejos problemas.* México City: Universidad Nacional Autónoma de México (UNAM), Instituto de Geografía, 2009.

Meyer Loy, Jane [now Rausch]. "Primary Education during the Colombian Federation: The School Reform of 1870." *Hispanic American Historical Review* 51, no. 2 (May 1971): 275–94.

Mijangos y González, Pablo. *The Lawyer of the Church: Bishop Clemente de Jesús Munguía and the Clerical Response to the Mexican Liberal Reforma.* Lincoln: University of Nebraska Press, 2015.

Millington, Thomas. *Debt Politics after Independence: The Funding Conflict in Bolivia.* Gainesville: University Press of Florida, 1992.

Molina, Gerardo. *Las ideas liberales en Colombia.* Bogotá: Ediciones Tercer Mundo, 1974.

Monmonier, Mark. *How to Lie with Maps.* Chicago: University of Chicago Press, 1991.

Morales Benitez, Otto. "Florentino González: Conspirador, periodista, hombre público y catedrático." *Credencial historia,* no. 9 (1990).

Morelli, Federica. *Territorio o nación: Reforma y disolución del espacio imperial en Ecuador, 1765–1803.* Madrid: Centro de Estudios Políticos y Constitucionales, 2005.

Mosquera, Tomás Cipriano de. "Carta autógrafa: T. C. de Mosquera Presidente de los Estados Unidos de Colombia a Su Santidad Pio IX, Pontífice Máximo." Facatativa: Imprenta de González, 1861. BLAA, LRM, Hojas Sueltas Independientes, HS10337.

———. *Memoria sobre la geografía física y política de la Nueva Granada, dedicada a la sociedad geográfica y estadística de Nueva York.* New York: S. W. Benedict, 1852.

Mundy, Barbara. *The Mapping of New Spain: Indigenous Cartography and the Maps of the Relaciones Geográficas.* Chicago: University of Chicago Press, 1996.

Múnera, Alfonso. *Fronteras Imaginadas. La construcción de las razas y de la geografía en el Siglo XIX colombiano*. Bogotá: Editorial Planeta, 2005.

Nieto Arteta, Luis Eduardo. *Economia y Cultura en la Historia de Colombia*. Bogotá: Ediciones Librería Siglo XX, 1942.

Nieto-Olarte, Mauricio. *La obra cartográfica de Francisco José de Caldas*. Bogotá: Universidad de los Andes, 2006.

———. *Orden natural y orden social: Ciencia y política en el Semanario del Nuevo Reyno de Granada*. Bogotá: Uniandes-Ceso, Departamento de Historia, 2007.

———. *Remedios para el imperio: Historia natural y la apropiación del Nuevo Mundo*. Bogotá: Universidad de los Andes, 2006.

Nieto Olarte, Mauricio, Paola Castaño, and Diana Ojeda. "Ilustracion y orden social: El Problema de la poblacion en el semanario del Nuevo Reyno de Granada (1808–1810)." *Revista de Indias* 65, no. 235 (2005): 683–708.

Nueva Granada. *Constitución poítica de la Neuva Granada sancionada el ano de 1853*. Bogotá: Imprenta Echevarria Hermanos, 1853. BNC, FPineda_3_pza11.

———. *Final controversia diplomática con relación a los sucesos de Panamá del dia 15 de abril de 1856*. Bogotá: Imprenta del Estado, 1857.

———. *Recopilación de leyes de la Nueva Granada, formada i publicada en cumplimento de la lei de 4 de Mayo de 1843 i por comisión del poder ejecutivo*. Compiled by Lino de Pombo. Bogotá: Imprenta de Zoilo Salazar, 1845. BNC, FPineda_505_pza1.

Nuijten, Monique. "Family Property and the Limits of Intervention: The Article 27 Reforms and the Procede Programme in Mexico." *Development and Change* 34, no. 3 (2003): 475–97.

Obregón Torres, Diana. "La sociedad de naturalistas neogranadinos y la tradición científica." Presented at 7th Congreso de Historia de Colombia, Popayán. Anuario Colombiano de historia social y de la cultura, 3 August 2012. Available at file:///Users/ld9277/Downloads/35810-142749-1-PB.pdf.

———. *Sociedades científicas en Colombia: La invención de una tradición, 1859–1936*. Bogotá: Banco de la República, 1992.

Ocampo Gaviria, José Antonio. *Café, industria y macroeconomía: Ensayos de historia económica colombiana*. México City: Fondo de Cultura Económica, 2015.

Orjuela, Héctor H. *Edda, la bogotana: Biografía de Rafael Pombo*. Bogotá: Editorial Kelly, 1997.

Ortiz, Venacio. *Historia de la revolución de l 17 de abril de 1854*. Bogotá: Imprenta Banco Popular, 1854.

Oslender, Ulrich. *The Geographies of Social Movements: Afro-Colombian Mobilization and the Aquatic Space*. Durham NC: Duke University Press, 2016.

Ospina, Joaquin. *Diccionario biográfico y bibliográfico de Colombia*. Vol. 3. Bogotá: Editorial De Cromos, 1927–39.

Ospina, Mariano. *Memoria del secretario de Estado . . . dirije al congreso constitutional de 1843*. Bogotá: Cualla, 1843. BNC, FPineda_802_pza1.

Ospina, Pastor. *Esposición del secretario de Estado del despacho de Gobierno de la Nueva Granada al Congreso Constitucional de 1855*. Bogotá, 1855.

Otero Muñoz, Gustavo. *Historia del periodismo en Colombia, Biblioteca Aldeana de Colombia*. Bogotá: Editorial Minerva, 1936.

Owensby, Brian. *Empire of Law and Indian Justice in Colonial Mexico*. Stanford: Stanford University Press, 2008.

Páez, Justiniano J. *Noticias históricas de la Ciudad y Provincia de Ocaña desde 1810 hasta la Guerra de tres años*. Biblioteca de autores ocañeros, vol. 9. Yerbabuena: Imprenta Patriótica Caro y Cuervo, 1972.

Palacio Fajardo, Manuel. *Outline of the Revolution in Spanish America; or, An Account of the Origin, Progress, and Actual State of War Carried on between Spain and Spanish America; Containing the Principle Facts Which Have Marked the Struggle, by a South American*. London: Longman, Hurst, Rees, Orme, and Brown, Paternoster-Row, 1817.

Palacios, Marco. *Between Legitimacy and Violence: A History of Colombia, 1875–2002*. Translated by Richard Stoller. Durham NC: Duke University Press, 2006.

———. *Coffee in Colombia: An Economic, Social and Political History*. Cambridge: Cambridge University Press, 1980.

Panamá (Estado: Confederado). *Disposiciones lejislativas i ejecutivas, del gobierno de la Nueva Granada, sobre creación del Estado de Panama*. Panama: Imp. El Centinela, n.d. HathiTrust, http://hdl.handle.net/2027/mdp.35112102275254.

Paquette, Gabriel. "The Dissolution of the Spanish Atlantic Monarchy." *Historical Journal* 52, no. 1 (March 2009): 175–212.

Park, James William. *Rafael Nuñez and the Politics of Colombian Regionalism, 1863–1886*. Baton Rouge: Louisiana State University Press, 1985.

Parra de Avellaneda, Prospera, and Luis Fernando Muñoz Patiño. "Aspectos de la agricultura y la desamortización en la sabana de Bogotá, 1860–1870." *Monografía de grado para optar el título de Licenciado en Ciencias Sociales*. Bogotá: Departamento de Historia, Universidad Nacional de Colombia, 1984.

Peloso, Vincent C., and Barbara Tenenbaum. *Liberals, Politics, and Power: State Formation in Nineteenth-Century Latin America*. Athens: University of Georgia Press, 1996.

Peña, Manuel. *Geometría práctica, lecciones de agrimensura, topografía y nivelación, dictadas en la Escuela de Ingenieros de Colombia*. Bogotá: Imprenta La Luz, 1887.

Peralta Ruiz, Victoria. "El impacto de las cortes de cadiz en el Peru: Un Balance Historiografico." *Revista de Indias* 68, no. 242 (2008): 67–96.

Péres Salas, María Ester. *Costumbrismo y litografía en México: Un nuevo modo de ver*. México City: Universidad Nacional Autónoma de México, 2005.

Pérez, Felipe. *Anales de la Revolución 1857–1861*. Bogotá: Imprenta de Estado de Cundinamarca, 1862.

———. *Compendio de jeografía jeneral de los Estados de Colombia*. Bogotá: Imprenta de Echeverria Hermanos, 1876.

———. *Geografía general física y política de los Estados Unidos de Colombia y geografía particular de la ciudad de Bogotá*. Vol. 1. Bogotá: Imprenta de Echevarria Hermanos, 1883.

———. *Jeografia física i política de los Estados Unidos de Colombia*. Bogotá: Imprenta de la Nacion, 1865.

———. *Jeografía jeneral de los Estados Unidos de Colombia escrita de orden de Gobierno por Felipe Pérez*. Paris: Libreria de Rosa y Bouret, 1865.

Pérez Aguirre, Antonio. *25 Años de historia colombiana, 1853–1878: Del centralismo a la federación*. Bogotá: Editorial Sucre, 1959).

Pérez Carrera, José Manuel. *Periodismo y costumbrismo en el siglo XIX*. Madrid: Santillana, 1996.

Phelan, John Leddy. *The People and the King: The Comunero Revolution in Colombia, 1781*. Madison: University of Wisconsin Press, 1978.

Pickles, John. *A History of Spaces: Cartographic Reason, Mapping, and the Geo-Coded World*. London: Routledge, 2004.

Pimentel, Juan. *La física de la monarquía: Ciencia y política en el pensamiento colonial de Alejandro Malaspina (1754–1810)*. Aranjuez, Spain: Doce Calles, 1998.

Plata, José María. *Informe del secretario de estado del despacho de Relaciones Esteriores de la Nueva Granada al Congreso Constitucional de 1853*. Bogotá, 1853.

Platt, Tristan. "The Alchemy of Modernity: Alonso Barba's Copper Cauldrons and the Independence of Bolivian Metallurgy (1770–1890)." *Journal of Latin American Studies* 32 (2000): 1–54.

Pohl Valero, Stefan. *¡Soy Caldas!: Biografía de Francisco José de Caldas*. Bogotá: Instituto Distrital de las Artes (IDARTES) and Universidad Distrital Francisco José de Caldas, 2016.

Pombo, Lino de. *Esposición del secretario de estado . . . 1834*. Bogotá: Espinosa por José Ayarza, 1834. BNC, FQuijano_26_pza1.

——. *Esposición del secretario de Estado . . . 1835*. Bogotá: Nicomedes Lora, 1835. BNC, FQuijano_27_pza1.

——. *Esposición del secretario de Estado . . . 1836*. Bogotá: Nicomedes Lora, 1836. BNC, FPineda_337_pza1.

——. *Esposición del secretario de Estado . . . 1838*. Bogotá: Nicomedes Lora, 1838. BNC, FQuijano_16_pza1.

——, ed. *Leyes i decretos expedidos por el Congreso Constitucional de la Nueva Granada, en el Ano de 1850*. Bogotá: 1850.

Poole, Deborah. *Vision, Race, and Modernity: A Visual Economy of the Andean Image World*. Princeton: Princeton University Press, 1997.

Portuondo, María. "Constructing a Narrative: The History of Science and Technology in Latin America." *History Compass* 7 no. 2 (2009): 500–522.

——. *Secret Science: Spanish Cosmography and the New World*. Chicago: University of Chicago Press, 2009.

Prakash, Gyan. *Another Reason: Science and the Imagination of Modern India*. Princeton: Princeton University Press, 1999.

Quijada, Mónica. "Sobre el origen y difusión del nombre 'América Latina': O una variación heterodoxa en torno al tema de la construcción social de la verdad." *Revista de Indias* 58, no. 214 (1998): 595–616.

Quijano, Aníbal. "América Latina en la economía mundial." *Problemas del desarrollo* 24 (1993): 5–18.

——. "Coloniality of Power, Eurocentrism and Latin America." *Nepantla: Views from South* 1, no. 3 (2000): 533–80.

Quintero, Inés, and Ángel Rafael Almarza. "Dos proyectos: Un solo territorio. Constitucionalismo, soberanía y representación. Venezuela 1808–1821." In *El laboratorio constitucional*, edited by Antonio Annino and Marcela Ternavasio, 55–70. Liverpool: Asociación de Historiadores Latinoamericanistas Europeos (AHILA), 2012.

Rappaport, Joanne. *The Politics of Memory: Native Historical Interpretation in the Colombian Andes*. Durham NC: Duke University Press, 1998.

Rausch, Jane [formerly Meyer Loy]. "Church-State Relations on the Colombian Frontier: The National Identity of Meta, 1909–1930." *Americas* 49, no. 1 (July 1992): 49–68.

——. *Colombia: Territorial Rule and the Llanos Frontier*. Gainesville: University Press of Florida, 1999.

Reeves, René. *Ladinos with Ladinos, Indians with Indians: Land, Labor, and Regional Ethnic Conflict in the Making of Guatemala*. Stanford: Stanford University Press, 2006.

Reinhardt, Nola. "The Consolidation of the Import-Export Economy in Nineteenth-Century Colombia: A Political-Economic Analysis." *Latin American Perspectives* 13, no. 1 (Winter, 1986): 75–98.

Restrepo, José Manuel. "Cotos: Articulo comunicado." *Gaceta de Colombia*, no. 26, 14 April 1822.

——. *Diario político y militar. Memorias sobre los sucesos importantes de la época para server a la historia de la revolución de Colombia y de la Nueva Granada desde 1849 para Adelante*. Vol. 4 (1 January–28 July 1858). Bogotá: Imprenta Nacional, 1954.

——. *Ensayo sobre la geografía: Producciones, industria, y población de la provincial de Antioquia en el Nuevo Reino de Granada*. Medellín: Fondo Editorial Universidad EAFIT, 2007.

——. *Exposición que el secretario de Estado del Despacho del Interior de la República de Colombia hizo al Congreso de 1824 sobre los negocios de su departamento*. Bogotá: Imprenta de la República por Nicomedes Lora, 1824.

——. *Historia de la Nueva Granada, 1845–1854*. Vol. 2. Bogotá: Editorial Cromos, 1963.

——. *Historia de la revolucíon de la República de Colombia*. 10 vols. and atlas. Paris: Librería Americana, 1827.

——. *Iglesia y estado en Colombia*. London: Gilbert and Rivington Ltd., St John's Square, 1885.

Restrepo Forero, Olga. "La Comisión Corográfica: Avatares en la configuración del saber Universidad Nacional de Colombia." Thesis, 1983. Published in *Monografías Sociológicas* no. 14. Bogotá: Facultad de Ciencias Humanas, Departamento de Sociología, 1988.

Restrepo Piedrahita, Carlos. *Constituciones de la primera República liberal, 1853–1856*. 4 vols. Bogotá: Universidad del Externado de Colombia, 1979–1985.

Reyes, Rafael. *Memorias de Rafael Reyes, 1850–1885*. Bogotá: Fondo Cultural Cafetero, 1986.

Rodríguez, Jaime O. *The Divine Charter: Constitutionalism and Liberalism in Nineteenth-Century Mexico*. Lanham MD: Rowman & Littlefield, 2004.

——. *The Independence of Spanish America*. Cambridge: Cambridge University Press, 1998.

Rodríguez Piñeres, Eduardo. *El olimpo radical: Ensayos conocidos e inéditos sobre su época, 1864–1884*. Bogotá: Editoriales de Librería Voluntad, 1950.

Rodríguez Plata, Horacio. *La inmigración alemana al Estado Soberano de Santander in el Siglo XX: Repercusiones socio-economicas de un proceso de tranculturación*. Bogotá, 1968.

Rodríguez Prada, María Paola. *Le musée national de Colombie, 1823–1830: Histoire d'une création*. Paris: L'Harmattan, 2013.

Rodríguez-Ruiz, Blanca, and Ruth Rubio-Marín, eds. *The Struggle for Female Suffrage in Europe: Voting to Become Citizens*. Leiden: Brill, 2012.

Rojas, Cristina. *Civilización y violencia: La búsqueda de la identidad en la Colombia del siglo XIX*. Bogotá: Grupo Editorial Norma, 2001.

Rojas Mix, Miguel. "Bilbao y el hallazgo de América latina: Unión continental, socialista y libertarian." *Cahiers du Monde Hispanique et Luso-Brasilien-Caravelle* 46 (1986): 35–47.

Romero, Mario Germán. *El héroe niño de la independencia, Pedro Acevedo y Tejada*. Bogotá: Editorial Kelly, 1962.

Rosenthal, Joshua. *Salt and the Colombian State: Local Society and Regional Monopoly in Boyacá*. Pittsburgh: University of Pittsburgh Press, 2012.

Ruiz, Adelia Esperanza. "El discurso costumbrista colombiano del siglo XIX: Instrumento ideologico idealizado." PhD diss., Florida International University, 2007.

Ruiz Gutierrez, Paola. "La génesis del federalismo en la Nueva Granada: Debate y práctica de la descentralización a mediados del siglo XIX: 1848–1863." Thesis, Colegio de Mexico, 2017.

Safford, Frank. *The Ideal of the Practical: Colombia's Struggle to Form a Technical Elite*. Austin: University of Texas Press, 1976.

———. "Race, Integration, and Progress: Elite Attitudes and the Indian in Colombia, 1750–1870." *Hispanic American Historical Review* 72, no. 1 (February 1991): 1–33.

———. "Social Aspects of Politics in Nineteenth-Century Spanish America: New Granada, 1825–1850." *Journal of Social History*, 5, no. 3 (Spring 1972): 344–370.

Safford, Frank, and Marco Palacios. *Colombia: Fragmented Land, Divided Society*. Oxford: Oxford University Press, 2002.

Safier, Neil. *Measuring the New World: Enlightenment Science and South America*. Chicago: University of Chicago Press, 2008.

Saldaña, Juan José. "Science and Freedom: Science and Technology as a Policy of the New American States." In *Science in Latin America*, edited by Juan José Saldaña and translated by Bernabé Madrigal, 151–62. Austin: University of Texas Press, 2006.

Saldarriaga Roa, Alberto, Alfonso Ortíz Crespo, and José Alexander Pinzón Rivera. *En busca de Thomas Reed: Arquitectura y política en el siglo xix*. Bogotá: Instituto Distrital de Patrimonio, 2005.

Samper, José María. "Cuaderno que contiene la esplicacion de los principios cardinales de la Ciencia Constitucional." Bogotá: Reimpreso en la Imprenta imparcial, 1852. BNC, FPineda_46_pza4.

———. *Ensayo Aproximado*. Bogotá, 1857. BNC, F.Pineda_215_pza11.

———. "España y Colombia." *La América. Crónica Hispano-Americana* 2, no. 5 (8 May 1858): 4.

———. *Historia de un alma*. Medellín: Bedout, 1971.

———. "La cuestión de las razas." *La América: Crónica Hispano-Americana* 2 (8 November 1858).

———. "La historia de un alma." In *Escritura autobiografica y conocimiento histórico, Colección memoria viva del bicentenario*, edited by Franz D. Hensel Riveros. Bogotá: Universidad del Rosario, 2009.

Sánchez, Efraín. *Gobierno y geografía: Agustín Codazzi y la Comisión Corográfica de la Nueva Granada*. Bogotá: Banco de la República y El Ancora Editores, 1999.

Sánchez Torres, Fabio, Antonella Fazio Vargas, and María del Pilar López-Uribe. "Land Conflict, Property Rights, and the Rise of the Export Economy in Colombia, 1850–1925." *Documentos CEDE*. Bogotá: Universidad del los Andes-Cede, 2006.

Sanders, James. "Belonging to the Great Granadan Family: Partisan Struggle and the Construction of Indigenous Identity and Politics in Southwestern Colombia, 1849–1890." In *Race and Nation in Modern Latin America*, edited by Nancy Appelbaum, Anne S. MacPherson, and Karin Alejandra Rosemblatt, 56–86. Chapel Hill: University of North Carolina Press, 2003.

———. *Contentious Republicans: Popular Politics, Race, and Class in Nineteenth-Century Colombia*. Durham NC: Duke University Press, 2004.

———. "The Vanguard of the Atlantic World: Contesting Modernity in Nineteenth-Century Latin America." *Latin American Research Review* 46, no. 2 (2011): 104–27.

―――. *The Vanguard of the Atlantic World: Creating Modernity, Nation, and Democracy in Nineteenth-Century Latin America*. Durham NC: Duke University Press, 2014.

Santander (Colombia: Department). *Codigos Lejislativos del Estado de Santander*. Vol. 1. Bogotá: Impr. De Medardo Rivas, 1870. BNC, FPineda_1_pza239.

Santamaría, Eustacio. *Primer libro de instrucción objetiva para el aprendizaje combinado del dibujo, la escritura i la lectura con nociones rudimentarias de historia natural, jeometría, aritmética, jeografía, i agricultura*. Havre: Impr. De A Lemale aîné, 1872.

Sartorius, David. *Ever Faithful: Race, Loyalty, and the Ends of Empire in Spanish Cuba*. Durham NC: Duke University Press, 2014.

Schneider, Ronald. *Comparative Latin American Politics*. Boulder: Westview Press, 2010.

Schwaller, John. *The Church and Clergy in Sixteenth-Century Mexico*. Albuquerque: University of New Mexico Press, 1987.

Schwartz, Roberto, and Victor Blumer-Thomas. *The Economic History of Latin America since Independence*. Cambridge: Cambridge University Press, 1995, 2004, 2014.

Scott, Heidi V. *Contested Territory: Mapping Peru in the Sixteenth and Seventeenth Centuries*. Notre Dame IN: University of Notre Dame Press, 2009.

Seth, Suman. *Crafting the Quantum: Arnold Sommerfeld and the Practice of Theory*. Cambridge MA: MIT Press, 2010.

Shapin, Steven. "The Invisible Technician." *American Scientist* 77, no. 6 (November–December 1989): 554–63.

―――. *A Social History of Truth: Civility and Science in Seventeenth-Century England*. Chicago: University of Chicago Press, 1994.

Shiels, Willima E. *King and Church: The Rise and Fall of the Patronato Real*. Chicago: Loyola University Press, 1961.

Silva, Renan. *Los ilustrados de Nueva Granada, 1760–1808: Genealogía de una comunidad de interpretación*. Medellín, Colombia: Universidad de EAFIT, 2002.

Skocpol, Theda. "Bringing the State Back In: Strategies of Analysis in Current Research." In *Bringing the State Back In*, edited by P. Evans, D. Rueschemeyer, and T. Skocpol. Cambridge: Cambridge University Press, 1985.

Slatta, Richard, and Jane Lucas De Grummond. *Simón Bolívar's Quest for Glory*. College Station: Texas A&M University Press, 2003.

Sommer, Doris. *Foundational Fictions: The National Romances of Latin America*. Berkeley: University of California Press, 1991.

Soriano Lleras, A. *Itinerario de la Comisión Corográfica*. Bogotá: Universidad Nacional de Colombia, 1968.

Soto Arango, Diana. "Aproximacion historica a la universidad Colombiana." *Revista histórica de la educación Latinoamericana* 7 (2005): 101–38.

―――. *Francisco Antonio Zea, Un criollo ilustrado*. Madrid: Doce Calles, 2000.

―――. *Recepción y difusión de la producción científica, filosófica y política Ilustrada en España, Portugal y América colonial*. Aranjuez, Spain: Doce Calles, 2003.

Sowell, David. *The Early Colombian Labor Movement: Artisans and Politics in Bogotá, 1832–1919*. Philadelphia: Temple University Press, 1992.

Steele, Arthur Robert. *Flowers for the King: The Expedition of Ruiz and Pavon and the Flora of Peru*. Durham NC: Duke University Press, 1964.

Stein, Stanley J., and Barbara H. Stein. *The Colonial Heritage of Latin America: Essays on Economic Dependence in Perspective*. Oxford: Oxford University Press, 1970.

Steiner, Claudia. *Imaginación y poder. El encuentro del interior con la costa en Urabá, 1900–1960*. Medellín, Colombia: Editoral de la Universidad de Antioquia, 2000.

Stock, Markus, and Nicola Vöhringer, eds. *Spatial Practices: Medieval/Modern*. Göttingen: V&R Unipress, 2014.

Stoller, Richard. "Ironías del federalismo en la provincial del Socorro, 1810–1870." *Fronteras de la historia* 2 (1998): 11–32.

Thurner, Mark. *From Two Republics to One Divided: Contradictions of Postcolonial Nationmaking in Andean Peru*. Durham NC: Duke University Press, 1997.

———. *History's Peru: The Poetics of Colonial and Postcolonial Historiography*. Gainesville: University Press of Florida, 2011.

———. "Peruvian Geneologies of History and Nation." In *After Spanish Rule*, edited by Mark Thurner and Andrés Guerrero. Durham NC: Duke University Press, 2003.

Tirado Mejia, Alvaro. *Introducción a la historia económica de Colombia*. Bogotá: Universidad Nacional de Colombia, 1971.

Topik, Stephen. "When Mexico Had the Blues: A Transatlantic Tale of Bonds, Bankers, and Nationalists, 1862–1910." *American Historical Review* 105 (2000): 714–38.

Torales Pacheco, María Cristina. *Ilustrados en la Nueva España: Los socios de la Real Sociedad Bascongada de los Amigos del País*. Mexico City: Universidad Iberoamericana, 2001.

Torget, Andrew. *Seeds of Empire: Cotton, Slavery, and the Transformation of the Texas Borderlands, 1800–1850*. Chapel Hill: University of North Carolina Press, 2015.

Torres Cendales, Leidy Jazmín. "Gazeta [Gaceta] de Colombia (1821–1826)." *Prensa Siglo XIX–XX, Programa Nacional de Investigación: Las Culturas Políticas de la Independencia, sus memorias y sus legados: 200 años de ciudadanías*. Bogotá: Universidad Nacional de Colombia. http://www.banrepcultural.org/blaavirtual/historia/prensa-colombiana-del-siglo-XIX/gazeta-de-colombia-1821-1826.

Torres Sánchez, Jaime, and Luz Amanda Salazar Hurtado. *Introducción a la historia de la ingeniería y de la educación en Colombia*. Bogotá: Universidad Nacional, 2002.

Tovar Mora, Jorge Andés, and Hermes Tovar Pinzón. *El oscuro camino de la libertad: Los esclavos en Colombia, 1821–1851*. Bogotá: Universidad de los Andes, 2009.

Tovar Pinzón, Hermes. *La formación social chibcha*. Bogotá: CIEC, 1980.

Trouillot, Michel-Rolph. *Silencing the Past: Power and the Production of History*. Boston: Beacon Press, 1995.

Turnbull, David. *Masons, Tricksters, and Cartographers: Comparative Studies in the Sociology of Scientific and Indigenous Knowledge*. London: Routledge, 2000.

Tyner, Judith. "Mapping Women: Scholarship on Women in the History of Cartography." *Terrae Incognitae: The Journal for the Society for the History of Discoveries* 48, no. 1 (2016): 7–14.

Uribe de Hincapie, María Teresa, and Liliana María Lópes Lopera. *La Guerra por las soberanias: Memorias y relatos en la Guerra civil de 1859–1862 en Colombia*. Medellín, Colombia: La Carreta Editores and la Universidad de Antioquia, 2008.

———. *Las Palabras de la Guerra: Un studio sobre las memorias de las guerras civiles en Colombia*. Medellín, Colombia: La Carreta Editores, 2006.

Uribe-Uran, Victor. *Honorable Lives: Lawyers, Family and Politics in Colombia, 1780–1850*. Pittsburgh: University of Pittsburgh Press, 2000.

Uribe Vargas, Diego, ed. *Las constituciones de Colombia*. Madrid: Ediciones Cultura Hispánica, 1977.

Urrutia, Miguel. *50 años de desarrollo económico colombiano*. Bogotá: La Carreta, 1979.

Valencia Llano, Alonso. "La revolución de Melo en las provincias del Cauca." In *Las guerras civiles desde 1830 y su proyección en el siglo XX: Memorias de la II Cátedra annual de Historia Ernesto Restrepo Tirado*. 2nd ed. Bogotá: Museo Nacional de Colombia, 2001.

Vanégas, Ricardo. *Proyecto de Constitución*. Bogotá: Imprenta de El Dia por José Ayarza, 1851. BNC, FPineda_164_pza4.

Van Mejil T., and F. Von Benda-Beckman, eds. *Property Rights and Economic Development: Land and Natural Resources in Southeast Asia and Oceania*. London: Kegan Paul International, 1999.

Vargas Martínez, Gustavo. *Colombia 1854: Melo, los artesanos y el socialismo (La dictadura artisanal de 1854, espresión del socialismo utópico en Colombia)*. Bogotá: Editorial la Oveja Negra, 1973.

Vélez Barrientos, Manuel. "Notice sur les Antiquités de la Nouvelle-Grenade." In *Bulletin de la Société de Géographie de Paris*, vol. 8 (1847).

Vila, Pablo. "Caldas y los origenes eurocriollos de la geobotanica." *Revista de la Academia Colombiana de Ciencias* 11 (1960): 16–20.

Villareal, José María. *Al criterio público*. Socorro: Imprenta de Gomez y Villareal, 1851. BNC, FPineda_573_pza359.

Villegas, Jorge. *Colombia: Enfrentamiento iglesia-estado, 1819–1887*. Bogotá: La Carreta, 1977.

Villoría, Ramón. "Estracto de la esposición de la provincial de Bogotá, presentado por su gobernador interino, Dr. Ramón Villoría a la cámara provincial en sus sesiones de este año." *Gaceta de la Nueva Granada* (Bogotá), 22 October 1837. BNC, FPineda_VFDUI–1574_pza1.

Viotti da Costa, Emilia. *The Brazilian Empire: Myths and Histories.*, Rev. ed. Chapel Hill: University of North Carolina Press, 2000.

Warf, Barney, and Santa Arias, eds. *The Spatial Turn: Interdisciplinary Perspectives*. London: Routledge, 2009.

Wiarda, Howard J., and Harvey Kline. *Latin American Politics and Development*. Boulder: Westview Press, 2014.

Williams, Raymond. *The Columbia Guide to the Latin American Novel since 1945*. New York: Columbia University Press, 2007.

Winichakul, Thongchai. *Siam Mapped: A History of the Geo-Body of a Nation*. Honolulu: University of Hawai'i Press, 1994.

Withers, Charles W. J. "The Social Nature of Map Making in the Scottish Enlightenment, c. 1682–1832." *Imago Mundi* 54 (2002): 46–66.

Wolf, Eric R., and Edward C. Hansen. "Caudillo Politics: A Structural Analysis." *Comparative Studies in Society and History* 9, no. 2 (1967): 168–79.

Wood, Denis. *The Power of Maps*. London: Guilford Press, 1992.

Wright, Thomas C. *Latin America since Independence: Two Centuries of Continuity and Change*. Lanham MD: Rowman and Littlefield, 2017.

Yannakakis, Yanna. "Beyond Jurisdictions: Native Agency in the Making of Colonial Legal Cultures." *Comparative Studies in Society and History* 57, no. 4 (2015): 1070–82.

Zahler, Reuben. *Ambitious Rebels: Remaking Honor, Law, and Liberalism in Venezuela, 1780–1850*. Tucson: University of Arizona Press, 2013.

Zubieta, Pedro. *Apuntaciones sobre las primeras misiones diplomáticas de Colombia*. Bogotá: Imprenta nacional, 1924.

Index